THE ADVENTUROUS TRAVELER'S GUIDE

by LEO LE BON

A Fireside Book
Published by Simon & Schuster, Inc.
New York

Published by Simon & Schuster, Inc.
Simon & Schuster Building
Rockefeller Center
1230 Avenue of the Americas
New York, New York 10020

FIRESIDE and colophon are registered trademarks of Simon & Schuster, Inc.
MOUNTAIN TRAVEL is a trademark of Mountain Travel, Inc.

Printed by DAI Nippon Printing, Japan

1 2 3 4 5 6 7 8 9 10

Library of Congress Cataloging in Publication Data

ISBN: 0-671-60447-3

The traditional Tibetan thanka style of painting has influenced Sherpa artists, who have evolved a special way of painting local scenes. Thubten Yeshi Sherpa, a lama at Thyangboche Monastery, created this painting showing Mountain Travel's tents watched over by a trio of yetis.

*Exhilaration follows a steep hike to a spectacular viewpoint in the high peaks of the Khumbu, Nepal/*Eric Sanford

THE ADVENTUROUS TRAVELER'S GUIDE

Acknowledgements

Our "wish book" is a result of the combined efforts of many people. Thanks to Managing Editor Pam Shandrick for writing and editing the text, and to Ken Scott for the book's design and production.

Thanks to others on the Mountain Travel staff: Dena Bartolome for the Adventure Travel Bibliographies and proofreading, Allen Bechky for Africa text, Linda Davis of Ann Flanagan Typography for typesetting, Gil Roberts, M.D., for Health Matters, Hugh Swift for map preparation and Dave Parker for ski program text.

And thanks to our extended family of trip leaders and associates who contributed their ideas to the "City Notes" sections: Iain Allan, Stan Armington, Mike Banks, Smoke Blanchard, John Cleare, Alfredo Ferreyros, Fikret Gurbuz, Pierre Jamet, Bonnie Kaden, Bruce Klepinger, Narinder Kumar, Mike Perry, Filippus Petersson, Bary Roberts, Gadi Sternbach, Allen Steck, Sara Steck, John Thune, Jaromir Wolf, and Jan Zabinski.

Thanks also to trip members, staff and leaders who contributed photographs to this production.

Above all, I'd like to express my gratitude to our trip members, those intrepid travelers who have participated in our adventures for the last 18 years. Without their interest and support, Mountain Travel would not exist. It is the sharing of some small, unique adventure somewhere on our planet with these people that has made it all worthwhile.

Leo Le Bon

Everest summiteers Sir Edmund Hillary and Tenzing Norgay, the first two men atop the world's highest peak/ *John Thune*

Trekking is one of the most agreeable pastimes that I know of. It is a healthy, vigorous and challenging activity which brings you close to nature and lets you share the beauty of the environment. You don't have to be a tough and hardy person to enjoy trekking. You can choose whatever you may wish to do from a relaxed stroll through the valleys and forests, a vigorous hike along a high mountain ridge, or the major effort involved in crossing a high alpine pass.

Nature can be very peaceful but it is rarely quiet. There may be the soft moaning of the wind over a ridge, the roaring of a foaming mountain stream, the sweet music of the birds in the forest, or the dull thunder of an ice avalanche tumbling down the high cliffs above. You have an astonishing sense of freedom—you are dependent only on your own two feet . . . no buses, trains, or planes to catch; no concrete jungles to traverse or gasoline fumes to breathe. The air is clean and fresh and you feel the stimulation of going wherever your own wishes may lead you.

Everest (29,028') in center viewed from Kala Patar, near the head of the Khumbu Glacier, Nepal/*Brian K. Weirum*

I have enjoyed trekking in many countries and in many types of terrain—up valleys, over hills, across deserts, through forests, along beaches, over the arctic tundra, and across high glacier plateaus. They all have their individual charm.

But perhaps I have enjoyed trekking in the Himalayas best of all. Such trekking can be energetic but very beautiful. The foaming mountain rivers sweep down and the icy summits thrust up towards the sky. And there is so much to see and do. The local people are friendly and warm; the cultures are varied and new; and although the villages may be poor according to our high standards, yet there is a feeling of peace and contentment. And that's what trekking is all about—beauty, peace and contentment!

Sir Edmund Hillary

SECTION I

HOW TO USE THIS BOOK

The 1986/87 Guide is divided into five major geographical regions: ASIA, AFRICA, EUROPE, SOUTH AMERICA and NORTH AMERICA. Each section begins with a general overview of Adventure Travel activities in that region.

Mountain Travel's own treks, outings and expeditions are presented by geographical region beginning with Asia and ending with North America.

The Calendar Index tells you what trips are leaving each month. The Quick-Reference Index will help you locate a trip which includes a particular outdoor activity (such as trekking, skiing or rafting).

Return the Trip Application at the end to sign up for an adventure of interest to you.

SECTION I — HOW TO USE THIS BOOK — 7
Activity Index, 8 • Calendar Index, 8 • Trip Grading, 10 • Adventure Travel Activities, 11

SECTION II — ASIA & THE PACIFIC — 17
Adventure Travel In Asia, 18 • Bibliography, 21 • Staying Healthy In Third World Countries, 22 • Essay: "A Skeptic Goes Trekking," 23 • Asia Leaders, 26 • Tibet, 27 • China, 33 • Mongolia, 36 • Nepal, 36 • Pakistan, 46 • India, 48 • Sikkim, 54 • Bhutan, 54 • Sri Lanka, 56 • Thailand, 56 • Japan, 57 • Marquesas, 58 • New Guinea, 58 • New Zealand, 59 • Australia, 60

SECTION III — AFRICA & THE SAHARA — 63
Adventure Travel In Africa, 64 • Bibliography, 66 • Essay: "Going Ape," 67 • Africa Leaders, 70 • Algeria, 71 • Sudan, 73 • Egypt, 74 • Kenya, 76 • Tanzania, 79 • Rwanda, 85 • Zimbabwe, 86 • Botswana, 86

SECTION IV — EUROPE & THE U.S.S.R. — 89
Adventure Travel In Europe, 90 • Bibliography, 92 • Essay: "Ascending Noah's Mountain," 93 • Europe Leaders, 96 • United Kingdom, 97 • Ireland, 99 • Iceland, 99 • Norway, 100 • Spain, 100 • Portugal, 101 • Czechoslovakia, 102 • Germany, 102 • Austria, 103 • Italy, 104 • France, 106 • Switzerland, 108 • Greece, 110 • Turkey, 111 • U.S.S.R., 111

SECTION V — SOUTH AMERICA & MEXICO — 115
Adventure Travel In South America, 116 • Bibliography, 118 • Essay: "Trekking Reminiscences and Rewards," 119 • South America Leaders, 122 • Antarctica, 123 • Chile, 123 • Argentina, 124 • Bolivia, 126 • Peru, 127 • Galapagos, 134 • Ecuador, 135 • Colombia, 136 • Costa Rica, 136 • Mexico, 137

SECTION VI — NORTH AMERICA & HAWAII — 141
Adventure Travel In North America, 142 • Essay: "Gathering at the River," 143 • North America Leaders, 144 • Hawaii, 145 • New Hampshire, 146 • Washington, 147 • Alaska, 147

SECTION VII — SKI ADVENTURES — 154
Downhill • Downhill Randonee • Cross Country • Cross Country Trail

SECTION VIII — MOUNTAIN TRAVEL GALLERY — 156
"The People & Art of Tibet" by Leo Le Bon

SECTION IX — PRACTICAL INFORMATION — 168
Health Matters, 168 • Equipment Checklist, 170 • Booking Information, 172 • About Mountain Travel, 174 • Trip Application, 175

Buddhist protector divinity, a detail on an ancient wall painting at Lamayuru Monastery, Ladakh, India/*Hugh Swift*

Activity Index

For detailed explanations of activities see pages 11–15.

Touring
Tibet 28, Marquesas 58, Papua New Guinea 58, Egypt 74, Britain 97, Ireland 99, France 106, Italy 104, Germany/Austria 102, Spain 100, Portugal 101, Czechoslovakia 102, Peru 127, Costa Rica 136, Mexico, 137, Antarctica 125, Alaska 147.

Cultural Expeditions
China 35, Tibet 30, Bhutan 55, India 49, Sahara 73, Egypt 75, Peru 127, Kenya 78.

Overland Journeys
Tibet 27, Pakistan 47, Patagonia 123, Iceland 99, Sudan 73, Hawaii 145.

Hut-to-Hut Hiking
New Zealand 59, Japan 57, France 107, Switzerland 108, Germany/Austria 103, Italy 104, Greece 110, Norway 100, New Hampshire 146.

Water Trips
Alaska 148, Peru 128, Zimbabwe 86, Sri Lanka 56, Marquesas 58, Australia 60, Egypt 74, Greece 110, Peru 130, Alaska 147.

Trekking
All China trips 33 to 35, Mongolia 36, all Nepal trips 37 to 45, most India trips 48 to 54, Bhutan 54, Pakistan 46, Sri Lanka 56, Thailand 56, Kenya 80, Tanzania 80, Sahara 73, Turkey 111, most Peru trips 129 to 132, Bolivia 126, Mexico 139.

Wildlife & Natural History Safaris
Sri Lanka 56, India 53, all trips in Kenya, Tanzania, Rwanda, Botswana 76 to 87, Galapagos 135, Peru 130, Argentina/Chile (Patagonia) 123, Costa Rica 136, Alaska 146, 152.

Backpacking
U.S.S.R. 112, Alaska 148, 152, Hawaii 145, Washington 152.

Camel Safaris
China 34, India 53, Sahara 41, Australia 61.

Mountaineering Seminars
Peru 133, Alaska 153, Washington 146.

Mountaineering Expeditions
China 31, Nepal 42, India 52, Switzerland 109, Austria/Germany 103, Turkey 111, U.S.S.R. 113, Bolivia 126, Peru 133, Ecuador 135, Mexico 138, Argentina 125, Alaska 153, Washington 146.

Skiing
France, Italy, Switzerland, Czechoslovakia, Norway, Lappland, U.S.S.R., Argentina, Washington , New Zealand, India, 154, & 155.

Calendar Index

Most of our 1986 trips will be repeated in 1987 on approximately the same dates.

January

Asia
The Annapurna Skyline Trek 45
Winter Festivals of Ladakh 50

Africa
Kenya Wildlife Safari 77
Tanzania Wildlife Safari 82
Climb Kilimanjaro 81
Wildlife Trekking Safari 78
Sahara Camel Safari 71

Europe
SKI: Italy: Monte Rosa 154
SKI: France: Val D'Isere-Tignes 154
SKI: Ski Holiday In Switzerland 154
SKI: Chamonix Ski Week 154
SKI: Ski Holiday In Switzerland 154

South America
Mountains Of Colombia 136
Patagonia Overland 124
Natural History Of Costa Rica 136
Discover Peru 127
The Aconcagua Expedition 123

North America
The Other Hawaii 145
SKI: Washington: Powder Skiing 154

February

Asia
The Nepal Adventure 41
Australia & Tanzania: Down Under 60
The Annapurna Skyline Trek 45
The Everest Escapade 39
Rajasthan Camel Safari 53

Africa
Discover Kenya 76
Neolithic Art Of The Sahara 73
Tanzania Wildlife Safari 82
Ancient Egypt 74
Kenya & Kilimanjaro Trek 80
Kenya Wildlife Safari 77
A Walk In The Sahara 73

Europe
SKI: Chamonix Ski Week 154
SKI: Italy: Monte Rosa 154
SKI: Norway: The Trails 154
SKI: U.S.S.R.: The Caucasus 154
SKI: Norway: The National Parks 154

South America
Patagonia Overland 123
Natural History Of Costa Rica 136
Volcanoes Of Mexico 138

March

Asia
The Everest Escapade 39
The Annapurna Skyline Trek 45
East Of Everest 41
Everest Walk-In Route 37
The Annapurna Skyline Trek 45
Sherpa Village Trek With Hillary 36
Papua New Guinea Patrol 59
Bhutan: The Chomolhari Trek 54

Africa
The Tanzania Express 83
Great Parks Of East Africa 79
Climb Kilimanjaro 81
Kenya Wildlife Safari 77
Botswana: Halley's Comet 87

Europe
SKI: Chamonix Ski Week 154
SKI: Switzerland: Engadin Ski Marathon 154
SKI: Italy: Monte Rosa 154
SKI: France: Val D'Isere-Tignes 154
SKI: Czechoslovakia: The Tatra Mts. 154

South America
Antarctica: The Bottom Of The World 123
Volcanoes Of Chile 123
Amazon Jungles & Inca Ruins 130
Volcanoes Of Mexico 138
The Peru Adventure 128
Discover Peru 127
The Galapagos Islands 134
Tarahumara Easter Fiesta 139

April

Asia
Tibet: Mt. Shishapangma Expedition 31
Family Trek In Nepal 39
Sherpa Village Trek With Hillary 36
Khumbu/Everest Exploration 38
Journey To The Marquesas 58
The Everest Escapade 39
Annapurna Sanctuary Trek 43
Around Annapurna 43
Tibet: Mt. Everest/ Shishapangma 31

Europe
SKI: Italy: Randonee Monte Rosa 154
SKI: France: Chamonix 154
SKI: Ski Lappland 154
SKI: Switzerland: The Haute Route 154

South America
Peru: Halley's Comet Tour 131
The Peru Adventure 128
The Other Mexico 127

North America
SKI: Alaska Spring Tour 154
The Other Hawaii 145

May

Asia
Tibet To Nepal Overland 27
Kun Lun Exploratory 34
Everest Base Camp 38
Temples/Monasteries Of Tibet 30
Trekkers' Holiday In Kashmir 48
Tibet: The Namche Barwa Trek 32
Pakistan: High Roads To Hunza 47
Trek To The Source Of The Ganges 52

Africa
The Zimbabwe Expedition 86

Europe
The Irish Countryside 99
The Other Italy 104

South America
Amazon Jungles & Inca Ruins 130
Ecuador Natural History 135
Peru: The Carabaya Trek 130

Pakistan *Sloane Smith* · ***Ecuador*** *Alla Schmitz* · ***China*** *Brian K. Weirum* · ***Kazakhstan*** *John Thune* · ***Tibet*** *Kurt Schwalbe* · ***Ladakh*** *Gordon Wiltsie* · ***Kenya*** *Allen Bechky* · ***China*** *Susan Thiele*

The Galapagos Islands 134
Walking Inca Trails 131
Highlands Of Bolivia 126
The Peru Adventure 128

North America

Mt. McKinley Expedition 153

June

Asia

Sia Kangri Expedition 52
Australia: The Outback Experience 61
Trekker's Holiday In Kashmir 48
Pakistan: The Baltoro/K2 Trek 46
Outback Camel Expedition 61
Tibet: Roof Of The World 28
Bhutan: The Lunana Trek 55
The Zanskar Trek 51
The Muztagata & Bogda Trek 34

Africa

Tanzania Wildlife Safari 82
Discover Kenya 76
The Botswana Safari 87
Climb Kilimanjaro 81
Kenya Wildlife Safari 78
Wildlife Trekking Safari 78

Europe

The Other Bavaria 102
The Other France 106
The Other Spain 100
The Other Britain 97
The Hills Of Czechoslovakia 102
Highland Hikes Of North Britain 98
Mont Blanc Circuit 108
Walks in Portugal & Madeira 101
Natural History Of Norway 100
Hiking In The Pyrenees 107
Ireland & Britain 98

South America

Andean Climbing Seminar 133
The Trans-Andean 132
Walking Inca Trails 131
The Peru Adventure 128
Cordillera Blanca Expedition 133

North America

McKinley Climbing Seminar 153
Noatak River By Canoe 151
Alaska Wildlife Safari 152
Canoeing Admiralty Island 149
Hawaii: Outer Island Adventure 145
The Inland Passage 146

July

Asia

Tibet: Roof Of The World 28
Trekkers' Holiday In Kashmir 48
Trekking In Kashmir & Ladakh 49
Trekking In Hunza 46
The Trans-Himalaya Trek 50
Zanskar: A Hidden Kingdom 49

Africa

Rwanda/Zaire Gorilla Expedition 85
The Tanzania Express 83
Kenya & Kilimanjaro Trek 80
Great Parks Of East Africa 79

Europe

The Greek Islands 110
Mont Blanc Circuit 108
Hiking The Haute Route 109
Alpine Hikes In Bavaria & Tyrol 103
Italy: The Val D'Aosta Hike 104
Exploring Iceland 99
Classic Climbs In The Alps 109
Italy: A Walk Through Piemonte 105
Italy: The Dolomites Hike 105
Ireland & Britain 98
Turkey: Mt. Ararat & The Taurus Mts. 111
The Pamirs & Peak Lenin 113

South America

The Peru Adventure 128
The Peruvian Highlands 129
Walking Inca Trails 131
SKI: Argentina: Bariloche 154
Bolivia 21,000 126

North America

North Cascades Seminar & Climb 146
The Inland Passage 146
Backpacking The Chilkoot Trail 148
The Arrigetch Wilderness 151
Kayaking In Glacier Bay 149
White Mountains Of New Hampshire 146
Canoeing Admiralty Island 149
Noatak Kayaking 150

August

Asia

Trekkers' Holiday In Kashmir 48
Trekking In Hunza 46
Tibet: Roof Of The World 28
Trekking In Kashmir & Ladakh 49
Pakistan: High Roads To Hunza 47
The Trans-Himalaya Trek 50
Tibet: Roof Of The World 28
K2 & The Chinese Karakorum 35
Tibet: Mt. Everest/Shishapangma 31

Africa

Botswana Camping Safari 86
Kenya Wildlife Safari 77
Climb Kilimanjaro 81
Discover Kenya 76
The Zimbabwe Expedition 86
Great Parks Of East Africa 79

Europe

Classic Climbs In The Alps 109
Eastern Alps Climbing Circuit 103
Hiking The Haute Route 109
Italy: A Walk Through Piemonte 105
Italy: The Val D'Aosta Hike 104
The Other Britain 97
Mont Blanc Circuit 108
Travels In Kazakhstan 111
Italy: The Dolomites Hike 105
The Irish Countryside 99
Mont Blanc Circuit 108
Hiking In The Pyrenees 107

South America

SKI: Argentina: Bariloche 154
The Peru Adventure 128
Walking Inca Trails 131
The Peruvian Highlands 129
Amazon Jungles & Inca Ruins 130
Peru: The Inca Legacy 132

North America

Tatshenshini/Alsek Rafting 148
Kayaking In Glacier Bay 149
Backpacking On McKinley 152
Kobuk River Kayaking 150
Canoeing Admiralty Island 149
White Mountains Of New Hampshire 146

September

Asia

Australia: The Outback Experience 61
The Silk Road 35
Trekking In Mongolia 36
Mt. Kailas: Holy Mountain Of Tibet 32
Tibet: Roof Of The World 28
North Alps Of Japan 57
Bhutan: The Chomolhari Trek 54
Bhutan:
Bumthang Cultural Tour 55
Bhutan: The Lunana Trek 55
SKI: Himalayan Ski Expedition 154
Trekkers' Holiday In Kashmir 48
Everest Walk-In Route 37
The Minya Konka Trek 33

Africa

Rwanda/Zaire Gorilla Expedition 85
Kenya & Kilimanjaro Trek 80
Kenya Wildlife Safari 77
The Botswana Safari 87
Kenya Cradle of Mankind 78
Great Parks Of East Africa 79

Europe

Hiking In Greece & Crete 110
The Other Italy 104
Highland Hikes Of North Britain 98
The Other France 106
The Other Bavaria 102
U.S.S.R.:
The Caucasus & Mt. Elbrus 112
Italy: A Walk Through Piemonte 105
The Other Spain 101

South America

The Peru Adventure 128
Discover Peru 127
The Other Mexico 107

October

Asia

Sacred Mountains
Of The Central Himalayas 53
Trekking In The Sigunian Valley 33
SKI: New Zealand Alps 154
Trekking In Sikkim 54
Around Annapurna 44
The Annapurna Skyline Trek 45
Tibet To Nepal Overland 27
Khumbu Himal & Mt. Mera 42
The Everest Escapade 39
Bhutan: The Chomolhari Trek 54
Khumbu/Everest Exploration 38
Expedition 20,000 42

Africa

The Zimbabwe Expedition 86
Botswana Camping Safari 86
Climb Kilimanjaro 81
Egypt & The Sinai 75
Discover Kenya 76
Kenya Wildlife Safari 77
Sahara Camel Safari 71

Europe

U.S.S.R.: Travels In Armenia 112
Walks In Portugal & Madeira 101

South America

Amazon Jungles & Inca Ruins 130
Painted Caves Of Baja 139
Volcanoes Of Mexico 138

North America

The Other Hawaii 145

November

Asia

The Annapurna Skyline Trek 45
Sri Lanka & The Maldives 56
Annapurna Sanctuary Trek 43
Buddhist Nepal: A Himalayan Trek 40
Tibet To Nepal Overland 27
The Everest Escapade 39
Rajasthan Camel Safari 53
The Manaslu Trek 43
East Of Everest 41
Tramping In New Zealand 59
Everest Base Camp 38

Africa

Sudan: The Nile & Nubian Desert 73
Ancient Egypt 74
Tanzania Wildlife Safari 82

South America

Antarctica:
The Bottom Of The World 125
Painted Caves Of Baja 139
Discover Peru 127
Mountains Of Ecuador 135

December

Asia

The Everest Escapade 39
The Nepal Adventure 41
Australia & Tasmania: Down Under 60
Journey To The Marquesas 58
The Annapurna Skyline Trek 45
Papua New Guinea Patrol 59
Thai Elephant Safari 56

Africa

Climb Kilimanjaro 81
Sahara Camel Safari 71
Discover Kenya 76
Tanzania Wildlife Safari 82

South America

Patagonia Overland 123
Discover Peru 127
Natural History Of Costa Rica 136
Volcanoes Of Mexico 138
The Galapagos Islands 134

North America

The Other Hawaii 145

Please Note:

We publish dates, prices and itineraries up to a year and a half in advance so you can formulate your travel plans with us well ahead of time. Since we do work so far in advance, there may be some changes in dates, prices and itineraries after the printing of this publication (August, 1985). All changes will be listed in the Trip Itineraries made up specifically for each trip.

Call or write our office for the most current information.

MOUNTAIN TRAVEL®

Write:
1398 Solano Avenue
Albany, California 94706

Call:
415 527-8100 (inside CA)
800 227-2384 (outside CA)

Nepal *Brian K. Weirum* · ***Tanzania*** *Allen Bechky* · ***Pakistan*** *Pam Shandrick* · ***Nepal*** *Charles Gay* · ***India*** *Jan Zabinski* · ***Peru*** *Sara Steck* · ***Pakistan*** *Jan Zabinski* · ***Tibet*** *Lanny Johnson*

Mountain Travel's Trip Grading System

Most commercial adventure travel firms have devised some kind of grading system to help deliniate the differences between trips.

Of course, the whole notion of "trip grading" should be considered in light of your own experience. Trips that may be strenuous for some are quite easy for others!

Even though we suggest pre-trip physical conditioning, we can't emphasize the following point strongly enough: the most important qualifications for any adventure travel trip are a positive mental attitude, a spirit of adventure, a sense of humor and a willingness to try new and different experiences. This can make all the difference!

Mountain Travel's trips are rated by both a letter and a number. The letter "B" or "C" denotes what altitude is reached on the trip (B is under 15,000 feet, C is above 15,000 feet) or if mountaineering experience is required (Grade D and E).

The number rating takes into account factors such as trail conditions and length of daily hikes.

1 EASY

2 MODERATE

3 STRENUOUS

Grade A
Allen Steck

Grade B
Dave Parker

Grade C
Hugh Swift

Grade D
Bruce Klepinger

Grade E
Gary Bocarde

A trips in the Mountain Travel system are "hiking optional" trips which can be undertaken by anyone who enjoys a moderately active life. These might include a walking tour of Ireland or a jeep safari in Africa.

B trips involve some required physical activity, such as hiking. Within the "B" category trips can run the gamut, since hiking time might vary from an easy three to a tough seven hours per day, depending on the particular trip. On B trips where you don't have to backpack, the rating is "B-1" or "B-2." Previous camping experience is recommended for B-1 and B-2 trips, but not required. If a trip requires backpacking, we call it "B-3" (strenuous).

C trips are different from "B" trips in that *some* of the hiking takes place at altitudes above 15,000 feet. The reason we separate them from "B" trips is that hiking at high altitudes is strenuous. However, most C trips are "treks," meaning that pack animals or porters carry all the loads and a staff of camp assistants does the cooking and camp chores. So a C-2 or C-3 trip might be *less strenuous* than a B-3 trip!

D trips require basic mountaineering skills. We assume that you are a strong, physically fit hiker who is familiar with the use of climbing equipment (ropes, ice axe, crampons) and has general mountain knowledge (use of small stoves, route finding, etc.).

E trips require advanced mountaineering skills, usually several years of solid background in the skills appropriate to the expedition combined with top physical condition. A detailed resume of your mountaineering background is required; we may require references.

Adventure Travel Activities

To help you identify the major activity focus of each trip listed in this book, we have assigned graphic symbols to represent each of the 12 Adventure Travel Activities (the activities are described on the following pages).

One of these symbols will appear with each trip description throughout the book. That way, you'll know immediately what the trip is all about, what qualifications are required, and you'll be able to find a trip which suits you.

Touring

An adventure travel "tour" is a sightseeing trip with travel by vehicle. These trips sometimes use an unusual mode of transport such as a landrover or even a *felucca* boat in Egypt, but *never* a huge "tour bus!" Group size is small, usually less than 15 members. Accommodations are in small hotels and inns.

Even though there is no camping, no required hiking and all travel is done by vehicle, an adventure company's "tours" are special: they visit locations which are well off-the-beaten-path of standard tour itineraries, such as the Marquesas, the mountain valleys of Bavaria, the Pyrenees of southern France.

A range of optional easy day hikes are made available for those who want to participate.

Overland Journeys

"Overlanding" is perhaps the original form of adventure travel. It means traveling on graded dirt roads in remote places through rugged terrain, often by four-wheel-drive vehicle or truck.

Since overland journeys usually visit very isolated places with few tourist facilities, camping is the usual type of accommodation, but sometimes these trips also stay in guest houses or "spontaneous" accommodations such as a village schoolhouse.

A range of easy-to-moderate day hikes are structured into the trips as an integral feature, but there is no required hiking.

When there are no local inns or restaurants, a cook accompanies the group to prepare camp meals *al fresco.*

'The Other Hawaii'/*Sara Steck*

'Patagonia Overland'/*Sara Steck*

'The Greek Islands'/*Allen Steck*

'The Other Britain'/*Mike Banks*

An adventure travel "tour" is a sightseeing trip with travel by an unusual mode of transport such as a landrover or even a felucca boat in Egypt.

'Ancient Egypt'/*Ray Jewell*

'Sudan: The Nile & Nubian Desert'/*Jean Ribat*

"Overlanding" is perhaps the original form of adventure travel. It means traveling on graded dirt roads in remote places through rugged terrain, often by four-wheel-drive vehicle or truck.

Hut-To-Hut Hiking

This is a favorite sport among mountain enthusiasts in Europe, where a system of inns, huts and refuges has been built throughout mountain regions of the Alps to accommodate hikers and climbers.

Since food and shelter is provided, hikers need not carry sleeping bags, tents, fuel, stove or food: just personal hiking clothes. Depending on what you like to bring with you in the way of clothing, your pack might weigh between 15 and 20 lbs.

Huts vary widely in the amenities they offer. Some are luxurious; others are rustic and offer just the basics. Some have dormitory-style accommodation, while others have two- or four-bed rooms. Private baths are not available.

A wide variety of hearty local cuisine is served, including soup, meat, vegetables, local breads, cheeses and good wine.

Huts accommodate up to 100 hikers or more and operate on a first-come, first-serve basis; no advance reservations can be made. No one is ever turned away, so some huts can be crowded on some popular routes (especially in July, when French and Italians take their annual vacations).

Trails of varying steepness connect the huts, which are usually a day's hike (four to six hours) apart.

If you go alone, you need to do advance planning including studying your route in guide books and maps. Speaking a few words of the local language is most helpful.

On a hut-to-hut trip with an adventure travel company, the trip is escorted by a guide who knows the area well and is with the group at all times. Outside Europe, good hut systems exist in New Zealand, Japan and New England's White Mountains.

'Hiking In The Dolomites'/ *Dick McGowan*

On a hut-to-hut trip with an adventure travel group outfitter, the trip is escorted by a guide who knows the area well and is with the group at all times.

Trekking

A group "trek" is a fully organized long-distance walk, with porters or pack animals carrying all equipment, tents, food and your personal gear for the entire trip. Trekking parties are self-sufficient "go-anywhere" units staffed by a leader and a local manager who directs a locally hired cook, camp assistants, porters or animal handlers (typically, Peru treks use mules as pack animals, India treks use horses, and Nepal treks use yaks). You don't have to carry anything.

Treks usually take place in undeveloped countries where salaries are low and large staffs can be hired. The range of "comforts" available on commercial treks will vary according to the price you pay. Top-of-the-line trekking companies will provide an experienced kitchen staff trained in hygiene, a trip physician, toilet tents, a dining tent, hot washing water and "bed tea." Less expensive outfitters provide a much more spartan experience.

Even though on a trek, all camp chores are done for you and all loads are carried by porters and/or pack animals, treks usually involve daily walks of five to eight hours, sometimes at altitudes above 10,000 feet, and often on hilly terrain.

So, treks are for people who are fit, in good health and who love walking, even long days of it. A properly designed trek route allows for gradual acclimatization to high altitudes.

'Everest Base Camp'/ *Brian K. Weirum*

'Peru Highlands'/ *Bruce Klepinger*

'Around Annapurna'/ *Charles Gay*

'Sherpa Villages'/ *Dick McGowan*

Top-of-the-line trekking companies will provide an experienced kitchen staff trained in hygiene, a trip physician, toilet tents, a dining tent, hot washing water and "bed tea."

Camel Safaris

Camels are exotic, picturesque and intelligent beasts whose antics and personalities add a special dimension to any trip.

On camel safaris, arrangements are much like a trek (see *Trekking*): the group is a self-contained unit traveling alone in the desert, with all gear and water carried by pack camels. There is a staff of camel handlers and camp assistants to do cooking and camp chores.

On a Sahara camel safari, the Touareg guides will show you how to gracefully (or sometimes not so gracefully!) mount and dismount, and even teach you how to get your camel to sit down and get up. Camels are trained with signals, like horses, and are usually very personable. Most of the bad "p.r." about camels is about animals which have been mistreated. A well-kept camel is a dignified animal of great character (ask any Touareg!).

Depending on the trip, you may ride part of the time and walk part of the time. You don't have to carry anything.

Deserts like the Sahara in Africa and the Thar in India can have extremes in temperature, but it never feels unpleasantly hot because the air is so dry. Nights are usually quite cold in the Sahara.

'Rajasthan Camel Safari'/*Marsha Parker*
Depending on the trip, you may ride part of the time and walk part of the time. You don't have to carry anything.

Backpacking

Backpacking is primarily an American sport. It means carrying *on your back* all you need to survive in the wilderness (your personal gear, such as sleeping bag, foam pad, clothes and equipment, plus a share of community gear such as tents, food, stoves, fuel). Going off for a week of backpacking means you might carry 40 to 50 lbs. depending on where you go, the local terrain and what climates you will encounter.

On an adventure travel company's backpack trips, the loads carried by participants are usually more moderate because caches of food may have been air-dropped or packed in by horses or other methods in advance of the trip (depending on the region).

When you sign up for a commercial backpack trip, check how much you will be carrying and whether the guides do the cooking and camp chores, as is often the case.

Backpack trips operate mostly in Alaska, Hawaii and the Lower 48 and are designed for strong and experienced hikers.

'The Caucasus & Mt. Elbrus'/
Dick McGowan
On an adventure travel company's backpack trips, the loads carried by participants are usually moderate.

Mountaineering
Expeditions

These vary widely in scope and in the skills required. Most commercial mountaineering trips climb peaks that are more physically than technically demanding.

For some climbs, participants should have at least three years of mountaineering experience and should know self-arrest, belays and other climbing techniques instinctively, as well as a thorough knowledge of the use of ice axe, crampons, anchors and other climbing tools.

If the expedition goes to altitudes over 18,000 feet (an arbitrary line), it's advisable to have previous climbing experience at high altitude before embarking.

Backpacking is required on the approach to some climbs, and all participants must be in top physical shape, able to carry loads of up to 60 lbs. at altitude.

In addition, it's important to be eager to do things the "expedition way," that is, to share the load carrying and camp chores including cooking, as well as lending support to others as needed.

Mountaineering
Seminars

Mountaineering seminars conducted by experienced alpinists offer the opportunity to learn the complete range of mountaineering skills including basic knots, belaying, basic rope handling, self arrest, glissading, snow climbing techniques, rappelling, use of ice axe and crampons, glacier travel techniques, crevasse rescue, avalanche rescue procedures, mountain safety, first aid and high altitude medical problems.

Also included may be technical ice climbing (instruction and practice using modern techniques and equipment), basic rock climbing (instruction and climbing techniques, use of pitons and chocks, setting up belay anchors, rapelling).

Usually, no prior climbing experience is necessary, but members must be very fit, since backpacking is often required on the approach to the site where the seminar is held.

'The McKinley Expedition'/*Gary Bocarde*

Ski Trips

Ski adventures are tours which include the services of a professional ski guide every skiing day and an itinerary designed to maximize the ski experience.

Downhill Skiing Tours: Visits to downhill ski resorts which share a vast variety of slopes for intermediates and experts alike. Add to this the company of an outstanding local guide, the ambience of world-class resorts like Val D'Isere in the French Alps and you have a skier's dream. Accommodations are in four-star hotels. Meals are usually included.

Randonee Skiing Tours: The sport of *randonee* is growing fast. It's a combination of downhill and cross-country skiing that gives access to the back-country far from ski lifts. Using light-weight equipment with skis, bindings and skins adapted for ascents and descents, you tour across the mountains and stay in a different hotel, lodge or camp each night. Simply put, *randonee* adds a touch of mountaineering to downhill skiing: a classic example is the Haute Route, the most famous *randonee* tour in the world.

'Skiing The Haute Route'/*Lanny Johnson*

The sport of randonee is growing fast. It's a combination of downhill and cross-country skiing.

Cross-Country Touring: Using medium-weight nordic equipment, this type of ski trip allows access to forests, national parks and glaciers and is primarily designed for the telemark enthusiast. Accommodations are in small hotels and ski lodges.

Cross-Country Trail Tours: Using light-weight nordic equipment, these tours take full advantage of the well-prepared and marked trails of Europe. These trail systems, designed exclusively for nordic skiers, connect villages and cross-country ski centers. Accommodations enroute range from quaint country inns to modern hotels.

'Norway: The Trails'/*Dave Parker*

Wildlife & Natural History Safaris

Led by professional or amateur naturalist guides, wildlife trips are informative adventures which pave the way for a greater understanding of the world's wild places.

Gameviewing is usually the most compelling reason to travel to Africa, and it can be fantastically rewarding. A wide variety of African safaris can be arranged: there are lodge safaris in Africa's classic game lodges, some of which are very deluxe, and from which one seeks game by vehicle.

There are also first-class camping safaris with a full staff of camp assistants, walk-in safari tents and travel by landrovers which hold 4 to 5 persons: this is perhaps the ideal "adventure safari" with the maximum chance of wildlife encounters and the most intimate contact with wild Africa.

Available in only two parks in Africa (Tsavo in Kenya and Luangwa in Zambia) are "foot safaris," the unique experience of seeking game on foot while on extended walks in bush country in the company of armed park rangers.

In the Amazon, the Galapagos Islands and in Southeast Alaska's Inland Passage, wildlife trips are best accomplished on small boats which allow minimum impact on the environment.

The key to getting the most from any safari or wildlife adventure is to have an experienced leader, one who knows wildlife biology and can plan a gameviewing strategy which maximizes your chances for observation.

'The Galapagos Islands'/*Alla Schmitz*

'Tanzania Wildlife Safari'/*Peter Ourusoff*

The key to getting the most from any safari or wildlife adventure is to have an experienced leader, one who knows wildlife biology and can maximize your chances for observation

'Wildlife Trekking Safari'/*Peter Ourusoff*

'Discover Kenya'/*Iain Allan*

Water Trips

River rafting comes in two categories: **"float trips"** on calm river with only brief stretches of small rapids, and **"whitewater trips,"** on which you can expect long periods of exciting waves. Commercial raft trips often use oar-frame rafts which hold 8 passengers and are fully operated by a skilled oarsman; he steers the boat with two large oars and you simply sit down, hang on and enjoy the excitement.

Kayaking: Most kayak outfitters use stable crafts designed for use by novices. These are usually inflatable or have built-in air sponsons for stability. They seat two people in comfort, with gear stowed in the bow and stern. The best of these easily-handled kayaks is the German-made Klepper brand (people have crossed the Atlantic in them!). They can be operated by anyone and do not require any special skills. At the start, the trip leader gives instruction in basic technique, which can be adequately mastered in a couple of hours.

Canoes: These trips feature safe, lightweight aluminum crafts which hold two people. Canoe trips usually take place on gentle rivers and lakes, so no previous "paddling" experience is necessary; you can pick up flatwater canoeing skills very quickly.

On group raft, kayak and canoe trips, camping equipment is carried on the boats in waterproof bags. The guides give instruction in river safety and all participants are required to wear life-jackets. Camp is set each night on a scenic and convenient spot along the shore. The guides cook the meals, and trip members may be asked to pitch in to help in setting up tents and doing some camp chores.

'Tatshenshini Alsek Rafting'/
Fred Faye-Hiltner

Cultural Expeditions

Cultural Expeditions are adventurous journeys **accompanied by a scholar/lecturer** whose academic expertise relates specifically to the remote centers of art and culture visited in the itinerary.

For example, a "cultural expedition" to the Silk Road in China may be accompanied by a professor of Chinese art and history, a Peru trip by a specialist in Inca and Pre-Inca history.

Throughout the trip, lectures by the leader and informal discussions with the group bring to life the great historic and artistic sights which are visited. Most cultural expeditions do not require hiking or trekking, except when that is the only means of access to an area of particular significance. Accommodations are as per *Touring* category unless there is trekking involved.

'Winter Festivals of Ladakh'/
Jim Gerstley

"Buddhist Nepal. A Himalayan Trek"/
Alla Schmitz

'Canoeing Admiralty Island'/*Leo Le Bon*

Camp is set up each night on a convenient spot along the shore. The guides cook the meals and trip members may be asked to pitch in to help in setting up tents and doing some camp chores.

'Temples & Monasteries of Lhasa & Central Tibet'/*Leo Le Bon*

Cultural Expeditions are adventurous journeys accompanied by a scholar/lecturer whose academic expertise relates specifically to the remote centers of art and culture visited.

SECTION II
ASIA & THE PACIFIC

"Nothing interrupted my view of the great amphitheatre about me. The cliffs and ridges of K2 rose out of the glacier in one stupendous sweep to the summit of the mountain, 12,000 feet above. The sight was beyond my comprehension and I sat gazing at it, with a kind of timid fascination, watching wreathes of mist creep in and out of corries utterly remote."

Eric Shipton,
Blank on the Map

Window detail, Nepal/*Hugh Swift*

Eric Shipton, last British consul assigned to Kashgar, Britain's most remote listening post in Central Asia, was one of the great explorers of modern times. He had one of his finest adventures among the northern solitudes of the Karakorum Range on a five-month-long expedition in 1937. He surveyed 1800 square miles and climbed up into the great amphitheatre under the forbidden north wall of K2, second highest mountain on earth.

It is incredible to think, now that we are in the age of satellites, that thousands of square miles of the earth still remained uncharted as late as 1937.

K2, Everest and Kanchenjunga, the supreme triumvirate, are the three highest mountains on earth. These mountains represent the magic of Asia and the dreams of those who seek that magic. It is toward these high and mighty mountains that all adventure and adventurous travelers to Asia seem to gravitate.

What diversity do we find in Asia! China is the land of more than 85 different nationalities, spread out over the 3,000-mile-long Silk Road, a caravan route linked by 2,000-year-old cities. In India, more than 100 tongues are spoken, 15 of which are recognized as national languages. In Pakistan there is the remote mountain Shangri La of Hunza, where people live to be 140! On the roof of Asia, there is long-forbidden Tibet— virtually closed to outsiders most of its history—with its magical capital of Lhasa and the fabulous gold-encrusted Potala Palace of the Dalai Lama.

Asia is also home to exotic wildlife, much of it endangered—including the mystical snow leopard of the Himalayas and the Royal Bengal tiger of the jungles. Asia has unique game parks where wildlife can be viewed from a very unique vantage point—from an elephant's back!

Throughout the Himalayas, there is magnificent trekking the entire 1,000-mile-length of the range, from Pakistan's Hindu Kush in the west to eastern Bhutan, a kingdom still lost in time and Buddhist tradition.

Whether a modern Asian adventure is an overland journey by minibus in Tibet, a camel caravan in Sinkiang on the Silk Road, or a trek among the colorful village of Hunza, it is certain to provide a rich and rewarding adventure.

Tibetan lama in Lhasa/*Lanny Johnson*

Floating market in Bangkok/*Sara Steck*

Baltoro Glacier, Pakistan. Besides keeping trekking expeditions on the move, Balti and Hunzakut porters add a cultural dimension to the trekking experience with their colorful traditions, dances and songs/*Dick McGowan*

Adventure Travel In Asia

Camels carry a trekking expedition's loads to K2 in the Chinese Karakorum. Travel in China's remote regions has been forbidden for many years, but this is rapidly changing as the Chinese get more accustomed to our strange (to them) requests to camp, trek and explore their remote areas/*Susan Thiele.*

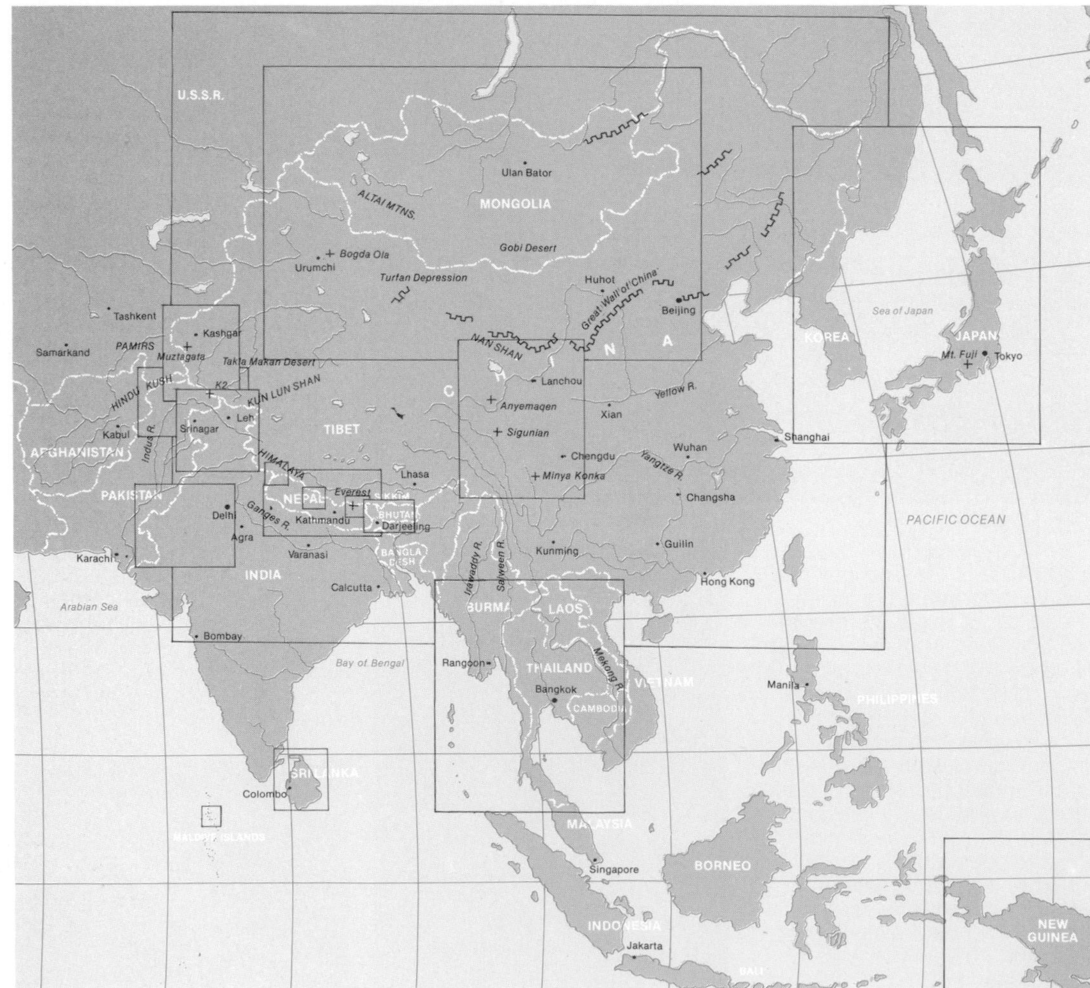

China:

Adventure travel is still in its budding stage in China, and new opportunities are becoming available all the time. In 1980, commercial adventure travel firms pioneered mountain exploration and trekking in the provinces of Sinkiang, Sichuan, Amdo and Tibet with great success.

Individual travel in these regions has been forbidden for many years but this is rapidly changing, as the Chinese get more accustomed to our strange (to them) requests to camp, trek and explore their remote areas. Bicycle trips in temperate regions such as the Yangtse Valley are available, and "mountain bike" tours may soon be popular in places like Tibet!

Trekking season generally runs from May through October.

Roof detail, Forbidden City, Beijing/ *Susan Thiele*

Golok woman of Tibet/*Kurt Schwalbe*

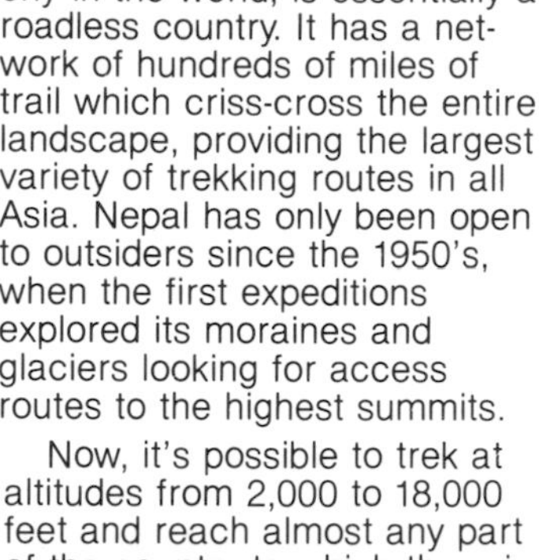

The Chukhung Valley, Nepal. Nepal has only been open to outsiders since the 1950's when the first expeditions explored its moraines and glaciers looking for access routes to its highest summits/Susan Linn

Sadhu, holy man in Kathmandu/ Alla Schmitz

Nepal:

Nepal, the only Hindu monarchy in the world, is essentially a roadless country. It has a network of hundreds of miles of trail which criss-cross the entire landscape, providing the largest variety of trekking routes in all Asia. Nepal has only been open to outsiders since the 1950's, when the first expeditions explored its moraines and glaciers looking for access routes to the highest summits.

Now, it's possible to trek at altitudes from 2,000 to 18,000 feet and reach almost any part of the country to which there is legal access (certain remote sections of east and west Nepal, however, are still off-limits).

Multi-day raft trips are possible on rivers such as the Sun Kosi and Trisuli. "Small peak" climbing is also permitted on dozens of non-technical "small" summits such as Island Peak and Mt. Mera (small by Himalayan standards—about 20,000 feet!). Special permits are required for the big mountains.

High season for trekking is mid-October to mid-December—with mild-to-cool weather. January and February are the coldest months, good for low altitude treks. March to May are excellent months, the warmest and most flower-filled season for trekking. Avoid June to September—that's monsoon season.

Summit of Island Peak, Nepal/ Eric Sanford

Pakistan:

Pakistan is less traveled by Westerners than most parts of Asia, even through there is superb trekking throughout its North West Frontier Province: Hunza, Chitral, Yasin, Baltistan and Swat are mountain valleys with cultures unique in Asia.

Trekking in northern Pakistan still affords much of the same excitement experienced by the early British explorers of the Western Himalayas: unmapped terrain, wild river crossings, villages where few Westerners have ever been, and some of the longest glaciers in the world outside the Polar regions. For those who don't like trekking, Pakistan offers overland jeep travel on the serpentine mountain roads which connect the villages of the North West Frontier Provinces.

The best season for northern Pakistan is May to September. Pakistan's mountain weather is very warm, so expect some hot-weather hiking during mid-day.

The trail above Namche Bazaar, Nepal/ Richard Irvin

Trekking in Pakistan still affords much of the same excitement experienced by the early British explorers of the Western Himalayas: unmapped terrain, wild river crossings, villages where few Westerners have ever been/ Bruce Klepinger

In Bhutan, a secluded Buddhist kingdom, only certain limited regions are open to trekking, and it is hard to get permission for individual treks/

Hugh Swift

'Winter Festivals of Ladakh'/ Siddiq Wahid

India:

Ladakh ("Little Tibet") offers a glimpse into a thriving Buddhist culture set in a high altitude plateau near the headwaters of the Indus. Here one can trek from monastery to monastery. Neighboring Kashmir offers a Moslem culture, dense conifer forests and great trout fishing. In times past, the British raj fled to Kashmir's cool, fragrant mountains in summer to escape the searing heat of India's plains. Fine treks can be accomplished in Himalchal Pradesh, the Kulu and Lahoul valleys, Garhwal in the central Himalaya, and in Darjeeing and Sikkim in the foothills of the Eastern Himalayas.

Alpine trekking and "small peak" mountaineering is available in Kashmir, Ladakh and Zanskar. Jeep expeditions are possible throughout many of India's mountain regions. Camel safaris are a wonderful way to travel the Thar Desert of Rajasthan. Game-viewing safaris by elephant or landrover are available in many wildlife parks such as Corbett, Kazirange (rhino!) and Kanha (the best place in India for catching a glimpse of a Royal Bengal tiger in the wild).

Trekking and mountaineering season in Kashmir/Ladakh is June to September. The season for Darjeeling and Sikkim runs from October to April (avoid the wet season between June and September).

Rajasthan's deserts and India's wildlife parks are best visited in the cooler winter months from November to February.

Sri Lanka:

Sri Lanka has trek routes in its delightful interior—terraced tea-growing country. There is fine wildlife viewing in its seaside settings such as Yala National park.

Bhutan:

In Bhutan, a secluded Buddhist kingdom, only certain limited regions are open for trekking. It is very hard to get permission for individual treks, as the Bhutanese infrastructure prefers to deal with groups. Trek routes are available to Chomolhari, the "divine" mountain of Bhutan, to Bhumthang in the eastern part of the country, and an extremely alpine route is open to Lunana on the Tibetan frontier. The trek season runs from November to April.

Mongolia:

Pony treks are available in the foothills of the Altai Mountains. Access is through the U.S.S.R.

Rangdum Monastery. Ladakh ("Little Tibet") offers a glimpse into a thriving Buddhist culture set in a high-altitude plateau/Hugh Swift

Mongolian family in "yurt"/Nigel Dabby

Camel trekking in Australia/ Warwick Deacock

New Zealand has extensive possibilities including trekking, mountaineering and ski touring, particularly in Mt. Cook National Park/Dick McGowan

South Korea, Japan, New Zealand:

These countries offer the only "hut to hut" hiking in Asia. Nightly accommodations are in mountain huts maintained by local mountain clubs. Japan's mountain huts are unique *ryokans* complete with *tatami* mats and futons. New Zealand has extensive possibilities, including trekking, mountaineering and ski touring, particularly rewarding at Mt. Cook National Park.

Papua New Guinea:

Only 30 years ago did outsiders penetrate the "green walls" of this island to encounter its lost Stone Age tribes. Adventure travel here takes place in "river trucks," motorized rafts which ply the interior rivers. This is the only way to gain access to many tribal villages.

Australia:

Perhaps the most enticing area of Australia for the adventurer is its great outback, a colorful desert where camel safaris from 7 to 22 days can be arranged. Jeep overlanding is also very popular.

Many visitors prefer the "underwater adventure" of the Great Barrier Reef, the world's greatest marine wildlife sanctuary, a paradise for snorkelers and scuba enthusiasts.

Only 30 years ago did outsiders penetrate the "green walls" of this island to encounter its lost Stone Age tribes/Dick McGowan

Asia Bibliography

Nepal

PEOPLE OF NEPAL
Dor Bahadur Bista, Ratna Pustak Bhandar, 1972.

THE ARUN: A NATURAL HISTORY OF THE WORLD'S DEEPEST VALLEY
Edward W. Cronin, Jr., Houghton Mifflin, 1979. Exploration of Nepal.

RHYTHMS OF A HIMALAYAN VILLAGE
Hugh R. Downs, Harper & Row, 1980. Village life of a Sherpa Buddhist community.

SHERPA HIMALAYA NEPAL
Mario Fantin, English Book Store, 1978.

BIRDS OF NEPAL
Robert L. Fleming, Sr. and Jr., Avalok, 1979.

PLANT HUNTING IN NEPAL
Roy Lancaster, Crook Helm, 1981. Adventures in Eastern Nepal.

STONES OF SILENCE: JOURNEYS IN THE HIMALAYA
George Schaller, Viking Press, 1980.

THE SHERPAS OF NEPAL
Christoph von Furer-Haimendorf, John Murray, 1964.

TREKKING IN THE HIMALAYAS
Stan Armington, Lonely Planet, 1982. Trekking in Nepal.

TREKKING IN THE NEPAL HIMALAYA
New edition of the above, 1985.

The following are mountaineering classics:

AMERICANS ON EVEREST
James Ramsey Ullman, Lippincott, 1964.

EVEREST: A MOUNTAINEERING HISTORY
Walt Unsworth, Houghton Mifflin, 1981.

India

HIMALAYAN WONDERLAND
Manohar Singh Gill, Vikas, 1972. Travels in Lahaul-Spiti.

BUDDHIST PARADISE: THE MURALS OF ALCHI
P. Pal, Nanda, 1982. A remote monastery in Ladakh.

LADAKH: BETWEEN EARTH AND SKY
Siddiq Wahid and Kenneth Storm, Jr. Edita, 1981. A beautiful portrait of this unique land.

THE TRAVELER'S KEY TO NORTHERN INDIA
Alistair Shearer, Knopf, 1983. A guide to the sacred places of northern India.

Pakistan

IN THE THRONE ROOM OF THE MOUNTAIN GODS
Galen Rowell, Sierra Club, 1977. American K2 expedition.

WHERE FOUR WORLDS MEET
Fosco Maraini, Harcourt, Brace & World, 1964. Hindu Kush.

KARAKORAM
Fosco Maraini, Viking, 1961. The ascent of Gasherbrum IV.

WHEN MEN AND MOUNTAINS MEET
John Keay, John Murray, 1981. Explorers of the Western Himalayas from 1820–1875.

THE GILGIT GAME
John Keay, John Murray, 1979. A companion volume to the above, exploration from 1865–1895.

CONTINENTS IN COLLISION
Keith Miller, George Philip, 1982. Hunza and Batura Glacier.

THE NAKED MOUNTAIN
Elizabeth Knowlton, Putnam, 1934. Nanga Parbat.

China

MOUNTAINS OF THE MIDDLE KINGDOM
Galen Rowell, Sierra Club, 1983. Exploration of Chinese mountain territory.

FOREIGN DEVILS ON THE SILK ROAD
Peter Hopkirk, University of Massachusetts Press, 1984. The search for the lost cities and treasures of Chinese Central Asia.

KONGUR, CHINA'S ELUSIVE SUMMIT
Chris Bonington, Hodder & Stoughton, 1982. Mountaineering.

MEN AGAINST THE CLOUDS
Richard Burdsall and Arthur Emmons, Mountaineers, 1980. The 1932 American expedition to Minya Konka.

BLANK ON THE MAP
Eric Shipton, Hodder & Stoughton, 1938. Explorations in Sinkiang, China.

Tibet

SEVEN YEARS IN TIBET
Heinrich Harrer, Houghton Mifflin, 1982. A vivid picture of Tibet before 1959. Reprint.

TRESPASSERS ON THE ROOF OF THE WORLD
Peter Hopkirk, Jeremy Tarcher, 1982. The opening up of Tibet during the 19th and 20th centuries.

TIBET
Ngapo Ngawang Jigmei. Jugoslovenska Revija, 1981.

ON TOP OF THE WORLD: FIVE WOMEN EXPLORERS IN TIBET
Luree Miller, Mountaineers, 1984.

A CULTURAL HISTORY OF TIBET
David Snellgrove and Hugh Richardson. Prajna Press, 1980.

TIBETAN BUDDHISM WITH ITS MYSTIC CULTS.
L. Augustine Waddell, Dover, 1972.

THE SACRED MOUNTAIN
John Snelling, East West Publications, 1984. Mt. Kailas.

A MOUNTAIN IN TIBET
Charles Allen, Andre Deutsch, 1982. The search for Mount Kailas and the sources of the great rivers of India.

Other & General Asia

ABODE OF SNOW
Kenneth Mason, Dutton, 1975. A history of Himalayan exploration and mountaineering.

FIRST ACROSS THE ROOF OF THE WORLD
Graeme Dingle and Peter Hillary, Hodder & Stoughton, 1982. Ten months trek across entire Himalaya.

TREKKER'S GUIDE TO THE HIMALAYAS AND KARAKORAM
Hugh Swift, Sierra Club, 1982. Covers the entire Himalayan system.

MOUNTAINS OF THE GODS
Ian Cameron, Century Publishing, 1984. History and exploration in the mountains of the Himalayas and Central Asia.

BHUTAN
Michael Aris, Aris & Phillips, 1979. History.

TWO AND TWO HALVES TO BHUTAN
Peter Steele, Hodder & Stoughton, 1970. A family journey in the Himalayas.

BHUTAN: A KINGDOM OF THE EASTERN HIMALAYAS
Francoise Pommaret-Imaeda and Yoshiro Imaeda. Shambhala, 1985.

TRACKS
Robyn Davidson, Pantheon, 1980. Australian outback.

JAPAN HANDBOOK
J.D. Bisignani, Moon Publications, 1983

ISLAND CIVILIZATIONS OF POLYNESIA
Robert C. Suggs, 1960.

Staying Healthy In Third World Countries

When you travel outside of the United States, Canada and Europe, you will probably be traveling in countries in which there are endemic health problems caused by poor-quality drinking water and inadequate sanitation. This is a problem both in the cities and in rural areas where "adventure travel" opportunities present themselves.

On Mountain Travel trips, food is prepared by experienced cooks using the highest possible degree of sanitation. We have a very good record of health on our trips.

However, anyone who travels in the "third world" is subject to getting the occasional bout with traveler's diarrhea and should take adequate measure to protect him or herself.

Here are a few basic rules of common sense: eat no food which is uncooked or which is bought from sidewalk vendors. Thoroughly cooked food which is still hot from a hotel kitchen is generally safe. Beware of salads. Custards, ice creams and creams in pastries are not safe in areas where refrigeration methods are primitive. Unboiled milk and its by-products are suspect.

Drinking tap water or even brushing your teeth in it is dangerous. At hotels, use the bottled water which is usually provided for you, preferably after adding your own disinfectant, such as iodine. Ice cubes are usually made from the local water supply, which may be contaminated. Streams may look enticing to drink from, but germs are invisible. Wash your hands before you eat. Don't eat food with your hands unless you have just washed them.

If you get diarrhea, don't let yourself get dehydrated. Keep drinking lots of liquids. Most cases of diarrhea are simply caused by a change in dietary habits and are nothing to worry about. Simple "traveler's diarrhea" will not last more than a week.

If your diarrhea lasts more than a week, you may have come in contact with a parasite and you may then require a week or ten days of treatment with antibiotics (tetracyline or sulfa drugs) or an antiparasitic drug (such as Flagyl.)

Discuss the pros and cons of medications with your physician before you start your trip. Medications of this sort are generally available without prescriptions in foreign countries. See the "Health Matters" section of this book for more information and a personal first aid kit list.

It's hard to advise exactly what physical shape you should be in for each different type of adventure travel activity (this is especially true for hiking trips, which vary greatly in what they demand of people). Read our descriptions in the *Activity* section at the front of the book (i.e., trekking, hut-to-hut hiking) and think about what these trips might involve.

The difference between being in great shape for a hiking trip and being only in fair shape basically means this: people in great shape will enjoy the hike more, get through the day's walk in a reasonable amount of time, spend less time worrying about breathing and more time enjoying the views and taking pictures. People who are only in fair shape will huff and puff, struggle on the uphills, get to the hut (or campsite) later than people in good shape, and might spend a lot of their vacation time feeling exhausted.

The hiking itself will probably get you in shape after several days of it, but why waste the first few days being uncomfortable? If you want to enjoy your hiking trip to the utmost, start pre-trip conditioning activities such as jogging, aerobics classes or bicycling. Begin about six weeks before the trip. Then *really* stick with your program right up until you go.

And remember, even if your "adventure" is only an easy trip with optional day hikes, travel itself can be wearing (airplanes, time changes, packing and unpacking, culture shock). Being in good physical shape will give you more stamina to enjoy every aspect of your journey.

High Altitude Acclimatization

The special problems of being at high altitiude are invariably a part of treks in the Himalayas and Andes.

Have you hiked at 10,000 feet or more? If so, you will probably find that hiking at 15,000 feet is simply an extension of your previous experience. You'll walk more slowly, rest more frequently, have some restlessness at night and be subject to headaches. However, if your previous reaction to altitude has been nausea or other unpleasant symptoms, trekking at high altitude may not suit you.

Neither age, gender nor previous experience at altitude has anything to do with whether or not you do well at high altitude. Obviously, it doesn't help if you are in bad shape, overweight and a heavy smoker.

Your trek should be designed for maximum altitude conditioning in the early days of the trek. That simply means don't go up too high too fast. However, be forewarned that there are no guarantees that your body will acclimatize properly.

To avoid severe cases of altitude sickness, *do not overexert yourself.* Take the day's hike at a slow pace, REST during rest stops, drink plenty of fluids.

Anyone who shows signs of potentially severe mountain sickness (such as H.A.P.E.—high altitude pulmonary edema) should immediately descend and remain at comfortable altitudes. Several excellent books and pamphlets are now available on high altitude medicine for trekkers and climbers. They include: *Mountain Sickness: Prevention, Recognition, & Treatment* by Peter H. Hackett, M.D. 1980. And for general wilderness emergencies, *Medicine For Mountaineering* by James A. Wilkerson, 1969.

Physical Conditioning For Adventure Travel

Who shouldn't go: people who are sedentary, senile or overweight; people with diabetes, high blood pressure, or significant heart, back or knee problems.

Who should go: people who enjoy being *active* in their everyday lives, whether their idea of "active" is just a simple one-hour walk before dinner or a whole weekend of bike riding in the hills. There is such a variety of adventure travel experiences to choose from that almost every healthy person can find *some* form of it to enjoy.

Trekkers on the Cho La Pass (17,800'), Nepal. Treks are designed for "altitude conditioning" in the early days of the trek. That simply means not going too high too fast/*Brian K. Weirum*

"A Skeptic Goes Trekking"

by Sarah Pearce

I'm coming out of the closet. A year ago, I was a Mountain Travel skeptic. Hadn't even heard of Mountain Travel. It was my father who started talking about Nepal last spring. He wanted to do a trek with Mountain Travel. Did I want to come?

"Dad", I said smugly, "You know me. I don't do *tours*. Nepal? Great! But I bet with a little research and some diligence, we could plan our own trip. . ."

He interrupted and said with some reverence, that this would be a *Mountain Travel* trek, not an ordinary tour.

I was not familiar with MT's reputation and I thought the whole thing reeked suspiciously of an organized tour. You know —a large group in day-old Adidas and Winnebago Glee Club windbreakers being herded frantically through exotic cities like they were visiting a local shopping mall. Not the style in which I pictured myself travelling. Nor, for that matter, how I imagined my seasoned, adventurous father would want to see Nepal.

In retrospect, however, my father fits the MT profile. He's been around the block a few times, knows what he needs to see but wants an experience he can sink his teeth into. Something slightly risky but with an element of style.

Yet, even after committing myself to the Mountain Travel Annapurna Sanctuary Trek, I remained hesitant. Something inside was fighting the ease with which MT took over and made all the arrangements. Was I missing something by not making the rounds of the airline offices, sending out queries to hotels, researching trekking companies in Kathmandu and blazing trails through equipment lists?

On a more serious and crucial issue, I became very familiar with the high degree of precautions MT takes to insure that any medical emergency on the trek can be met adequately. My father would be going as trek physician and, as a nurse, I helped him organize an impressive amount of medical supplies as required by MT for physicians. It was evident that MT puts safety above all else in a country where medical attention, if available at all, can be several days away. On foot.

Trekkers climbing up to the lush alpine grasslands of the Annapurna Sanctuary in Nepal/*Lanny Johnson*

On the way to Kathmandu, my father and I spent a good deal of in-flight time in conjecture over the type of person our leader, Scot Macbeth, might turn out to be. I was expecting someone along the lines of a character Victor Mature might have played in a safari film—arrogant, aloof, mysterious about why he takes on these trips into remote areas, hints of intrigue in his life and way above the common weekend hoofer.

Once I met Scot Macbeth, standing in the thundering mob outside the airport, I began to get an inkling of what MT was all about. Away from the gloss and slick of advertising brochures, MT has only its guides to rely on in terms of delivering the quality trip expected. From the start, Scot was personable, intuitive and quite down to earth. I don't think anyone in our group had anything but the utmost confidence in this man's ability to deliver us a first rate experience. No detail was too small for him to attend to personally. We were impressed right from the beginning and we continued to be warmed by his humor and energy.

The first time the group all met together, I glanced briefly at the strange faces around me. I realized that these were strong, experienced travellers. For the most part, each person had a varied background in mountaineering. One entire family on the trek had climbed the Matterhorn and completed several Outward Bound courses. My own tentmate was an Outward Bound instructor in New Zealand. Another guy had just completed a six-month traverse of the Continental Divide—this was his *vacation?* One woman had returned the previous day from a trek to the Everest Base Camp.

I looked across at my father. Dear old dad. He'd been running 5-7 miles a day, hiking, biking and doing weight training. I wanted to strangle him for being in such good shape. What if he had to quit the trek and accompany his exhausted daughter back to civilization? There goes his lifelong dream of seeing the Himalayas. What had I gotten myself into?

Two days later, we began walking.

The trailhead was just outside Pokhara, a one-hour flight from Kathmandu. In the beginning, we walked easily along a river valley, the Seti Khola, surrounded by green Himalayan foothills. The sharp Himalayan peaks in the distance were obscured by cloud-cover except in the early morning. Passing through villages, we were surrounded by children returning home from school. But in these low altitude populations so near the trailhead, we were not much of a curiosity.

At the end of the first day, I looked back laughingly over my previous doubts. We had had an easy walk in good weather and, with light daypacks, it had been more like a stroll. Lunch had been ready and waiting along the trailside. Spread out picnic style on a blue tarp, our meal was not the usual trail fare I was used to fixing: it was onion omelettes, cheese, potatoes, bread, oranges and tea.

Our campsite for the night was by the river. Our tents were already up and tea was waiting for us as we walked into camp.

As the days passed, the amenities I enjoyed took on greater meaning as I came to know some of the Sherpas and helpers who provided these nice extras.

Annapurna villager/*Barb Kaplan*

Each member of the kitchen staff had a specific routine. In the morning, it was Wan Chu and Rotni, two of the Sherpa guides, who would come to wake us.

"Good morning, *Didis,*" Wan Chu would say to Judy and I as he unzipped our tent flat. *Didi* is the Nepali word for older sister or a woman a little older than you. "Coffee or tea or cocoa?"

We were practicing our Nepali, so Judy would ask for *taato paani* or hot water for her own tea bags and I would ask for *chiyaa* or tea.

The steaming mugs were thrust through the tent door and we sipped while still in our sleeping bags. Our morning ritual was to take a few moments to warm up with our cups and stare at the Himalayas, clear from cloud cover and highlighted with the alpenglow of dawn.

Wan Chu made a second round of the tents distributing *dhune paani* or warm washing water in tin bowls. We were expected to be washed and packed fairly quickly in the morning. Antare, another Sherpa guide, would stroll by the tents after Wan Chu's washing water tour, reminding us that the porters needed to pack up and leave for our next campsite. If someone needed help stuffing a bag or zipping a duffel, Antare would smile and help.

The day would take on a cadence dictated by walking and the interludes of conversation, chance meetings with other passing trekkers or rest stops at tea houses along the trail.

Many conversational inhibitions disappear when you talk for hours at a time while walking. Talk quickly drifts to topics that, outside the confines of such a trip, would demand more than being just a passing acquaintance. Yet when you eat, sleep, walk, share sickness, physical exertion and a travel experience, companions become much more than passing acquaintances. Life stories come out easily during a level traverse through a cool, bamboo forest. Travel adventures keep the steady push on a steep uphill from being sheer torture. And at the top of that

Village woman, Naudanda/Susan Thiele

uphill, sweating and gasping as you share water with a companion, it's as if you've known them all of your life.

One day, my tentmate Judy and I stopped on a high ridge to eat some trail mix. We looked back to where we'd been and what the trail was like ahead. Behind us was some of the hardest walking we'd done in a long time. Staircases! Hours and hours worth of handhewn staircases! In front of us is a misted, narrow canyon lined at the bottom with a glacial-blue river. Around the upper edges is a ridge of screaming-tall snow-capped peaks—we guess that they're over 20,000 feet. It's a site I might see (minus the 20,000 foot range) if I hiked days into the wilderness of California. But there's a catch. In the near distance is an oasis. There's a town. We can see where the trail turns into a lane between gleaming white-washed houses with thatched roofs. A small farm nearby is busy—three oxen are hitched to a pivot pole and are threshing some kind of grain. The family driving the oxen are singing and working in their colored clothes of scarlet, goldenrod and mauve. Cast against the deep flaxen backdrop of their crops, it's almost perfect choreography. A photograph taken now could be nothing but splendid. But Judy and I are silent—no camera shutters for the present. We are trying to fathom a country where a town and people can exist five days hard hiking from the nearest road, electric light or phone.

The green foothills below Machapuchare/Hugh Swift

At every village, we stopped for tea or Lemu (the Indian equivalent of Squirt). This was a good place to meet other trekkers. On our route to the Annapurna Sanctuary, we met people coming back from the Sanctuary. We got a pretty good idea about the place long before we actually saw the Sanctuary based on the reports we received.

On Day 9 of the trek, we reached the Sanctuary. Our campsite was at 9,900 feet, the Machupuchare Base Camp. The actual Sanctuary is 3,400 feet higher at 13,000 feet. We had a welcome layover day here. There was a small tea house just inside the glacial bowl that is called the Annapurna Sanctuary View Lodge. I spent most of the day lying in the sun near the teahouse, resting in the thin air, watching the mountains of the Annapurna Himal glow.

Our pace quickened as we left the Sanctuary and headed back to Pokhara. The much talked about Fishtail Lodge, where hot showers were waiting, became our new goal. We were able to have one more layover day near the village of Dhampus due to our new-found energetic pace.

We arrived in Dhampus on Thanksgiving Day. There was the usual afternoon routine. The tents were waiting for us on a grazing field near the village. Wan Chu brought us our washing water and we had much-needed sponge baths.

Our Thanksgiving dinner included chicken, mashed potatoes, dichon and a pumpkin pie, specially baked by our cook. Someone had placed candles and flowers on the table. Scot provided *rakshi,* beer and rum for the many toasts offered that evening.

In a sense, it was a fitting way for the trek to draw to a close, the Thanksgiving holiday. Be it trekkers in Nepal or pilgrims in the New World, travelers like to band together and consume good food when a goal has been met.

Ms. Pearce was a member of our ANNAPURNA SANCTUARY TREK in Nepal.

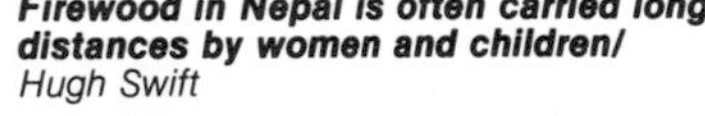

Firewood in Nepal is often carried long distances by women and children/ Hugh Swift

Asia Leaders

Trip leaders are an important part of what makes a Mountain Travel trip special. Our Asia leaders come to us with a wide variety of backgrounds. Some are chosen for their knowledge of the language or culture, some for their mountaineering experience, but above all, for their ability to assure a safe, enjoyable and successful trip.

Bruce Klepinger

Lanny Johnson

Richard Irvin   Dick McGowan

Scot Macbeth

Charles Gay   Daku Tenzing Norgay

Ray Jewell

Warwick Deacock   Jerry Coe

Mike Perry   Bob Bates

ROBERT E. BATES, originally from Australia, came to Papua New Guinea in 1964 as an engineer for the Papua New Guinea government. He has lived in the highland town of Mt. Hagen for the last 15 years and has climbed most of Papua New Guinea's major mountains.

SMOKE BLANCHARD, 66, is a mountaineer with over 40 years of guiding and climbing experience. He has completed extensive mountain walks throughout Japan, Nepal, India and Alaska and his autobiography, *Walking Up And Down In The World,* was recently published by the Sierra Club.

JERRY COE, 34, is a mountaineer, woodworker and blacksmith. He is conversant in Japanese and Chinese and leads mountain treks in China and the Himalayas. When not on trek, he designs metal sculptures and ornamental architectural ironwork.

WARWICK DEACOCK, 58, is the founder of Ausventure, Australia's oldest adventure travel company. Retired from the British Army, he set up the Australian Outward Bound School in 1959 and has led 67 Himalayan treks and 13 major expeditions. His favorite among them was a 10,500-mile sale on a 63-foot gaff-rigged schooner to make a first ascent of Big Ben on Heard Island in the sub-Antarctic. Warwick is a Fellow of the Royal Geographic Society and Consul General for Nepal in Australia.

CHARLES GAY, 37, lived in Nepal for several years as a Peace Corps volunteer, speaks fluent Nepali, and is a very experienced trek leader.

RICHARD IRVIN, 55, has been leading Mountain Travel treks in Nepal, India and Pakistan since 1979. A former mathematics teacher and recent ecology graduate from the University of California, Davis, he has more than 30 years of mountain exploration and climbing experience and is a veteran of nine major expeditions.

RAY JEWELL, 52, has been with Mountain Travel ever since its inception, and was a member of our very first trip (the first group of Americans ever to trek in Nepal). A former physicist, Ray has over 50 Mountain Travel trips to his credit, specializing in leading treks in Asia.

LAURIE JEAYS, 47, is a master mariner. He comes from Queensland, Australia, and has a long background of outings in the Northern Territory, New Guinea and the Himalaya. He has built his own 35-foot yacht and is a full time adventure travel guide.

LANNY JOHNSON, 30, is a professional mountaineer and skier. He has led many treks in Nepal for Mountain Travel and has participated in major Himalayan expeditions, including the International Expedition on Makalu in 1977. In 1984, he led our attempt on Changtse (24,868′), north peak of Everest, in Tibet. Lanny has also climbed and taught downhill and nordic skiing for many years in the U.S. and Canada.

BRUCE KLEPINGER, 44, has led more than 80 Mountain Travel treks in Asia and South America. His mountaineering background includes over 1,000 climbs, and he has led numerous expeditions on Aconcagua (highest peak in the Western Hemisphere), Huascaran (highest peak in Peru), and peaks in Nepal and India. He has also spent many years as a senior boatman on the Grand Canyon of the Colorado River.

LEO LE BON, 51, president and founder of Mountain Travel, has more than 25 years of professional experience in all phases of the travel industry, both in his native Europe and in the U.S. His early interest in wilderness travel led him to the creation of Mountain Travel in 1967. An avid sailor, skier and mountaineer, he has made exploratory expeditions on five continents in search of unusual forms of adventure travel.

SCOT MACBETH, 55, is a field geologist by profession, mountaineer by avocation, and founder of the Alpine Stomach Club. He has spent years leading treks in Nepal, calls the Khumbu region his "second home," and was a member of the 1981 American Everest Expedition in Tibet.

DICK McGOWAN, 52, Mountain Travel's vice president and general manager, has climbed and trekked throughout the world. He led the first guided ascent of Mt. McKinley and was Chief Guide on Mt. Rainier from 1956 to 1965 (with 83 ascents of that mountain!). He has also been on ten major expeditions, including Everest-Lhotse in 1955 and Masherbrum in the Karakorum in 1960. Dick has a lengthy business background as administrator, consultant and manager of several equipment firms.

MIKE PERRY, 29, a New Zealander, is a photographer by profession and has climbed extensively in the Southern Alps of New Zealand for the last ten years.

John Thune

Susan Thiele

Hugh Swift

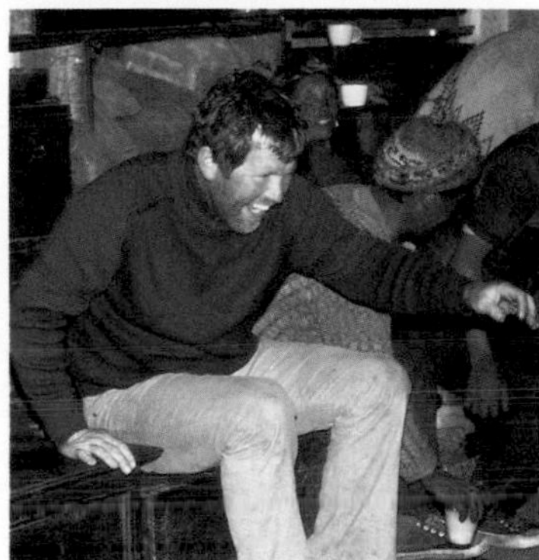
Brian K. Weirum

Jan Zabinski

HUGH SWIFT, 42, author of *The Trekker's Guide to the Himalaya and Karakoram,* has visited just about every nook and cranny of the Himalaya and leads treks in Nepal, India and Pakistan. In 1981–82 he walked from Bhutan to Pakistan, a ten-month journey with 231 camps.

DAKU TENZING NORGAY, 45, is a Sherpani born in the Everest region of Nepal. Wife of Everest summiteer Tenzing Norgay, she is an experienced mountain guide and manages a trekking agency in Darjeeling.

SUSAN THIELE, 37, Mountain Travel's equipment manager, has been a mountain guide for five years. She spent a summer in Beijing, China, studying Chinese language, and her Chinese travels have taken her from China's heartland to the remote mountains of Sinkiang, China's westernmost province. She is conversant in basic Mandarin. She has also trekked with Mountain Travel in Nepal and the European Alps.

JOHN THUNE, 68, is a mountain enthusiast, skier and runner. A former Park Ranger in Yellowstone, Survival Training Officer in Naval Aviation and a long-time member of the National Ski Patrol, he is a noted photo-lecturer and has trekked extensively in China and Nepal.

BRIAN K. WEIRUM, 41, has a graduate degree in South Asian Political Development from U.C. Santa Barbara and has traveled in Asia for the past 20 years. He has lived and hiked extensively in Nepal during the last 15 years and speaks fluent "hill Nepali." He has yet to climb Rum Doodle.

JAN ZABINSKY, 36, is a ski instructor, mountaineer and school teacher. He taught for three years at the American School in Lahore, Pakistan, and in 1982 completed a 4,000-km, four-month walk from the southern tip of India to Kashmir in the north. He speaks Urdu and Hindi, and has travled extensively in Asia.

Tibet To Nepal Overland

Driving from Kathmandu to Lhasa

In 1985, a long-awaited travel opportunity finally presented itself: a motorable road from Tibet to Nepal was officially opened, giving relatively easy access between Lhasa, the long-forbidden city which is the birthplace of Tibetan Buddhism, and Kathmandu, the 1,000-year-old capital of the Hindu kingdom of Nepal, replete with bazaars, pagodas and temples.

Trip #1 begins in China and ends in Nepal. We first visit Hong Kong and Chengdu (capital of Sichuan Province), then fly to Lhasa for three days of touring its renowned monasteries and the Potala Palace.

Boarding mini-buses, we drive south from Lhasa for several days across the high plains, stopping at the isolated Tibetan towns of Shegar and Shigatse.

Crossing the border into Nepal at the "friendship bridge" near Nilamu, we'll find a change in scenery: a green, welcoming, fertile valley surrounded by high mountains and populated by a diverse mix of Nepalis and Tibetans. A 70-mile drive from the Nepal/Tibet border brings us to Kathmandu.

Enroute between Lhasa and Kathmandu, our accommodations are in simple government-constructed guest houses. Once in Nepal, we stay in a First Class hotel and have two days to enjoy the endless delights of Kathmandu.

Trip #2 travels in the opposite direction, from Nepal to China, visiting Kathmandu first, then Lhasa, Chengdu and Hong Kong.

Itinerary (Trips #1 and #3):
Day 1: Leave U.S.
Day 2: Arrive Hong Kong.
Day 3 and 4: In Hong Kong.
Day 5: Travel to Canton.
Day 6: Fly to Chengdu.
Day 7: In Chengdu.
Day 8: Fly to Lhasa.
Day 9 to 11: In Lhasa.
Day 12: Drive to Gyantse.
Day 13: Drive to Shigatse.
Day 14: In Shigatse.
Day 15: Drive to Shegar.
Day 16: In Shegar.
Day 17: Drive to Nilamu.
Day 18: Go through border formalities and continue to Kathmandu.
Day 19 and 20: In Kathmandu.
Day 21: Fly to Bangkok.
Day 22: Depart Bangkok and arrive U.S.

Trips #2 and #4:
Day 1: Leave U.S.
Day 2: Arrive Bangkok.
Day 3: Fly to Kathmandu.
Day 4 and 5: In Kathmandu.
Day 6: Drive across the border and continue to Nilamu, Tibet.
Day 7: Drive to Shegar.
Day 8: In Shegar.
Day 9: Drive to Shigatse.
Day 10: Drive to Gyantse.
Day 11: Drive to Lhasa.
Day 12 to 14: In Lhasa.
Day 15: Fly to Chengdu.
Day 16: In Chengdu.
Day 17: Fly to Canton.
Day 18: Fly to Hong Kong.
Day 19 and 20: In Hong Kong.
Day 21: Depart Hong Kong on homeward-bound flights.

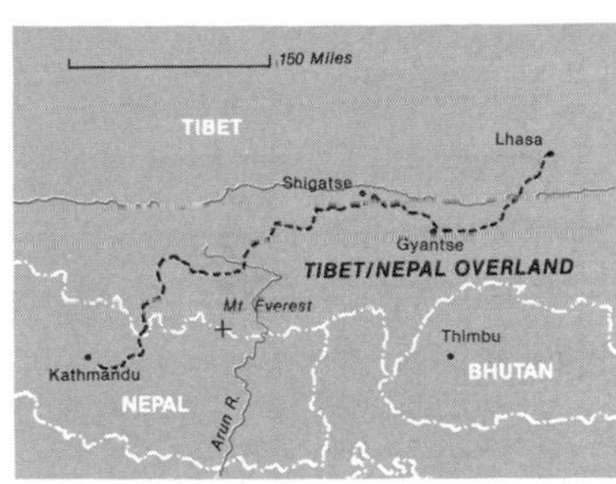

Dates: #1 May 1–May 22 (22 days) (Lhasa/Kathmandu)
#2 May 13–Jun 2 (21 days) (Kathmandu/Lhasa)
#3 Oct 20–Nov 10 (22 days) (Lhasa/Kathmandu)
#4 Nov 2–Nov 22 (21 days) (Kathmandu/Lhasa)
Leader: to be announced
Grade: A-3
Land Cost: $3975 (10 or more members)
Single Supplement: not available
IT6PA1SFAA

Tibet: Roof Of The World

Overland on the Qinghai/ Tibet Plateau

Join a unique high altitude overland adventure which crosses the very "roof of the world," the vast Qinghai/Tibet Plateau, one of the most remote and least known regions on earth.

We travel these reaches for five days by mini-bus with truck support, starting in Xining in northeast China and ending in Lhasa, captial of Tibet. There will be optional day hikes from our off-road camps enroute.

From Lanzhou, capital of Gansu Province, we take the train to the city of Xining on the fringe of the Tibetan Plateau. Taking with us tents, food, camping gear, as well as a liaison officer and a cook, we set out from here into the open wilderness of the Tibetan Plateau.

The road takes us along Qinghai Lake at 10,500 feet, largest lake in China and known for its birdlife, and across the Chaidam, the largest salt basin in Asia, where the one-lane road is built over a foundation of salt crystals.

Reaching Golmud, a staging area for trucks bound for Lhasa, we continue south across feeder streams of the Yangtse River, entering Tibet itself as we cross the Tangu Pass (17,390′), less than 60 miles from the source of the Yangtse.

Further south, we reach our first Tibetan settlements and begin to see yak and sheep herders. Crossing the snow-capped Tanglha Shan peaks, we finally descend to Lhasa, at 11,000 feet, on the 8th day of our crossing.

In Lhasa, we spend our days touring the Potala, the Jokhang and other sites.

Trips #1, #3 and #5 begin in Xining and travel to Lhasa. Trips #2, #4 and #6 begin in Lhasa and travel to Xining.

Itinerary (Trips #1, #3, #5):
Day 1 and 2: Leave San Francisco. Arrive Beijing.
Day 3: In Beijing.
Day 4: Fly to Lanzhou.
Day 5: By train to Xining.
Day 6 to 10: Drive to Lhasa.
Day 11 to 14: In Lhasa.
Day 15: Fly to Chengdu.
Day 16: Fly to Beijing.
Day 17: Depart Beijing and connect with homeward-bound flights.

Itinerary (Trips #2, #4, #6):
Day 1 and 2: Leave San Francisco. Arrive Beijing.
Day 2: In Beijing
Day 4: Fly to Chengdu.
Day 5: Fly to Lhasa.
Day 6 to 9: In Lhasa.
Day 10 to 13: Drive to Xining.
Day 14: Arrive Xining.
Day 15: Train to Lanzhou.
Day 16: Fly to Beijing.
Day 17: Depart Beijing and connect with homeward-bound flights.

Dates: #1 Jun 15–Jul 1 (17 days)
#2 Jul 2–Jul 18
#3 Jul 20–Aug 5
#4 Aug 6–Aug 22
#5 Aug 24–Sep 9
#6 Sep 10–Sep 26
Leader: to be announced
Grade: A-3
Land Cost: $3850
(10–20 members)
Single Supplement: not available
IT6PA1SFAA

China trips include: airfare within China, good hotels with private bath where available, all meals, airport transfers, sightseeing, transport by bus, truck or other conveyance, entrance fees, leadership, guides, visas, permits, government taxes. On treks (if applicable), all arrangements including camp meals, guides, pack animals, services of camp and commissary crew.

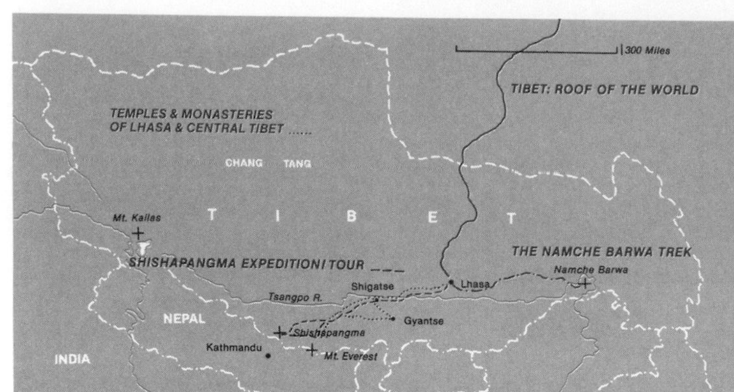

Yak herder from Kharta, Tibet/Leo Le Bon

Roof detail, Potala Palace/ Dick McGowan

Women of Lhasa/Dick McGowan

Taking with us tents, food, camping gear, as well as a liaison officer and a cook, we set out into the open wilderness of the Tibetan Plateau/Leo Le Bon

The Great Wall of China near Beijing/Leo Le Bon

The 13-story Potala Palace, architectural centerpiece of Tibet, is said to contain 1,000 rooms and completely covers the mountain it stands upon. It contains hundreds upon hundreds of brilliant thankas, frescoes and images built in an era when religious art was created anonymously as a means of gaining merit for future lives/John Thune

"Just passing through..."

BEIJING

City notes by John Thune

Walking/jogging routes:

The people of Beijing are accustomed to seeing athletic activities as part of street life. Feel free to practice your tai-chi in the streets at dawn; you'll blend in with many Chinese doing the same thing. If you run, plan to do so early in the morning; after that, the streets are packed with bikes, buses and trucks. Jog in the Temple of Heaven Park, Taoranting Park (both have a small admission fee). You can rent bicycles near the Friendship Store but beware of traffic. Carry a card from your hotel that gives the hotel's name in both Chinese and English so you can find your way back!

Special Markets:

With free enterprise on the move, entrepreneurs have opened stands in many parts of the city, selling a variety of things from clothing to fruit and vegetables.

Restaurants:

Any of countless small, private family restaurants are now open. You might also try Fan Shan, the finest restaurant in Beijing, located in Bei Hai Park (advance reservations necessary).

About Trekking In The People's Republic

Our China trips are accompanied by a Mountain Travel leader plus a Chinese team of three: a liaison officer from the Chinese Mountaineering Association, an interpreter who has studied English at college level, and a cook.

No camp assistants are available in China, so trip members will be expected to pitch their own tents. All camp gear is transported by horses, camel or yaks (porters are not usually available).

Food served in camp will be Chinese, supplemented by supplies from the U.S. (cheese, salami, granola, etc.).

Please note that trek itineraries in China are subject to change due to the complex nature of negotiations with the Chinese Mountaineering Association. Contact us for the latest information on each trek.

Cultural Expedition:

Temples & Monasteries Of Lhasa & Central Tibet

The cultural heritage of an ancient kingdom

This is the most comprehensive cultural tour of Tibet available anywhere, visiting all the historic and religious sites currently open in Tibet, including the Samye, Ganden and Zhalu monasteries.

In our 20 days in Tibet, we focus on the art and history of Buddhism. We begin in the Yarlung Valley, which holds the burial sites of the Tibetan kings, and Samye Monastery.

Traveling next into the Lhasa Valley, we explore its major temple complexes including the 7th century Jokhang, principal Buddhist temple of Lhasa, as well as all of Tibet, with its large gold image of Sakyamuni Buddha.

The 13-story Potala Palace, architectural centerpiece of Tibet, is said to contain 1,000 rooms and completely covers the mountain it stands upon. It contains hundreds upon hundreds of brilliant *thankas,* frescoes and images built in an era when religious art was created anonymously as a means of gaining merit for future lives.

We also visit Norbulingka, the traditional summer palace of the Dalai Lamas, a richly decorated complex located in a beautiful garden setting. This is the place from which the Dalai Lama fled to exile in 1959.

We also visit Sera and Drepung, two of the three large monasteries in the Lhasa area. Sera, founded in 1419, is a monastery of the Gelugpa order. Guilded, bell-shaped *gyamtschens* grace the roofs of many of the larger buildings. Drepung used to have 8,000 monks who were taught in the traditions of Vajrayana, Tantra and Sutra.

We then journey by bus along the Tsangpo Valley to Shigatse and Gyantse (with its unique Kumbum Stupa), then onward by truck over several high passes to Shegar and Tingri, villages within miles of the great Himalayan crest.

Our ultimate destination is the site of Rongbuk Monastery, situated at 16,500 feet near the foot of Mt. Everest. Rongbuk, now being rebuilt and inhabited, was at one time the highest inhabited dwelling on earth. After a day at Rongbuk, we retrace our drive back to Lhasa, visiting Tashilumpo Monastery in Shigatse and the nearby Zhalu Monastery.

There is no required hiking or trekking on the trip, but there will be camping at Tingri and Rongbuk.

Lecturer/Leader: James F. Fisher, Ph.D., professor of anthropology and director of Asian Studies at Carleton College, Northfield, Minnesota, has completed extensive research on Himalayan anthropology, including fieldwork on the trans-Himalayan traders of northwest Nepal. He is conversant in Nepali and in basic Tibetan.

Itinerary: Day 1 and 2: Leave U.S. Arrive Beijing.

Day 3 and 4: Sightseeing in Beijing.

Day 5: Fly to Chengdu.

We visit Sera and Drepung, two of the three largest monasteries in the Lhasa area. Sera was founded in 1419. Drepung used to have 8,000 monks who were taught in the Buddhist traditions of Vajrayana, Tantra and Sutra/ *Leo Le Bon*

Day 6: Fly to Lhasa and drive to Tsetang.

Day 7 and 8: Explore by minibus in the Yarlung Valley, site of the burial sites of the Kings of Tibet.

Day 9: By ferry and donkey cart to the Samye Monastery. Return to Tsetang.

Day 10: Drive to Lhasa.

Day 11 to 14: Tour the Jokhang Temple, the Potala, monasteries of Sera, Drepung and Ganden.

Day 15: Drive to Shigatse, Tibet's second largest city.

Day 16: By bus to Gyantse, crossing the central Tibetan plains.

Day 17: By bus to Shegar.

Day 18: Drive to Tingri, a small farming community on the Tingri Plain.

Day 19: Over the 17,300-foot Pang La Pass to the ruins of Rongbuk Monastery, founded about 300 years ago.

Day 20: At Rongbuk.

Day 21 to 24: Return to Lhasa via Shegar and Shigatse.

Day 25: Fly to Chengdu.

Day 26: In Chengdu.

Day 27: Fly to Beijing.

Day 28: Depart Beijing and connect with homeward-bound flights.

Dates: May 4–May 31 (28 days)
Grade: A-3
Land Cost: $6400 (10–15 members) $6900 (6–9)
Single Supplement: not available
IT6PA1SFAA

Ours is the most comprehensive cultural tour of Tibet available anywhere, visiting all the historic sites currently open in Tibet, including the Samye, Ganden and Zhalu monasteries/*Leo Le Bon*

To reach the mountains, we drive down the valley of the Yarlung Tsangbo to Shigatse and Shegar (14,500′), site of a historic walled village/Leo Le Bon

Tibet: The Mt. Everest/ Shishapangma Tour

Visit Lhasa and northern flanks of the Himalayas

"Tibet, forbidden and forbidding, the land of vast sweeping plateaus and giant ranges crowned with eternal snows, the land of a strange and colorful people. From the time of Marco Polo, it has drawn men of the Western Hemisphere to probe its mysteries. . . ."—R. Burdsall, *Men Against The Clouds.*

Of all the places we visit in China, only one can claim the magic and mystery of Tibet. The aim of our Tibetan travels will be visits to the bases of Mt. Everest (29,028′), known to Tibetans as Chomolungma, and to Mt. Shishapangma (26,291′), one of the last 8,000-meter peaks to be climbed. We arrive at both base camps by truck and have several days for optional day hikes, photography and enjoying the spectacular scenery.

First touring Lhasa, Tibet's capital, we visit the legendary Potala Palace, the very symbol of Tibet, a thousand-room hilltop citadel which was the traditional seat of 13 successive Dalai Lamas, God-Kings of Tibet. We also visit Drepung (the world's largest monastery), and Jokhang, holiest shrine in Tibet and equivalent of Mecca for Tibetan Buddhists.

To reach the mountains, we drive down the valley of the Yarlung Tsangpo to Shigatse and Shegar (14,500′), site of an historic walled village, then further by truck over rough tracks to the base of Shishapangma, where we spend two days taking local walks.

Continuing by truck to the beautiful Tingri Valley, with views of Cho Oyo (26,750′) and Gyanchun Kang (26,140′), we drive over the 17,000-foot Pang La Pass and reach the Rongbuk Valley ("Valley of Precipices"), at the head of which stands Mt. Everest.

At the site of the old Rongbuk Monastery (16,500′), we have four days to explore the area and feast our eyes on the mountain views. Those who are very fit and well acclimatized can hike up the Rongbuk Glacier to advance base camp and Camp I of the historic Everest expeditions of the 1920's.

Itinerary: Day 1 and 2: Leave U.S. Arrive Beijing. Transfer to hotel.

Day 3: Sightseeing including the Great Wall and the Ming Tombs.

Day 4: Fly to Chengdu.

Day 5: Fly to Lhasa on one of the most spectacular mountain flights in the world.

Day 6 to 9: Four sightseeing days in Lhasa, with visits to the Potala, the Norbulingka, and the three great monasteries of Lhasa (Ganden, Sera, and Drepung), and time to stroll in the bazaar.

Day 10: All-day bus ride to Shigatse (12,500′), with a ferry ride across the Tsangbo River. In Shigatse, second largest city in Tibet, we will visit Tashllumpo Monastery, the former seat of the Panchen Lama and one of the most important religious centers in central Tibet.

Day 11: All-day bus ride to the town of Shegar ("White Crystal") at 14,500 feet, crossing the Gyatso La (17,300′).

Day 12: In Shegar.

Day 13: Drive to Shishapangma Base Camp.

Day 14 and 15: At Shishapangma Base Camp.

Day 16: By truck to Rongbuk (16,500′), over the Pang La (17,300′). Spectacular views of the north side of the Himalaya from Makalu to Cho Oyu, including Mt. Everest.

Day 17 to 20: Four layover days at Rongbuk area.

Day 21: By truck to Shegar.

Day 22: By bus to Shigatse.

Day 23: By bus to Gyantse. Visit site of Younghusband's Fort and Kumbum stupa (largest in Tibet).

Day 24: By bus to Lhasa.

Day 25: Fly to Chengdu.

Day 26: Fly to Beijing.

Day 27: Depart Beijing and connect with homeward-bound flights.

Dates: #1 Apr 27–May 23 (27 days)
#2 Aug 31–Sep 26
Leader: #1 to be announced
#2 John Thune
Grade: A-3/C-2
Land Cost: $5900 (10–15 members)
$5900 (6–9)
Single Supplement: not available
IT6PA1SFAA

Yak herders on the Rongbuk Glacier/Lanny Johnson

At the site of the old Rongbuk Monastery (16,500′), we have four days to explore the area and feast our eyes on the mountain views. Those who are very fit and well acclimatized can hike up the Rongbuk Glacier to advance base camp/Leo Le Bon

Tibet: Mt. Shishapangma Expedition

Ascent of world's 14th highest peak

This expedition will attempt to climb Mt. Shishapangma (26,291′), an "8,000-meter" peak and 14th highest mountain in the world. It is located wholly in Tibet, 80 miles northwest of Mt. Everest. We will attempt the standard route.

Even though Shishapangma is considered one of the easier of the 8,000-meter peaks, it is nevertheless a difficult and formidable ascent. All experienced mountaineers know the implications of climbing an 8,000-meter peak. Persons applying for this expedition must have extensive climbing experience.

Itinerary: Day 1 and 2: Leave San Francisco. Arrive Beijing.

Day 3: Fly to Chengdu

Day 4: Fly to Lhasa, Tibet.

Day 5: In Lhasa.

Day 6 to 9: Drive toward Shishapangma by truck and bus with yaks to advance base camp.

Day 10 to 17: Carry loads with yaks to advance base camp.

Day 18 to 53: On the mountain.

Day 54 to 56: Return drive to Lhasa.

Day 57: Fly to Chengdu.

Day 58: Fly to Beijing.

Day 59: Depart Beijing and connect with homeward-bound flights.

Dates: Apr 9–Jun 6 (59 days)
Leader: to be announced
Grade: E-3
Land Cost: approx. $10,000 (10–12 members)
Single Supplement: not available
IT6PA1SFAA

Tibetan man in Shigatse/Lanny Johnson

Tibet: The Namche Barwa Trek

Visit to lush southeastern highlands

Namche Barwa (25,445′), highest unclimbed peak in the world, is considered to be the last great rampart of the Eastern Himalaya. It is a lovely icy pyramid standing above the gorge of the mighty Tsangpo River, which curls around its foot and doubles back on itself to become the Brahmaputra. Just seven miles across the river, Gyala Peri (23,458′), another impressive unclimbed peak, rises toward the mountains of China.

The focus of this trip is a 7-day visit to the base of Namche Barwa with a chance to hike and explore extremely remote and unvisited portions of the southeastern Tibetan highlands.

After a three-day visit to Lhasa, capital of Tibet, we drive for two days by truck to southeastern Tibet, arriving by road at Namche Barwa Base Camp at 9,000 feet. Vegetation around base camp will be lush and subtropical, in great contrast to the peak which rises 15,000 feet above it.

Botanists take a special interest in this region, which is one of the world's great centers of temperate plants, as documented in the 1930's by British botanists.

We spend a week at and above base camp for trekking and local exploration. Stronger trekkers can hike up to Camp II on Namche Barwa at 14,800 feet.

Itinerary: Day 1 and 2: Leave U.S. Arrive Beijing. Transfer to hotel.

Tibetan children at Shegar/ *Lanny Johnson*

Day 3: Sightseeing including the Great Wall and Ming Tombs.

Day 4: Fly to Chengdu.

Day 5: Fly to Lhasa (11,700′).

Day 6 to 8: Sightseeing in Lhasa.

Day 9 and 10: Drive southeast by truck and arrive at Namche Barwa Base Camp.

Day 11 to 17: A week at and around base camp.

Day 18 and 19: Return drive to Lhasa.

Day 20: In Lhasa.

Day 21: Drive to Gyantse via Yamdrok Lake.

Day 22: Morning in Gyantse. Afternoon to Shigatse (12,500′), second largest town in Tibet.

Day 23: Sightseeing in Shigatse.

Day 24: Drive to Lhasa.

Day 25: Fly to Chengdu.

Day 26: In Chengdu.

Day 27: Fly to Beijing.

Day 28: Depart Beijing and connect with homeward-bound flights.

Dates: May 18–Jun 13 (27 days)
Leader: to be announced
Grade: B-2
Land Cost: $6400
(10 or more members)
$6700 (6–9)
Single Supplement: not available
IT6PA1SFAA

After a three-day visit to Lhasa, capital of Tibet, we drive for two days by truck to southeastern Tibet, arriving by road at Namche Barwa Base Camp at 9,000 feet/*Leo Le Bon*

Cultural Expedition:

Mt. Kailas: Holy Mountain Of Tibet

Overland through West Tibet

Mt. Kailas is the holy mountain of Tibet, a 19,910-foot peak revered alike by Hindus and Tibetan Buddhists. They consider Kailas to be the sublime "throne of the gods" and center of the world, both physically and spiritually.

The Kailas region is in fact the source of four great rivers: the Indus, Brahmaputra, Sutlej and Karnali. It is the ultimate pilgrimage center for Hindus and Buddhists who believe that by devoutly circling Mt. Kailas on foot (with Hindus also taking a ritual bath in the glacial waters of serene Lake Manasarovar below it), they will be cleansed of all earthly sins and reach ultimate freedom: Moksha (liberation) to Hindus and Nirvana (extinction) to Buddhists.

To get to West Tibet, we first tour Beijing and Chengdu, then fly to Lhasa. Traveling by minibus from Lhasa, we visit the towns of Shigatse and Shegar, crossing a 17,400-foot pass with views of Mt. Everest.

Continuing by mini-bus (with truck support) on dirt roads which twist through the northern flanks of the Great Himalayan Range, we reach two high lakes near Mt. Kailas. At mountain-ringed Lake Manasarovar ("lake of the mind") at 13,000 feet, we enjoy supreme mountain grandeur in an unbelievably isolated and serene setting. This region is virtually unpopulated, although we may see nomadic herders at the lake and possibly pilgrims on spiritual journeys.

Driving a day towards Mt. Kailas itself, we will make an optional three day, 32-mile walk around the mountain, crossing an 18,000-foot pass and following a pilgrimage route.

Lastly, we drive the Tibetan-Sinkiang highway to the ancient Guge kingdom of West Tibet to visit the ruins of Tsaparang, a crumbling site of deserted shrines and mountain-top monasteries with unique Tibetan Buddhist wall paintings and statues.

Most of this trip is spent at altitudes above 12,000 feet.

There are many long days of travel by minibus on rough roads. We estimate the road travel portion of the trip to be 25 days and 2,175 miles!

Lecturer/Leader: Ed Bernbaum, M.A. and author of *The Way To Shambhala,* a book about Tibetan myth, is writing his doctoral dissertation at the University of California, Berkeley, on pilgrimage and holy mountains in the Himalaya.

Itinerary: Day 1 and 2: Fly U.S. to Beijing.

Day 3: Tour Beijing.

Day 4: Fly to Chengdu.

Day 5: Fly to Lhasa, Tibet.

Day 6 to 8: Tour Lhasa and acclimatize.

Day 9: Drive to Shigatse.

Day 10: Drive to Shegar.

Day 11 to 16: Drive to Lake Manasarovar.

Day 17: Drive to Kailas.

Day 18 to 20: Three-day trek around Mt. Kailas.

Day 21: Spare day.

Day 22 and 23: Drive to Tsaparang.

Day 24 and 25: Return to Lake Manasarovar.

Day 26 to 31: Return to Shegar.

Day 32: Return drive to Shigatse.

Day 33: Visit Gyantse.

Day 34: Return to Lhasa.

Day 35: Fly to Chengdu.

Day 36: Fly to Beijing.

Day 37: In Beijing.

Day 38: Depart Beijing and connect with homeward-bound flights.

Dates: Sep 7–Oct 14 (38 days)
Grade: A-3 (C-3 optional)
Land Cost: $9,360
(10 or more members)
Single Supplement: not available
IT6PA1SFAA

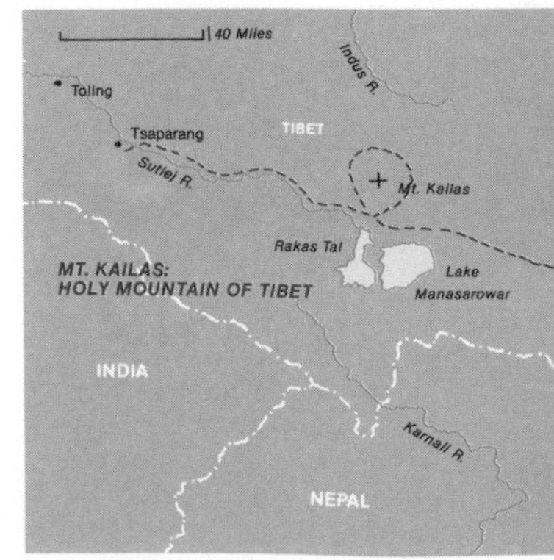

The Minya Konka Trek

13-day trek in the "Alps of Chinese Tibet"

Mt. Minya Konka is the most beautiful mountain in China, a mountain so awesome that "to behold the peak is worth ten years of meditation." This is written on an inscription in the now-restored Konka Gompa ("Snow Monastery") at the foot of the peak.

Mt. Minya Konka—located in the Alps of Chinese Tibet—was truly unknown and unexplored until about 50 years ago. In the early part of this century, a few travellers reported the distant sight of a great mountain in western Sichuan, on the edge of the Tibetan Plateau. Some thought it might be higher than Mt. Everest. It wasn't until the epic National Geographic Society Expedition of 1927–30, led by Dr. Joseph Rock, that the stupendous range called Minya Konka was definitely located and explored. Its highest peak, Mt. Minya Konka (also called Mt. Minya Gongga) towers 24,950 feet, its base drained by the Tatu River at 3,000 feet, less than 20 miles away.

We'll make our own explorations in this region, completing a 13-day trek through remote "Greater Tibet," an autonomous district in western Sichuan, with a visit to the base camp below Minya Konka, and an optional hike up to "Rock's Ridge" at 17,000 feet for spectacular views.

Before the trek, we visit Kanding, a small town nestled in the mountain valleys of western Sichuan, and Chengdu, capital of Sichuan Province.

Itinerary: Day 1 and 2: Leave San Francisco. Arrive Beijing. Transfer to hotel.

Day 3: Sightseeing including the Great Wall and Ming Tombs.

Day 4: Fly to Chengdu. Afternoon tour of city.

Day 5: In Chengdu.

Day 6 to 8: Drive to Kanding via Ya'an and Luding, and on to starting point of trek at Yue Ling at 10,000 feet.

Day 9 and 10: With horses carrying equipment, walk through a landscape dotted with Tibetan houses and tents and striking mountain scenery. Camp at about 13,000 feet.

Mt. Minya Konka is the most beautiful mountain in China, a mountain so awesome that "to behold the peak is worth ten years of meditation"/*Leo Le Bon*

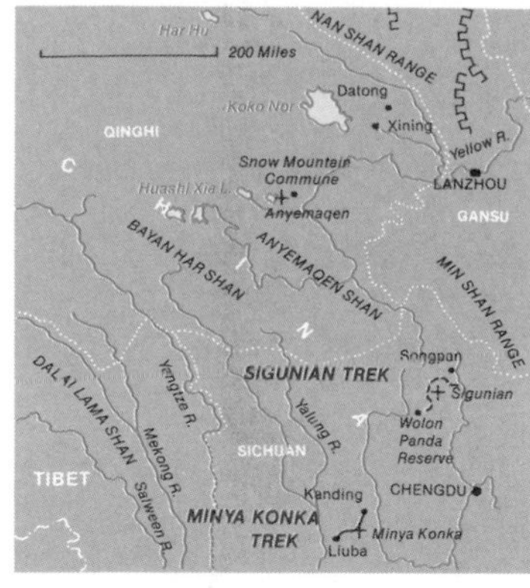

Day 11 and 12: Trek over Sam Pan San Pass (also called Djezi La) at 15,685 feet, then walk down Yulongshi Valley through wild country.

Day 13 and 14: Walk through small Tibetan villages where there has been little contact with foreigners. Layover day.

Day 15 and 16: Up and over the Tsumei La (15,288') and on to Minya Konka base camp and the site of Konka Gompa at 12,300 feet. Magnificent views of Minya Konka.

Day 17 and 18: Layover days to photograph, explore, hike to Rock's Ridge and advance base camp for the standard route on Minya Konka.

Day 19 to 21: Walk back down to Tsumei, once again cross over the Tsumei La to the Yulongshi Valley. Continue past the Sorbu Gompa to Tibetan village of Liuba at the roadhead.

Day 22: Drive to Kanding.

Day 23 and 24: Drive to Chengdu via Ya'an.

Day 25: Fly to Beijing.

Day 26: In Beijing.

Day 27: Depart Beijing and connect with homeward-bound flights.

Dates: Sep 28–Oct 24 (27 days)
Leader: John Thune
Grade: C-3
Land Cost: $3500 (10–15 members) $3800 (7–9)
Single Supplement: not available
IT6PA1SFAA

Trekking In The Sigunian Valley

6-day natural history trek

This trip features a six-day natural history trek in the foothills of the Sigunian Alps, a very beautiful region of granite peaks which rise out of heavily forested valleys. The highest peak in the area is Sigunian (21,600'—"Four Sisters Peak"), one of the most impressive granite spires in the world.

Our trek, which takes place at an average altitude of about 11,000 feet, takes us through rhododendron country, up into green meadows and through deep conifer forests draped with Spanish moss

Birdlife in the region is prolific, including raptors, griffon vultures, lammergeiers, Chinese goshawks and redstarts. We have a good chance of sighting bharal (blue sheep) and musk deer. Higher in this region (although we probably won't be lucky enough to spot them) the forest gives cover to golden-faced monkeys, wild yaks and snow leopards.

We also stop for a visit at Wolon Panda Reserve, a sanctuary established to protect the giant panda and other species.

There is no difficult hiking on the Sigunian trek, but those wishing to see wildlife must be prepared for some steep walks/*Bruce Klepinger*

Woman at village of Shamoju/
Leo Le Bon

Much research on pandas has been done here by naturalist/author George Schaller.

Our approach to Sigunian is via Chengdu, one of China's most historic cities, called the "Storehouse of Heaven," a center for hand-crafted treasures including embroidery, baskets and pottery.

There is no difficult hiking on the trek, but those wishing to see wildlife must be prepared for some steep walks. Horses carry the gear on trek.

Itinerary: Day 1 and 2: Leave U.S. Arrive Beijing. Transfer to hotel.

Day 3 and 4: Sightseeing at the Great Wall, Ming Tombs and Forbidden City.

Day 5: Fly to Chengdu.

Day 6: Sightseeing in old Chengdu.

Day 7: Drive to Wolon (6,435'), through agricultural plains and small villages. Overnight at guest house.

Day 8: By special permit, we visit the Wolon Panda Research Station. There are some pandas living in nearby enclosures which we may be able to visit.

Day 9: All-day drive over Palung Pass (14,500') down to Zelun (10,500') with fine views of the Sigunian Alps.

Day 10: Begin six-day trek into the Sigunian Alps.

Day 11: Camp at about 12,500 feet in a meadow below the impressive northern face of Mt. Sigunian (21,600').

Day 12 to 14: Day hikes in the area, or optional backpacking to a spectacular side canyon that leads to Celestial Peak, a granite pyramid of about 18,500 feet.

Day 15: Return to Zelun.

Day 16: In Zelun, a commune of about 800 people.

Day 17: Drive to Wolon.

Day 18: Drive to Chengdu, with a picnic stop at Two Kings Temple (Erwangsi) built during the Qing Dynasty (221–206 B.C.).

Day 19: Fly to Beijing.

Day 20: Depart Beijing and connect with homeward-bound flights.

Dates: Oct 5–Oct 24 (20 days)
Leader: to be announced
Grade: B-2
Land Cost: $2800 (10–15 members) $3100 (7–9)
Single Supplement: not available
IT6PA1SFAA

Exploring The Kun Lun

China's most mysterious peaks

Of the five great mountain chains of Asia—the Hindu Kush, the Himalaya, the Karakorum, the Tien Shan and Kun Lun, the latter is the least known.

As of this writing (May 1985), no Westerner has ever reached this range of mountains, nor been given access to it via the southern Takla Makan route.

The Kun Lun is a very long range dividing Tibet and western China's Sinkiang Province. Its highest peak is Ulug Mustagh (25,337′), reputed to be one of the highest unclimbed peaks in the world, located in the center of the range at the southern fringe of the fierce Takla Makan Desert, over which Marco Polo traveled on his way from Venice over 800 years ago.

Mountain Travel's proposed exploratory journey starts from Urumchi, capital of Sinkiang. From here we travel south by bus and truck for five days across the Lop Desert, visiting forgotten oases along the way.

Reaching a roadhead at the foothills of the mighty Kun Lun, we will trek for about 12 days to a base camp at 13,000 feet, making a non-technical ascent of a satellite peak of Ulug Mustagh called Mugh Mustag from which we hope to observe and photograph the highest peaks and valleys of the mysterious Kun Lun.

Itinerary: Day 1 and 2: Leave San Francisco. Arrive Beijing.
Day 3 and 4: In Beijing.
Day 5: Fly to Urumchi.
Day 6: In Urumchi.
Day 7 to 11: By bus across Lop Desert.
Day 12 to 23: Exploratory trek in the Kun Lun.
Day 24 to 28: Return drive to Urumchi.
Day 29: Fly to Beijing.
Day 30: Depart Beijing and connect with homeward-bound flights.

Dates: May 2–May 31 (30 days)
Leader: Leo Le Bon
Grade: D-1
Land Cost: approx. $5200 (10–15 members)
Single Supplement: not available
IT6PA1SFAA

Sinkiang: The Muztagata & Bogda Trek

In the Tien Shan and Chinese Pamirs

The western corner of Sinkiang Province, where the borders of Russia, Pakistan and China meet, is the very heart of Central Asia. This is as far away as one can travel from Beijing (3,000 miles) and still be in China! In the heyday of the Silk Road, western Sinkiang was known as High Tartary, Chinese Turkestan, and Kashgaria.

Our Sinkiang journey features two relatively easy treks in two very different mountain regions.

From Beijing, we fly to Urumchi, capital of Sinkiang Province. Driving to Tien Schi Lake (6,000′) in the foothills of the Tien Shan, not far from Urumchi, we make a leisurely four-day trek to the base of Mt. Bogda (17,900′), highest peak in the Tien Shan. Kazakh horsemen carry our gear and we have two layover days at base camp for day hikes in an alpine setting.

For our second trek, we fly to Kashgar, an ancient oasis town in the Takla Makan Desert and last stop on the Silk Road in China. We explore Kashgar's fantastic bazaar (among the most authentic in Central Asia) then drive up into the mountains to a lake at 12,000 feet on the rolling steppes below Mt. Muztagata (24,757′), a Central Asian giant called "the father of ice mountains."

In seven days of easy trekking, we hike to a high camp on Muztagata at 14,750 for wide-ranging views of the snowy summits of Muztagata and nearby Kongur (25,320′) and distant views into the brown vastness of the Soviet Pamirs. We also visit scattered Kirghiz settlements and get a glimpse into the nomadic life that predominates the Central Asian grasslands. Bactrian (two-hump) camels carry all our gear.

At the end of the trek, we may sponsor a "bushkashi," a wild polo-like horse-chase event during which we'll admire the renowned horsemanship of the Kirghiz.

On both treks, we will visit nomadic families (both Kazakh and Kirghiz) in their *yurts,* portable dome-shaped homes made of felt.

Itinerary: Day 1 and 2: Leave U.S. Arrive Beijing.
Day 3 and 4: Sightseeing including the Great Wall and Ming Tombs.
Day 5: Fly to Urumchi.
Day 6: In Urumchi.
Day 7: Drive to Tien Schi Lake.
Day 8: Walk toward Bogda base camp.
Day 9: Arrive at base camp.
Day 10 and 11: Layover days for hikes and exploration.
Day 12: Walk out to the lake.
Day 13: Drive back to Urumchi.
Day 14: Fly to Kashgar.
Day 15: In Kashgar.
Day 16: Drive to Karakol Lake (12,000′) and camp.
Day 17: Trek with camels up to Muztagata Base Camp at 14,750 feet.
Day 18: Optional hike from high camp.
Day 19 to 22: Leisurely trekking to Subashi village, through meadows along the Konsiver River, along rolling grasslands with views of Kongur and Muztagata.
Day 23: Drive back to Kashgar.
Day 24: Fly to Urumchi.
Day 25: Fly to Beijing.
Day 26: In Beijing.
Day 27: Depart Beijing and connect with homeward-bound flights.

Dates: Jun 29–Jul 25 (27 days)
Leader: Susan Thiele
Grade: C-2
Land Cost: $4100 (10–15 members) $4600 (7–9)
Single Supplement: not available

We visit scattered Kirghiz settlements and get a glimpse into the nomadic life that dominates the Central Asian grasslands/*Pam Shandrick*

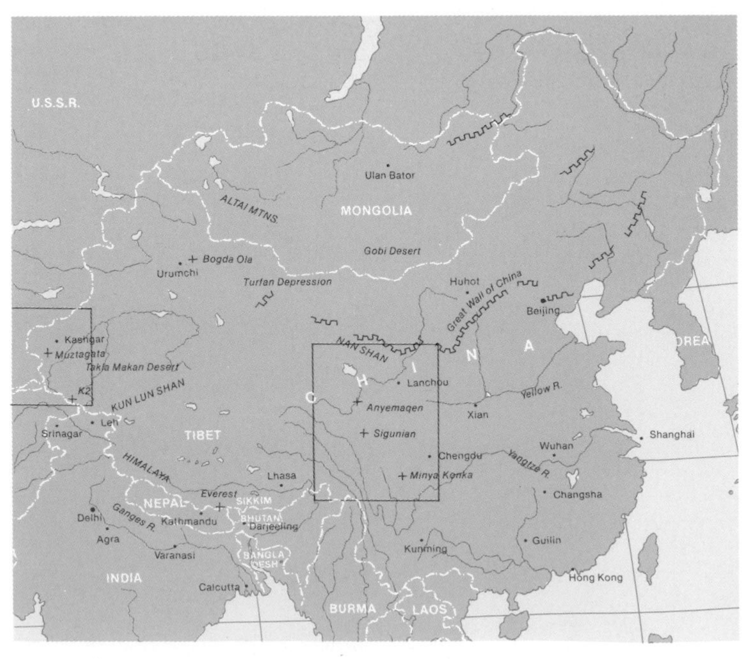

During the heyday of Western exploration of this area, such men as Sven Hedin, Sir Aurel Stein, Albert Von Le Coq and others uncovered much of the lost artistic heritage of early Buddhism (5th to late 16th century)/Susan Thiele

Cultural Expedition

The Silk Road: Ancient Highway Of Central Asia

To the devotee of Buddhist art, no other region on earth offers such a vast treasure of early Buddhist relics as does China's Silk Road. During the heyday of Western exploration of this area at the turn of the century, such men as Sven Hedin, Sir Aurel Stein, Albert Von le Coq and others uncovered much of the lost artistic heritage of early Buddhism (5th to late 16th century).

Our tour, which takes us from the windswept heights of the Muztagata plateau where Marco Polo entered China, to the empty sprawl of the great Takla Makan and Gobi deserts, explores this extraordinary heritage.

We will be privileged to visit the great oasis-cities of Central Asia—Kashgar, Turfan, Dun Huang—and we hope we may also be able to visit such unique sites as Kizil and Kotcho (permits pending).

A two-day tour of Xian, beginning of the Silk Road and ancient capital of China, will also be a tour highlight.

Accommodations will be in simple hotels or guesthouses, except at the base of the snowy giant, Mt. Muztagata, where we will stay in a tented camp at 12,000 feet near Lake Karakol. Some optional hiking is available during the camping portion

Lecturer/Leader: Patricia Berger, Ph.D. is assistant professor of Chinese Art at U.S.C. and Curator for Chinese Art at the Asian Art Museum of San Francisco.

Itinerary: Day 1 and 2: Leave U.S. Arrive Beijing.

Day 3: Sightseeing in Beijing.

Day 4: Fly to Urumchi.

Day 5: In Urumchi.

Day 6: Fly to Kashgar, once Britain's most remote listening post in Central Asia.

Day 7: In Kashgar, wandering in the bazaar, a medieval scene of craftsmen making things by hand—blacksmiths, coppersmiths, cobblers, woodworkers and other artisans who supply the local farmers and shepherds with the wares of daily life.

Day 8: Drive to tented camp near Karakol Lake (about 12,500').

Day 9: An optional day's walk toward the base of Mt. Muztagata, the "Ice Mountain Father."

Day 10: Drive back to Kashgar.

Day 11: Fly to Urumchi.

Day 12: By bus to the Silk Road oasis of Turfan.

Day 13: In Turfan.

Day 14: Drive to Dun Huang and visit Magao Grottoes, a great repository of Chinese cave art spanning the period from the Northern Wei to the Yuan dynasties.

Day 15 and 16: At Dun Huang.

Day 17: Fly to Lanzhou, capital of Gansu Province.

Day 18: Boat cruise on the Yangtse to visit the spectacular Buddhist temples at Bingling.

Day 19: Fly to Xian, the beginning of the Silk Road.

Day 20 and 21: Tour Xian, visiting its major archaeological site, the tomb of Shi Huang Di, with its countless life-size terra cotta statues of warriors and horses from about 200 B.C.

Day 22: Fly to Taiyuan.

Day 23: In Taiyuan.

Day 24: By train to Datong.

Day 25: In Datong.

Day 26: Train to Beijing.

Day 27: In Beijing.

Day 28: Depart Beijing on homeward-bound flights.

Dates: Sep 3–Sep 30 (28 days)
Grade: A-2
Land Cost: $4425
(10 or more members)
$4650 (6–9)
Single Supplement: not available
IT6PA1SFAA

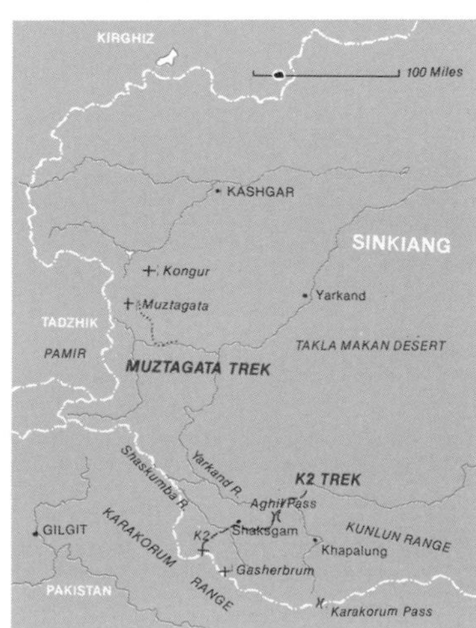

We ford the Shaksgam River by camel, then continue farther to K2 base camp at 12,900 feet on the banks of the Sarpo Laggo River/Susan Thiele

K2 & The Chinese Karakorum

18-day trek to north side of K2

On this spectacular hiking expedition in far western China, we will approach the base of K2 (28,741'), 2nd highest peak in the world, set in the majestic grandeur of the Chinese Karakorum.

Explorer Eric Shipton wrote eloquently about the northern flanks of K2 in his classic book, *Blank On The Map,* written about his 1936 travels in this region. ". . . Nothing interrupted my view of the great amphitheatre about me. The cliffs and ridges of K2 rose out of the glacier in one stupendous sweep to the summit of the mountain, 12,000 feet above. The sight was beyond my comprehension."

Shortly after Shipton's visit, the Chinese Karakorum and the province of Sinkiang became inaccessible to outsiders. The trekking route to K2 was just opened in the summer of 1983.

Our approach to K2 begins from the Silk Road city of Kashgar (4,000'), then takes us by road along the southern edge of the great Takla Makan Desert to Khargalik, an extremely remote Silk Road stopover.

Driving to the Yarkand River, we meet our Kirghiz camel drivers and the camels which carry our trek gear.

The trek begins with a hike over the historic Aghil Pass (15,700'), first crossed by Sir Francis Younghusband on his epic journey from Beijing to India in 1887, then a fording of the Shaksgam River by camel, and further to K2 base camp at 12,900 feet on the banks of the Sarpo Laggo River.

The trek length is a total of 18 days: six days to hike in to K2 base camp, six to hike back out, and, once at the base camp, six days to relax, take day hikes or a strenuous backpacking trip along moraine and glaciers to advance base camp on K2, which has splendid views.

Itinerary: Day 1 and 2: Leave U.S. Arrive Beijing. Transfer to hotel.

Day 3 and 4: Sightseeing in Beijing including the Great Wall and Ming Tombs.

Day 5: Fly to Urumchi.

Day 6: Day for sightseeing.

Day 7: Fly to Kashgar in far western Sinkiang.

Day 8: Sightseeing in Kashgar.

Day 9 to 11: Drive along the great Takla Makan desert to Karghalik, over 10,800-foot Akazu Pass and then the 16,200-foot Chiragsaldi Pass, one of the highest road passes in China. Descend to Yarkand Valley and camp at Mahza (12,375').

Day 12 to 17: Six-day hike to K2 base camp begins along the banks of the Yarkand River, Surukat River and then over Aghil Pass (14,650').

Day 18 to 23: Six days at or above camp. Those wanting to go to Advance Base Camp on K2 Glacier must be capable of a six-day round trip backpack trip (carrying 20 lbs. or more). Mountaineering boots and an ice axe (but not crampons) are required for this.

Day 24 to 28: Return trek to Mazha.

Day 29: By bus to Khargalik.

Day 30: By bus to Kashgar.

Day 31: Fly to Urumchi.

Day 32: Fly to Beijing.

Day 33: Free day in Beijing.

Day 34: Leave Beijing. Arrive Tokyo and continue to San Francisco.

Dates: Aug 24–Sep 26 (34 days)
Leader: Jerry Coe
Grade: C-2/C-3
Land Cost: $6100
(10–15 members)
$6300 (6–9)
Single Supplement: not available
IT6PA1SFAA

Trekking In Mongolia

7-day walk in the High Altai

Mongolia is the land of Genghis Khan, whose fierce nomadic warriors once ranged from the Black Sea to the Pacific.

Our Mongolian visit begins with a long flight from Moscow across Siberia, to Ulan Bator, Mongolia's capital, set in grasslands at 5,000 feet. Here we visit Ganden Monastery, where there are several resident lamas and very impressive Buddhist art and artifacts.

From Ulan Bator, we fly to Kobdt, across the sands of the Gobi Desert and up to the lake-strewn northern forests for a seven-day trek in the High Altai, a remote mountain range which rises from the steppes of Central Asia.

With horses to carry our gear, we hike over hills and ridges, occasionally visiting the yurt dwellings of nomadic Kazakh shepherds, seeing beautiful wildflowers in bloom on the hillsides and, with luck, catching a glimpse of some rare Central Asian wildlife such as Argali sheep and ibex.

After the trek, we visit the ruins of Karakorum, Genghis Khan's original capital, abandoned in 1260 A.D. when his son, Kublai Khan, moved the Mongol capital to Beijing.

Our last day in Ulan Bator coincides with festive annual "independence day" celebrations, where we can watch demonstrations of the traditional Mongolian sports of wrestling and archery.

Itinerary: Day 1 and 2: Leave U.S. Arrive Moscow and continue on flight to Ulan Bator.

Day 3: Arrive Ulan Bator. Transfer to hotel.

Day 4: Fly to Kobdt, then drive to Sert along the base of the High Altai Mountains.

Day 5 to 12: On seven-day trek.

Day 13: Drive to Kobdt and fly to Ulan Bator.

Day 14: Visit Ganden Monastery, and Bogda Khan's winter palace.

Day 15: Fly to Khujert and drive to Karakorum. Overnight in yurt camp.

Day 16: Fly back to Ulan Bator.

Day 17: Watch Independence Day celebrations.

Day 18: Fly to Moscow. Overnight in hotel.

Day 19: Sightseeing in Moscow.

Day 20: Depart Moscow and connect with homeward-bound flights.

Day 21: Arrive home.

Dates: Sep 6–Sep 26 (21 days)
Leader: to be announced
Grade: B-2
Land Cost: $3950
(6–15 members)
Single Supplement: not available
IT6AF155UG

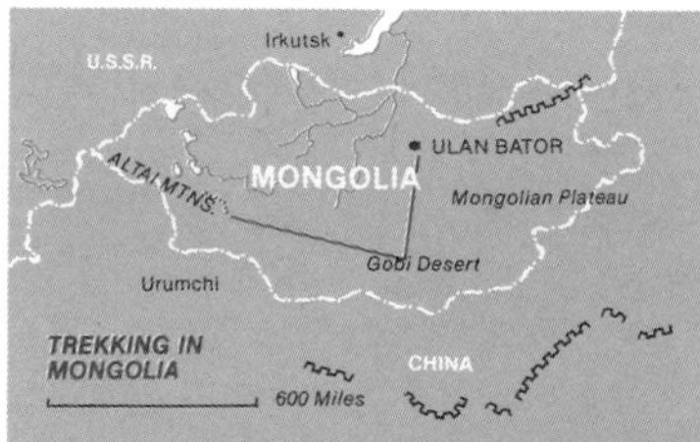

Sherpa Village Trek With Sir Edmund Hillary

To support Himalayan assistance program

This 10-day trek is a fund-raising event for the American Himalayan Foundation and a unique opportunity to meet and trek with Sir Edmund Hillary, who will host visits to schools and hospitals built by the Himalayan Trust, of which he is chairman.

Hillary's Himalayan Trust has undertaken a long and vigorous assistance program to the Sherpa community and we are pleased to be able to help the American Himalayan Foundation contribute to funding efforts.

Ed Hillary is one of the Khumbu's most well-known and well-loved figures, and to travel with him in this region, where he has spent much of the last 30 years, is a very special opportunity.

We visit all the major Sherpa villages including Namche Bazaar, Thame, Khumjung, and the famed Thyangboche Monastery (12,700′), where there are views of Everest.

$1000 of the Land Cost of the trip will be your direct tax-deductible donation to the American Himalayan Foundation, which supports Hillary's Himalayan Trust.

Itinerary: Day 1 to 3: Leave U.S. Arrive Kathmandu. Transfer to hotel.

Day 4: Sightseeing in Kathmandu. Briefing on the trek arrangements.

Sir Edmund Hillary with Mountain Travel's Vice President, Dick McGowan, at the Himalayan Trust's hospital at Khunde, Nepal/*Wayne Smith*

Day 5 and 6: Fly to Lukla (9,300′), weather permitting, and trek to Namche Bazaar (11,300′), main trading center for the Khumbu area.

Day 7: Trek to the village of Thame (12,500′).

Day 8 and 9: Visit Thame Monastery then trek to Khumjung (12,500′). Rest day at Khumjung, with time to visit the Hillary school.

Day 10 and 11: At Thyangboche Monastery.

Day 12: Trek to Pangboche.

Day 13: Trek back to Khunde and visit the Hillary hospital.

Day 14: Trek to Lukla.

Day 15 to 17: The next few days will be spent either in Kathmandu or Lukla, depending on flying weather. Arrive in Kathmandu, transfer to Malla Hotel.

Day 18: Transfer to airport. Leave Kathmandu on homeward-bound flights.

Day 19: Arrive home.

Dates: Apr 5–Apr 23 (19 days)
Leader: Leo Le Bon
Special Guest: Sir Edmund Hillary
Grade: B-2
Land Cost: $1800
(6–15 members)
Single Supplement: $265
IT5TG1MT04

Winter Palace, Ulan Bator/*Nigel Dabby*

Archery contest/*Nigel Dabby*

From Ulan Bator, we fly to Kobdt across the sands of the Gobi Desert and up to the lake-strewn northern forests for a seven-day trek in the High Altai/*Richard Irvin*

Our Khumbu treks visit all the major Sherpa villages including Namche Bazaar, Thame, Khumjung, and of course the famous Thyangboche Monastery pictured above, where there are views of Everest/*Eric Sanford*

Everest Walk-In Route

The traditional trek to Base Camp

Mt. Everest (29,028′), the world's highest mountain, is known to the Nepalese as Sagarmatha, "Mother Goddess of the Earth." It is a mountain to describe in superlatives—the most photographed and most written about mountain on earth.

The region below Mt. Everest is now designated as Sagarmatha National Park. It is Nepal's most popular trekking destination. Although the walk from the 4,000-foot lowlands near the Kathmandu Valley to Everest Base Camp at 18,000 feet is long and demanding, the experience of gazing on the majesty of Everest is an indescribable thrill and the realization of a dream for many.

The 25-day *Everest Walk-In Route* follows the traditional base camp march from the south used by most Everest expeditions. Many trekkers like the continuity of a walk-in (as an alternative to starting with a flight to Lukla at 9,000 feet), and other than the *East of Everest* trek, this is the only walk-in we offer.

We spend the first six days on a special out-of-the-way route used by few trekkers, then on the seventh day, we join the traditional Everest expedition walk-in route. Since the deep valleys which drain the Himalaya lie north to south, we'll be cutting "across the grain," in the first two weeks, hiking up and down over many ridges in subtropical scenery of bamboo thickets and rhododendron forests. The villages are inhabited by a variety of Hindu hill tribes.

After about two weeks of walking (great for later altitude acclimatization), we enter the Buddhist culture of the Khumbu region, the Sherpa homeland, and spend the rest of our trek in a wonderland of alpine Himalayan grandeur, culminating in a hike up to Kala Patar (18,192′) for classic Everest views near the site of Everest Base Camp.

The trek ends with a walk down to Lukla and a flight to Kathmandu.

Itinerary: Day 1 to 3: Leave U.S. Arrive Kathmandu. Transfer to hotel.

Day 4: Sightseeing in Kathmandu. Briefing on trek arrangements.

Day 5 to 10: Drive to Barabhise at 2,600 feet. Walk steeply up and down ridges high above the Sun Kosi River on a trail used by few trekkers and villagers. Cross Tingsang La at 10,889 feet and proceed to Mali.

Day 11 to 15: Along the river to Shivalaya, over Chyangma Pass (8,900′) and Lamjura Pass (11,600′) to Junbesi (8,800′). Beautiful mountain views including Numbur.

Day 16 to 19: Enter the Sherpa-inhabited Solu Valley for a first glimpse of Mt. Everest. Up and down the Dudh Kosi canyon and ascend to Namche Bazaar (11,300′).

Day 20 to 22: On past the village of Khumjung and the Thyangboche Monastery (12,700′) to the village of Dingboche.

Day 23 to 25: To the yak grazing pastures at Lobouje (16,200′) and up to Gorak Shep (17,000′), walking on boulder fields and glacial debris to the edge of the Khumbu Glacier. Hike up Kala Patar (18,192′) for classic views of Mt. Everest, or hike to base camp itself. Return to Lobouje.

Day 26 to 29: Back down the Khumbu on a scenic high trail to Dingboche (14,500′) and around a steep mountainside to Phortse, then through Khumjung and down to Lukla (9,300′), the mountain airstrip where we fly out to Kathmandu.

Day 30 to 32: The next few days will be spent either in Kathmandu or Lukla, depending on flying weather.

Day 33: Depart Kathmandu on homeward-bound flights.

Day 34: Arrive home.

Dates: #1 Mar 8–Apr 10 (34 days)
#2 Sep 27–Oct 30
1987: Mar 7–Apr 9
Leader: #1 Richard Irvin
#2 Charles Gay
Grade: C-3
Land Cost: $2090
(6–15 members)
Single Supplement: $265
IT5T61MT04

Nepal trips include: twin accomodations in Kathmandu with breakfasts, flights within Nepal (if applicable), sightseeing in Kathmandu, visas, trek permits, airport transfers, trek arrangements including all meals on trek, leadership, guides, porters, tents, foam sleeping pads, community cooking gear, services of camp and cooking crew, baggage porterage.

About Trekking in Nepal

In addition to a professional Mountain Travel leader, each trekking expedition is accompanied by Sherpa guides, kitchen staff and porters, all under the direction of a *sirdar*, or Sherpa leader.

All camp gear and your own duffle bag of personal gear will be carried by hired porters or yaks; you carry only a small daypack for your water bottle, camera and jacket.

The daily schedule is usually as follows: up at 6 a.m., pack up your duffle and have a light breakfast of oatmeal and tea. The Sherpas take down the tents and the porters head up the trail with their assigned loads. Trekkers and Sherpas start on the trail around 7 a.m.

Despite the fact that there may be about a dozen trekkers in the group, it is always possible to walk alone if one chooses, since everyone is encouraged to walk at his/her own pace.

The afternoon walk begins around 1 p.m. and continues until 4:30, when camp is reached. While camp is being set up by the sherpas, light snacks and tea are served. Dinner is served around 6:30 in a dining tent with a dinner table and small rattan stools.

After dinner one can linger in the dining tent to talk about events of the day, or retire to read or write by flashlight. We provide large, comfortable tents specially designed for us.

Food on the trek will be plentiful. Fresh vegetables, eggs, chickens and other foodstuffs are purchased as available. Meals are supplemented with tinned foods, such as peanut butter, fruit, coffee and fish. The Sherpa cook and his staff are trained professionals.

Private Treks In Nepal

In addition to our scheduled Nepal treks, we can arrange treks for private groups and individuals. Ideally, a group of four or more persons is the best number from a cost standpoint, but we can make arrangements for fewer than that.

Since there are so many wonderful trekking routes in Nepal, selecting a trek itinerary can be bewildering! We suggest that you read the descriptions of the treks listed here and pick the one that sounds best for you, according to your time schedule. We can then adapt the itinerary to suit your specific needs.

Dates:
September through May (8 to 36 days)
Leader:
Sherpa sirdars
Land Cost:
Depends on number in party and services requested.

Porters on the trail to Namche/*Susan Linn*

Trailside sculpture/*Charles Gay*

All camp gear and your own duffle bag of gear will be carried by hired porters or yaks. You carry only a small daypack for your water bottle, camera and jacket/*Brian K. Weirum*

Khumbu-Everest Exploration

Base Camp plus visits to Gokyo and Chhukhung Valley

This adventurous 22-day trek is the ultimate opportunity for trekkers to explore the entire Mt. Everest region of Nepal, walking through and around all the glacial valleys of the Khumbu, gaining a look into the life of the Sherpas, and being continually bombarded by views of the densest concentration of high and beautiful mountains on earth.

Besides visiting the base of Mt. Everest, we plan a visit to Gokyo, with its turquoise-blue alpine lake and high vantage points which give sensational views of the Everest "trinity"—Everest (29,028'). Lhotse (27,890'), Nuptse (25,850') as well as Makalu (27,805') and Cho Oyu (26,750')—four of the eight highest peaks on earth! Leaving the Gokyo Valley, we hike across the snow-covered South Cho La Pass (17,800'), an adventurous way to approach the upper Khumbu Valley enroute to Everest Base Camp.

Another dramatic side trip leads up the Chhukhung Valley to a viewpoint at 17,000 feet with superb vistas of Makalu, Ama Dablam, Island Peak and a close-up view of the incredible rock wall that links the peaks of Nuptse and Lhotse.

The trek begins and ends with flights to Lukla.

Itinerary: Day 1 to 3: Leave U.S. Arrive Kathmandu. Transfer to hotel.

Day 4: Sightseeing in Kathmandu. Briefing on trek arrangements.

Day to 5 to 7: Fly to Lukla, weather permitting. Trek to Namche Bazaar. Spare day here for acclimatization.

Day 8 and 9: Ascend the Bhote Kosi Valley and trek to Thame (12,500'). Visit Thame Monastery, known for its frescoes, and trek to Khumjung (12,500'), a beautifully situated village.

Day 10 to 14: Trek gradually up Gokyo Valley, through birchwoods with fine views of Kangtega. Continue up a rocky gulch beside the Ngozumba Glacier to beautiful Gokyo Lake (15,800'). Rest day and optional hike up Gokyo Ri.

Sherpani porter/*Brian K. Weirum*

Day 15 and 16: Cross the Ngozumba Glacier and ascend the 17,800-foot South Cho La pass on boulder fields and a steep, but short, snow slope. Descend the glacier to the beautiful glen of Dzonglha (15,900').

Day 17: Contour the steep, grassy hillsides above Tshola Lake, enter the upper Khumbu Valley and walk to Lobouje (16,200').

Day 18 to 20: To the yak grazing pastures at Lobouje (16,200') and up to Gorak Shep (17,000'), walking on the edge of the Khumbu Glacier. Hike up Kala Patar (18,192') for classic views of Mt. Everest, or hike to base camp itself. Return to Lobouje.

Day 21 and 22: Walk to Chhukhung for the dramatic Chhukhung ridge hike.

Day 23 to 26: Back down the Khumbu through Khumjung to Lukla (9,300'), the mountain airstrip where we fly out to Kathmandu.

Day 27 to 29: The next few days will be spent either in Kathmandu or Lukla, depending on flying weather.

Day 30: Depart Kathmandu on homeward-bound flights.

Day 31: Arrive home.

Dates: #1 Apr 5–May 5 (31 days)
#2 Oct 30–Nov 29
Leader: Scot Macbeth
Grade: C-3
Land Cost: $2090
(6–15 members)
Single Supplement: $265
IT5TG1MT04

Everest Base Camp

Trek from Lukla to Base Camp

The 17-day trek to Everest Base Camp bypasses the lowland scenery and begins with a flight to Lukla airstrip at 9,300 feet, just a two-day walk from Khumbu. The trek route heads directly from Namche Bazaar to Gorak Shep for a hike up Kala Patar (18,192') with classic views of Everest.

Most of the trek is spent above altitudes of 11,000 feet in the Khumbu and Imja valleys, surrounded by the major peaks of the Khumbu.

Although this is our shortest trek to the base of Everest, there will be ample time to enjoy the Sherpa culture of the Khumbu, to stop in tea houses to sip a glass of *chang,* to visit monasteries and see the prayer flags and beautifully-carved *mani* stones which decorate every trail and hillside, and to learn how Lamaistic Buddhism influences Sherpa life.

The trek begins and ends with flights to Lukla.

Itinerary: Day 1 to 3: Leave U.S. Arrive Kathmandu. Transfer to hotel.

Day 4: Sightseeing in Kathmandu. Briefing on the trek arrangements.

Day 5 to 8: Fly to Lukla, weather permitting. Trek to Namche Bazaar (11,300'), the Sherpa "capital." Spare day at Namche.

Day 9 to 12: Trek to Thyangboche Monastery, Pangboche and Dingboche.

Day 13 and 14: Trek to Lobouche. Rest day for acclimatization.

Day 15: To Gorak Shep (17,000'), up and down by the Khumbu Glacier passing over a tangle of moraine.

Day 16: Morning hike to the summit of Kala Patar (18,192') and walk back down to Lobouje.

Day 17 to 19: Down past the Trekkers' Aid Post at Pheriche to the Imja Khola, on to Pangboche (12,800'), then continue down to Thyangboche Monastery (12,700'). Spare day at Thyangboche.

Day 20 and 21: Down to Namche Bazaar and continue along the gorge of the Dudh Kosi to Lukla.

Day 22 to 24: The next few days will be spent either in Kathmandu or Lukla, depending on flying weather.

Day 25: Depart Kathmandu on homeward-bound flights.

Day 26: Arrive home.

Dates: #1 May 3–May 28
(26 days)
#2 Nov 28–Dec 23
Leader: Charles Gay
Grade: C-3
Land Cost: $1850
(6–15 members)
Single Supplement: $265
IT5TG1MT04

Besides visiting the base of Everest Khumbu/Everest Exploration visits Gokyo, with its turquoise-blue alpine lakes and high vantage points which give sensational views of the Everest "trinity": Everest, Lhotse and Nuptse, as well as Makalu and Cho Oyu—four of the eight highest peaks on earth!/*Catherine Perrodin*

The Everest Escapade

Short walk in the Khumbu

For those who can't take our longer "base camp" treks, we offer a seven-day trek which visits the major Sherpa villages of the Khumbu and famous Thyangboche Monastery for mountain views including Everest and a fantastic panorama of Khumbu giants such as Kangtega (22,340'), Thamserku (22,208') and the obelisk of Ama Dablam (22,494').

The villages we visit lie between 11,000 and 13,000 feet, and are connected by well-trodden paths.

Although this short trek doesn't visit Everest Base Camp, it is nevertheless a fantastic opportunity to enjoy unbeatable mountain scenery, meet Sherpas, and enjoy the quiet beauty of the Buddhist culture which so pervades the northern flanks of Nepal's Himalayas.

The trek begins and ends with flights to the mountain airfield at Lukla.

Itinerary: Day 1: Leave Seattle or Dallas on Thai Airways International.
Day 2: Arrive Bangkok. Overnight.
Day 3: Fly to Kathmandu.
Day 4: Sightseeing in Kathmandu.
Day 5: Fly to Lukla, weather permitting, and begin trek.
Day 6 and 7: To Namche Bazaar and Thyangboche Monastery.
Day 8: To Pangboche (12,800') to visit Pangboche Monastery, oldest in the Khumbu.
Day 9: To Phortse (12,500').
Day 10 and 11: Return to Namche Bazaar and Lukla.
Day 12: Fly to Kathmandu, weather permitting.
Day 13 and 14: In Kathmandu (or Lukla, if flight doesn't go).
Day 15: Fly to Bangkok. Overnight.
Day 16: Fly to Seattle or Dallas.

The Everest Escapade *is a fantastic opportunity to enjoy unbeatable mountain scenery, meet Sherpas, and appreciate the quiet beauty of the Buddhist culture that so pervades Nepal's Himalayas*/Sara Steck

***Street scene, Kathmandu*/**Alla Schmitz

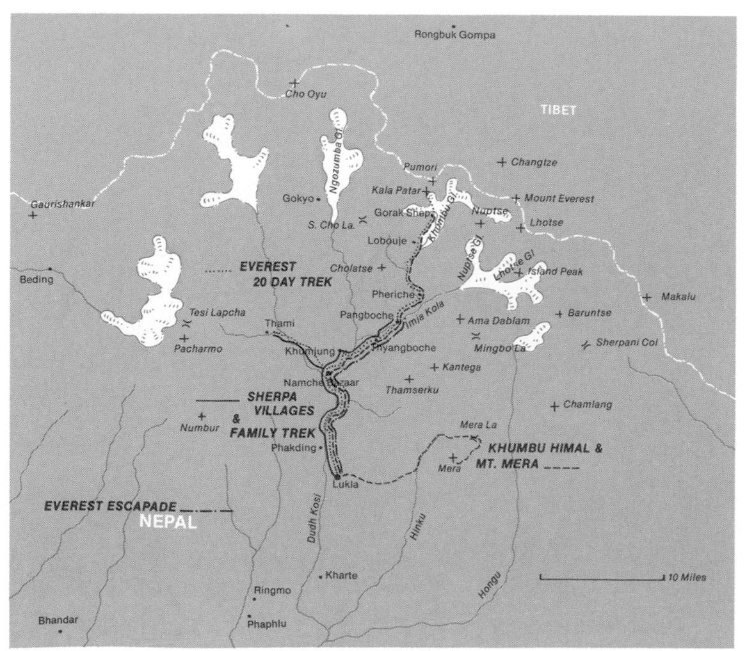

Dates: #1 Feb 15–Mar 2 (16 days)
#2 Mar 1–Mar 16
#3 Mar 15–Mar 30
#4 Mar 29–Apr 13
#5 Apr 12–Apr 27
#6 Apr 26–May 11
#7 Oct 25–Nov 9
#8 Nov 8–Nov 23
#9 Nov 22–Dec 7
#10 Dec 6–Dec 21
#11 Dec 20, 1986–Jan 4, 1987
1987 trips depart Feb 14, Feb 28, Mar 14, Mar 28
Leader: to be announced.
Grade: B-2
Tour Cost:
From Seattle: $2690
From Dallas: $2920
INCLUDING round trip economy class airfare on Thai Airways International.
Single Supplement: $110
IT5TG1MT04

"Just passing through..."

KATHMANDU

City notes by Stan Armington

Walking, jogging, getting around: Taxis (metered) are cheap and reliable and are your best bet for getting around. Bikes can be rented in the Thamel area near the Kathmandu Guest House. If you want to "adventure" by public transportation, be prepared for the sardine concept: Kathmandu's auto rickshaws hold up to 7 passengers plus driver in a 4-square-foot compartment! The Chinese trolley buses to Bhaktapur that start from near the Blue Star Hotel are more reasonable.

Some of the best places to go jogging are: through paddy fields (in season) from Budhanilkantha to Naraythang, a Hindu temple (round trip about two hours). Or from the historic city of Bhaktapur, architectural showplace of Nepal with is its 17th century carved wooden temples, you can jog through green wooded hills up and down to Nalacha (about 1-½ hours). You can always escape a bit of downtown auto pollution by running on the "ring road" outside Kathmandu.

Day trips:

Hire a car and driver and go to Budhanilkantha, then hike three hours round trip to Shivapuri (7,000 feet). Or drive to Godavari Botanical Gardens and walk up from St. Xaviers School to an altitude of 9,000 feet at Pulchowki (hiking time five hours). This is the highest point you can reach in the Kathmandu Valley and the view is outstanding. Or drive to Balaju, get out at the Nagarjun gate and start walking until you come to Jamachho. This three-hour walk is especially quiet and peaceful but don't go on Saturdays and holidays as then it is crowded with people.

Drive to Panhkhal, about 1-½ hours from Kathmandu, and hike uphill through wooded terrain until you come to Palanchowk Bhagvati, one of Nepal's most famous temples. Walking time is 2-½ hours. Tuesdays and Saturdays are the best times for this particular day trip. Birding enthusiasts will be certain to see a fine selection of Nepal's 800 bird species on any of these excursions

"Flightseeing":

Morning "flightseeing" trips to view Mt. Everest depart daily (weather permitting) from Kathmandu Airport. It's also possible to fly round trip to Pokhara for a day of sightseeing in that small town. The flight, which skims along the foothills of the Himalayas, is worthwhile in itself just for the views.

Shopping:

Hand-woven rugs made by Tibetan refugees are one of the best buys in Nepal. Visit the Tibetan Refugee Center at Patan (there are many shops surrounding it). Shipping rugs from these shops via air or sea to your home is reliable and easy to do; inquire from the shopkeeper.

Restaurants:

In Kathmandu, you can find authentic Nepali, Indian, Tibetan, Chinese, Russian, Japanese, German, French and even American cuisine at an amazing variety of restaurants. In the Thamel area, you can swap tall tales with fellow trekkers over cool drinks at the Rum Doodle, where the menu includes such things as spaghetti, steak and ice cream. Also in Thamel, try Red Square for Russian Kabobs and the Utse for Chinese and Tibetan food. The Indira, on New Road, serves good Indian food, and the Sun Kosi, on the same block as the Annapurna Hotel, has Tibetan and Nepali specialties.

Cultural Expedition:

Buddhist Nepal: A Himalayan Trek

Lamaistic culture of Nepal

The ideal way to experience or study Buddhism is to combine lectures and discussions with visiting the sites where this ancient religion is practiced today, as it has been for hundreds of years.

The Solu-Khumbu region of Nepal provides an excellent opportunity for this type of experience. This is the home of the Sherpas, who belong to the Nyingma-pa Buddhist sect. People of Tibetan stock who practice their own special version of Buddhism, Sherpas maintain many of the customs they brought with them on their migration from eastern Tibet.

The actual trek will take 20 days and will combine visiting monasteries (including viewing daily activities, worship practices and ritual practices) with meeting the lamas, monks, nuns and lay practitioners. This should provide a comprehensive picture of this Buddhist culture. We visit five different monasteries over the 20-day period, and in the process cover a lot of the Solu-Khumbu region.

This trek is not intended to be an intensive course in Buddhism but rather is for people who wish to visit a thriving Buddhist culture and see how much a part of Sherpa life it is.

Lecturer/Leader: to be announced.

Itinerary: Day 1 to 3: Leave U.S. Arrive Kathmandu.

Day 4: Tour Kathmandu.

Day 5: Drive to Jiri and begin trek.

Day 6 and 7: Trek to Thodung Monastery.

Day 8 to 10: Trek to the beautiful village of Junbesi (8,000′).

Day 11: At Tupten Choling Monastery.

Day 12: Rest day.

Day 13: Trek to Takshindu Monastery (10,000′).

Day 14 to 18: Trek via Namche Bazaar to Thyangboche (12,700′). one of the most impressively situated monasteries in all of the Himalayas.

Day 19 and 20: At Thyangboche.

Day 21: Trek to Pangboche Monastery (13,000′).

Day 22 and 23: Trek to Lukla (9,300′).

Day 24: Fly to Kathmandu, weather permitting.

Day 25 and 26: In Kathmandu (if Lukla flight not delayed).

Day 27: In Kathmandu.

Day 28: Depart Kathmandu on homeward-bound flights.

Day 29: Arrive home.

Dates: Nov 1–Nov 29 (29 days)
Grade: B-3
Land Cost: $1990
(6–15 members)
Single Supplement: $245
IT5TG1MT04

Family Trek In Nepal

10-day Sherpa culture trek

This special trek visits the Sherpa villages of the Mt. Everest region. It is a wonderful opportunity for parents and children to share the fun of a Nepal trek.

On a very relaxed trekking schedule, the 10-day trek begins at Lukla (9,300′) and circles up into the Khumbu region at a moderate pace. Certain extra amenities will be added to help make things run as smoothly as possible (i.e., extra Sherpa staff and porters to carry the children when necessary).

Much of the emphasis will be on interaction with the Sherpa population. Sherpa families are close-knit and they love being with children. They and their own children are always fascinated to meet "foreign" youngsters, a relative rarity in the Khumbu.

Itinerary: Day 1 to 3: Leave U.S. Arrive Kathmandu. Transfer to hotel.

Day 4: Sightseeing in Kathmandu. Briefing on trek arrangements.

Day 5: Begin trek. Fly to Lukla (9,300′), weather permitting, and trek for a few hours to the village of Phakding (8,700′).

Day 6 and 7: To Namche Bazaar (11,300). Rest day at Namche.

Day 8: Trek to the village of Thame (12,500′) and visit Thame Monastery.

Day 9: Trek to Khumjung (12,500′) or Namche.

Day 10 and 11: At Thyangboche Monastery, the best-known monastery in Nepal.

Day 12: Up the Khumbu Valley to Pangboche (12,800′).

Day 13: Return to Thyangboche and Khunde (12,500′) via the steep Dudh Kosi gorge.

Day 14: Down past Namche Bazaar to Lukla.

Day 15 to 17: The next few days will be spent either in Kathmandu or Lukla, depending on flying weather.

Day 18: Transfer to airport. Leave Kathmandu on homeward-bound flights.

Day 19: Arrive home.

Dates: Apr 2–Apr 20 (19 days)
Leader: Wayne Smith, M.D.
Grade: B-2
Land Cost: $1570
(6–15 members)
Children: ages 7–14: $785
2–6: $695
Single Supplement: $245
IT5T61MT04

On our Family Trek, extra Sherpa staff and porters carry the children when necessary/*Dick McGowan*

The Buddhist Nepal trek will take 20 days and will combine visiting monasteries (including viewing daily worship and ritual practices) with meeting the lamas, monks, nuns and lay practitioners/*Brian K. Weirum*

After crossing the Arun (most likely by dugout), the East of Everest trek heads northwest along the Irkhua River valley over narrow bamboo bridges and among millet and rice fields./
Charles Gay

East Of Everest

To Base Camp via the remote Arun Valley

This approach to Everest's base is different from other base camp treks in its remoteness and distance from well-trodden paths.

We begin in eastern Nepal, following small paths through the green tropics of the Arun Valley which drain the slopes of Makalu (27,825′), fifth highest mountain in the world.

We follow these remote trails for the first two weeks—the same trails used by the lowland porters who supply Namche Bazaar (the Sherpa capital) with its food grains, and the same historic path walked by the first Mt. Everest reconnaissance expedition from the south in 1950, led by British explorer Eric Shipton.

After crossing the Arun (most likely by dugout), we head northwest along the Irkhua River valley, walking over narrow bamboo bridges and among millet and rice fields.

We cross three passes before reaching Khumbu. The first is the 11,400-foot Salpa Bhanjang. Descending into the deep Hongu Valley, we trek for several days across two steep gorges before finally arriving in the Dudh Kosi Valley south of Mt. Everest.

Here, perhaps for the first time on our trek, we begin to see other trekkers as we join the well-traveled path north of the Lukla airfield.

The last twelve days of the trek follow the regular hiking route into the Khumbu region and up to Kala Patar (18,192′) for superb views of Everest.

Itinerary: Day 1 to 3: Leave U.S. Arrive Kathmandu. Transfer to hotel.

Day 4: Sightseeing in Kathmandu. Briefing on trek arrangements.

Day 5: Fly to Biratnagar and drive to Dharan (1,200′) at the edge of the low Siwalik hills.

Day 6: Drive to the roadhead and begin trek.

Day 7: Ascend to the village of Hile (6,100′) on a ridgetop with its Bhotia community and new monastery.

Day 8 to 10: Magnificent distant views of Makalu as we descend to the hot Arun Valley floor at about 850 feet and cross the Arun River in a dugout "ferry."

Day 11: Passing lush fields, we ascend the Irkhua Valley populated by people of the Brahmin, Chettri and Rai clans. Reach Phedi (6,500′).

Day 12: Cross the Salpa Bhanjang (11,400′) and descend to Sanam village.

Day 13 and 14: Down into the Hongu gorge with views of snow peaks up-valley and across Sipkie Pass (10,120′).

Day 15 and 16: We are now in the Inukhu (also called Hinku) Valley. Climb to the Pangum La (10,400′) and descend to the Dudh Kosi Valley, south of Khumbu.

Day 17 to 20: Join the trail beyond Lukla airfield to Namche Bazaar, Khumjung and Thyangboche (12,700′).

Day 21 to 23: Trek to Pheriche (14,000′), Lobouje (16,200′) and Gorak Shep (17,000′).

Day 24: Hike to top of Kala Patar (18,192′) for classic Everest views.

Day 25 to 28: Retrace our steps back down through Khumbu and down the Dudh Kosi Valley to Lukla.

Day 29 to 32: The next few days will be spent either in Kathmandu or Lukla, depending on flying weather.

Day 33: Depart Kathmandu on homeward-bound flights.

Day 34: Arrive home.

Dates: #1 Mar 8–Apr 10 (34 days)
#2 Nov 15–Dec 18
1987: Mar 7–Apr 9
Leader: #1 Charles Gay
#2 Hugh Swift
Grade: C-3
Land Cost: $2090
(6–15 members)
Single Supplement: $265
IT5TG1MT04

The Nepal Adventure

Annapurna foothills and terai *jungle wildlife*

This journey follows the scenic trekking paths of the Annapurna region then heads south to discover the superb Asian wildlife habitat hidden in the tall "elephant grass" jungles of Chitwan National Park.

We begin with a pleasant six-day Annapurna foothills trek circling up through cool forests and lovely Gurung villages such as Ghandrung (6,400′), to feast our eyes on a classic Himalayan panorama including Annapurna, Dhaulagiri and Machapuchare, the "Matterhorn of Nepal."

Driving south from the town of Pokhara to rustic Gaida Wildlife Camp, named for *gaida,* the endangered Indian one-horned rhinoceros, we spend several days searching for game on elephant-back, by dugout canoe, and on foot in the deep *terai* jungle, haunt of elusive "big cats" such as leopards and Bengal tigers, and enough exotic tropical birds to delight any ornithology buff.

Itinerary: Day 1 to 3: Leave U.S. Arrive Kathmandu. Transfer to hotel.

Day 4: Morning sightseeing tour of Kathmandu.

Village of Naudanda/*Susan Thiele*

Day 5: Spectacular flight along the Himalayan skyline to the little town of Pokhara and begin trek.

Day 6: Across rice fields to the small village of Suikhet, climb a steep crest to 6,500 feet then descend to Landrung (5,280′).

Day 7: Down to the Modi Khola River, then up 2,300 feet to a grazing pasture above Ghandrung (6,400′).

Day 8: Back down to the Modi Khola to Birethanti (4,300′).

Day 9: Cross the Modi Khola and ascend to the hamlet of Chandrakot to Naudanda (4,800′).

Day 10: End trek in the afternoon, arrive in Pokhara and check into Fishtail Lodge on Phewa Lake.

Day 11: Drive to Gaida Wildlife Camp. Check into cabins and take an afternoon jungle walk.

Day 12: Game viewing on the river by dugout canoe, nature walks, afternoon game viewing by elephant.

Day 13: Morning game viewing then five-hour drive to Kathmandu.

Day 14: In Kathmandu.

Day 15: Depart Kathmandu on homeward-bound flights.

Day 16: Arrive home.

Dates: #1 Feb 1–Feb 16 (16 days)
#2 Dec 6–Dec 21
1987: Jan 31–Feb 15
Leader: to be announced
Grade: B-1
Land Cost: $1595
(8–15 members)
Single Supplement: $295
IT5TG1MT04

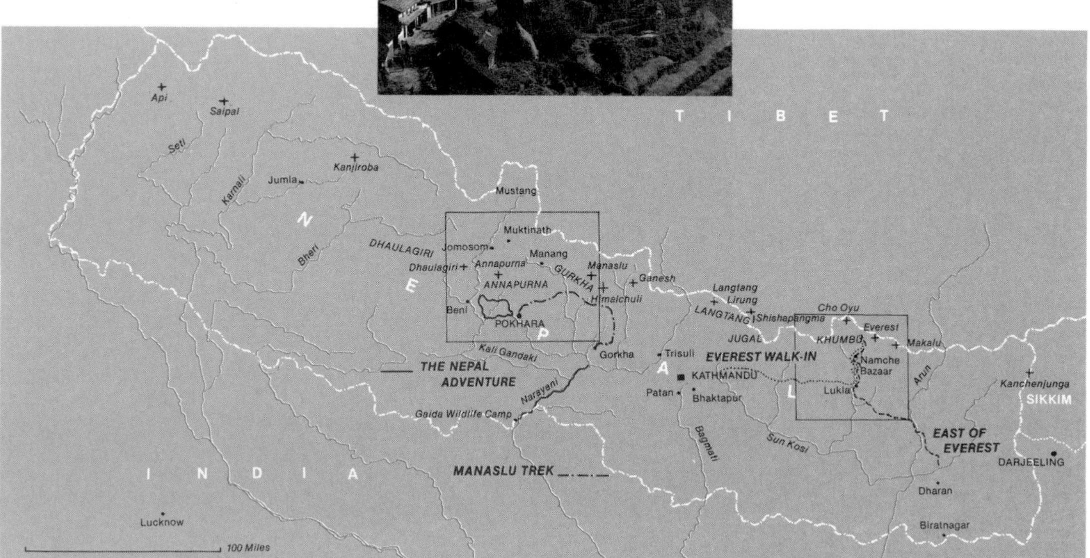

Expedition 20,000

30-day Khumbu climbing circuit

A 30-day climbing adventure, *Expedition 20,000* will attempt ascents of Pokhalde (19,044′), Island Peak (20,238′) and Parcharmo (21,097′)

Island Peak is a moderately technical snow climb in an unbelievably magnificent setting at the foot of the huge Lhotse Wall. Pokhalde stands to the southwest of the Lhotse Wall, east of the Khumbu Glacier, and Parcharmo is situated above the Tesi Lapcha Pass on the edge of the Rolwaling Valley.

The peaks are very challenging but not technically demanding. The itinerary includes a visit to Everest Base Camp and the crossing of two rarely-used passes, the Changri La and Kongma La.

Itinerary: Day 1 to 3: Leave U.S. Arrive Kathmandu. Transfer to hotel.

Day 4: Sightseeing in Kathmandu. Briefing on trek arrangements.

Day 5 to 17: Fly to Lukla (weather permitting). Trek to Gokyo Lake (15,800′), cross Ngozumba Glacier and Changri La Pass to Changru Nup Glacier. Arrive at Everest Base Camp.

Day 18: Ascend Pokhalde.

Day 19 to 21: Hike up Imja Khola.

Day 22 and 23: Climb Island Peak.

Day 24 to 27: Trek to Thame.

Day 28 to 32: To Glacier Camp and ascend Parcharmo.

Day 33 and 34: Trek to Lukla.

Day 35 to 37: The next few days will be spent either in Kathmandu or Lukla, depending on flying weather.

Day 38: Leave Kathmandu on homeward-bound flights.

Day 39: Arrive home.

Dates: Oct 30–Dec 7 (39 days)
Leader: Lanny Johnson
Grade: D-2
Land Cost: $2690
(6–12 members)
Single Supplement: $265
IT5TG1MT04

Khumbu Himal & Mt. Mera

Trekking and climbing in the Everest region

One of our most popular alpine trips since we first began offering it 11 years ago, this trek and climb combines a visit to Everest Base Camp and an ascent of Mt. Mera (21,247′), from which one can see four of the five highest mountains in the world: Everest (29,028′), Kanchenjunga (28,208′), Lhotse (27,923′) and Makalu (27,825′).

The first half of our trek, which begins with a flight to Lukla, takes us to the base of Everest via the spectacular Gokyo Valley.

The second half takes us back down to Lukla then east into the high Hinku Valley, a wild and uninhabited area. The entire trip from Lukla to Mera and back is one of high adventure amidst superb mountain wilderness.

We'll establish a high camp on the Mera La, an 18,000-foot pass from which qualified trip members can don crampons for an attempt on Mera's snowy summit. The climb is not a technical one but the altitude makes it physically demanding.

Itinerary: Day 1 to 3: Leave U.S. Arrive Kathmandu. Transfer to hotel.

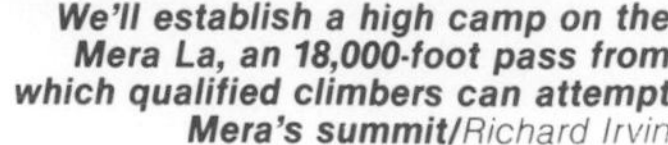
We'll establish a high camp on the Mera La, an 18,000-foot pass from which qualified climbers can attempt Mera's summit/Richard Irvin

Day 4: Sightseeing in Kathmandu. Briefing on trek arrangements.

Day 5 to 7: Begin trek. Fly to Lukla (9,300′) (weather permitting) and trek to Namche Bazaar and Khumjung (12,500′).

Day 8 to 10: Trek up the Gokyo Valley to Gokyo Lake at 15,800 feet. Optional hike to Gokyo Ri (18,000′).

Day 11 and 12: Cross the Ngozumba Glacier and the snow-covered South Cho La Pass (17,800′). Descend to Dzonghla.

Day 13 to 15: Trek to the yak pastures of Lobouje (16,200′), then Gorak Shep (17,000′) along the edge of the Khumbu Glacier and the summit of Kala Patar (18,182′) or Everest Base Camp itself. Return to Lobouje.

Day 16 to 18: Trek down to Thyangboche Monastery (12,700′), Namche Bazaar and back to Lukla where we prepare for the second stage of the trek.

Day 19 and 20: Climb through pine and rhododendron forests, then yak pastures and a series of three passes at about 14,900 feet. Descend to Chetara (13,700′).

Day 21 to 23: Climb up over a rocky spur and descend into the Hinku Valley.

Day 24 to 26: Ascend to the Mera La (18,000′) and prepare for the climb. Extra days here to allow for acclimatization and inclement weather.

Day 27 and 28: Establish high camp at approximately 19,500 feet and make a summit attempt.

Day 29 to 33: Trek back out to Lukla.

Day 34 to 37: The next few days will be spent either in Kathmandu or Lukla, depending on flying weather.

Day 38: Depart Kathmandu on homeward-bound flights.

Day 39: Arrive home.

Dates: Oct 23–Nov 30 (39 days)
Leader: Richard Irvin
Grade: C-3/D-2
Land Cost: $2690
(6–15 members)
Single Supplement: $265
IT5T61MT04

The peaks are very challenging, but not technically demanding. The Expedition 20,000 itinerary includes a visit to Everest Base Camp and the crossing of two rarely used passes, the Changri La and Kongma La/Eric Sanford

The Manaslu Trek: Ridge Walking In Central Nepal

Exploring the Gurkha Himalaya

This 22-day "ridge walking" trek in central Nepal is for people who want to explore a region where virtually no other trekkers go.

In fact, we probably won't see another Westerner on the entire trek until we join the busy "Around Annapurna" trail on our 17th day of walking.

Our trek starts at Gorkha (4,000′), home of the 17th century founder of a united Nepal, Prithvinarayan Shah. From here, we trek through Brahmin and Chettri villages and then up to the remote and uninhabited forested ridges coming off the magnificent "Gurkha Himal": Manaslu (26,760′), Himalchuli (25,895′) and Peak 29 (25,705′).

During the middle ten days of the trek, there are no villages, just an idyllic Himalayan landscape of rhododendron forests, alpine meadows and upland grazing pastures.

We reach our highest point on an optional hike up the Rupina La (15,400′), an unfrequented pass near Manaslu with views across all of central Nepal.

Our return route takes us down through thick rhododendron forests to the chartreuse-hued rice fields of the Annapurna foothills.

Itinerary: Day 1 to 3: Leave U.S. Arrive Kathmandu. Transfer to hotel.

Day 4: Sightseeing in Kathmandu. Briefing on trek arrangements.

Day 5 and 6: Drive to Gorkha and begin trek.

Day 7 to 9: Hike north along a single ridgeline, leaving the last village we'll see for some days.

Day 10 to 12: Into the upper gorge of the Darondi Valley. Optional hike to the top of the 15,000-foot Rupina La.

Day 13 and 14: Out onto a high ridge called Topche Danda.

Day 15 and 16: Contour westerly across the upper basin of the Chep Valley then a long day down to the village of Simi, the first village in some time. Friendly locals and rakshi *(the local home-brew) available here!*

Day 17 and 18: Down the Dordi Valley to the base of Bara Poharki Lekh, our last and highest ridge.

Day 19 and 20: To a campsite with views of Manaslu, Peak 29, Himalchuli and the Annapurna and Lamjung massifs.

Day 21 and 22: Trek to Marsyandi Valley and join the busy Annapurna trekking route.

Day 23 and 24: Trek to the Gurung town of Ghanpokhara.

Day 25 to 27: Down into the Pokhara Valley. Overnight at Fishtail Lodge.

Day 28: Fly or drive to Kathmandu. Transfer to hotel.

Day 29: Day free in Kathmandu.

Day 30: Transfer to airport. Depart Kathmandu on homeward-bound flights.

Day 31: Arrive home.

Dates: Nov 8–Dec 8 (31 days)
Leader: Jan Zabinski
Grade: B-3
Land Cost: $1890
(6–15 members)
Single Supplement: $245
IT5TG1MT04

Annapurna Sanctuary Trek

15-day trek to a spectacular mountain amphitheatre

The Annapurna Sanctuary is a glacier-covered amphitheatre at 13,300 feet formed by a circle of the principal peaks of the western Annapurna Range—including Annapurna South (23,814′), Fang (25,089′), Annapurna I (26,545′), Gangapurna (24,458′), Annapurna III (24,787′) and the spire of Machapuchare (23,942′).

This spectacular mountain-ringed basin can be reached on a relatively short trek (15 days) that goes right to the base of some of the most famous peaks in the Himalaya.

We trek steeply up the Modi Khola valley through forests of bamboo, rhododendron and oak, and villages of the Gurung and Tamang clans. We'll reach the Sanctuary on about the 7th day and spend two days within its spectacular confines with a possible visit to Annapurna South Base Camp.

Return to Pokhara is via the Gurung settlements of Landrung and Ghandrung, with a final grand mountain panorama from our last campsite.

The Annapurna Sanctuary is a spectacular mountain-ringed basin that can be reached on a short trek/ *Jan Zabinski*

Itinerary: Day 1 and 3: Leave U.S. Arrive Kathmandu. Briefing on trek arrangements.

Day 4: Sightseeing in Kathmandu. Briefing on trek arrangements.

Day 5: Drive to Pokhara, and trek to Henja (3,500′), on the outskirts of the Pokhara Valley.

Day 6 to 8: Cross the Yangri Khola river and wind through rice fields, climb up a steep hill to Naudanda and continue on to Khare (5,600′). Drop down to the Modi Khola and climb very steeply uphill through forests to Ghorapani Pass (9,300′).

Day 9: Early morning visit to Poon Hill for a spectacular view of Dhaulagiri. Trek eastward along the ridge to forest camp at 9,500 feet.

Day 10 and 11: Cross the pass leading to Ghandrung and then steeply down to a bridge at about 6,000 feet, then back up high above the Modi Khola, through forests of rhododendron, oak, and hemlock to Kuldi Ghar (7,000′)

Day 12: Climb steeply high above the river in a bamboo forest to the tiny campsite at Hinko (9,900′).

Day 13 and 14: A short walk to Annapurna Sanctuary (13,300′) and spend these days exploring, photographing and enjoying the mountain scenery.

Day 15 to 18: Retrace our steps back down through Kuldi Ghar and Ghandrung.

Day 19: Down the Yangri Khola valley to Pokhara. Overnight at Fishtail Lodge.

Day 20: Fly or drive to Kathmandu. Transfer to hotel.

Day 21: In Kathmandu.

Day 22: Depart Kathmandu on homeward-bound flights.

Day 23: Arrive home.

Dates: #1 Apr 12–May 4 (23 days)
#2 Nov 1–Nov 23 (23 days)
Leader: Charles Gay
Grade: B-3
Land Cost: $1650
(6–15 members)
Single Supplement: $245
IT5TG1MT04

On the Manaslu trek we walk through terraced fields and villages and up to remote, uninhabited ridges/ *Hugh Swift*

Trekking routes from Pokhara pass through the colorful Gurung settlements of Landrung and Ghandrung/ *Alla Schmitz*

Around Annapurna

A classic Himalayan trek

One of our favorite treks and a classic walk in Nepal is the 24-day circuit around Annapurna, circling north of the Annapurna massif via the Thorong La (17,771′).

The walk begins in the lush valley of the Marsyandi River, which cuts steeply between the Annapurnas to the west and the Manaslu/Himalchuli peaks to the east.

Turning west into the Manang Valley, a longitudinal gorge which makes a deep furrow behind the Annapurnas, we'll find ourselves in an increasingly Buddhist culture.

The Manang Valley is inhabited by gypsy traders of Tibetan origin whose villages are striking clusters of medieval stone dwellings often nestled into eroded sandstone cliffs. The main villages are Chame, Pisang, Braga (where there is a magnificent monastery) and Manang.

Above Pisang, there is a sudden environmental transition as the dense forests of the lower valley give way to rocky and arid Tibetan scenery and high yak pastures.

The Manang Valley is walled on the south by Annapurnas II and IV, Annapurna III (24,787′), Gangapurna (24,458′) and Glacier Dome (23,191′); to the north, and barring the way to Tibet, is a long ridge of 20,000 to 22,000-foot peaks.

At the head of the valley we cross north of the Annapurnas at the Thorong La and descend by way of the Hindu and Buddhist shrines at Muktinath. Now in the deep gorge of the Kali Gandaki, we descend gradually into green, terraced hillsides and the rhododendron groves of Lete. There are continuous and beautiful views of Dhaulagiri (26,810′), Tukche and the Annapurnas all the way back to Pokhara.

Itinerary: Day 1 to 3: Leave U.S. Arrive Kathmandu. Transfer to hotel.

Day 4: Sightseeing in Kathmandu. Briefing on the trek arrangements.

Day 5 to 9: Begin trek, hiking gently upward through lush subtropical vegetation and the cultivated fields along the Marsyandi River. Excellent views of Manaslu, Peak 29, Himalchuli, Annapurnas II and IV, Lamjung and Machapuchare.

Day 11 and 12: Enter the heavily wooded lower Manang Valley and pass the villages of Chame (8,800′) and Pisang (10,450′).

Day 13 and 14: A beautiful walk on easy terrain through forests to the upper Manang Valley. Rest day at the village of Braga (11,250′).

Day 15: Past Manang village and continue up past yak huts to Chakar Dhunga (13,500′).

Day 16: Continue through alpine country past Leder (14,200′) to a high camp at Phedi (14,500′), just at the foot of the climb to the Thorong La.

Day 17: Long day, ascending steeply on a yak and pony trail. Cross Thorong La and descend steeply to Muktinath (12,500′).

Day 18: Rest day at Muktinath. Visit Hindu and Buddhist shrines and enjoy views of Dhaulagiri.

Day 19: Descend about 3,000 feet down the Jhong Khola canyon. Camp at the medieval village of Kagbeni (9,000′).

Day 20: Down along a level but rocky trail through juniper thickets to Jomosom and then Marpha (8,760′), a large Thakali village with an important monastery.

Day 21 and 22: Continue down the Kali Gandaki flood plain to Larjung (8,400′). Rest day or optional hike to the Dhaulagiri icefall at 12,000 feet.

Day 23 to 25: Through pine woods to Ghasa (6,400′), descend lower into the Kali Gandaki canyon, through Tatopani to Ghorapani and over Deorali Pass (10,000′), with views of Dhaulagiri and Annapurna South.

Day 26 to 28: Through rhododendron forests to Ghandrung (6,400′) and the Modi Khola, up to Landrung, another Gurung village, then descend to the Yangri Khola valley and walk along flat fields to Pokhara (2,800′). Overnight at Fishtail Lodge on the shores of Phewa Lake.

Day 29: Fly or drive to Kathmandu. Transfer to hotel.

Day 30: Day free in Kathmandu.

Day 31: Depart Kathmandu on homeward-bound flights.

Day 32: Arrive home.

Dates: #1 Apr 12–May 13 (32 days)
#2 Oct 11–Nov 11
#3 Oct 18–Nov 18
#4 Oct 25–Nov 25
Leaders: #1 Richard Irvin
#2 Jan Zabinski
#3 Brian Weirum
#4 Susan Thiele
Grade: C-3
Land Cost: $2090 (6–15 members)
Single Supplement: $245
IT5TG1MT04

The Manang Valley village of Braga is a striking cluster of medieval stone dwellings nestled into eroded sandstone cliffs/*Hugh Swift*

Above Pisang, there is a sudden environmental transition as the dense forests of the lower valleys give way to rocky and arid Tibetan scenery/ *Hugh Swift*

The Annapurna Skyline Trek

4-day ridge walk

A short walk in the Annapurna foothills is as good an introduction to the Nepal Himalayas as there is. There may be no other place in the world from which great Himalayan peaks can be admired so easily from such a close distance.

The "skyline" trek lasts four days, and travels a special route which is used by virtually no other trekkers. We start in a subtropical valley at about 2,000 feet from which there are fine views of Annapurna (26,545′), Dhaulagiri (26,810′) and a marvelous view of the "fishtail" peak of Machapuchare (22,943′), only 20 miles away.

Our route follows trails along intricately terraced rice and mustard fields, groves of citrus and banana, up into rhododendron and oak forests, and through small villages which show us part of the remarkable ethnic diversity of Nepal. We'll see the villages of Brahmin and Chetri hill people as well as Gurungs and Magars.

Views from the highest point on the trek (about 6,000 feet) include Annapurna II (26,040′), Annapurna III (24,787′), Annapurna IV (24,688′), Gangapurna (24,458′) and Lamjung (22,910′)

Itinerary: Day 1: Depart Seattle or Dallas on Thai Airways International.
Day 2: Arrive Bangkok. Overnight.
Day 3: Fly to Kathmandu.
Day 4: Sightseeing.
Day 5: Travel to Pokhara and begin trek.
Day 6 and 7: On trek.
Day 8: Return trek to Pokhara.
Day 9: Travel to Kathmandu.
Day 10: Fly to Bangkok. Overnight.
Day 11: Sightseeing.
Day 12: Fly to Seattle or Dallas.

Dates: #1 Jan 11–Jan 22 (12 days)
#2 Jan 25–Feb 5
#3 Feb 8–Feb 19
#4 Feb 22–Mar 5
#5 Mar 8–Mar 19
#6 Mar 22–Apr 2
#7 Oct 18–Oct 29
#8 Nov 1–Nov 12
#9 Nov 15–Nov 26
#10 Nov 29–Dec 10
#11 Dec 13–Dec 24
#12 Dec 27, 1986–Jan 7, 1987
1987: trips depart Jan 10, Jan 24, Feb 7, Feb 21, Mar 7
Leaders: to be announced
Grade: B-2
Tour Cost:
From Seattle: $1990
From Dallas: $2220
INCLUDING round trip economy-class airfare on Thai Airways International
Single Supplement: $105
IT5TG1MT04

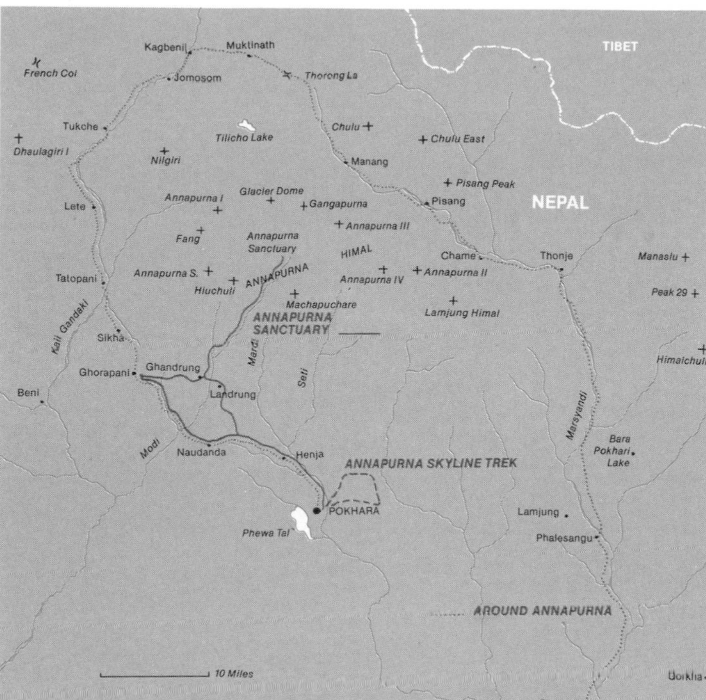

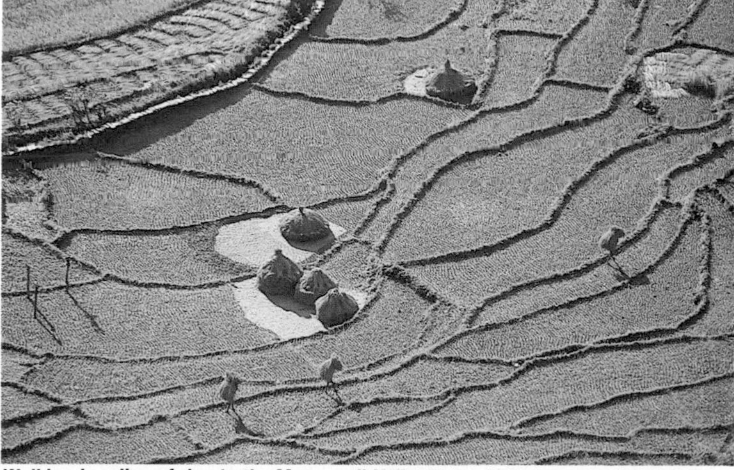
Walking bundles of rice in the Marsyandi Valley/*Brian K. Weirum*

Temple fountain, Kathmandu/*Alla Schmitz*

Kathmandu /*Alla Schmitz*

Our route follows trails through small villages which show us part of the remarkable ethnic diversity of Nepal. We'll see the villages of Brahmin and Chettri hill people as well as Gurungs and Magars/*Susan Thiele*

Our man in Nepal

Stan Armington was, by coincidence, one of Mountain Travel's very first trip members (number five, we think). He was a member of one of our 1969 Nepal treks and, since then, has spent most of his time in Nepal, developing one of the best trekking operations anywhere. Since his professional background is in computer science, he owns and programs a special computer (one of the few in Nepal) with which he keeps up with such complexities as gear and food inventory, Sherpa assignments, and members' arrival information. He is well acquainted with Sherpa and Nepali culture, speaks fluent Nepali, and is author of the guidebook, *Trekking in The Himalayas.* Stan can frequently be found at *The Rum Doodle,* his own bar and restaurant in Kathmandu.

The Baltoro/K2 Trek

"The world's greatest museum of shape and form"

"The whole itinerary along the Baltoro seems to have been devised by some prince-poet who had used his genius to hand down to posterity a work whose like was never seen . . . In the mighty mass of the whole, each single part seems so finely wrought, each one a telling note in a mighty cord; and in the patterning of ridge, couloir, rock face and icefall, thrusting inexorably upwards to the peak, there is the logic of a Bach fugue." Fosco Maraini, *Karakorum.*

The Baltoro Glacier has long been the expedition route to the great 8,000-meter peaks of the Karakorum including K2 (Chogori), the second highest mountain on earth.

The goal of our 28-day trek is that spectacular conjunction of the Godwin-Austen and Baltoro glaciers called Concordia (14,500′). Here, within a radius of about twelve miles, rise six peaks over 26,000-feet. Author and mountaineer Fosco Maraini was not exaggerating when he referred to it as "the world's greatest museum of shape and form."

Setting out with our 100 expedition porters, we begin successive one-day marches to the villages of Chakpo, Changpo and then Askole (10,000′), the last village we will see for three weeks. After Askole, human habitation ends and one enters an incredible wilderness of ice, rock and sky.

Reaching Paiju Camp (11,000′) at the foot of the Baltoro, one begins to feel the pulse of creation: the ice melts, the rocks roll, the glacier creaks and groans, rearranging its icy rivers.

At Concordia, we will be surrounded by K2 (28,741′), Broad Peak (26,400′), Gasherbrum IV (26,180′), Sia Kangri (24,350′), the Golden Throne (23,989′), and razor-edged Mitre Peak (19,718′) —undoubtedly one of the most majestic mountain sites in the world.

While in the uninhabited wilderness of the Baltoro, we will have with us a colorful part of Karakorum culture: our 100 expedition porters, the lively Baltis and Hunzakuts who carry all our group trekking gear. We will spend many memorable evenings listening to their songs and watching (and perhaps joining in) their dances.

The trek is graded "C-3," but it is really a true expedition, with all the difficulties and rewards one might expect. The rewards are too numerous to mention; the difficulties will include rough glacier travel, wild river crossings, and possible delays in the mountain flights in and out of Skardu.

Itinerary: Day 1 to 3: Leave U.S. Arrive Rawalpindi. Transfer to hotel.

Day 4: In Rawalpindi.

Day 5: Fly to Skardu (weather permitting). Overnight in guest house.

Day 6: In Skardu at 8,850 feet on the banks of the Indus River.

Day 7: Jeep to Basha and hike to Dasso.

Day 8: to 19: Hike to the Biafo Glacier, up the Braldu Valley, cross the Dumordo River, ascend the north bank of the Baltoro Glacier and reach Concordia, one of the world's most spectacular places.

Day 20 to 22: Side trips from Concordia.

Day 23 to 33: Return down the Baltoro Glacier and Braldu Valley to Dasso.

Day 34: Meet jeeps and drive to Skardu. Overnight at guest house.

Day 35: Fly to Rawalpindi, weather permitting.

Day 36: Leave Rawalpindi and connect with homeward-bound flights.

Dates: Jun 7–Jul 12 (36 days)
Leader: Richard Irvin
Grade: C-3
Land Cost: $3950
(11–15 members)
Single Supplement:$230
IT5BA1YO45

Porters on the Baltoro Glacier/ Dick McGowan

Trekking in Hunza/ Pam Shandrick

At Concordia, pictured above, we will be surrounded by K2, Broad Peak, Gasherbrum IV, Sia Kangri, the Golden Throne and razor-edged Mitre Peak—undoubtedly one of the most majestic mountain sites in the world/ Bruce Klepinger

Trekking In Hunza

Legendary "kingdom" of the Karakorum

Legendary Hunza, which explorer Eric Shipton called "the ultimate manifestation of mountain grandeur," is known for its glacier-covered peaks (including 25,500-foot Rakaposhi), fragrant apricot orchards and the longevity of its people.

The people of Hunza, many of whom are green-eyed and fair-skinned (with blue-eyed boys often named Sikander, for Alexander), are thought to be descendants of a lost column of the army of Alexander the Great, who passed through here around 350 B.C., leaving many stragglers behind as he spread Greek culture from Asia Minor to India.

Our approach to Hunza is by jeep through the Hunza Gorge, the only gorge which actually cuts through the Karakorum Range, linking the ancient trails of the Gilgit-to-Kashgar caravan route, part of the Silk Route from western China.

We drive high above the dizzying gorge of the Hunza River to the picturesque village of Gulmit, then further to the roadhead at Pasu, about 70 miles from the 16,000-foot Khunjuerab Pass into China (and as far north as foreigners are currently permitted to go).

Here we begin a nine-day trek which takes us to shepherds' settlements alongside the 25-mile long Batura Glacier. There are spectacular views of the 25,000-foot Batura-area peaks and from our highest camp at 12,000 feet, we can hike to the uppermost pastures just below snowline for views extending into China and over the vast glacier-wilds of the Karakorum.

Itinerary: Day 1 to 3: Leave U.S. Arrive Rawalpindi. Transfer to hotel.

Day 4: In Rawalpindi.

Day 5: Fly to Gilgit, weather permitting.

Day 6: Scenic drive to Gulmit in upper Hunza. First views of Rakaposhi.

Day 7: Drive to Pasu. First views of the Batura Glacier. Walk to Yonz (9,570′) and camp beside glacier.

Day 8 to 11: Traverse moraine-covered glacier and shepherds' paths at 11,000 feet to Guchashim (12,276′), a meadow with views of the fantastic Batura Peaks and Disteghil Sar.

The people of Hunza, many of whom are green-eyed and fair-skinned are thought to be descendents of a lost column of the army of Alexander the Great/*Pam Shandrick*

Day 12 to 15: Outbound trek via Fatimahel, Yashpirt and Pasu.

Day 16 and 17: Drive to Karimabad. Vist the Mir of Hunza's former palace.

Day 18: Afternoon drive to Gilgit.

Day 19: Fly to Rawalpindi, weather permitting.

Day 20: In Rawalpindi.

Day 21: Depart Rawalpindi and connect with homeward-bound flights.

Dates: #1 Jul 12–Aug 1 (21 days)
#2 Aug 2–Aug 22
Leader: Richard Irvin
Grade: B-3
Land Cost: $2290
(11–15 members)
$2590 (6–10)
Single Supplement: $150
IT5BA1YO46

Alongside the 25-mile-long Batura Glacier, there are spectacular views of the 25,000-foot Batura-area peaks/*Leo Le Bon*

High Roads To Hunza

Overland tour of Swat, Gilgit and Hunza

To tour the "northwest frontier province" of Pakistan is to discover some of the most beautiful and least spoiled mountain regions in the world: Swat, Gilgit, and Hunza.

We first drive to Swat via Malakand Pass, near which Winston Churchill served his military apprenticeship. The Swat Valley was a semi-autonomous princely state until the 1960's. Its scenery is alpine and Swiss-like, with fast-moving streams fed by glaciers from 19,000-foot mountains. Swat is rich in archaeological remains dating from the Gandhara period of Buddhist art.

Next we drive the twisting gorge of the mighty Indus River to Gilgit, around which British and Russian explorers played "the Great Game" of exploration of *terra incognita* between India and Central Asia in the 19th century.

From here, we approach Hunza. Not by the dangerous trails of yore, but by jeep on the Karakorum Highway, a two-lane road that pushes through hundreds of miles of seemingly impossible terrain between Pakistan and China, perhaps some of the most rugged terrain on earth. The KKH, as the highway is known, was completed in the late 1970's after almost 20 years of work.

Arriving in Hunza, one of the most impressive mountain communities in the world, we drive along the precipitous Hunza Gorge to visit Karimabad, the "capital" and site of the Mir of Hunza's former palace. Driving as far north as we are allowed on the KKH (70 miles from Kashgar in Sinkiang Province of China), we enjoy views of the 25,000-foot Batura Peaks and snout of the 25-mile-long Batura Glacier.

The trip also visits the wonderful frontier town of Peshawar, home of the swashbuckling Pathans, and the very old city of Lahore, a Moghul city of brick ramparts, moats, mosques and bazaars which Kipling used as a setting for his classic novel of India, *Kim*.

Itinerary: Day 1 to 3: Leave U.S. Arrive Karachi. Transfer to hotel.

Day 4: Fly to Rawalpindi and drive to Peshawar via archaeological site at Taxila.

Day 5: Sightseeing in Peshawar.

Day 6: Drive to Saidu Sharif, capital of Swat.

Day 7: All-day drive to Gilgit on the Karakorum Highway (KKH).

Day 8: By jeep to Karimabad, Hunza. First views of snow-capped Rakaposhi (25,550') today.

Day 9: Excursion to view glaciers in the Nagar Valley, then drive north to village of Gulmit.

Day 10: Drive past spectacular peaks to the northernmost point open to foreigners. Return to Gilgit.

Day 11: Fly to Rawalpindi (weather permitting!).

Day 12: Fly to Lahore. Afternoon sightseeing.

Day 13: In Lahore, with evening flight to Karachi. Overnight in hotel.

Day 14: Depart on homeward-bound flights, arriving same day.

Dates: #1 May 20–Jun 2 (14 days)
#2 Oct 12–Oct 25
Leader: #1 to be announced
#2 Richard Irvin
Grade: A-2
Land Cost: $1550
(11–15 members)
$1690 (7–10)
Single Supplement: $145
IT5BA1YO44

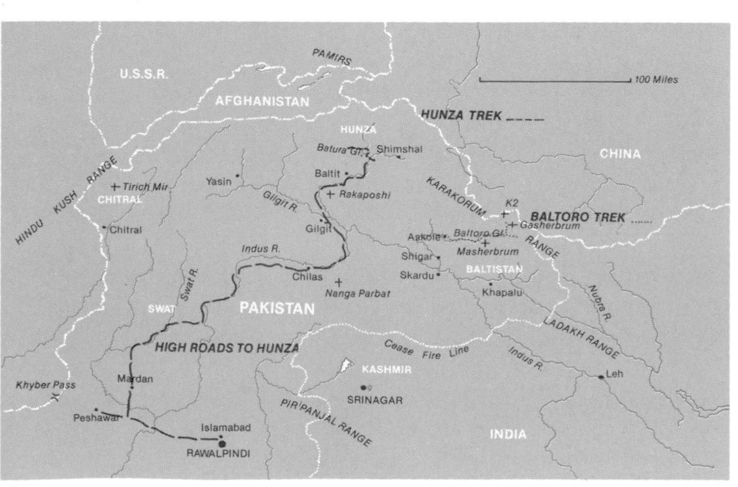

Pakistan trips include: twin accommodations in hotels, all meals (except in cities), mountain flights within Pakistan (if applicable), visas (if required), permits, leadership, sightseeing, ground transportation. On trek (if applicable), all arrangements including tents and commissary gear, all camp meals, services of camp and commissary crew, porters.

"Just passing through..."

ISLAMABAD/ RAWALPINDI

City notes by Pam Shandrick

Walking/jogging:

It's usually too hot and humid to jog in this city, but die-hards could jog the road to the hilltop overlook above Islamabad for views of the huge Saudi-funded mosque which, when completed, will be the world's largest.

Shopping:

Good quality rugs from Afghanistan and the Middle East are sold in shops near the major hotels in both the "twin cities" of Islamabad and Rawalpindi. Stroll the Raja Bazaar in 'Pindi to buy a *shalwar kamis*, the Pakistani national costume of knee-length tunic and baggy drawstring pants—the ideal garment for trekkers (both men and women) in Pakistan's warm weather mountains.

Day Trips:

Take a short, inexpensive flight (or drive three hours each way) to Peshawar to stroll its unforgettable bazaars for great bargains on Afghan rugs (much better prices than in Rawalpindi/ Islamabad), Afghan jewelry and much more. The Peshawar Museum, with its Gandhara art collection, is also a must. Or hire a car to drive from Islamabad to the archaeological site at Taxila and the famous Attock Fort built by Emperor Akbar. Escape the heat with a round-trip drive to Muree, a cool 7,500-foot British-style hill town 42 miles from Islamabad which was the colonial summer capital for the Punjab beginning in 1850.

About Trekking In Pakistan

To make your Pakistan trek as comfortable as possible, all camping gear is carried by porters we hire from local villages. Pack animals are not normally available in these regions. You will only need to carry a light day-pack for your jacket, camera, and water bottle.

In addition to a Mountain Travel leader, there will be a camp staff including a cook. Breakfast and dinner are hot meals served in camp. A cold lunch (with hot tea) is served picnic-style each day.

Trekkers' Holiday In Kashmir

5-day trek plus tour of historic Rajasthan

The Vale of Kashmir—its very name conjures up visions of Moghul princes escaping the mid-summer heat of the plains in their lavish Kashmiri gardens and palaces, and of the British Raj floating up-river on Victorian-style houseboats.

The 85-mile-long Kashmir Valley is the largest within the Himalayan chain. With its Swiss-like scenery of green meadows and white peaks, poets have called Kashmir "an emerald set in pearls." To us, it's a delightful Himalayan retreat and a good place for a short, easy trek.

This trip features a five-day trek beginning at the village of Pahlgam at 7,000 feet. The walk takes place on pleasant trails through valley orchards, flower-filled meadows, and cool woods of pine and birch at 9,000 feet.

The alpine hills of Kashmir are populated in summer by nomadic herders. Most are Gujars and Bakarwals. The Gujars herd horses, cattle and water buffalo; the Bakarwals herd sheep and goats.

When European residents of India began to discover the delights of Kashmir hundreds of years ago, a law was passed forbidding foreigners to own land here. The British got around this by making their summer homes on elegant Victorian houseboats in the lakes around Srinagar, Kashmir's capital. It is on such houseboats that we will relax, Raj-style, at the finish of our trek. In Srinagar, we'll appreciate the quality and variety of Kashmir's handicrafts (carved woodwork, leather, papier-mache, carpets and silver).

The trip ends with visits to some of the most beautiful sites in Rajasthan, the ancient desert province which was home to dynasties of warrior-kings, rajas and maharajas. In Agra, we visit the incomparable Taj Mahal a "vision in white marble" which really must be seen to be believed, and nearby Fatephur Sikri, the haunting abandoned 15th century capital of Emperor Akbar. We also travel to Jaipur, with its 18th century rose-colored palaces and courts, and to Amber Palace, a 12th century fortress to which we ascend in grand style: on elephant-back!

With its Swiss-like scenery of green meadows and white peaks, poets have called Kashmir "an emerald set in pearls." To us, it's a delightful Himalayan retreat and a good place for a short, easy trek/*Hugh Swift*

Itinerary: Day 1: Depart Seattle.
Day 2: Arrive Bangkok. Overnight.
Day 3: Sightseeing.
Day 4: Fly to Delhi.
Day 5: Fly to Srinagar.
Day 6 to 9: On trek.
Day 10: End trek in Srinagar.
Day 11: Fly to Delhi.
Day 12: Drive to Agra, visit Taj Mahal.
Day 13: Fly to Jaipur, visit palaces.
Day 14: Visit Amber, drive to Delhi.
Day 15: Depart Delhi.
Day 16: Arrive Seattle.

Dates: #1 May 10–May 25 (16 days)
#2 Jun 7–Jun 22
#3 Jul 5–Jul 20
#4 Aug 2–Aug 17
#5 Aug 30–Sep 14
#6 Sep 27–Oct 12
Leader: to be announced
Grade: B-2
Tour Cost:
From Seattle: $2690
From Dallas: $2920
INCLUDING round trip economy-class airfare on Thai Airways International
Single Supplement: $275
IT5TG1MT05

India, Sikkim, Bhutan and Sri Lanka trips include: twin accommodations in hotels, all meals (except in Delhi or Calcutta), leadership, visas, permits, airport transfers, ground transportation. On treks, all arrangements including tents and commissary gear, all meals on trek, services of camp crew, porters or pack animals, ground transportation, sightseeing.

Lamayuru Monastery, Ladakh/ *Marsha Parker*

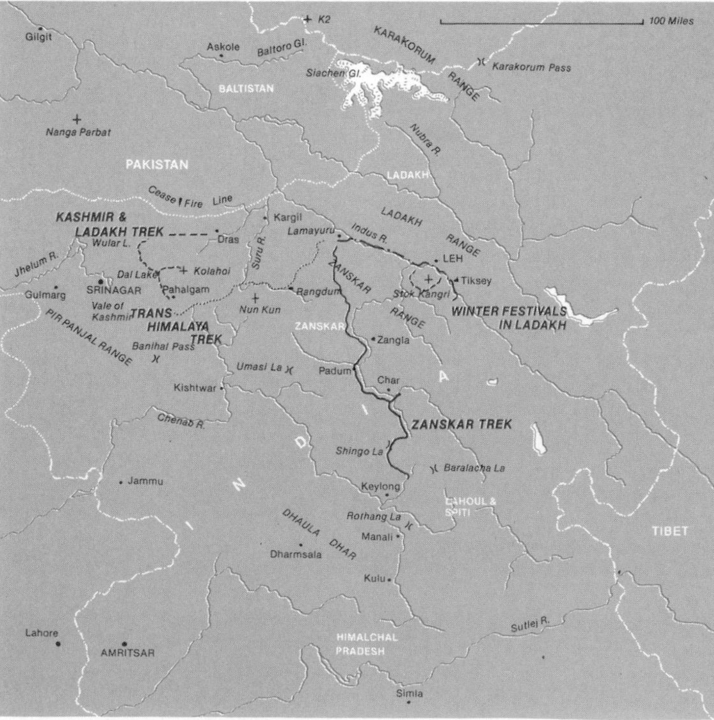

The Zanskari people are among the most colorfully dressed of Himalayan peoples, especially the women with their massive turquoise-encrusted headdresses/*Leo Le Bon*

Floating market, Dal Lake, Srinagar/ Ken Scott

Trekking In Kashmir & Ladakh

A perfect introduction to the Western Himalayas

The Kashmir Valley is cool, green and lush in summer, its gentle mountains and hillsides dense with evergreen forests, birch groves and wildflowers. It is ideal terrain for a first trek in the Himalayas because of its relatively moderate elevation.

The arid mountains of Ladakh, just across the Himalayan watershed, present an interesting counterpart to Kashmir, both scenically and culturally. Kashmir's culture is Islamic and its mountains are verdant; Ladakh's culture is Buddhist and its landscape is windswept and arid, lying on the edge of the Tibetan Plateau.

After an overnight on a houseboat in Srinagar, we drive to Pahlgam and begin our first trek, hiking through remote forested valleys inhabited by a few colorful Gujar nomads. Views include a close look at precipitous Kolahoi Peak (17,800′) and the distant giant Nanga Parbat (26,660′). Highest altitude reached on this trek is 13,500 feet, the crossing of the Yemnher Pass into the Sind Valley.

Driving across the Zoji La Pass (11,580′) over the Himalayan crest and passing over the Himalayan rain shadow, we find ourselves in the extremely arid mountain landscape of Ladakh.

At Leh and in the Indus Valley, we visit some of the most beautiful Buddhist monasteries in existence, including spectacular Lamayuru, then make a four-day trek on the flanks of the Indus Valley towards the peak of Stok Kangri (21,000′) for grand panoramas of the Indus Valley and mountains of Ladakh from a pass at 16,000 feet.

Itinerary: Day 1 to 3: Leave U.S. Arrive Delhi. Transfer to hotel.

Day 4: Fly to Srinagar (5,200′) and transfer to houseboat on Dal Lake.

Day 5 and 6: Drive to Pahlgam (7,800′) and begin trek. Hike to Aru (7,850′), then to a large open valley above the Lidder River, passing Gujar shepherd huts and forests of Kashmiri maple, pine and fir to Satlanjan (10,050′).

Day 7: Optional hike up the valley to the snout of the Kolahoi Glacier.

Day 8 and 9: Back through Lidderwat, climb toward Sekiwas (11,150′) and cross Yemnher Pass (13,500′) and descend into the Sind Valley.

Day 10: Descend the whole day, sometimes steeply, to a meadow near Zaivan (9,300′).

Day 11: Walk to Sonamarg and drive to Kargil (9,000′). Overnight at hotel.

Day 12: Continue the spectacular drive over the mountains to Leh (11,000′). Transfer to hotel.

Day 13: Visit the Tiksey and Hemis monasteries.

Day 14: Begin four-day trek with a hike up through the village of Stok (11,500′) and into a long, winding canyon.

Day 15: Trek towards the peak of Stok Kangri, climbing steadily all day to a camp at about 14,000 feet just below the Matho La Pass.

Day 16: A short but steep climb up to the Matho La Pass (16,000′). Fine views of snowy 20,000-foot Ladakh ranges. Descend to camp at about 14,000 feet with views of surrounding glaciers.

Day 17: Descend through a beautiful canyon and end the trek near the village of Matho. Drive to Leh. Overnight at hotel.

Day 18: Fly to Srinagar (weather permitting) and transfer to houseboats on Dal Lake.

Day 19: Free day in Srinagar.

Day 20: Fly to Delhi and transfer to hotel.

Day 21: Transfer to airport and connect with homeward-bound flights.

Dates: #1 Jul 5–Jul 25 (21 days)
#2 Aug 16–Sep 5
Leader: to be announced
Grade: B-2
Land Cost: $1790
(12–15 members)
$2095 (9–11)
Single Supplement: $225
IT6PA1SFMT5

Pam Shandrick

Cultural Expedition:

Zanskar: A Hidden Kingdom

Ancient Buddhist culture of the Western Himalayas

Zanskar has kept alive an archaic form of Buddhism which flourishes in craggy stone fortress-monasteries, well guarded by the high passes of the Great Himalayan Range.

To reach the inner sanctum of Zanskar, we trek for twelve days along paths lined with *mani* walls and white-washed chortens, to hidden monasteries which are evidence of the areas' total immersion in Buddhist culture.

Driving to the Lahoul Valley, we hike over the Shingo La (16,400′), descending into Zanskar. As we trek towards Padum (11,000), the "capital," we take side trips to Phuktal, a monastery perched on a steep hillside at the mouth of a cave, to Bardun Gompa, atop a rock above the Tsarp River, and to Karsha, Zanskar's largest monastery complex.

We end the trek at Padum and drive to Leh via fantastic Lamayuru Monastery. In Leh, we spend our time visiting important Indus Valley monasteries such as Tiksey, Hemis and Alchi, the most artistically complex monastery in Ladakh.

Lecturer/Leader: Tadeusz Skorupski is director of the Institute of Buddhist Studies at the University of London and co-author, with David Snellgrove, of *Cultural Heritage of Ladakh.*

Itinerary: Day 1 to 3: Depart U.S. Arrive Delhi.

Day 4: In Delhi.

Day 5: Fly to Kulu, drive to Manali (6,000′).

Day 6: In Manali.

Day 7: All-day drive over the Rothang Pass (13,100′) to Lahoul Valley. Camp at Darcha (10,580′).

Day 8 to 19: 12-day trek through Zanskar via the Shingo La (16,000′).

Day 20 to 22: Visit Karsha Monastery complex and serene Thonde, with its seven temples.

Day 23: Drive to 18th century Rangdum Compa.

Day 24: Drive to Kargil.

Day 25: Visit Lamayuru Monastery.

Day 26: Drive to Leh.

Day 27 and 28: Drive to Srinagar via Kargil.

Day 29: Fly to Delhi.

Day 30: Depart Delhi and connect with homeward-bound flights.

Dates: Jul 26–Aug 24 (30 days)
Grade: $2690
(12–15 members)
$3100 (9–11)
Single Supplement: $260
IT6PA1SFMT9

"Black Hat" dance drama, Ladakh/ Siddiq Wahid

Zanskar has kept alive an archaic form of Buddhism which flourishes in craggy stone fortress-monasteries well-guarded by the high passes of the Great Himalayan Range/Siddiq Wahid

The Trans-Himalaya Trek

19-day trek from Kashmir to Ladakh

There are few places on earth where it is possible to experience the diversity of landscape seen on this 19-day foot journey, which travels from the densely forested Kashmir Valley to the desert of Ladakh. Moreover, this trek provides an ethnic odyssey, from the Moslem herders' hamlets of Kashmir to the medieval Buddhist villages of Ladakh, known as "Little Tibet."

Trekking through the deep forests for which Kashmir is famous, we hike over the Pir Panjal Range at Shilshar Pass (11,760′), passing shepherds' meadows of the Warwan Valley, a place of Moslem culture and Gujar nomad camps.

Reaching the head of the Warwan Valley, we cross the Great Himalayan Range at Lonvilad Gali Pass (14,530′) into the watershed of the Indus River and enter the Suru Valley, a semi-arid canyon populated by Baltis (who are ethnically Tibetan but long ago converted to Islam). The Suru Valley is cradled between the snowy flanks of the Himalaya and the parched rock of the Zanskar Range to the north.

Continuing up the Suru Valley with views of massive Nun Kun (23,410′), we enter a landscape of dry and windswept mountains and reach our first lamaistic temple, Rangdum Gompa, on the outskirts of Zanskar.

Crossing the Zanskar Range by the rocky Kanji La Pass (17,240′), we descend past the medieval village of Kanji, a cliff-side settlement whose inhabitants dress in thick red robes, goatskin shawls and winged stovepipe hats. Our last days take us past the multi-colored cliffs of Kang Nalla and to the ancient Lamayuru Monastery (11,300′) from where we drive to Leh, capital of Ladakh. We spend three days visiting monasteries of the Indus Valley before flying to Srinagar and homeward.

Itinerary: Day 1 to 3: Leave U.S. Arrive Delhi. Transfer to hotel.

Day 4: Fly to Srinagar. Transfer to houseboats on Dal Lake.

Day 5: Sightseeing in Srinagar (5,300′), capital of Kashmir.

Day 6: Drive to Lihenwan and camp.

Day 7 to 10: Hike across Shilshar Pass (11,760′), through forests and meadows, descend to Inshan (8,000′) on the Warwan River, and trek past a number of villages, to Sokhniz (9,100′), the highest village in the Warwan Valley.

Day 11 to 14: Through lovely countryside leaving behind the forests and walking through rocky meadows and over Lonvilad Gali Pass (14,530′) along the terminal moraine and glacier.

Day 15 and 16: Descent to the Suru River. The countryside, now in the Himalayan rain shadow, is noticeably drier and more barren. First views of Nun Kun and the Zanskar Range. Continue over the Pukartse La (12,500′) and descend to Parkachick, a fascinating adobe village at the foot of the Zanskar Range.

Day 17 and 18: An easy walk along a road to camp at Golmatung Meadow (12,650′) and a rest day.

Day 19 and 20: Trek to beautifully situated Rangdum Gompa, a Buddhist monastery, then walk to the Kanji La South Base Camp (13,900′).

Day 21: A long and gradual hike up to the Kanji La where there are breathtaking views of the peaks of the Karakorum.

Day 22 and 23: An easy walk down a dramatic maze of canyons to camp near the medieval village of Kanji, a classic Ladakhi town at about 12,000 feet. Rest day at Kanji.

Day 24 and 25: Emerge at Hiniskut from between high, steep ridges and drive to Leh via Lamayuru Monastery.

Day 26: Visit Hemis, Tiksey and other monasteries.

Day 27: Fly to Srinagar (weather permitting). Transfer to houseboats on Dal Lake.

Day 28: Free day in Srinagar.

Day 29: Fly to Delhi. Transfer to hotel.

Day 30: Depart Delhi and connect with homeward-bound flights.

Dates: #1 Jul 26–Aug 24 (30 days)
#2 Aug 23–Sep 21
Leader: Jan Zabinski
Grade: C-3
Land Cost: $2180 (12–15 members)
$2450 (9–11)
Single Supplement: $215
IT6PA1SFMT4

Our Cultural Expedition will join the Ladakhis for their festivities to witness dance dramas, to see rare works of art displayed only on these special occasions, and to hear their haunting chants accompanied by cymbals, drums and horns/Jim Gerstley

Cultural Expedition:

Winter Festivals In Ladakh

Dance dramas at ancient monasteries

Ladakh's high valleys can be at their most brilliant in winter, when a dusting of snow enhances spectacular vistas of high desert mountains. This is also the time when the great monasteries come alive with religious festivals that few outsiders have a chance to see. With tourists gone and fields lying fallow, the people of Ladakh have time to gather and watch the sacred dances of Lamaistic Buddhism, performed by lamas in ornate robes and magnificent painted masks.

We will join the Ladakhis for their festivities to witness dance dramas, to see rare works of art displayed only on these special occasions, and to hear their haunting chants accompanied by cymbals, drums and horns.

Our trip centers around Leh (11,000′), the capital, from which we take day trips to monasteries and other places of interest, returning to a small hotel each night.

Lecturer/Leader: Michael Aris, Ph.D., is Research Fellow in Himalayan and Tibetan Studies at Wolfson College, Oxford, England. He lived for more than five years in Bhutan and is the author of two books on the history of that country. He has travelled extensively in the Himalayas, India, Tibet and China.

Itinerary: Day 1 to 3: Leave U.S. Arrive Delhi.

Day 4: In Delhi.

Day 5: Fly to Leh. Overnight in hotel.

Day 6 and 7: At Likir Monastery.

Day 8: In Leh.

Day 9: Visit Hemis, Tiksey and Shey monasteries.

Day 10: Visit Alchi and Rizong monasteries.

Day 11: In Leh.

Day 12: Drive to Lamayuru Monastery for overnight.

Day 13: Return to Leh.

Day 14: In Leh.

Day 15 to 17: Visit Stok village.

Day 18: In Leh.

Day 19: Fly to Delhi.

Day 20: In Delhi.

Day 21: Depart Delhi on homeward-bound flights.

Dates: approx. Jan 24–Feb 13 (21 days)
1987: Jan 23–Feb 12
Grade: A-2
Land Cost: $1990 (12–15 members)
$2250 (9–11)
Single Supplement: $265
IT6PA1SFMT2

There are few places on earth where it is possible to experience the diversity of landscape seen on the Trans-Himalaya trek, 19-day foot journey which travels from the densely forested Kashmir Valley to the desert of Ladakh/Hugh Swift

The Zanskar Trek

Inner canyons of the Western Himalayas

This rugged 18-day trek in the Great Himalayan Range traverses the parched canyons of the ancient "kingdom" of Zanskar, once part of western Tibet.

Zanskar is a fascinating Buddhist enclave which historically has had little contact with the outside world—indeed, even the famous Himalayan caravan routes didn't pass this way, since snows keep Zanskar's high passes inaccessible most of the year. Two ceremonial monarchs still reside here, one in Padum and one in the tiny hamlet of Zangla. There are several ancient monasteries in Zanskar, including the large and spectacularly-situated complex at Karsha.

We approach Zanskar by flying to the verdant Kulu Valley hill town of Manali (6,000'). From here we drive over the spectacular Rothang La (13,050') into the arid setting of the Lahoul Valley. The trek begins at Darcha (11,000'), where we quickly leave the Lahoul Valley via the steep Shingo La (16,700').

Descending into Zanskar, we spend the next two weeks following a precipitous course along twisting river gorges and over rocky passes.

The arid Zanskari landscape is brightened by shimmering willow groves, glacier-irrigated fields of yellow buckwheat and green pea patches. At every turn, we'll see dramatically-situated medieval villages—many nestled into cliffsides—and trails lined with some of the most exquisitely-carved *mani* stones in the Himalayas. We'll also meet the handsome Zanskari people, among the most colorfully dressed of Himalayan inhabitants, particularly the women with their massive turquoise-encrusted headdresses.

The trek ends at Lamayuru, the spectacular monastery situated on the Leh-to-Srinagar road.

Itinerary: Day 1 to 3: Leave U.S. Arrive Delhi. Transfer to hotel.

Day 4: Fly to the Kulu Valley and drive to the hill station of Manali (6,000').

Day 5: In Manali.

Day 6: All-day drive over Rothang Pass (13,100') crossing the Great Himalayan Range to the Lahoul Valley. Camp at Darcha (10,580').

Day 7 to 10: Trek towards and over the Shingo La (16,700'). Rest day after the pass.

Day 11 to 13: Descend past the first Zanskari chortens to the village of Kargiakh at 13,000 feet, past many mani walls built of beautifully carved slate stones, and over a swinging bridge to Phuktal Monastery (12,500'), one of the most dramatically situated of the Zanskar gompas.

Day 14 and 15: Visit Mune (12,200'), a village with a 200-year-old monastery, and the 17th century Bardan Gompa (11,800'), perched like a medieval fortress above the river.

Day 16 to 20: Trek to Padum, capital of Zanskar, then continue to the little hamlet of Zangla, and cross Hanuma La (16,000'), with its breathtaking views of the jagged ranges of the Zanskar Himalaya.

Day 21 to 24: Trek over Kuba La (12,500'), Shingi La (17,060'), and Sirsir La (16,000').

Day 23 and 24: Trek to Wanla, like a green oasis in the desert landscape, with its lovely apricot orchards. Cross the Prinkiti La to Lamayuru Monastery.

Day 25: Drive to Leh. Overnight in hotel.

Day 26: Sightseeing including major monasteries such as Tiksey and Hemis.

Day 27: Fly to Srinagar (weather permitting). Transfer to houseboats on Dal Lake.

Day 28: Free day in Srinagar.

Day 29: Fly to Delhi. Transfer to hotel.

Day 30: Depart Delhi on homeward-bound flights.

Dates: Jun 27–Jul 26 (30 days)
Leader: Jan Zabinski
Grade: C-3
Land Cost: $2090
(12–15 members)
$2290 (9–11)
Single Supplement: $345
IT6PA1SFMT2

Girl from Kanji village/*Ray Jewell*

The arid Zanskari landscape is brightened by shimmering willow groves, glacier-irrigated fields of yellow buckwheat and green pea patches/*Jan Zabinski*

"Just passing through..."

DELHI

City notes by Colonel N. Kumar and Jan Zabinski

Jogging/walking tours;

The "Raj Path," a road from the Presidential Palace to the National Stadium, is a nice morning run. The Lodi Gardens are a good place for early morning walks; many of Delhi's professional community take their daily exercise here.

Day trips:

Kurkushetra, north of Delhi on the Grand Trunk Road, would be a nice alternative if you've already seen the Taj. It's a pilgrimage center with pools and temples. Basic Hindu beliefs articulated here by Krishna to Arjuna, as told in the Bhagavad Gita.

Museums:

Gurudwara Sis Gang on Chandi Chowk Road is a good little-known museum: downstairs it preserves the tree under which Guru Tech Bahadur was martyred. The Indian Mountaineering Foundation's museum is at Juraj Benito Road in New Delhi.

Special markets:

Day or night, you can always find adventures on Chandi Chowk and its side bazaars, a microcosm of India!

About Trekking In Kashmir & Ladakh

Most of our India treks take place in portions of the Great Himalayan Range such as Ladakh and Zanskar, sparsely populated and arid regions, usually at 10,000 feet or higher. Campsites are chosen for their scenic beauty as well as their proximity to sources of water and fodder for the pack animals.

All camping gear is carried by pack animals (porters are not a tradition in this region of the Himalaya). You will only need to carry a light daypack for your jacket, camera, and water bottle.

There will be a Mountain Travel leader, a camp manager and a small local camp staff including a cook. Breakfast and dinner are hot meals served in a dining tent. Pack lunches are carried on the trail.

The Third Pole Expedition

Ascent of Sia Kangri (24,350′)

We are pleased to announce the fielding of the first-ever Western expedition to the Siachen Glacier, the high altitude mountain wilderness of the Eastern Karakorum of India, which contains the longest glaciers in Asia as well as the largest body of continuous ice in the Greater Himalayas. This region is known as "the Third Pole."

Preceded only by the 1912 expedition of Bullock-Workman (read *Two Summers In The Ice-Wilds Of the Karakorum*), our expedition will be the first to ascend the entire 47-mile Siachen glacier from its snout to its source, the Indira Col at 20,000 feet.

Traveling on the glacier by cross-country or mountaineering skis, the expedition will then attempt the first American ascent of Sia Kangri (24,350′).

From Delhi, we fly to Leh, capital of Ladakh, and spend several days acclimatizing to the high altitude (11,000′). From here, we travel by truck over the 18,200-foot Khardung La, highest road pass in the world, crossing the Nubra Valley to the roadhead at Sasoma.

From here, we trek for two weeks up the Siachen Glacier to Sia Kangri base camp.

Even though Sia Kangri is not technically difficult, it is a high peak commanding the utmost respect. From the summit, one can look into Afghanistan, Russia, Chinese Turkistan, Tibet, Pakistan and India.

Looking at Saltoro Kangri II (also known as Peak 35). Traveling on glaciers by cross-country skis, the Third Pole Expedition will attempt the first American ascent of Sia Kangri (24,350′)/*Colonel N. Kumar*

Our expedition will travel to the head of the Siachen Glacier jointly with the first party to attempt the difficult and unclimbed east face of Peak 35 (Saltoro Kangri II—25,278′), which may be the highest unclimbed peak in the world (after Namche Barwa in Tibet). An Indian climbing team will also join the party.

Itinerary: Day 1 to 3: Leave U.S. Arrive Delhi. Transfer to hotel.
Day 4: In Delhi.
Day 5: Fly to Leh.
Day 6 and 7: Acclimatization in Leh.
Day 8: By truck to Sasoma over the Khardung La (18,200′).
Day 9 to 11: Trek to snout of glacier.
Day 12 to 14: On the lower glacier to base camp at 16,000 feet.
Day 15 to 19: On the upper glacier using skis to advance base camps below the pass.
Day 20 to 30: Attempts on Sia Kangri.
Day 31 to 37: Return to roadhead.
Day 38: Return to Leh.
Day 39: Fly to Delhi
Day 40: Depart Delhi on homeward-bound flights.

Dates: Jun 1–Jul 10 (40 days)
Leader: Leo Le Bon
Grade: E-2
Land Cost: approx. $8000 (6 members)
Single Supplement: $200
IT6PA1SFMT6

Trek To The Source Of The Ganges

Pilgrim trails to the abode of Shiva

The holy Ganges River, mother of India, springs from the high peaks and melting glaciers of the Garhwal Himalaya, where the contrast of green, monsoon-watered valleys and soaring rock and ice peaks produces one of the most impressive sections of the Great Himalayan Range.

The Vedas, ancient sacred books of Hinduism, deemed the Garhwal Himalaya as the abode of Shiva and other major dieties. For thousands of years, pilgrims, *sadhus* and assorted mystics have walked the trails to the sacred places of the Garhwal to meditate and pray.

A six-day trek to the very source of the Ganges is not just a mountain experience; it's a unique cultural experience—a chance, if you will, to make your own pilgrimage *(yatra).*

We fly to Dehra Dun and drive to the old British "hill station" of Mussoorie at 6,000 feet, escaping the searing summer heat of the Indian plains. Driving further north to Gangotri (10,300′), we'll find several ashrams and a temple built in the 18th century.

From here we hike to Gaumukh ("the cow's mouth"), snout of the 25-mile-long Gangotri Glacier. A day's walking across the glacier itself, which may be snow-covered at this time of year, takes us to Tapovan, within sight of Shivling, a peak with mythic associations.

In the words of author Marco Pallis in his book, *Peaks and Lamas,* "It is useless to try to describe the grandeur of the scene; there are perfections about which the only eloquence is silence."

Our return drive takes us through the ashram-filled town of Rishikesh ("place of the seekers of truth") to Dehra Dun and Delhi.

Itinerary: Day 1 to 3: Leave U.S. Fly to Delhi. Transfer to hotel.
Day 4: In Delhi.
Day 5: Fly to Dehra Dun and drive to Mussoorie.
Day 6: 130-mile drive to Lanka along the banks of the Ganges and camp.
Day 7: Drive and walk to Gangotri.
Day 8: Exploring Gangotri and its ashrams.
Day 9 and 10: Trek to Chirbasa and Gaumukh at 13,000 feet.
Day 11: Trek to Tapovan across Gangotri Glacier at 13,800 feet.
Day 12: Exploring Tapovan.
Day 13 and 14: Return trek to Chirbasa and Gangotri.
Day 15: Drive to Chamba and camp.
Day 16: Drive to Rishikesh.
Day 17: Drive to Dehra Dun.
Day 18: Fly to Delhi.
Day 19: In Delhi.
Day 20: Depart Delhi on homeward-bound flights.

Dates: May 20–Jun 8 (20 days)
Leader: Jan Zabinski
Grade: B-3
Land Cost: $1490 (12–15 members) $1690 (9–11)
Single Supplement: $225
IT6PA1SFMT1

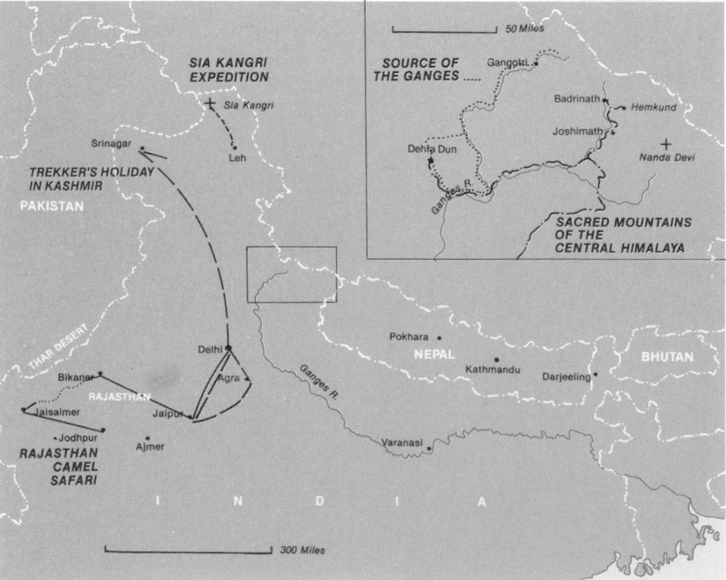

A Shivite flagellant. For thousands of years, pilgrims sadhus and assorted mystics have walked to the sacred places of the Garhwal annually to meditate and pray/*Jan Zabinski*

Sacred Mountains Of The Central Himalayas

The Kumaon trek: a microcosom of Hindu and Buddhist culture

The Kumaon region of the central Himalayas has the distinction of having India's holiest and highest peaks, including 25,645-foot Nanda Devi (highest in India), Trisul (23,406′), and Kamet (25,477′).

But the Kumaon Himalaya has much more than just famous peaks: its pilgrim trails lead us through a veritable microcosm of Indian and Himalayan cultures.

Beginning in the Pindar Valley, whose rivers drain the peak of Trisul ("Trident of Shiva"), we trek for 7 days among shrine-filled villages, finding a melting pot of Hindu and Buddhist cultures.

We encounter Bhotia tradesmen (people of Tibetan descent who have adopted Hindu religion and dress), and we see Hindus on the pilgrim trails to holy mountains and shrines.

Nanda Devi tops the Kumaon Himalaya. It is a sacred peak whose name means "bliss-giving goddess," and was the highest mountain in the British Empire for 100 years of the Raj.

Trisul, first climbed in 1907 by Longstaff, was climbed and descended *on skis* in 1977 by Mountain Travel's "man in India" (and leader of this trek), Indian mountaineer "Bull" Kumar.

After the trek we drive to two special pilgrimage sites: Hemkund, a lake at 14,200 feet which is the holiest pilgrimage site for Sikhs, and fascinating Badrinath (10,300′), birthplace of Shiva, a shrine of great sanctity and India's most popular Hindu pilgrimage center.

Nanda Devi, a sacred peak whose name means "bliss-giving goddess," was the highest mountain known in the British Empire for 100 years of the Raj/ Hugh Swift

Colonel Narinder Kumar

Itinerary: Day 1 to 3: Leave U.S. Arrive Delhi. Transfer to hotel.

Day 4: Day free in Delhi.

Day 5: Fly to Pant Nagar and drive to Ranikhet (6,500′) and camp.

Day 6: Visit the Kumaon Regiment Museum and drive to Gwaldam (6,600′) with first views of Trisul.

Day 7 to 14: On trek at altitudes of about 9,000 feet.

Day 15: Drive to Badrinath.

Day 16 and 17: Visit Hemkund.

Day 18: Drive to Joshimath.

Day 19: Drive to Dehra Dun and fly to Delhi.

Day 20: Depart Delhi and connect with homeward-bound flights.

Day 21: Arrive home.

Dates: Oct 1–Oct 21 (21 days)
Leader: Colonel N Kumar
Grade: B-2
Land Cost: $1650
(12–15 members)
Single Supplement: $215
IT6PA1SFMT25

Our Man In India

Colonel Narinder ("Bull") Kumar, 52, now retired after a distinguished career in the Indian Army, is director of our trekking operations in India. He has led and participated in more than ten major Himalayan climbs, including successful expeditions on Everest, Kanchenjunga and Nanda Devi, and has been awarded his nation's highest awards for his achievements. A frequent visitor to our office in California and a long-time friend and associate, Colonel Kumar knows the Indian Himalayas intimately—probably better than anyone else in the world—and provides the finest trekking services available in the Indian Himalyas. He is the author of five books on his expeditions.

Rajasthan Camel Safari

Exploring a history-filled desert province

Before India's independence in 1947, Rajasthan ("land of princes") consisted of 18 princely states, some of the oldest monarchies in India and perhaps the world.

The Rajput *rajas* and *maharajas* had a long tradition of martial valor and this desert is still dotted with palaces and fortresses that are reminders of that romantic, turbulent era.

Our Rajasthan explorations center around a seven-day camel safari in the Great Indian Desert. We ride (or walk if preferred) from one village to another, camping enroute. An ancient civilization once flourished here, as is apparent from archaeological finds such as Kaligangan. The desert's current inhabitants are pastoral tribes who tend livestock and ride camels with colorful tasseled saddles.

The trip also includes visits to the city of Jaisalmer, a 12th century desert stronghold, Jaipur, a city of rose-colored stone buildings built in 1721, and Amber, where we ascend to the Amber Palace on elephant-back to view its lavish workmanship.

In Jodphur, Jaipur, Gajner and Bikaner, our accommodations are in *maharajas'* palaces which have been converted to hotels.

Note: dates and itinerary of Trip #2 will be adjusted to accommodate a visit to the colorful annual Puskhar Camel Fair.

Itinerary: Day 1 to 3: Leave U.S. Arrive Delhi. Transfer to hotel.

Day 4: Sightseeing in Delhi.

Day 5: Fly to Jaipur. Sightseeing at Amber.

Day 6: Drive to Dunlod Castle for overnight.

Day 7: Drive to Bikaner Palace for overnight.

Day 8: Visit Gajner Wildlife Sanctuary.

Day 9: Drive to camp at Bithnok.

Day 10 to 15: On camel safari.

Day 16: Drive to Jaisalmer. Overnight at palace.

Day 17: Sightseeing in Jaisalmer. Night train to Jodphur.

Day 18: Sightseeing in Jodphur.

Day 19: Fly to Delhi. Transfer to hotel.

Day 20: In Delhi.

Day 21: Transfer to airport and connect with homeward-bound flights.

Dates: #1 Feb 15–Mar 7 (21 days)
#2 Nov 8–Nov 28
Leader: to be announced
Grade: B-2
Land Cost: $1690
(12–15 members)
$1790 (9–11)
Single Supplement: $265
IT6PA1SFMT7

Villagers of the Thar Desert/ Marsha Parker

On the Rajasthan Camel Safari, we ride (or walk if preferred) from one village to another, camping enroute/ Marsha Parker

Trekking In Sikkim

12-day trek to Kanchenjunga

The summit crest of Mt. Kanchenjunga (28,208′), third highest mountain in the world, forms the border between Sikkim and Nepal. Its satellite peaks —Jannu (25,294′), Tent Peak (24,089′), Siniolchu (22,610′) and Kangbachan (25,925′)—are called "The Five Treasures of the Great Snows."

From Gangtok, capital of Sikkim, we begin our 12-day trek near the great monastery at Pemyangtse, one of 60 monasteries in Sikkim. The walk begins at 6,000 feet and takes us through moss-laden forests of pine, magnolia and rhododendron, venturing gradually up into high alpine country. At mid-point in the trek from a camp at 13,000 feet, we make an optional hike up to the Goecha La (16,400′) for classic views of Kanchenjunga.

The trip begins with a visit to Darjeeling (8,000′), queen of the British colonial hill stations, where we walk its steep, narrow streets, and from Tiger Hill, glimpse the famous sight of sunrise reflected on mighty Kanchenjunga, just 50 miles away.

Itinerary: Day 1 to 3: leave U.S. Arrive Delhi. Continue by air to Bagdogra. Drive to Darjeeling.

Day 4: Sightseeing in Darjeeling.

Day 5: Drive to Gangtok, Sikkim.

Day 6: Sightseeing in Gangtok.

Day 7: Drive to Pemyangtse.

Day 8: All-day drive to Yoksum (6,000′). Overnight at Dak Bungalow.

Day 9 to 11: Trek to 9,000 feet, then higher through yak and sheep grazing areas to Dzongri (13,221′), with its awe-inspiring views of the Sikkimese Himalaya.

Day 12 and 13: Continue through the great Onglathang Valley, past spendid glacial lakes and numerous glaciers to Chemathang (15,748′).

Day 14: Optional Goecha La hike.

Day 15 to 18: Descend to Yoksum.

Day 19: Trek to Tashiding Monastery.

Day 20: End trek and drive to Darjeeling.

Day 21: Sightseeing in Darjeeling. Afternoon drive to Bagdogra and fly to Delhi.

Day 22: Depart Delhi and connect with homeward-bound flights.

Dates: Oct 11–Nov 1 (22 days)
Leader: Daku Tenzing Norgay
Grade: B-2
Land Cost: $1695
(12–15 members)
$1795 (9–11)
Single Supplement: $175
IT6PA1SFMT10

From Chemathang, we hike up to the Goecha La (16,400′) for classic views of Kanchenjunga/*Ken Scott*

Trip leader Daku Tenzing Norgay on the Rathong Glacier, Sikkim/*Ken Scott*

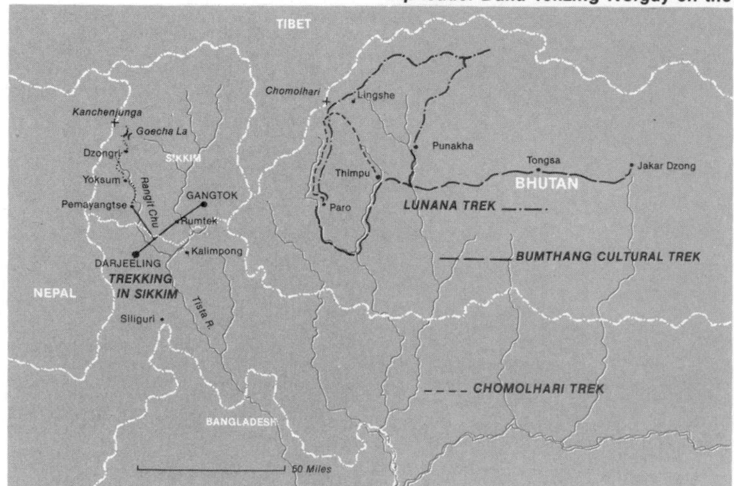

From Paro we trek for seven days, hiking through pine forests and yak herders' settlements and enjoying views of Chomolhari (23,977′), seen above, the "divine mountain" of Bhutan/
Leo Le Bon

The Chomolhari Trek & Paro Festival

Bhutan, "Land of the Peaceful Dragon," is a Himalayan monarchy whose quiet ways and Buddhist culture are still thriving in enormous medieval fortress-monasteries where red-robed lamas continue traditions of manuscript illustration and scroll painting.

Our Bhutan visit begins in the Shangri La setting of the Paro Valley, where we ride by pony up to cliff-side Taksang Monastery, the legend-filled "Tiger's Nest."

From Paro, we trek for seven days, hiking through pine forests and yak herders' settlements and enjoying views of Chomolhari (23,977′), the "divine mountain" of Bhutan. The highest altitude reached on the trek is Yalila Pass (15,800′).

Our visit to Paro coincides with the festivities of the annual Paro Festival, a lively Buddhist celebration. Another special plus on this trip is that we'll be here in April, prime season for rhododendrons, national flower of Bhutan.

Itinerary: Day 1 to 3: Leave U.S. Arrive Delhi. Continue by air to Bagdogra and drive to Phuntsoling, Bhutan. Overnight at hotel.

Day 4: Drive on a twisting mountain highway to Paro (7,000′). Overnight at hotel.

Day 5 and 6: Paro Festival and pony excursion to Taksang.

Day 7 to 11: Trek along the Paro River through pine and juniper forests and over Nyela Pass (13,940′) and Yalila Pass (15,800′).

Day 12 and 13: Trek through rhododendron forests past the ruins of Barshong Dzong and drive to Thimphu (7,600′), capital of Bhutan.

Day 14: Sightseeing in Thimphu.

Day 15: All-day excursion by road to Punakha Dzong.

Day 16: Drive to Phuntsoling.

Day 17: Drive to Bagdogra and fly to Delhi.

Day 18: Depart Delhi and connect with homeward-bound flights.

Dates: #1 Mar 22–Apr 8 (18 days)
#2 Oct 25–Nov 11
1987: Mar 28–Apr 14
Leader: to be announced
Grade: C-2
Land Cost: $2590
(10–15 members)
$2790 (6–9)
Single Supplement: not available
IT6PA1SFMT25

There is considerable wildlife on the Lunana Trek, with a good chance of seeing Himalayan blue sheep. There is also an abundance of wonderful flowers from rhododendrons to Himalayan blue poppies/ John P. Evans

Bhutan: The Lunana Trek

The ultimate *trek in the Eastern Himalayas*

We are pleased to offer the *ultimate* journey in Bhutan (and perhaps the entire Eastern Himalayas): an 18-day trek among the peaks and glaciers of remote Lunana in northern Bhutan.

This is the most alpine trek route in Bhutan, covering 200 miles and 8 passes below the Bhutan/Tibet frontier.

Though alpine in nature, this trek has incredible cultural attractions. Lunana, like its counterparts such as the long-restricted valleys of Dolpo in Nepal and Shimshal in Hunza, is one of those rare, isolated regions where the oldest and most authentic culture still remains. Most of northern Bhutan has rarely, if ever, been visited by outsiders.

The Bhutanese Himalayas are particularly rich in myths. In Lunana, it is believed that the highest hill forests are inhabited by seven brother-demons from Tibet. Consequently, no axeman has dared cut the trees and marvelous juniper forests at 13,000 feet survive intact (wood for village use is carried from distant regions). We'll see much other evidence of animistic, pre-Buddhist (Bon) traditions as we hike from one remote village to the next.

There is wildlife on this trip, with a good chance of seeing Himalayan blue sheep. There is also an abundance of wonderful flora, ranging from rhododendrons (national flower of Bhutan) to Himalayan blue poppies.

Itinerary: Day 1 to 3: Leave U.S. Arrive Calcutta. Overnight at airport hotel.

Day 4: Fly to Paro, Bhutan.

Day 5: Excursion to Taktsang Monastery.

Day 6: Drive to Thimphu, Bhutan's capital.

Day 7: Drive to Punakha. Camp.

Day 8 to 17: Trek over Pari La (12,450'), Tsumi Pass (16,000'), Karakachu Pass (17,300').

Day 18 to 20: Arrive in Lunana proper. Visit villages of Woche, Ledi and Thanza. Fantastic views of unknown 24,000-foot peaks on the Bhutan/Tibet border.

Day 21 to 27: Depart Lunana via Jaze La (17,500'), Loju La (17,100'), Rinchen Zoe Pass (17,780'), and Tampe La (14,900') to Tongsa in the Bumthang region.

Day 28: Drive to Thimphu.

Day 29: In Thimphu.

Day 30: Drive to Paro. Fly to Calcutta. Connect with homeward-bound flights.

Day 31: Arrive home.

Dates: Sep 25–Oct 25 (31 days)
Leader: Bruce Klepinger
Grade: C-3
Land Cost: $4390 (12–16 members)
$4575 (8–11)
Single Supplement: not available
IT6PA1SFMT25

Lunana, like its counterparts such as the long-restricted valleys of Dolpo in Nepal and Shimshal in Hunza, is one of those rare, isolated regions where the oldest and most authentic culture still remains intact. Most of northern Bhutan has rarely, if ever, been visited by outsiders/C. Hollister

Cultural Expedition:

Inner Bhutan: Bumthang Cultural Tour & Thimphu Festival

Visit historic central valleys

This non-trekking tour focuses on Bhutan's thriving Tantric Buddhist culture and the pastoral valleys of Bumthang, one of Bhutan's most historic regions.

We begin by spending a day in Thimphu (Bhutan's capital) to see the Tsechu Festival, an annual four-day event complete with masked dance-dramas. The Tsechu Festival celebrates various events in the life of Padmasambhava, the 8th century Indian-born tantrist who introduced Buddhism in its tantric form to Bhutan and Tibet.

Driving to Bumthang (central Bhutan), we explore by mini-bus on winding country roads and find beautiful scenes of white-washed farmhouses set amidst fields of barley and buckwheat. We stay in the remote towns of Punakha, Jakara and Tongsa (from where Bhutan's royal lineage originated), and visit an astounding array of medieval fortresses, temples and monasteries which played an important part in Bhutan's colorful history.

Leader/Lecturer: Professor Alexander W. MacDonald taught Ethnology and Comparative Sociology at Tribhuvan University in Kathmandu, Nepal, for two years and currently holds the same position at the University of Paris, France. He speaks fluent Tibetan, Hindi and Nepali and is a distinguished scholar on Tibet and Himalayan Buddhism.

Itinerary: Day 1 to 3: Leave U.S. Arrive Calcutta. Overnight at hotel.

Day 4: Fly to Paro, Bhutan. Overnight in hotel.

Day 5 and 6: Sightseeing in Paro.

Day 7: Drive to Thimphu. Overnight at hotel or camp.

Day 8: Day at Tsechu Festival.

Day 9: Drive to Punakha. Camp nearby.

Day 10: Drive to Tongsa. Overnight at guest house.

Day 11: Visit Tongsa Dzong, largest fortress in Bhutan, and continue to the town of Jakar. Overnight at guest house.

Day 12 and 13: Visit Jakar Dzong, Jambe Lhakhang, Kuje Lhakhang Monastery.

Day 14: Drive back to Tongsa. Overnight at guest house.

Day 15: Drive to Thimphu.

Day 16: Sightseeing in Thimphu.

Day 17: Drive to Phuntsoling.

Day 18: Drive to Bagdogra (India) Airport and fly to Delhi. Overnight at hotel.

Day 19: Transfer to airport and connect with homeward-bound flights.

Dates: Sep 7–Oct 8 (19 days)
Grade: A-1
Land Cost: $2590 (11–15 members)
$2750 (6–10)
Single Supplement: $75 (Calcutta and Delhi only)
IT6PA1SFMT12

The Tsechu Festival celebrates various events in the life of Padmasambhava, the 8th century Indian-born tantrist who introduced Buddhism in its tantric form to Bhutan and Tibet/Leo Le Bon

Taksang Monastery, "The Tiger's Nest"/ Leo Le Bon

Sri Lanka & The Maldives

5-day highland trek, 3-day wildlife safari, 4-day sailboat excursion

Although Sri Lanka is an island off the southeast tip of India, it is *not* an extension of India. It is a beautiful, diverse country with a unique culture all its own.

Its Buddhist history goes back 2,500 years, as we will see in the ancient ruined city of Polonnaruwa. Early Arab travelers came upon Sri Lanka and called it "Serendib" (from which was coined "serendipity," the aptitude for making happy discoveries accidently). The British called this island Ceylon and started world famous tea plantations here.

One of the highlights of our visit will be a leisurely five-day trek across Sri Lanka's green terraced hillsides. Our walk takes place in the interior: delightfully cool and lush terrain at 6,000 to 7,000 feet. This is tea country; we'll walk among many beautiful plantations where close-cropped tea bushes are harvested by Tamil women carrying wicker baskets. We also walk up and into untouched mountainous jungle (with great birdwatching possibilities). Local porters will carry our goods; a cook and assistant round out the camp staff. After the trek, we visit Nuwara Eliya, a colorful town set amid tea plantations and reminiscent of the British era in Sri Lanka.

Driving to the southeast coast, we spend three days in one of Sri Lanka's finest wildlife reserves, 420-square-mile Yala National Park. By night we stay in rustic bungalows and by day we travel by landrover with a local tracker-guide, exploring a protected wilderness park which is teeming with elephant, sambar, buffalo, wild boar and a huge variety of birdlife, all in a unique seaside setting (we might even see herds of wild elephants roaming the deserted beach!).

The last portion of our trip takes us to the remote Maldive Islands, a snorkeler's paradise where the coral reef wildlife is on a par with the Great Barrier Reef. There are 1800 islands in the Maldives, only 200 of which are inhabited. We'll spend four days exploring by *dhonie,* local sailing crafts which accommodate six people and a crew of three plus cook. We camp at night in secluded lagoons and travel by day among remote islands, taking time to swim, enjoy fresh seafood and snorkel in the crystal clear waters of the Indian Ocean.

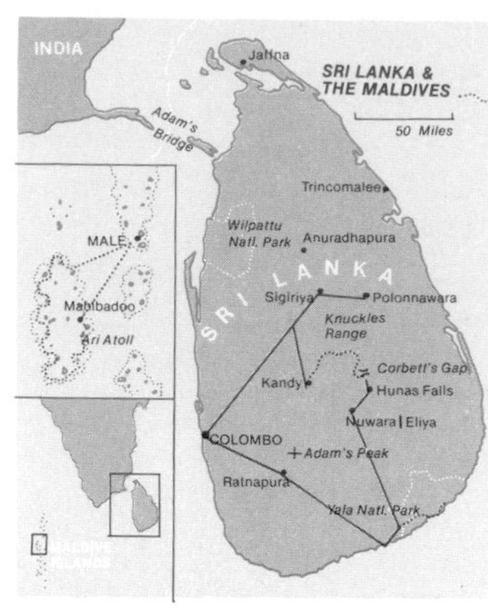

Itinerary: Day 1 to 3: Leave U.S. Arrive Colombo, Sri Lanka. Transfer to hotel.

Day 4: Visit Polonnaruwa, 11th century capital of Sri Lanka.

Day 5: Drive to Kandy, visiting Sigiriya, 5th century fortress of the reclusive kings of Sri Lanka.

Day 6 to 9: Drive to Bambarella and make five-day trek, walking through forest and cardamom plantations.

Day 10: Trek to a tea plantation and drive to Nuwara Eliya. An evening to sip brandy and play billiards in the game room of the private Hill Club.

Day 11: Drive to Yala National Park and check into park bungalow.

Day 12 and 13: Game drives in open landrovers with a tracker-guide.

Day 14: Drive to Colombo.

Day 15: Fly to Maldive Islands. Check into Ihuru Island Resort

Day 16 to 18: Board dhonies *and sail to Ari Atoll.*

Day 19: Sail back to Male and check into resort.

Day 20: Fly to Colombo. Late evening departure on homeward-bound flights.

Day 21 Arrive home.

Dates: Nov 1–Nov 21 (21 days)
Leader: to be announced
Grade: B-1
Land Cost: $1690
(12–15 members)
$1840 (8–11)
+ $130 Maldives flight
Single Supplement: $265
IT5TG1MT07

Fresco at Sigiriya/*Ken Scott*

Elephant "school" *Ken Scott*

Our walk takes place in the interior, delightfully cool and lush terrain at 6,000 to 7,000 feet. This is tea country; we'll walk among many beautiful plantations where close-cropped tea bushes are harvested by Tamil women carrying wicker baskets/*Ken Scott*

Thai Elephant Safari

Exploring northern Thailand

North Thailand was, until the early part of this century, accessible from Bangkok only by a complex river journey or by several weeks of hard travel by elephant. Not until the 1920's did a railway come to this isolated region, so not surprisingly, "the north" has a distinct flavor all its own.

Flying from Bangkok to Chiang Mai and onward to Mae Hong Son in the *very* north near the Burmese border, we spend three days on an elephant safari through beautiful forests and peaceful valleys dotted with villages.

We walk part of the way and ride part of the way, staying in simple village houses and enjoying "mountainous jungle" scenery that is the most breathtaking in all Thailand. Thailand's highest mountain, heavily-forested Doi Inthanon (8,517′) is in this region.

Of particular fascination will be our encounters with the Tibeto-Burmese hill tribes who add so much interest to this area, the nomadic Karen, the Shan, and Lawa to name a few, with their almost-medieval traditional embroidered costumes (sometimes including turbans) and heaps of silver bangles and jewelry which are still their every-day dress.

Beforehand, we tour the city of Chiang Mai, "Flower Of The North," with its amazing array of hill tribe handicrafts, impressive mountain scenery and historic temples.

Our trip ends with a two-day river trip by small thatch-roof bamboo rafts and a relaxing visit to the tropical splendor of Koh Samui, an off-the-beaten-path island in the gulf with some untouched beaches and the best coconuts in Thailand!

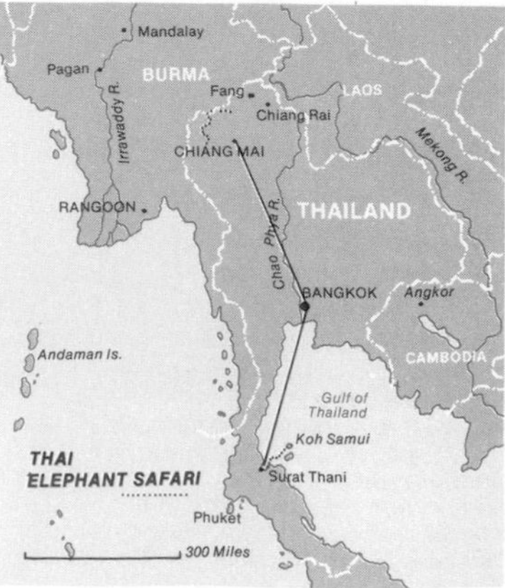

Itinerary: Day 1 and 2: Leave U.S. Arrive Bangkok.
Day 3: Tour Bangkok. Overnight train to Chiang Mai.
Day 4: Tour Chiang Mai.
Day 5: Fly to Mae Hong Son. Overnight in a Karen hill tribe village.
Day 6 to 8: Elephant safari through the mountainous jungle. Accommodations in hill tribe villages.
Day 9 and 10: By thatch-roof bamboo rafts down the Nam Haw River. Stops enroute for swimming and fishing. Overnight at hill tribe villages.
Day 11: Drive to Chiang Mai.
Day 12: Fly to Bangkok. Sleeper train to Surat Thani on the gulf.
Day 13: Arrive and ferry to island of Ko Samui. Overnight at small hotel.
Day 14: At leisure.
Day 15: By boat and plane to Bangkok.
Day 16: Depart on homeward-bound flights.

Dates: Dec 19, 1986–
Jan 3, 1987 (16 days)
Leader: Bruce Klepinger
Grade: B-2
Land Cost: $1590
(10–15 members)
$1890 (6–9)
Single Supplement: $60
IT5TG1MT04

North Alps Of Japan

9-day mountain walk

Japan is one of the most mountainous countries on earth, with more than 80% of its total terrain too steep for habitation. This trip features a nine-day walk across Japan's most beautiful and precipitous mountain range, the North Alps.

This trip is for people who want to experience Japan exactly as the Japanese do. In the places we go, there is almost no English spoken or written. There are no Western-style accommodations, no Western-style food (and virtually no Westerners!)

Although less than 10,500 feet high, the North Alps rise over a vertical mile above their immediate bases. Their cliff-hung sides are draped with dense forests which at the time of our visit will be covered with wild splashes of red and yellow autumn coloring.

In general, the trails are steep, rocky, narrow and exposed. Japanese literature lists these walks as "climbing" but all of it can be done on what we call a trail in the U.S. Hiking time will be about 6 or 7 hours a day. We prefer to have strong, experienced hikers but we have taken brave novices.

In addition to our time in the mountains, we will have two days in the famous mountain town of Takayama and three full days to enjoy the gardens, palaces and gourmet dining of Kyoto.

We can arrange an optional climb of Mt. Fuji before or after the trip

Japanese literature lists these walks as "climbing" but all of it can be done on what we call a trail in the U.S. Hiking time will be about 7 or 8 hours a day/ Rick McGowan

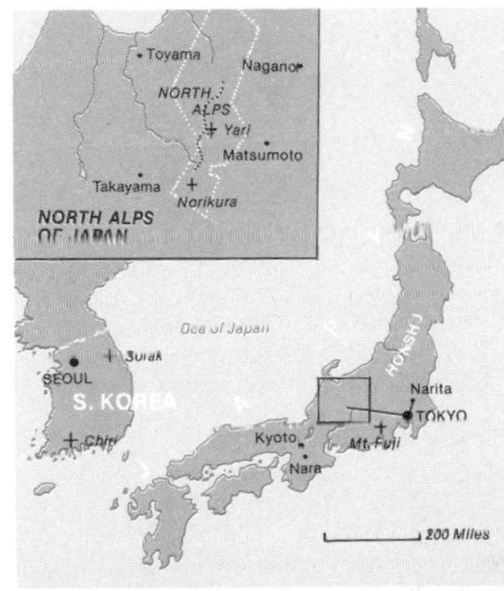

Itinerary: Day 1 and 2: Leave U.S. Arrive Tokyo. Transfer to hotel.
Day 3 and 4: Sightseeing or optional two-day climb of Mt. Fuji.
Day 5: By train through the mountains to Ariake. By taxi to trailhead at Nakabusa Onsen (Nakabusa Hot Springs).
Day 6 to 13: Walking hut to hut in the Japanese Alps.
Day 14: End trek at Nakao Onsen (Nakao Hot Springs). Overnight at inn in Nakao.
Day 15: Bus to Takayama, a spectacular ride through the mountains. Overnight at inn.
Day 16: Another day to enjoy Takayama. Evening train to Kyoto.
Day 17 to 19: In Kyoto for sightseeing and shopping.
Day 20: By "bullet" train to Tokyo. Overnight at hotel.
Day 21: Depart Tokyo and connect with homeward-bound flights.

Dates: Sep 13–Oct 3 (21 days)
Leader: Smoke Blanchard
Grade: B-3
Land Cost: $2175
(12–15 members)
$2350 (8–11)
Single Supplement: $150
IT6PA1SFMT13

Karen woman/Ken Scott

Lasu women. In Northern Thailand there will be fascinating encounters with the Tibeto-Burmese hill tribes, the nomadic Karen, the Shan and Lawa to name a few, with their traditional embroidered costumes and heaps of silver bangles and jewelry which are still their everyday dress/Ken Scott

Saffron-robed monks of Bangkok. Burma, Thailand and Sri Lanka practice Hinayana Buddhism, a branch that stresses the original monastic discipline and the attainment of nirvana by the individual through meditation/Ken Scott

Journey To The Marquesas

14-day cruise on the Aranui

Few places have such universal appeal as do the remote Marquesas Islands, "mystic isles of the South Seas" celebrated by Gauguin, Conrad and Melville. Just the name "Marquesas" evokes visions of handsome people, sparkling coral beaches, gentle island music and steep green mountains lying in tranquillity beneath the Southern Cross. This vision is still a reality on the isolated Marquesas, which are relatively untraveled by visitors to the South Pacific.

We journey to the Marquesas on a two-week cruise on the *Aranui,* a handsome 264-foot German-built passenger/cargo ship. Although this is primarily a cargo ship, passenger comfort, air conditioned cabins and a good restaurant are priorities on board.

The ship holds 20 passengers in cabins and 20 more on open deck space (this space is usually all Polynesian villagers).

As a cargo ship carrying essential goods for the local residents, the *Aranui* is a life line to the islands and its arrival in ports of call is frequently a cause for celebration. Passage on the *Aranui* offers the adventurous traveler a unique experience: contact with everyday life on remote Polynesian islands.

The ship visits almost the entire archipelago, from Nuku Hiva to Fatu Hiva, sailing from island to island or bay to bay each night. During the daytime, passengers go ashore with the ship's English-speaking escort and enjoy hill walks, visits to villages, strolls along white sand beaches, shopping, and perhaps lunch in a local restaurant.

The Marquesas are renowned for the spectacular landscape, and we see the valleys and villages which inspired Robert Louis Stevenson, discover the sites of ancient stone *tikis* in the valleys of Paumau where Gauguin's descendents still live, and visit Taipivai, made famous by Herman Melville.

Note: Early booking is strongly advised due to very limited cabin space.

Itinerary: Day 1 and 2: Leave U.S. Arrive Papeete, Tahiti. Board the Aranui, *departing at noon.*

Day 3: To Rangiroa.

Day 4: To Takapoto.

Day 5: At sea.

Day 6: To Ua Poa.

Day 7 to 9: At Nuku Hiva.

Day 10: To Ua Huka.

Day 11 and 12: At Hiva Oa.

Day 13: To Fatu Hiva.

Day 14 to 16: At sea.

During the daytime, passengers go ashore with the ship's English-speaking escort and enjoy hill walks, visits to villages, strolls along white sand beaches, shopping and perhaps lunch in a local restaurant/*Rodolphe Buntz*

Day 17: Evening arrival in Papeete. Overnight at hotel.

Day 18: In Papeete.

Day 19: Depart Papeete on homeward-bound flights.

Dates: #1 Apr 7–Apr 25 (19 days)
#2 Dec 12–Dec 30
Leader: Local escort
Grade: A-1
Land Cost: $990 to $2280 depending on type of cabin
Single Supplement: available on request

IT5TE10V0502

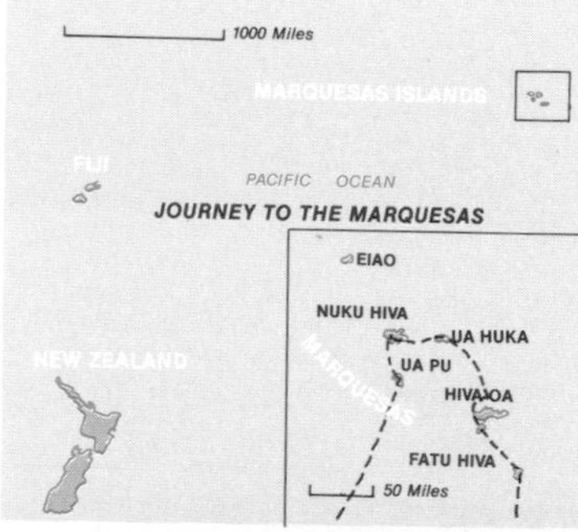

Papua New Guinea Patrol

Entering Stone Age villages

A trip to Papua New Guinea is "an adventure among peoples," a chance to stand in a *haus tambaran* (spirit house), to watch a *singsing,* to visit highland country so rugged and remote that first contact with "white man" wasn't made until the 1930's.

Despite the fact that some roads, airstrips and missions have been built in the New Guinea highlands, the basic structure of one of the oldest tribal societies in the world—just 40 years from the Stone Age—remains untouched.

We spend our first week here on a camping and hiking adventure, taking us for four days across the surrealistic landscape of mist-shrouded alpine grasslands surrounding Mt. Giluwe (14,483′), an extinct volcano, and for two more days through heaths and mires to the summit of Mt. Wilhelm (14,895′), New Guinea's highest peak, with its unusual mountain flora.

Our last week is spent in the Sepik Basin, cultural center of Papua New Guinea, where spectacular traditional spirit houses and exquisite carvings (including canoe shield masks, decorated hand drums and woven masks) are still made exactly as they have been for hundreds of years. Primitive art from the Sepik Basin is recognized as among the best in the world.

Here we spend time at Karawari Lodge, a remote inn accessible by light aircraft, with time to visit villages and witness enactments of tribal skin-cutting initiations and truly impressive ceremonies performed by feathered and painted warriors. We'll also find dazzling flora and fauna around the lodge including the famous Sepik Blue Orchid and Bird of Paradise.

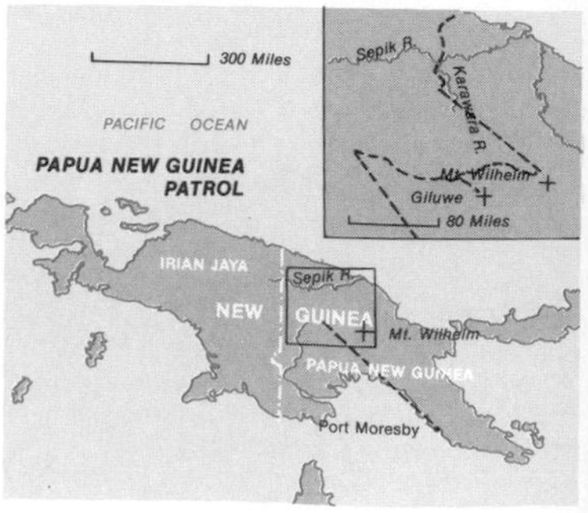

We spend our first week on a camping and hiking adventure, hiking for two days through heaths and mires to the summit of Mt. Wilhelm (14,895′) seen here, New Guinea's highest peak/ *Bob Bates*

Primitive art from the Sepik Basin is recognized as among the most intriguing in the world/Bob Bates

Moving to houseboats on the Sepik River, we explore its reaches by "river truck," small motorized rafts which enable us to reach nearby villages. The Sepik (called "Amazon of the Pacific") forms a natural highway into the remote interior of Papua New Guinea, where there are no roads and villages are only accessible by river.

Itinerary: Day 1 and 2: Leave Honolulu.

Day 3: Arrive Port Moresby, Papua New Guinea.

Day 4: Fly to Ambua Lodge at Tari.

Day 5: Day tour.

Day 6 to 9: Four-day Mt. Giluwe trek, camping at altitudes of about 10,000 feet.

Day 10: Drive to roadhead at Mt. Wilhelm and hike to Lake Piunde.

Day 11: Hike to summit of Mt. Wilhelm and return.

Day 12: Drive to town of Mt. Hagen.

Day 13: Fly to Karawari Lodge.

Day 14: At Karawari Lodge.

Day 15: Travel by river truck towards the Sepik. Overnight on houseboat.

Day 16: Visit villagers of the Iatmul tribe. Overnight on houseboat.

Day 17: By river truck and bus across the Sepik Plains to Wewak. Overnight in hotel.

Day 18: Fly to Port Moresby.

Day 19 and 20: In Port Moresby.

Day 21: Depart Port Moresby for Cairns, Australia. Overnight.

Day 22: Depart Cairns and connect with homeward-bound flights.

Dates: #1 Dec 14, 1985–Jan 4, 1986 (22 days)
#2 Mar 26–Apr 16
#3 Dec 17, 1986–Jan 7, 1987
1987: Mar 25–Apr 15
Leader: Robert E. Bates
Grade: B-2
Land Cost: $2490 (8–15 members) + $285 domestic flights
Single Supplement: $160
IT5QF1MT1

We explore the Sepik River by "river truck," small motorized rafts which enable us to reach remote villages/Dick McGowan

Feathered and painted dancer/warriors of the Sepik Basin/Dick McGowan

Tramping In New Zealand

Routeburn Walk, Milford Track, Mt. Cook National Park

New Zealand's Southern Alps offer a variety of opportunities for the trekking enthusiast. This trip has magnificent hiking in lush rainforest terrain, the challenge of glacier travel, and optional guided snow climbs at moderate altitudes.

We begin on the world-famous Milford Track in Fjordland National Park, trekking for three days through rainforest vegetation in steep valleys with 5,000-foot walls and wonderful birdlife. Our accommodations here (as on the rest of the trip) are in well-stocked and convenient wilderness huts.

After a visit to the serene mountain-ringed fjord at Milford Sound, we move to Mt. Aspiring National Park for three days on the Routeburn Walk, little known outside New Zealand and Australia, but an extremely beautiful hike along 25 miles of high trails with views down into luxuriant beech forests and out over four or five different mountain ranges.

Our Milford and Routeburn walks will be appropriate warm-up for our activities in Mt. Cook National Park. We fly by ski-plane to the head of the Tasman Glacier, where there is a small and spectacularly situated lodge for climbers and trekkers.

Based in the lodge, we spend two days making non-technical guided climbs on the surrounding snow and ice peaks (choosing peaks according to the degree of difficulty desired). Those who don't want to climb can sunbathe and enjoy the alpine setting.

The culmination of our mountain experience is a spectacular trek of about 15 miles (taking two days) along the snow-and-ice-covered Tasman Glacier with views all along the way of the icefalls and summits of New Zealand's highest peaks.

Itinerary: Day 1 to 3: Leave U.S. Arrive Auckland and continue by air to Christchurch. Overnight at hotel.

Day 4: Fly to Te Anau. Transfer to hotel.

Day 5: Afternoon ride by motor launch to the head of Lake Te Anau. Begin hike on the Milford Track.

Day 6 to 8: Hiking via Pompolona Hut and Quintin Hut, over MacKinnon Pass to Milford Sound. Overnight at hotel.

Day 9: Launch cruise on Milford Sound. Afternoon flight around the coast to Martins Bay.

Day 10: Jet-boating, local bush walks, or beachcombing.

Day 11: Short flight up the valley and drive to start the Routeburn Walk.

Day 12: Hike across Harris Saddle to Routeburn Falls Hut.

Day 13: Free day at Routeburn Falls.

Day 14: Hike out to the trailhead and drive to Queenstown.

Day 15: Drive to Mt. Cook National Park. Overnight in chalets.

Day 16 to 19: Optional non-technical snow climbs and 15-mile trek down the Tasman Glacier.

Day 20: Morning tour of a high country sheep station, then fly to Christchurch. Overnight at hotel.

Day 21: Depart Christchurch and connect with homeward-bound flights.

Dates: Nov 20–Dec 10 (21 days)
Leader: Mike Perry
Grade: B-2
Land Cost: $1990 (9–12 members) $2290 (5–8)
Single Supplement: available on request
IT5TE10VO501

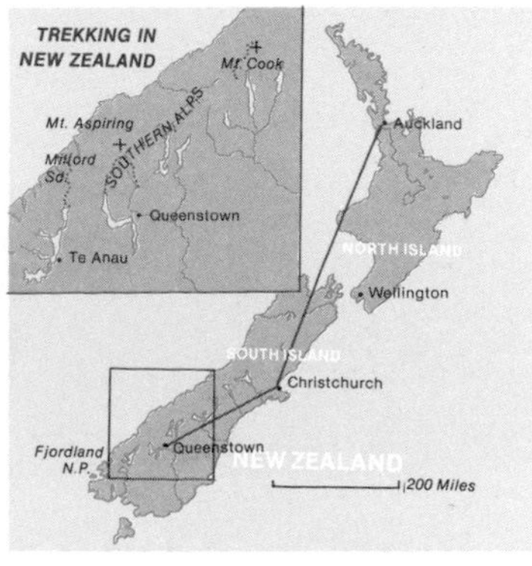

Based in the lodge on Tasman Glacier, we spend two days making non-technical climbs on the surrounding snow and ice peaks/Dick McGowan

Australia & Tasmania: Adventure Down Under

Hiking, camping, canoeing and reef-walking

We begin our trip by exploring the Great Barrier Reef, 1,200 miles of coral wonderland stretching along Australia's eastern seaboard. We cruise the reef for three days by small yacht with a glass-bottom tender for coral viewing. There will be ample time for reef walking, sunbathing and enjoying "catch-of-the day" meals on board.

Next, we travel to Kosciusko National Park, one of the world's largest national parks. Within its boundaries are the highest mountains and most extensive snowfields in Australia.

Our time in the park will be spent on a leisurely three-day trek in the Snowy Mountains, hiking the 5,000 to 7,000-foot terrain around Mt. Kosciusko (7,316′) Australia's highest peak. We'll carry only light day packs and sleep in park lodges at night.

Driving to Tumut, we paddle the Tumut River for three days in two-person canoes, with our guides teaching us all we need to know to become efficient on a river holiday. At night, we camp by the river banks, which are lined with stately gum and willow trees.

Our last adventure is a four-day camping sojourn in Lake St. Clair National Park, Tasmania, with an optional hike up Mt. Ossa (5,305′), Tasmania's highest peak. The Tasmanian wilderness presents an exotic environment of deep rain forest, thundering waterfalls and high alpine lakes. Wildlife here is mainly nocturnal, including such unique "down under" creatures as wombat, wallaby and Tasmanian devil.

We paddle the Tumut River for three days in two-person canoes, with our guides teaching us all we need to know to become efficient on a river holiday/Warwick Deacock

Itinerary: Day 1 and 2: Leave U.S. Arrive Cairns.

Day 3 and 4: Board the M. V. Boomerang. *Three-day cruise on the Great Barrier Reef.*

Day 5: End cruise and fly to Sydney.

Day 6: In Sydney.

Day 7: Drive and fly to Kosciusko National Park Headquarters and continue to lodge at Guthega.

Day 8 to 11: On trek in the Snowy Mountains. Nights in lodges.

Day 12: Drive to Tumut for canoe trip.

Day 13 and 14: Canoeing on the Tumut.

Day 15: Afternoon drive to Melbourne.

Day 16: Fly to Devonport, Tasmania. Begin Mt. Ossa trek.

Day 17 to 19: On trek.

Day 20: End trek and return to Davenport.

Day 21: Fly to Melbourne.

Day 22: Depart Melbourne on homeward-bound flights.

Dates: #1 Feb 5–Feb 26 (22 days)
#2 Dec 10–Dec 31
1987: Feb 4–Feb 25
Leader: #1 Warwick Deacock
#2 Laurie Jeays
Grade: B-2
Land Cost: $2450 (10–14 members)
$2680 (6–9
Single Supplement: $260
IT5QF1MT3
**Cost of flights within Australia not included.*

A camel trek in the Flinders is a leisurely experience—riding saddles are available every day. The weather is warm and sunny with cold, crisp nights. We sleep in "swags" at night (bed rolls on stretchers or mattresses)/
Warwick Deacock

Great Barrier Reef/Warwick Deacock

Australia: The Outback Experience

7-day camel trek, 3-day cruise on the Great Barrier Reef

On a seven-day camel trek in the Flinders Range, we'll discover Australia's most colorful and spectacular outback mountains.

The Flinders Range has been described as "an exhilarating experience in form and color," with its peaks and ridges rising like brick-red battlements. Huge "gum creeks" (dry water courses of sand or rocks in which enormous "river-red" gum trees grow) wind their way through the rugged mountains of the Flinders Range and provide pleasant natural "roads" through the area.

Scattered along the gum creeks are water holes and springs which maintain a large variety of wildlife, varying from feral donkeys and goats to giant red or western grey kangaroos, euros (a hill kangaroo) and the delightful but rare yellow-footed rock wallaby. We might also see emus (Australia's flightless birds), wedge-tailed eagles, enormous flocks of carellas (a white cockatoo) and gallahs (rose and grey cockatoo).

A camel trek in the Flinders is a leisurely experience—riding saddles are available every day. The weather is warm and sunny with cold, crisp nights. We sleep in "swags" at night (bed rolls on stretchers or mattresses). Tents are not used, and we'll appreciate the serenity of camping in the open. We spend the last night in shearers' quarters in a sheep station.

We also visit Ayer's Rock, the 1140-foot high fortress-like monolith which is Australia's most famous natural feature, and the historic town of Alice Springs, set in the gnarled grandeur of the MacDonnell Ranges.

Before our outback experience, we enjoy the pleasures of a three-day cruise on a glass-bottom boat on the Great Barrier Reef, with plenty of time for coral viewing, reef walking and snorkeling.

Itinerary: Day 1 to 3: Leave U.S. Arrive Cairns.
Day 4: Board the M.V. Boomerang *and begin a three-day cruise on the Great Barrier Reef.*
Day 5: On cruise.
Day 6: End cruise and transfer to hotel in Cairns.
Day 7: Fly to Adelaide.
Day 8: Drive to Flinders Ranges. Camp.
Day 9 to 14: Camel trek in the Flinders Ranges.
Day 15: End camel trek at sheep shearers station and drive to Adelaide.
Day 16: Fly to Alice Springs.
Day 17: Tour Ayers Rock
Day 18: Fly to Alice Springs.
Day 19: Fly to Sydney.
Day 20: Evening departure on homeward-ward bound flights.

Dates: #1 Jun 4–Jun 23 (20 days)
#2 Sep 3–Sep 22
Leader: #1 Warwick Deacock
#2 Laurie Jeays
Grade: B-2
Land Cost: $1990 (10–14 members)
$2390 (6–9)
Single Supplement: $270
IT5QF1MT2
**Flights within Australia not included in Land Cost.*

Australia and New Guinea trips include: twin accommodations in hotels, camp meals (meals in cities and towns on your own), leadership, entrance fees, permits, airport transfers, baggage porterage, ground transport, sightseeing as noted in itinerary, camping arrangements (if applicable) including camp meals, group commissary gear and camping equipment. Domestic flights within Australia or New Guinea not included.

King Billy pines, Tasmania/ W. Deacock

Sam, the lead camel/Warwick Deacock

'Bush tucker,' food that sustains Aborigines on their walkabouts/ Carla Dole

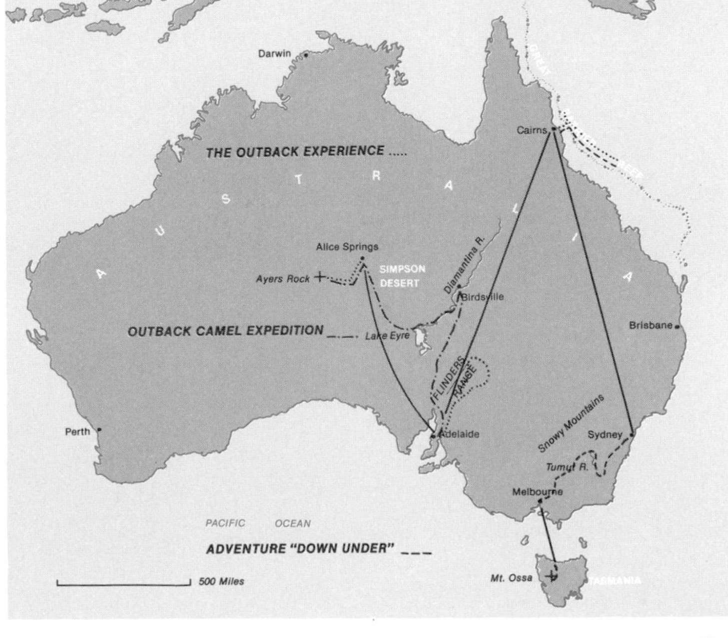

Outback Camel Expedition

22-day crossing of the Simpson Desert

Australia's Simpson Desert—indeed any desert—is an environment where nature's extremes, such as heat and cold, aridity and floods, come together in harmony, and any time spent by man in attempting to understand this duality is a rare privilege.

A 22-day crossing of the Simpson Desert is a challenging participatory adventure on which each trip member will assist in expedition tasks (cooking, wood gathering, loading gear on the camels). Riding is not possible on the first week of the trip, because we use all the camels to carry food and water. Daily walking distance averages about 15 miles.

The route follows the Diamantina River downstream along a string of waterholes, shaded by picturesque "coolibah" gum trees. We also pass several huge cattle stations enroute. One of them, Clifton Hills, is the largest single pastoral lease in the world: 6,500 square miles in area. Eventually the stations are left behind as the river enters true desert, near the northern end of Lake Eyre. The expedition ends at the 3,000-square-mile Macumba Station.

Itinerary: Day 1 to 3: Leave U.S. Arrive Adelaide, Australia.
Day 4 to 6: Drive the rough 4-wheel-drive "service run" past the Flinders Ranges and up the historic Birdville Track.
Day 7 to 28: 22-day camel expedition across the Simpson Desert.
Day 29 and 30: Drive to Alice Springs.
Day 31: Tour Ayers Rock
Day 32: Return to Alice Springs.
Day 33: Fly to Melbourne.
Day 34: Depart on homeward-bound flights.

Dates: Jun 14–Jul 17 (34 days)
Leader: Ray Johnston & Rex Ellis
Grade: B-3
Land Cost: $2490 (10–14 members)
Single Supplement: $145
IT5QF1MT4

The wooded Tsavo bush country still renews itself from the moveable feast of its elephant inhabitants, and the African night, its sensuous serenity only deepened by the punctuations of the distant lion's roar, still beckons of the mystery of creation/*Allen Bechky*

SECTION III
AFRICA & THE SAHARA

"Then they began to climb and they were going to the East it seemed, and then it darkened and they were in a storm, and rain so thick it seemed like flying through a waterfall, and then they were out and Compie turned his head and grinned and pointed and there, ahead, all he could see, as wide as all the world, great, high, and unbelievably white in the sun, was the square top of Kilimanjaro. And then he knew that there was where he was going."

Ernest Hemingway, excerpted from "The Snows of Kilimanjaro" in *The Short Stories of Ernest Hemingway.* Copyright 1938 Ernest Hemingway; copyright renewed © 1966 Mary Hemingway. Reprinted with the permission of Charles Scribner's Sons.

Kibo, the summit dome of Kilimanjaro/ *Allen Bechky*

Kilimanjaro, highest mountain in Africa, the symbol of African adventure. It is a huge mountain massif, rising in volcanic isolation from other ranges. Its feet rest on the timeless African plain, the domain of Africa's incomparable wildlife.

Here life pulses to an older rhythm than most of us know today. The march of seasons from wet to dry stimulates animal migrations on a Pleistocene scale. The columns of wildebeest and zebra still march in their hundreds of thousands over the endless, unpeopled Serengeti Plains. The wooded Tsavo bush country still renews itself from the moveable feast of its elephant inhabitants, and the African night, its sensuous serenity only deepened by the punctuations of the distant lion's roar, still beckons of the mystery of creation.

Kilimanjaro's flanks are another Africa. Volcanic soil and mountain rains have produced verdant African forests, which have since succumbed to the axe to make way for *homo sapiens.* The lower slopes of the mountain are covered by the *shambas* of the Chagga tribe. Each *shamba* is a luxuriant

Masai at Lake Natron/ *W. Berg*

tangle of corn, beans and vegetables which feed people where coffee trees are the cash crop. The Chagga, lively, friendly, holding on to traditions at the same time they are aggressively pursuing a materially better future, could symbolize the African people of today. They are vibrant, agriculturally-based people whose sheer numbers will shape the Africa of tomorrow. They know little of wildlife and have abandoned their old gods who inhabited the inhospital world of rock and ice at the mountain's head.

Of course Kilimanjaro and the gamelands which surround it are just one piece of a "continental pie," delicious with adventure. Taste again and you sample the

Sunset silhouettes a baobab tree/ *Allen Bechky*

romance of a camel safari through the immense Sahara, riding with Touaregs, blue men of the desert. Or taste the world of the Okavango, a sea of grass where a mighty river drowns in Kalahari sands, giving life to a uniquely African community of hippos and hoopoes, crocs and jumbos, lechwe and lion, all dwelling in a great wetland wilderness.

There are many tastes to the African pie, and many different ways to take the bite.

Most visitors to Africa take a "holiday safari." Mini-vans whisk them into the bush for morning and evening game drives, and much time is spent in luxurious lodges which are really resort hotels. The buffet tables groan, the atmosphere is relaxing, and the animals are a sure-fire hit.

The only thing that is missing is contact with Africa.

A *camping safari,* on the other hand, offers close contact with the African bush, which is the core of African experience. The distractions and tourists at the lodge pale in contrast with the comraderie of a private camp. Camping safaris are the supreme adventure travel experience for wildlife enthusiasts.

Adventure Travel In Africa

Elephants at Samburu. Quality camping safaris are hard to find but worth it just for their depth of leadership/ *Iain Allan*

Serengeti, Tanzania. Here life pulses to a different rhythm than most of us know today. The march of seasons from wet to dry stimulates animal migrations on a Pleistocene scale/ *Allen Bechky*

Kenya:

Game viewing in the national parks are easily arranged by many tour operators. Car rentals are available and camping on your own in the parks is allowed. Quality camping safaris are hard to find but worth it just for their depth of leadership.

Mt. Kenya is the setting for trekking trips across high moorlands up to Point Lenana at 16,355 feet, highest point accessible to walkers. Technical rock climbers ascend Nelion and Batian, the two summits of Mt. Kenya.

Kenya's coast is highly developed for tourism, but good snorkeling and dhow adventures can be found.

Kenya's best seasons are Christmas to mid-March and June to mid-October. April and May are the "long rains," October and November are the "short rains."

Tanzania:

Short game viewing trips can be arranged locally as few local agents do camping trips which get off the well-worn tracks. Kilimanjaro is the ultimate trek in Africa, culminating in a hike to Uhuru Peak (19,340′), roof of the continent. The southern parks of the Selous Game Reserve, Ruaha and Mikuni National Parks are excellent and highly recommended but difficult to get to.

Tanzania's best seasons for visiting are the same as Kenya's (above).

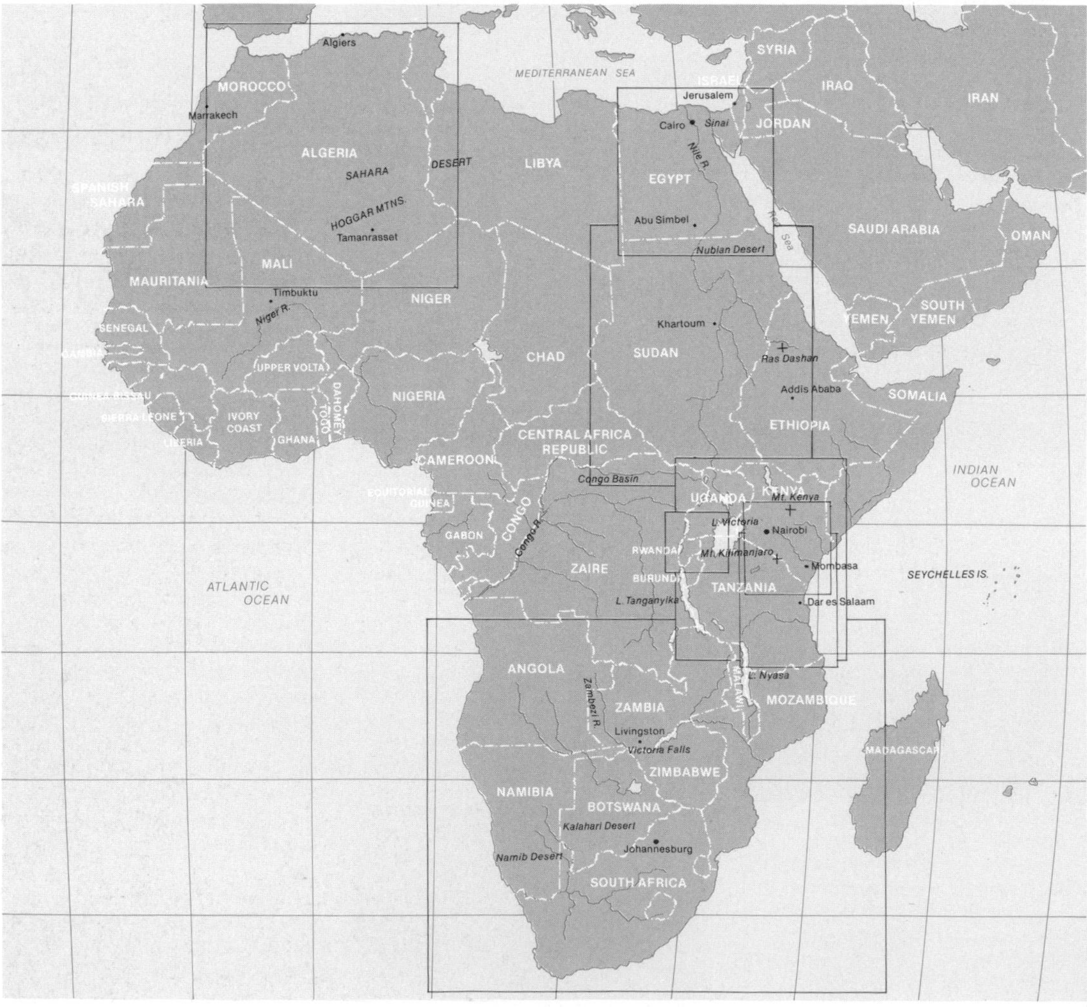

Porters on Kilimanjaro (Mawenzi in background)/*Allen Bechky*

Rwanda:

Gorilla tracking! The number of permits issued is strictly limited to 12 a day. They are extremely difficult to get. Unless you are prepared to camp at Parc des Volcans for days or weeks waiting for a cancellation to come up, better book with a group before you leave home. Many a traveler, on arrival in Rwanda, has had their inquiries answered with: "Gorilla permits—don't leave home without them!" Rwanda is best from December to March and June to October.

Zaire:

A difficult country to travel in on your own *or* with a group. There are hassles with language, officials, transportation and the economy. The long journey down the Congo on a riverboat crowded with natives is a great adventure but it takes time and endurance. The east has much to offer: the Virunga Volcanoes (and the wealth of their wildlife) and the Ruwenzoris, "Mountains of the Moon," the pygmies of the Ituri forest and gorillas at Bukavu.

Kenya's tropical coast/*Allen Bechky*

The number of permits issued for gorilla tracking is strictly limited to 12 a day. They are extremely difficult to get/*Allen Bechky*

Botswana:

The marshes of the Okavango Delta offer fishing, game viewing, and paddling native dugout canoes in an unique Eden-like atmosphere. The neighboring Chobe National Park features "Big Game." The Kalahari Desert is basically accessible only to self-sufficient four-wheel-drive expeditions.

Zambia

The Luangwa Valley National Park allows foot safaris in a wooded riverine habitat well populated with game. A rafting trip on the Zambesi River at the foot of Victoria Falls is one of the ultimate one-day whitewater experiences!

Social weaver bird nest, Kalahari Desert/*Allen Bechky*

Zimbabwe:

Its national parks are excellent and include Hwange and the Mana Pools, where foot safaris are allowed. Canoe trips down the mightly Zambesi River are an excellent way to arrive at Mana Pools. The 14th century ruins of Great Zimbabwe are *the* archaelogical site of Black Africa. Zimbabwe's long dry season is May through the end of October, when all the parks and attractions can be visited.

South Africa:

A very developed, Westernized pace where most of the country has been tamed, but which has a good park system which preserves much wild beauty. There is a major trail system for hiking the wild coast of Transkei, the mountains of the Natal Drakensburg, the bushlands of the eastern Transvaal and the Karoo deserts of the western Cape.

Lunch spot along the Zambesi River/*Dick McGowan*

Zulu villagers/*Dick McGowan*

The nomadic Masai of Tanzania fatten up their big herds of cattle and goats by following seasonal rainfalls, drifting from the Rift Valley to the dry weather ranges in the Crater highlands/*Allen Bechky*

Temple of Ramses at Abu Simbel, Egypt/*Allen Bechky*

Egypt:

After 5,000 years of history, Egypt is still an adventure. Fascinating and chaotic, it boasts the most amazing archaeological wonders in the world: the Great Pyramids, Abu Simbel, the temples and tombs of Luxor. Spice up your visit by seeing "the other Egypt" on a *felucca* sail down the Nile or a camel trek with Bedouins on the path of Moses through the Sinai. In Egypt, October through April is the best season (the Sinai is good throughout the year).

Morocco:

Morocco has such a vibrant cultural scene that virtually any visit is an adventure. Try trekking the High Atlas Mountains with donkeys for pack animals, visiting the *souks* and bazaars of Marrakech and Fez, and, yes, experiencing the seedy romance of Casablanca.

Algeria:

The adventure here is getting into the heart of the Sahara. This is most romantically accomplished by riding a camel with blue-robed Touareg nomad guides in the desert fasts of the Hoggar Mountains from Tamanrasset, the key oasis in southern Algeria. The variety of desert landscapes is astounding, ranging from great "oceans" of sand dunes called *erg,* to acacia-thorn-covered *wadis* and boulder-strewn desert plateaus called *tassilis,* replete with neolithic paintings and carvings. Generally, the best season is from October to March, when it is dry and comparatively cool. The summer months are to be avoided because of the heat, especially at lower elevations.

Touareg guide preparing tea. Adventure in the heart of the Sahara is most romantically accomplished by riding a camel through the desert fasts of the Hoggar Mountains/*Alla Schmitz*

Africa Bibliography

GUIDE TO MT. KENYA & KILIMANJARO
Iain Allan, Mountain Club of Kenya, 1981. Complete guide for hikers and climbers.

WILDFLOWERS OF KENYA
Michael Blundell, Collins, 1982.

OUT OF AFRICA
Isak Dineson, Random House, 1937. Life on a farm in Kenya from 1914–1931.

KILIMANJARO
John Reader, Universe Books, 1982. Portrait of the mountain.

THE TREE WHERE MAN WAS BORN.
Peter Matthiessen, Dutton, 1983. Tanzania, Kenya and Masai.

SERENGETI SHALL NOT DIE
Bernard Grizimek, Dutton, 1959. Tanzania.

ONE LIFE
Richard Leakey, Michael Joseph, 1983. Autobiography.

THE SERENGETI LION
George Schaller, University of Chicago Press, 1972. Study of predator-prey relationships.

FIELD GUIDE TO THE BIRDS OF EAST AFRICA
John G. Williams, Collins, 1980.

FIELD GUIDE TO THE NATIONAL PARKS OF EAST AFRICA
John G. Williams and Norman Arlott, Collins, 1981.

FIELD GUIDE TO THE MAMMALS OF AFRICA, INCLUDING MADAGASCAR.
Theodor Haltenorth and Helmut Diller, Collins, 1980.

PORTRAITS IN THE WILD
Cynthia Moss, University of Chicago, 1982. Review of wild animal behavior.

AMONG THE ELEPHANTS
Iain and Oria Douglas-Hamilton, Viking, 1975. Tanzania.

THE WHITE NILE
Alan Moorehead, Vintage, 1983. History of exploration in Central Africa.

GORILLAS IN THE MISTS
Dian Fossey, Houghton Mifflin, 1983. Field study of gorillas in Zaire, Rwanda and Uganda.

YEAR OF THE GORILLA
George Schaller, Ballantine, 1964. Studies in East Central Africa.

MAASAI
Tepilit Ole Saitoti and Carol Beckwith, Harry Abrams, 1980. Definitive Masai book.

NEWMAN'S BIRDS OF SOUTHERN AFRICA
Kenneth Newman, Macmillan S.A., 1983.

OKAVANGO
Peter Johnson and Anthony Bannister (Creina Bond, text), C. Struik, 1977. Botswana.

THE LOST WORLD OF THE KALAHARI
Laurens Van der Post, William Morrow & Co., 1958. Journey into the African desert.

LORDS OF THE ATLAS
Gavin Maxwell, Dutton, 1966. Morocco, history.

MOUNTAINS IN THE DESERT
Louis Carl and Joseph Petit, Doubleday, 1954. Adventure in Central Sahara.

THE FEARFUL VOID
Geoffrey Moorhouse, J.P. Lippincott, 1974. Crossing of the Sahara.

SAHARA HANDBOOK
Simon and Jan Glen, Roger Lascelles, 1980.

THE TUAREG
Jeremy Keenan, Allen Lane, 1977. People of the Sahara.

VOICES FROM THE STONE AGE.
Douglas Mazonowicz, Crowell, 1974. Cave art of Tassili and around the world.

DESERT, MARSH & MOUNTAIN
Wilfrid Thesiger. Adventures in Africa and Asia.

WHERE MOUNTAINS ROAR
Lesley Hazelton, Holt, Rinehart & Winston, 1980. Sinai and Negev desert.

ANCIENT EGYPT
Lionel Casson, Time/Life Books, 1965.

SNOW ON THE EQUATOR
H.W. Tilman, Bell, 1937. Climbs on Mt. Kenya, Kilimanjaro and the Ruwenzori.

GREEN HILLS OF AFRICA
Ernest Hemingway, various editions. Fiction.

NORTH OF SOUTH
Shiva Naipaul, Simon & Schuster, 1978. A view of modern Africa.

"I was on my hands and knees, crawling through jungle, and five feet in front of me sat a two-hundred-and-fifty-pound female gorilla. She was contentedly eating a large white African mushroom...." */Allen Bechky*

Going Ape

by Michael Callahan

Maybe it was the altitude. Maybe I was hyperventilating. I remember difficulty in breathing and sweating profusely. I was about as excited as I've ever been.

I was on my hands and knees, crawling through jungle, and five feet in front of me sat a two-hundred-and-fifty-pound female gorilla. She was contentedly eating a large white African mushroom. As I looked down I could see droplets cascading from the tip of my nose, forming a small pool in the mud between my hands. I wasn't afraid, rather exhilarated to be in the midst of wild mountain gorillas. They were foraging in the bamboo jungle at the base of Mt. Sabinio, a volcano in the Virunga chain in Rwanda, Africa. Of course most wild animals would never allow man to get this close, but these are most unusual animals.

Gorillas travel in extended families ranging in size from a few individuals to a couple of dozen. Usually there is a dominant male, "The Old Man", or "silverback" (at sexual matuity, age nine or ten, the hair on the backs of males turns grey). He may have some male subordinates, advisors if you will, and is responsible for the females and juveniles. Occasionally groups consist solely of males, either immature or otherwise unfit for command. Because they are the largest primates, with adult males five to six feet tall and four to five hundred pounds, mythical legends about their ferocity were inevitable and abounded. Until George Schaller arrived.

He came in 1959. He spent two years and recorded his observations in his excellent book *The Year of the Gorilla*. He found gentle, loyal, and intelligent creatures (terribly miscast in "Planet of the Apes" as sour-faced enforcers, Pacifists would have been more appropriate. Indeed, when hunted for meat or trophies by natives, there were instances where, cornered and terrified, they refused to fight and sat down and accepted a cruel death by club and spear).

Schaller was like a distant cousin to the gorillas, reluctantly accepted, and welcomed for short visits only. It was different with Dian Fossey. They adopted her.

She came in 1967. Like Schaller she spent a great deal of time alone on their periphery. She learned that their vocabulary is limited. Not because of any biological or intellectual factors. No none knows why. Perhaps it's due to superior intelligence: the knowledge that a belch is a more satisfying statement than "Have a nice day", and a subtle look says more than "You question my authority?". She learned their social customs: staring is considered impolite.

She found postures are important: standing upright with one's chest out is considered aggressive, bent over is more acceptable. By mimicing these traits she was able to win complete acceptance from certain groups. Then she was able to study them from a unique perspective, as an actual family member. This was no frivolous task. It took fourteen years.

Obviously her purpose was to study mountain gorillas scientifically; not to make them a tourist attraction (the ultimate Disneyland exhibit, "Z tickets please"). Tourists are allowed with reluctant approval.

When he began his study, Schaller estimated the gorilla population of the Virunga volcano region at over 400. Today that figure has been halved. While there is less poaching now, the dense population of Rwanda continues to expand, relentlessly appropriating land and driving the animals higher and higher up the volcanoes. Conservationists and government officials hope that permitting tourism will bring some revenue into Rwanda and also provide some "P.R." for the *Gorilla gorilla beringei.* If some jobs are created for guides and porters around gorilla territory, the local people may feel it is in their best interest to ensure that the tourist attraction remains in existence.

Tourists must get a permit from the Rwanda National park Administration prior to visiting any of the three acclimated groups. Only small groups of five or six people are allowed to visit, and only for an hour or so each day. Fortunately for us Mountain Travel had made all arrangements.

Ten of us, mostly strangers, had signed up. Our group consisted of an older grey-haired lawyer, five somewhat younger males, four females, and no juveniles.

We had permits for two days to see groups 11 and 13. We would divide in half and alternate visits each day. That evening Allen Bechky, our Mountain Travel guide, briefed us.

"Tomorrow we will be doing steep hiking above 9000 feet. Be careful to avoid stinging nettles and thorns. They are everywhere. Watch out for safari ants. No, they do not travel about with tiny knapsacks. Yes, their bites are most painful. Bring raingear. It's normally wet and slippery and even worse when it rains." He looked around the room. "Although these are gentle, placid animals, we do have some Dont's—with capital D's.

"Don't touch the gorillas; they are susceptible to human diseases. Don't stare directly at individuals, particularly the silverback; this is considered aggressive. Don't stand erect; this is considered a confrontation and may cause retaliation."

"What kind of retaliation?" asked a quiet voice.

"The Silverback Charge. When aggravated one of these four-hundred-pound animals comes charging through the jungle directly at you. You won't see him. But you will hear him crashing the brush, roaring savagely, making a colossal racket. When he gets within ten yards or so, he stops and peers through the foliage. If you have run he chases you with wicked delight, running on feet and knuckles. When he catches you, as is likely, you may receive a nasty nip on your rear end. Then you will be permitted to leave, properly chastised."

"Long ago when the natives shared the land and lived more intimately with wild animals," Bechky went on, "such an encounter could be doubly painful. When a tribesman returned to his village with a buttock wound, he was likely to be teased and ridiculed. You see, these natives knew the truth: The Old Man is just a big bluffer. When he completes his fierce charge and peeks through his green curtain, he is really determining the effectiveness of a theatrical performance. If the object of his derision has not moved, he quickly turns and quietly leaves in the opposite direction. Those who run have shown cowardice. Which leads us to our final Don't: DON'T RUN! If a gorilla should charge you, hold your ground! But avert your eyes and crouch down."

Contemplation of this last command kept me awake most of the night.

The next morning we met our native guides and porters at the base of Mt. Sabinio. Group 13 has nine members: one silverback, five females, and three juveniles. Each morning a young American resident naturalist from the Karisoke Research Center locates them and spends the day studying them.

The gorillas' daily routine is one many of us might envy. They rise after the sun, between seven and eight, leisurely. Many take breakfast in bed, reaching for the vegetation just outside. After a decent interlude, say an hour or so, they begin their daily constitutional. Led by the Old Man (who never abrogates the responsibility of his position) they travel a half-mile to a mile before lunch. This foraging is informal with the family dispersed over approximately fifty yards. Everyone dawdles, stopping every few minutes to snack on roots, bamboo, bark, foliage, perhaps a mushroom or two. When the Old Man moves, the rest follow. He selects the noontime picnic site. After lunch, like sensible people, they nap.

In the afternoon they will travel another half-mile or so and then prepare nests by bending bushes, branches or bamboo, and covering the top with leaves. These look like large comfortable hammocks. After dinner, when dusk comes, they retire. Mothers and juveniles may sleep together. With the exception of an occasional foolish leopard tempted by a youngster, they have no natural enemies.

We found the gorillas by locating their last campsite and following their trail. Because of their peculiar squat, on short legs with the knuckles of their massive long arms touching the ground, at a distance gorillas

"Close up, a gorilla's face is remarkable. Instead of the fierce look you might imagine, there is a most poignant sadness. The corners of his mouth are turned down in what seems to be a pout. His sensitive brown eyes have a hurt look—on the verge of tears it seems. It is an effort not to reach out and offer consolation...."*/Allen Bechky*

Allen Bechky

tend to look like large brown balls. The American naturalist was with them when we arrived.

He was a large red-headed fellow with stern blue eyes. He quickly whispered instructions in French, Rwanda's official language. Unfortunately most of us couldn't understand a word but assumed it was the usual "Don't touch, stare, stand, or run." Oddly no one asked him to speak English. Then, crouched over, we set off after the gorilla family.

They were spread out, travelling slowly, and we caught up quickly. I was at the rear of our small column, not the best position for a close-up view. However I consoled myself with a pleasant thought: should the silverback charge, I would have a head start when we all turned and ran.

Suddenly gorillas were all around us. The red-head kept motioning with looks and gestures to keep low. Finally I found it easiest to crawl on my hands and knees.

Close up, a gorilla's face is remarkable. Instead of the fierce look you might imagine, there is a most poignant sadness. The corners of his mouth are turned down in what seems to be a pout. His sensitive brown eyes have a hurt look—on the verge of tears it seems. It is an effort not to reach out and offer consolation. With the exception of their pitiful expressions they exhibit a remarkable calmness.

They seem so different from their lowland cousins in the zoo. Those poor lifers tend toward obesity and generally look terribly bored (too much beer and TV, I guess).

The mountain gorillas accepted us quietly, without notice—except for the juveniles. These truants raced about, wrestling, climbing trees, jumping on each other, and running in circles around us. In general, roughhousing just like any three-year olds. Occasionally they tried to grab camera equipment. The youngest, one or two years old, rode on his mother's back, his arms wrapped tightly around her neck.

Allen Bechky

Every ten or fifteen minutes the silverback would get up and move on. Everyone followed. The red-head kept us behind him, occasionally casting sharp looks at individuals and motioning them down. I noticed he always positioned himself between us and the silverback, although the Old Man acted impervious.

The experience began to take on a surrealistic quality. Images seemed to focus brighter. We were giggling like school girls at nonsensical things: The red-head pointing and motioning violently, while I was on my hands and knees in the mud wondering how I could possibly get any lower, and almost being stepped on by a gorilla wandering by from the rear; pulling my camera away as one of the juveniles tried to grab it; the clouds opening and a sunlight blessing through bamboo shutters; being showered by twigs, leaves, and dust as a female climbed a tree next to me and giggling hysterically feeling faint from the altitude and euphoria.

When it was time to go some of us shook the red-haired's hand and thanked him. He smiled shyly, and seemed genuinely pleased. We never did get his name. I don't know why I felt so sad. Too soon we were on the farmland below.

Group 11 had stopped for lunch when we located them the next day. The dominant male and one juvenile were missing their right hands, and the other male's right hand was crippled and useless. They were victims of our common curiosity, having caught their hands in poachers' snares. The snares are wire loops made to catch small game for sale to local restaurants. The lucky ones lose a hand. The others get gangrene and die.

It's easy to condemn poachers and farmers for the loss of wildlife, but hunting is a way of life in Africa and these are hungry people.

Some people have said, "So what if gorillas and other wild animals are driven out? Man's needs are more important. If possible, we could still keep them in zoos. If not, would it really be that great a loss? After all, other animals, such as the dinosaur, have become extinct and the world doesn't seem to be any worse off."

Who knows? Would it really have been a great loss if there had never been a Michelangelo or Beethoven? Do we really understand the ecological repercussions of the loss of a species and its environment? Are not all species important? Don't they have a right to live here too? Besides . . . I like gorillas.

So like us. But with faces capable of diverse expression, why the haunting pathos? Perhaps with that innate knowledge some animals seem to possess, they have a prescience. Maybe they have seen their destiny.

Mr. Callahan was a member of our RWANDA GORILLA SAFARI.

Michael Callahan is a 6'1" male primate weighing approximately 180 lbs. While his primary habitat is the southwestern coast of the U.S. he has been known to wander as far as India, Turkey, Africa, and Alaska. He is a solitary male and belongs to no group.

His eating preference is green vegetation, with occasional meat, fowl, or fish but, when hungry, he will eat anything. He also exhibits curious strutting and sermonizing behavior most noticeable after consumption of foamy liquids. A clever ruse, knowledge of computers, enables him to secure these foodstuffs without foraging.

He enjoys social grooming with members of the species, and noon naps. His brown, generally matted, hair is in contrast to most middle-aged males, who tend to grey, and is possibly indicative of general immaturity.

Michael cares about all animals, even man.

Whether the journey's emphasis is wildlife, natural history or cultural exploration, our African trip leaders bring a special dimension to African travel with their extensive experience.

IAIN ALLAN, 36, has lived in East Africa most of his life. A journalist by profession and one of Kenya's leading mountaineers, he is author of the definitive *Guide to Mt. Kenya and Kilimanjaro.* He has pioneered new climbing routes on both mountains and is also an experienced safari leader.

ALLEN BECHKY, 38, is an expert naturalist and avid ornithologist who knows Africa from Capetown to Cairo. Manager of our African operations, he spends most of his year guiding in East Africa and scouting new trips. Allen speaks Swahili and has a decade of experience as a professional safari guide.

COLIN BELL, 31, was raised in the Southern Kalahari and Western Cape. A keen wildlife photographer, hiker and ornithologist, he has traveled extensively throughout southern and central Africa. He led his first Botswana safari in 1977.

JEAN-LOUIS & ODETTE BERNEZAT, ages 46 and 40, are professional Sahara adventurers who have spent more than 15 years exploring the expanses of this great desert, which they love with a passion. Odette is the author of two books on Touareg nomads.

DAVID BUITRON, 36, has traveled extensively all over the continent and has managed road-building camps in remote parts of Kenya and Sudan. He speaks Swahili and leads many of our trekking programs in East Africa.

Jean-Louis and Odette Bernezat

Allen Bechky

Jim Gardiner

JIM GARDINER, 35, was born in Zimbabwe and has spent his life in Africa as a farmer, soldier and professional safari guide. Now a Swahili-speaking resident of Kenya, he is at home in the bush and specializes in conducting our Kenya foot safaris.

MATTANYAH ZOHAR, 46, leader of our Egypt trips, has completed studies in archaeology and Assyriology at the Hebrew University, Jerusalem. Matti's expertise ranges over a variety of aspects of Middle Eastern culture, with a particular emphasis on the Turkish/Ottoman empire. He was born in Berlin, spent his youth in Istanbul and Asia, and in 1972, immigrated to Israel. He is fluent in English, Hebrew, German and Italian, and has a strong background in many languages including Turkish, Persian, Arabic and Hindustani.

David Buitron

Iain Allan

Mattanyah Zohar

Sahara Camel Safari

13-day trek with Touareg nomads

The Sahara, the largest desert in the world, is not an unending sea of sand, as fiction and film would have us believe. It has an infinite variety of landscapes: rock-ribbed plateaus, sandstone canyons, the volcanic Hoggar Mountains, beach-like golden washes filled with oleander, tamarisk and acacia-thorn trees, date palms and many wildflowers.

We journey for 13 days across the most mountainous region of the Sahara—the Hoggar Mountains. We travel by camel and on foot, enjoying the mystique of the Sahara and experiencing the way of life of our nomadic Touareg guides, the blue-robed "nobles of the desert."

Depending on personal preference, we can walk or ride part of each day. Enroute, we circle around the central Atakor pillar, a geological remnant dating from the pre-Cambrian era. We stop to examine many prehistoric rock paintings and view unclimbed domes, basalt gorges, awesome volcanic spires and erosion-carved river beds.

Each night, we sleep under a brilliant canopy of stars (there is no need for tents), perhaps gaining a better understanding of the mysterious power which the desert has always had over the human soul.

During the trip, several interesting non-technical climbs are possible enroute for those who are interested.

We also hike up to the famous hermitage of Father Charles de Foucauld, 10,000 feet high on the summit of the Assekrem Plateau.

This is our 12th successful year of offering this very unusual trip.

NOTE: no previous camel riding experience is required!

Itinerary: Day 1 and 2: Leave U.S. Fly Paris/Algiers, Algeria. Transfer to hotel.

Day 3: Fly to Tamanrasset. Overnight at hotel.

Day 4 to 8: Traverse the plain of Tam and along the base of the rocky hills of Aleheg, where there are neolithic engravings and graffiti in Tifinar (the written langauge of the Touaregs). Cross Aleheg Mountain towards the beautiful peak of Aguelzam.

Touareg saddle/*Alla Schmitz*

Day 9 to 11: Walk into the gorge of Terara, with its fine neolithic drawings of giraffes. Cross a narrow pass where an epic battle among the Touaregs took place around 1880. Reach the base of the Tezouiag (9,000'), among the most beautiful summits of Atakor.

Day 12 to 15: Cross Aril Pass and descend past the site of a battle between Touaregs and the French Foreign Legion, then descend the canyon called Oued Terhenanet.

Day 16: Arrive in Tamanrasset. Overnight at hotel.

Day 17: Fly to Algiers. Overnight in hotel.

Day 18: Fly Algiers/Paris and connect with homeward-bound flights.

Dates: Oct 30–Nov 16 (18 days)
Leader: Jean-Louis Bernezat
Grade: B-2
Land Cost: $2100
(8–15 members)
Single Supplement: not available
IT6PA1SFMT16

Sahara Camel Safari

8-day trek with Touareg nomads

This is an 8-day camel safari, a shorter version of the 13-day trek, visiting the exact same area as the longer trip (see *Sahara Camel Safari* 13-day trek for description of route).

Itinerary: Day 1 and 2: Leave U.S. Fly Paris/Algiers, Algeria. Transfer to hotel.

Day 3: Fly to Tamanrasset. Overnight at hotel.

Day 4 to 11: 8-day camel trek across the Hoggar Mountains.

Day 11: Arrive in Tamanrasset. Overnight at hotel.

Day 12: Morning flight to Algiers. Overnight in hotel.

Day 13: Fly Algiers/Paris and connect with homeward-bound flights.

Dates: #1 Jan 15–Jan 27
(13 days)
#2 Dec 7–Dec 19
Leader: Jean-Louis Bernezat
Grade: B-2
Land Cost: $1550
(8–15 members)
Single Supplement: not available
IT6PA1SFMT16

"Just passing through..."

ALGIERS

City notes by Leo Le Bon

Walking/jogging routes:
There are two interesting parks: the "Bois de Boulogne" and the Jardin D'Essai, both on the outskirts of town. Take a taxi to visit good beaches at Boroj El Kiffan, 10 miles from Algiers, and at Djemila, also about ten miles from town.

Day trips:
Tipasa, an important Roman ruin (a favorite haunt of Albert Camus), is perhaps the most interesting all-day excursion out of Algiers (about 70 km. west).

Special markets:
Hire a guide from your hotel and visit the famous Kasbah, built in the 16th century.

Museums:
Khedaouej El Amiia, a Turkish palace, houses masterpieces of Algerian handicrafts. Also visit the Bardo Museum of ethnography.

Restaurants:
Try El Bacour for Algerian specialities.

Alla Schmitz

Desert village/*Alla Schmitz*

Alla Schmitz

We travel for 13 days across a mountainous region of the Sahara—the Hoggar Mountains—by camel and on foot/*Alla Schmitz*

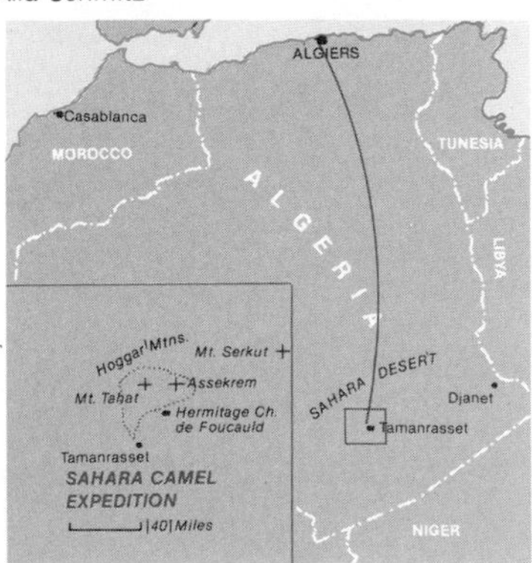

In an overwhelming landscape of stone forests, spires, dry river beds, cliffs and dunes, we'll follow our mysteriously veiled guides, Touaregs from the oasis of Ahorar, for only they know where to find the N'Immidir's painted caves, scant waterholes and passes/
Alla Schmitz

A Walk In The Sahara

Desert exploration in the Tassili N'Immidir

This is a true voyage of discovery, an 8-day walk in a virtually unexplored region of the Sahara, the world's largest and most magnificent desert.

Starting from the large administrative center of Tamanrasset, a city of brown mud-walled houses, we travel by landrover for two days across a magnificent desert landscape to the Touareg village of Ahorar.

From here, our walk takes us across the Tassili N'Immidir, a region so unknown that our friend and trip leader Jean-Louis Bernezat believes that members of his 1983 reconnaissance party were the first non-Touaregs ever to visit the region, and the first to view its beautiful neolithic art—walls and caves decorated with scenes of combat and hunting dating to 6,000 B.C.

In an overwhelming landscape of stone forests, dry river beds, cliffs and dunes, we'll follow our mysteriously-veiled guides, Touaregs from the oasis of Ahorar, for only they know where to find the N'Immidir's painted caves, scant waterholes and the passes which lead to the upper plateaus for scenic vistas of this enchanted land.

Camels (dromedaries) carry our gear but are not available for riding because the terrain is too rough on their feet. We walk an average of six to eight hours a day.

We sleep under the stars, as we do on all our Sahara camel expeditions, in a balmy climate that is a unique experience in itself.

Trip #2 is a Cultural Expedition, with a guest lecturer who is a specialist in Neolithic art of the Sahara/*Alla Schmitz*

Mountain Travel is the only U.S. organization which offers unique and totally authentic walks and camel safaris in the Sahara Desert of Algeria.

**Trip #2* is a Cultural Expedition with a guest lecturer who is a specialist in Neolithic art of the Sahara.

Itinerary: Day 1 and 2: Leave U.S. Fly Paris/Algiers, Algeria. Transfer to hotel.

Day 3: Fly to Tamanrasset.

Day 4 and 5: By landrover towards the settlement of Ahorar, camping enroute.

Day 6 to 12: Walking and exploring the Tassili N'Immidir.

Day 13: Return to Ahorar in the morning. Afternoon at the oasis.

Day 14 and 15: Return drive to Tamanrasset by landrover across the open desert.

Day 16: Fly to Algiers for overnight.

Day 17: Depart Algiers and arrive home.

Dates: #1 Feb 26–Mar 14 (17 days)
**#2 Feb 12–Feb 23*
Leader: #1 Jean-Louis Bernezat
#2 to be announced
Grade: B-3
Land Cost: #1 $2250 (8–15 members)
**#2 $2730 (8–15)*
Single Supplement: not available
IT6PA1SFMT15

Sudan: The Nile & The Nubian Desert

Landrover exploration of ancient civilizations

We invite you to discover Sudan, a country visited often by archaeologists and ethnologists, and seldom (if ever) by tourists.

The beauty of this country lies not just in the wild Nubian Desert with its volcanic summits, and the ever-changing patterns of its ochre and yellow dunes, but in its civilizations, past and present.

As we journey for eleven days by landrover along the Nile and across the desert, we'll see the impressive remains of royal cities, pyramids and temples dating back 5,000 years, the vestiges of such kingdoms as Meroe and Kush.

At Naga, we'll see surprising ruins which combine the art of Rome, Greece and Egypt. At the royal city of Meroe, we'll walk amidst Roman baths and hundreds of pyramids and try to imagine how verdant and populous this land once was.

Crossing the Nile, we'll admire temples to the God Amun. Further along in Argo, we'll see wonderful Nubian clay houses and find the oldest ruin in Sudan: Kerma, built around 4,000 B.C. and still an enigma to archaeologists.

People of the Sudan/*Jean Ribat*

We'll also have a look at present-day civilization in Sudan, as we wander through the villages of the Nile, seeing the rich riverside gardens and orchards and enjoying the celebrated hospitality of the Nubian people.

Itinerary: Day 1 and 2: Leave U.S. Arrive Paris. Overnight at hotel.

Day 3: Fly to Khartoum, Sudan.

Day 4: Visit the wonderful museum of Khartoum, then travel by landrover to the 6th cataract on the Nile.

Day 5 and 6: Explore the ruins of the kingdom of Meroe.

Day 7: Cross the Nile to the Bayuda Desert.

Day 8: Visit the high pyramid of Taharka, Nubian pharoah of Egypt.

Day 9: Explore the villages along the banks of the Nile.

Day 10: Leave the Nile Valley and head through the desert to the city of Argo.

Day 11: Visit Kerma, the oldest ruin in Sudan.

Day 12: Onward to the Third Cataract, with its Egyptian temple sites.

Day 13 and 14: Cross the Nile once more and reach Dongola, the main city of northern Sudan.

Day 15 and 16: Drive back to Khartoum through the desert.

Day 17: Free day in Khartoum.

Day 18: Fly Khartoum/Paris and connect with homeward-bound flights.

Day 19: Arrive home.

Dates: Nov 13–Dec 1 (19 days)
Leader: to be announced
Grade: A-2
Land Cost: $1900 (8–15 members)
Single Supplement: not available
IT6PA1SFMT26

This is a true voyage of discovery, an 8-day walk in a virtually unexplored region of the Sahara, the world's largest and most magnificent desert/*Alla Schmitz*

At the royal city of Meroe, we'll walk amidst Roman baths and hundreds of pyramids and try to imagine how verdant and populous this land once was/*Jean Ribat*

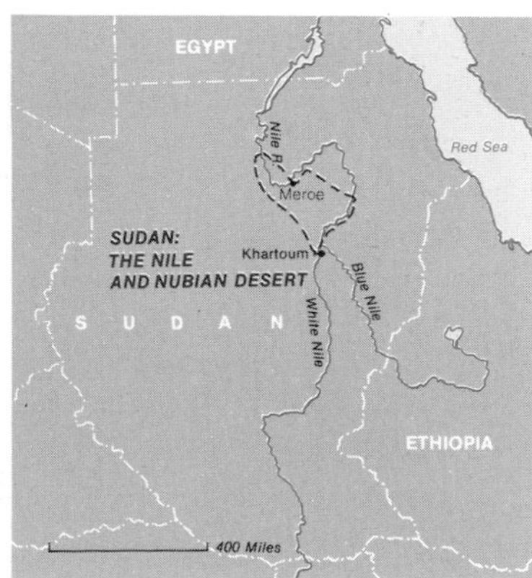

Ancient Egypt

Camping and sailing on the Nile

Herodotus wrote of Egypt in the 5th century A.D., "there is no other country which possesses such wonders." And that is still true today.

In Cairo, we visit the Great Pyramids, the Sphinx and the Egyptian Museum of Antiquities (filled with King Tut's treasures). From Aswan, we visit Abu Simbel, site of the Nile-side temples of Ramses II.

We then begin a special part of our Egypt tour, a leisurely four-day sail on the Nile from Aswan to Luxor. Our vessels for the sail will be *feluccas,* the traditional native sailboats. Living on these little boats involves "roughing it" by Western standards. Toilet facilities are primitive, privacy is limited, and since there are no berths on the boat, we will sleep in tents on the beaches at night. What the boats lack in comfort, they make up for in flexibility. We think they provide a far better Nile experience than the sterile cruise ships which are floating hotels.

Egyptian sailors handle the boat and do all the cooking. We'll have a relaxed pace on the river, visiting the major temples enroute, and meeting white-robed Nubians as they conduct the commerce of the Nile from their *felucca* boats.

Arriving at Luxor, where the legacy of the pharaohs is at the most astonishing, we'll discover the world of ancient Thebes, visiting the Valley of the Kings, Tutankhamen's tomb and other wonders.

All trips are escorted by a professional Egyptologist. Travel between Cairo and Aswan is by sleeper train.

Itinerary: Day 1 and 2: Leave U.S. Arrive Cairo and transfer to hotel.

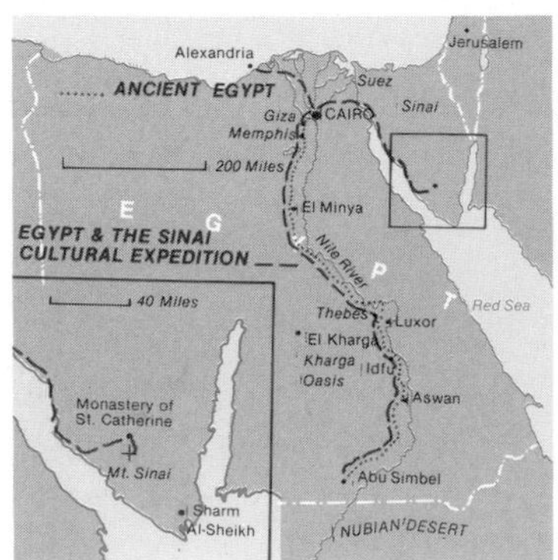

Day 3 and 4: Two full days sightseeing. Evening of Day 4, board the night train to Aswan.

Day 5: Arrive in Aswan about noon. Visit Kitchener Island, Elephantine Island and the Mausoleum of the Aga Khan.

Day 6: Short morning flight to Abu Simbel, Nile-side temples saved by an international engineering project from the rising waters of Lake Nasser. Fly back to Aswan and take a short sail to Philae, site of a lovely temple to Isis.

Day 7 to 10: Board the feluccas *and enjoy the quiet pleasures of the Nile, a beautiful river whose waters are edged by green palm thickets and flanked by golden desert escarpments. We stop each day to visit the major temples enroute. We also have close contact with the friendly Nubian people living along the banks of the Nile, getting a glimpse into the lives of Egyptian shepherds and farmers. This experience is totally different than a Nile cruise in a big luxury liner.*

Day 11: Arrive in Luxor, bid our felucca *crew goodbye, and transfer to a hotel for showers and cleanup.*

Day 12 and 13: Visit the incredible funerary temples of Queen Hatshepsut and Ramses III, the tombs of Ramses IV and Tutankhamen, and temples of Karnak and Luxor.

Day 14: Afternoon departure on the overnight train to Cairo.

Day 15: Arrive in Cairo and transfer to hotel. Day free.

Day 16: Depart Cairo and connect with homeward-bound flights.

Dates: #1 Feb 15–Mar 2 (16 days)
#2 Nov 15–Nov 30
Leader: Mattanyah Zohar
Grade: A-2
Land Cost: $1890 (10–16 members)
$2090 (6–9)
Single Supplement: $275

IT6TW15639

Arriving at Luxor, where the legacy of the Pharoahs is at its most astonishing, we'll discover the world of ancient Thebes, visiting the Valley of the Kings, Tutankhamen's tomb and other wonders/
Bruce Klepinger

Cultural Expedition:

Egypt & The Sinai: 5,000 Years of History

Cairo, Alexandria, Luxor, Abu Simbel, Mt. Sinai

This tour offers an in-depth experience in the land of Egypt, from the astounding pharaonic sites of the Nile Valley to the Sinai Coast.

After touring Cairo and Alexandria, we travel through the Fayum oasis with its ancient monuments and unique irrigation systems.

In Luxor (ancient Thebes) we explore Karnak, the most impressive of Egyptian temple sites, and the famous sites of the New Kingdom on the west bank of the Nile, including the tomb of King Tut-Ankh-Amon, mortuary temple of Queen Hatshepsut, and the Ramesseum, mortuary temple of King Ramses the 2nd.

In Aswan, we spend a relaxing day on *feluccas,* the small sailboats of the Nile, touring to the Nubian village of Suheil and walking up to Qubet el Hawa for a breathtaking view of the Nile.

After a day tour to Abu Simbel, eternal temple of King Ramses the 2nd, we drive southward along the Sinai Coast, to visit St. Catherine's Monastery (with its Byzantine treasures) and hike (or ride camels) up Mt. Sinai. The trip finishes with a day of swimming among the spectacular coral reefs of Nabq on the Sinai Coast.

Leader/Lecturer: Mattanyah Zohar's expertise ranges over a variety of Middle Eastern cultures. He has completed studies in archaeology at Hebrew University in Jerusalem, and has guided cultural groups in Egypt and Turkey for many years.

Itinerary: Day 1 and 2: Leave U.S. Arrive Cairo.

Day 3 and 4: Tour Cairo and environs.

Day 5: Drive to Alexandria on the Mediterranean.

Day 6: Tour Alexandria, largest sea port of the Greek world, and return to Cairo.

Day 7: Drive to Al Miniya in the Fayum oasis.

Day 8: Tour the painted rock-cut tombs of Beni Hassan, dating to the Middle Kingdom.

Day 9: Drive to Luxor via the temple sites of Abidos and Dendera.

Day 10 and 11: Tour Luxor.

Day 12: Drive to Aswan via the Nile-side temple at Edfu.

Day 13: Spend a day on the Nile in feluccas.

Day 14: Visit Aswan High Dam, tour Abu Simbel, take sleeper train to Cairo.

Day 15: Tour Cairo.

Day 16: Drive across the Suez Canal to the Sinai Coast and camp at an oasis.

Day 17: Drive to St. Catherine's Monastery.

Day 18: Hike or ride camels up Mt. Sinai, then drive to the Gulf of Aqaba and camp at the oasis of Nabq.

Day 19: Morning swimming at the beach, then fly to Cairo.

Day 20: In Cairo.

Day 21: Depart Cairo and connect with homeward-bound flights.

Dates: Oct 4–Oct 24 (21 days)
Grade: A-1
Land Cost: $2390 (10–16 members) $2590 (6–9)
Single Supplement: $345
IT6TW15640

Temples at Abu Simbel/Bruce Klepinger

Mortuary temple of Queen Hatshepsut/ Allen Bechky

Nubian village/Bruce Klepinger

A special part of our Egypt tour is a leisurely four-day sail on the Nile from Aswan to Luxor. Our vessels for the sail will be feluccas, the traditional native sailboats/*Allen Bechky*

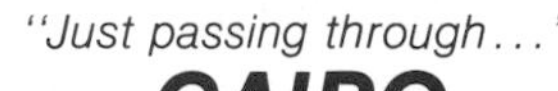

"Just passing through..."

CAIRO

City notes by Gadi Sternbach

Walking/jogging routes:

At sunrise or by moonlight, circle on foot around the Great Pyramids at Giza, a crowdless and romantic time to be there. Walk through Ataba market to Al Azhar Square and through the endless Khan al Khalil Bazaar and adjacent silver, gold and spice markets. Walk to the Muhamad Ali Mosque via Cairo's Mamluke cemetery, the famous "City of the Dead" which is also a city of the living, because many Egyptians have taken up residence in the tombs and catacombs.

Day trips:

Rent a taxi for the day and visit Faiyum, a large oasis 56 miles southwest of Cairo; interesting birdlife and several adjacent archaeological sites are enroute. Visit the pyramid of Meidum on the way. Another worthwhile destination is Wadi Natron, an oasis on the road to Alexandria. There are several Coptic monasteries enroute.

Special museums:

Besides the famed Egyptian Museum, which houses King Tut's treasures, visit the Gezira Museum for another view of Egyptian civilization, the Coptic Museum in Old Cairo and the Museum of Islamic Art.

The Sphinx at Giza/Allen Bechky

The bazaar in old Cairo/Allen Bechky

Discover Kenya

Mountain trek, foot safari, landrover game viewing

Discover the amazing diversity of Kenya the Mountain Travel way: trek across Mt. Kenya, travel the game-filled Masai Mara by landrover, track animals on foot in the bush country of Tsavo National Park, then taste the tropical exuberance of the historic Kenyan coast. This is an African safari for the adventurer.

On a five-day hiking traverse of Mt. Kenya, we explore the forest (home of the leopard, buffalo and elephant), the moorlands, and the peak-studded alpine zone. The trail scales Point Lenana (16,355′), highest point accessible to walkers, then descends into the beautiful Teliki Valley on the southwest side of the peak.

From our private camp in the fantastic Masai Mara, our landrovers carry us to close encounters with elephant, cheetah, giraffe, and the whole range of plains animals.

In the deep bush country of Tsavo National Park, we make a four-day "foot safari" along the banks of the Tsavo River to experience intimately the sight, sound and feel of the African bush. Game seen on this non-strenuous trek will include hippo, crocodile and elephant.

On Kenya's coast at Mombasa, we take time for beachcombing and shopping. Return to Nairobi by way of an overnight train ride on the turn-of-the-century "Lunatic Express."

Itinerary: Day 1 to 3: Leave U.S. Arrive Nairobi. Transfer to Norfolk Hotel.

Day 4: Drive to Mt. Kenya. Overnight at Sirimon Camp (8,000′).

Day 5: Hike for five miles across open moorland. Camp by a stream at 13,000 feet.

Day 6: Trek to the head of the Mackinder Valley.

Day 7: Making a pre-dawn start, we ascend Point Lenana from the north, reaching the summit at about 9 a.m. Descend to the Teliki Valley on the south side of the mountain. (We grade this trip a "B-2/C-2" because members who don't want to make the Point Lenana hike can traverse around the mountain by a different route, catching up with the group at Teliki Camp.)

Three days of trekking along the Tsavo River, a warm-water river through Tsavo's semi-desert bush, is a totally different wildlife experience/*Leo Le Bon*

Day 8: Descend the Teliki Valley to the roadhead and transfer to Mountain Lodge. Enjoy nighttime game viewing from the lodge.

Day 9: Drive to Lake Naivasha.

Day 10 to 12: Superb game watching in Masai Mara, camping in classic African savannahs.

Day 13: Fly to Nairobi. After lunch, drive to Tsavo National Park.

Day 14 to 17: Three full days of trekking along the Tsavo River, a warm-water river through Tsavo's semi-desert bush. This is a totally different wildlife experience, tiptoeing quietly through the rugged bush country and meeting wildlife on its own terms. An armed park ranger will be with us at all times for our protection.

Day 18: We complete our trek, then leave the desert for the inviting tropical coast at Mombasa. Stay at Nomad Tented Camp, with walk-in tents with twin bed and private showers.

Day 19: Day free for beachcombing and shopping.

Day 20: Free day in Mombasa, then board overnight train to Nairobi in the late afternoon.

Day 21: Arrive in Nairobi in the morning. Late evening departure from Nairobi on homeward-bound flights.

Day 22: Arrive home.

Dates: #1 Feb 1–Feb 22 (22 days)
#2 Jun 7–Jun 28
#3 Aug 2–Aug 23
#4 Oct 4–Oct 25
#5 Dec 13, 1986–Jan 3, 1987
Leader: #1 Jim Gardiner
#2 & #3: Iain Allan
#4 & #5: to be announced
Grade: B-2/C-2
Land Cost: $2490 (10–15 members)
Single Supplement: $350
IT5BA1YO50

Masai woman/*Allen Bechky*

Our Discover Kenya trip scales Point Lenana (16,355′), highest point accessible to walkers, then descends into the beautiful Teleki Valley shown above, on the southwest side of the peak/*Iain Allan*

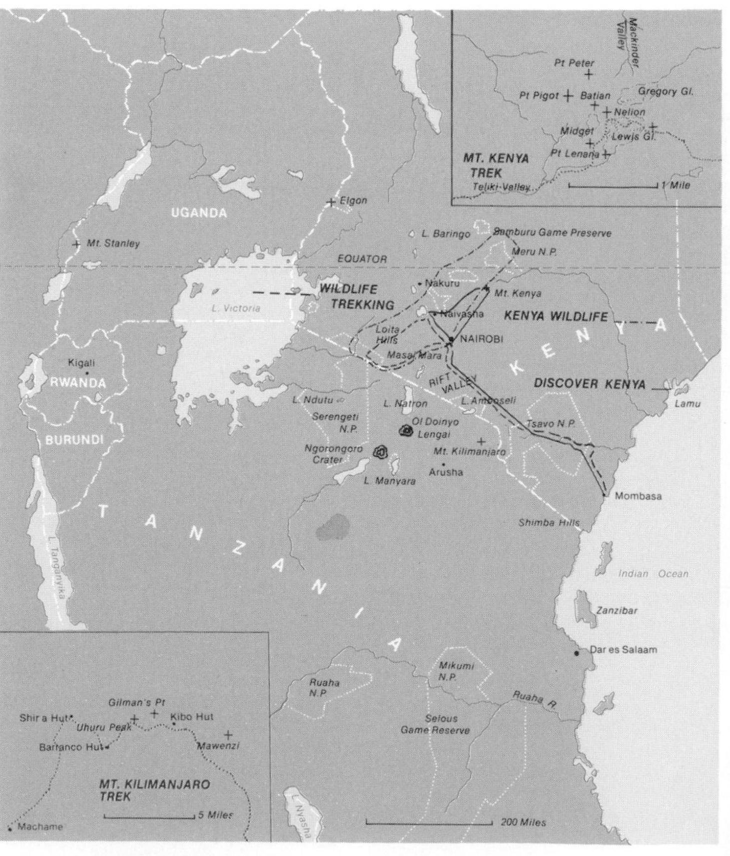

Kenya Wildlife Safari

To Masai Mara, Samburu and the Aberdares

This safari visits the very best parks in Kenya: Meru National Park, Samburu Game Reserve, the Aberdares and fantastic Masai Mara.

Like our other Kenya safaris, it is a deluxe camping adventure, complete with full camp staff, cook, large walk-in tents (plus shower tent and bathroom tent). All these "creature comforts" afford us the convenience of a game lodge while allowing us the privacy of our own camp in the wilds. We will travel by landrover, with four or five persons plus driver, and, of course, we will always be in the company of an expert safari guide.

Meru National Park was once home to Elsa, the famed lioness of *Born Free*. Elsa is gone, but her descendants remain, as do elephant and buffalo. Many antelope species such as oryx and dikdik are found here. Meru's Tana River shelters many hippos and crocodiles.

Samburu Game Reserve is part of the range of the nomadic Samburu tribe (we may visit one of their villages). It is also the habitat of celebrated desert species such as reticulated giraffe, Grevy's zebra and gerenuk.

Aberdares National Park features the wildlife of the high mountain moorlands and forest.

The Masai Mara is one of the finest wildlife areas in all Africa, a classic African savannah covered with roving herds of antelope—certainly the best bush country in Kenya for finding big predators such as lion, cheetah, hyena and the always-elusive leopard.

Itinerary: Day 1 to 3: Leave U.S. Arrive Nairobi. Overnight Norfolk Hotel.

Day 4 and 5: Camp in Meru National Park, an extraordinarily beautiful landscape of wooded plains and palm-bordered rivers. Meet our first elephants, giraffes and lion and have a chance to see rare species such as white rhino and lesser kudu.

Day 6: Camp in the private game reserve at Lewa Downs and visit Samburu Reserve, meeting the exotic species of Kenya's northern desert.

Day 7 and 8: Enter the forests of Aberdares National Park for nighttime game viewing of such oddities as giant forest hog and bongo, plus elephant and rhino at the Ark Lodge.

Day 9: Travel over the Aberdares moorlands to Lake Naivasha.

Day 10 to 12: Camp in the fabulous Masai Mara, observing all the creatures of this rich savannah country and meeting the Masai at their manyattas.

Day 13: Fly to Nairobi. Evening departure on homeward-bound flights.

Day 14: Arrive home.

Dates: #1 Jan 5–Jan 18 (14 days)
#2 Feb 23–Mar 8
#3 Mar 16–Mar 29
**#4 Jun 29–Jul 12*
#5 Aug 2–Aug 15
#6 Sep 7–Sep 20
#7 Oct 12–Oct 25

**Trip #4 set aside as "Family Safari" with special rates for children. Ask for itinerary.*

Leader: #1 David Buitron
#2 to #7: to be announced

Grade: A-1

Land Cost: $1690
(9–15 members)

Single Supplement: $310

IT5BA1Y052

Kenya & Tanzania trips include: twin accommodations in hotels, all meals (except in Nairobi), leadership, local transport, visas for Kenya and Tanzania, airport transfers for those using the group flights, camping accommodations including camp meals, safari staff and community camping equipment (if applicable).

Deluxe safari camp in Kenya's national parks/*Leo Le Bon*

Giraffes at Masai Mara/*Allen Bechky*

Red-billed hornbills/*Allen Bechky*

We travel by landrover, with four or five persons plus driver, and of course, we will always be in the company of an expert safari guide/*Leo Le Bon*

Female elephant and calf/*Allen Bechky*

Wildlife Trekking Safari

On foot in Tsavo National Park

Tracking game on foot allows for extraordinary wildlife encounters, an intimate appreciation of the African bush environment, and a chance to experience the real Africa in the style of explorers of the last century.

Our foot safari leads us on an extended exploration of Kenya's wildest country, the bushland tracts of Tsavo National Park.

Starting in the thornbush thickets of the Tsavo River, we stalk elephant, rhino and hippo through riparian forest. Moving eastward, we trek the semi-desert country along the Galana River, which attracts grazing animals such as zebra and gazelle, as well as the big cats. Resident lion prides range territories along both rivers. Their often invisible presence, as well as that of buffalo and elephant, lends another dimension to this uncommon safari experience. Armed rangers and experienced guides are with us every step of the way.

We round out the exciting foot safaris with classic game viewing from four-wheel-drive vehicles while we camp in the beautiful Masai Mara Reserve, plus nighttime viewing of rare mountain species in the Aberdares, and a coastal stay north of Mombasa at beautiful Watamu Beach.

Itinerary: Day 1 to 3: Leave U.S. Arrive Nairobi. Overnight at Norfolk Hotel.

Day 4: To the Ark Lodge for nighttime game viewing in the forests of the Aberdares.

Day 5: Drive over the Aberdares moorlands to Lake Naivasha.

Day 6 to 9: Four days to really explore the Masai Mara. We can expect to see all the great African wildlife: elephant, giraffe, zebra, lion and a vast array of antelopes, all present in unbelievable numbers.

Day 10: Fy to Nairobi and drive to a lodge in Tsavo West National Park.

Day 11 to 13: Camp along the Tsavo River, exploring on foot.

Day 14: Drive to Tsavo East, another section of Kenya's largest wildlife reserve.

Day 15 and 16: Trek the semi-desert country fringing the Galana River.

Day 17 and 18: Drive to the coast, resting at lovely Watuma Beach. Explore the reefs of the Marine Park.

Day 19: Roam historic Mombasa and take an overnight train ride to Nairobi.

Day 20: In Nairobi. Evening departure on homeward-bound flights.

Day 21: Arrive home.

Dates: #1 Jan 12–Feb 1 (21 days)
#2 Jun 29–Jul 19
Leader: #1 David Buitron
#2 to be announced
Grade: B-2
Land Cost: $2350
(10–16 members)
Single Supplement: $360
IT5BA1YO53

Tracking game on foot allows for extraordinary wildlife encounters, an intimate appreciation of the African environment, and a chance to experience Africa in the style of the explorers of the turn of the century/Nadia Le Bon

Cultural Expedition:

Kenya: Journey To The Cradle Of Mankind

A study tour focusing on human evolution

In the last decade, the search for the origins of mankind has focused dramatically on the parched desert lands of East Africa's Rift Valley. The quest for the missing links in human evolution is to African research in this century what the search for the Nile was to the last.

At the epicenter of research activity is Lake Turkana, the "Jade Sea" in the desert of northern Kenya where Dr. Richard Leakey directs ongoing investigations of the ancient fossil record. We will visit his site at Koobi Fora, where he will lend us his insights into the significance of his work.

As we drive to Lake Turkana, a journey which takes us through the wildest parts of the Kenyan desert, we visit and study a fascinating collection of modern-day inhabitants of the "Cradle of Mankind": cattle-tending Samburu, war-like Turkana, Rendille camel herders, and the fishing El Molo of the lake. In the company of expert anthropologists, we shall learn to see the desert through these nomads' eyes.

We round out our cultural sojourn with a stay on the Indian Ocean island of Lamu, which unpretentiously preserves the 15th century Swahili coastal city states, and a visit to the Masai Mara Reserve for superb game viewing.

Special Guest Lecturer: Richard E. Leakey has been instrumental in making Kenya one of the world's major centers for the study of evolution and human origins. Born and raised in Kenya, he learned about prehistoric Africa from the work of both his parents, Louis and Mary. Dr. Leakey is now director of the National Museum of Kenya. His book, *The Making of Mankind* and the 7-part BBC television series of the same name, have contributed to a greater understanding of the search for the origins of human ancestry.

In the company of expert anthropologists, we shall learn to see the desert through these nomads' eyes/Allen Bechky

Masai manyatta/Allen Bechky

Itinerary: Day 1 to 3: Leave U.S. Arrive Nairobi. Transfer to Norfolk Hotel.

Day 4: Visit national museum and Olorogasalie Prehistoric Site.

Day 5: Drive to Hyrax Hill Prehistoric Site (excavated by Louis Leakey) enroute to camp at Lake Baringo.

Day 6: Visit local Njemps and Pokot tribes.

Day 7 to 10: Journey through Kenya's northern desert, in the company of specialist guides, visiting traditional nomad camps.

Day 11 and 12: Reach Lake Turkana and study the tiny El Molo tribe, dependent entirely on harvesting the lakes' fish, hippo and crocodile.

Day 13 and 14: Fly to Koobi Fora, where Richard Leakey will be our guide for exploration of this celebrated site.

Day 15 and 16: Fly to Lamu. Visit archaeological site of Takwa, a 10th century Swahili town, and relax on gorgeous beaches.

Day 17 to 19: Fly to Masai Mara Game Reserve for a classic African camping safari.

Day 20: Fly to Nairobi. Evening departure on homeward-bound flights.

Day 21: Arrive home.

Dates: Sep 21–Oct 11 (21 days)
Leader: David Buitron
Grade: A-2
Land Cost: $3850
(10–15 members)
+$500 donation to the National Museum of Kenya
Single Supplement: $350
IT5BA1YO48

Great Parks Of East Africa

Classic game viewing in Masai Mara, Samburu, Serengeti, Ngorongoro

This grand safari features the best of both Kenya and Tanzania. Here the superlative African bestiary can be appreciated in all its diversity among landscapes of legendary tranquility and beauty.

The great parks of both countries are now "household names": Serengeti, Ngorongoro, Masai Mara, Samburu. They have become such by virtue of the countless researchers and cinematographers who have recorded the wonder of these places. The wonder is still there, and the time to go is now.

Many companies offer tours to the parks of Kenya and Tanzania, but few offer the superlative experience of a camping safari, and none in the style of Mountain Travel. This trip combines the outdoor integrity of a real camping safari with a few nights in scenic game lodges.

No zebra-striped mini-vans trundle us from one resort hotel to the next, nor lumbering overland trucks crowded with camping gear. We still offer the niceties of the traditional camping safari: we travel in rugged four-wheel-drive landrovers which really do have the capability to go anywhere. Our support vehicle goes ahead to set up camp and our safari staff takes care of all chores, from preparing appetizing meals to fixing up hot camp showers. All this attention allows you the time to do what you came to do—to savour the African experience.

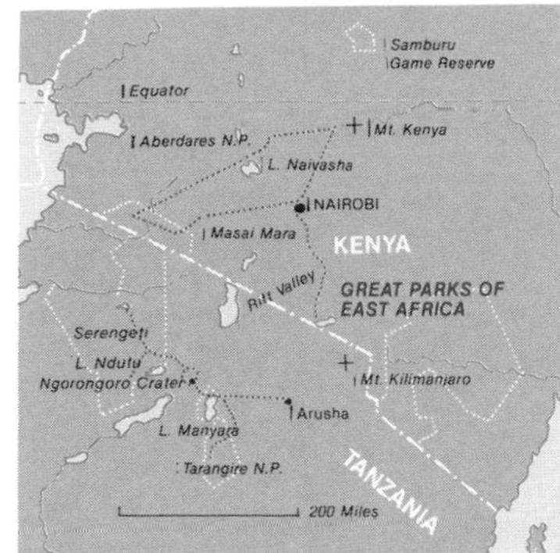

Itinerary: Day 1 to 3: Leave U.S. Arrive Nairobi. Overnight at Norfolk Hotel.

Day 4 to 6: Fly to our exclusive camp in the Masai Mara Game Reserve, celebrated for its lion prides which flourish due to the presence of abundant resident antelopes. Along the Mara River, we'll see pools of sleepy hippos and basking crocodiles. The plains abound with grazers: gazelle, zebra, topi and gnu.

Day 7 and 8: Drive to Nairobi, then on to Amboseli, where dry bush country features oryx and gerenuk, and marshes are home to rhino and elephant, all with snow-topped Kilimanjaro in the background.

Day 9: Drive to Tanzania. Visit Lake Manyara Park for close-up encounters with elephant and baboons. Note: we alter the Tanzania portion of the itinerary in accordance with seasonal animal migrations.

Day 10 and 11: Explore the grasslands of the Serengeti, encountering immense herds of wildebeest, zebra and gazelle. Lion and cheetah are commonly seen. Overnight at Ndutu Lodge.

Day 12 and 13: Cross the plains to Seronera for more gameviewing. Overnight at Seronera Lodge.

Day 14 and 15: Visit Olduvai Gorge enroute to the "Eden like" Ngorongoro Crater, a complete collection of African animals found in a setting of dazzling beauty.

Summer Departures:

Day 10 and 11: Cross the Serengeti to Seronera, where we find resident game.

Day 12 and 13: At Ngorongoro Crater.

Day 14 and 15: Visit Tarangire, home to thousands of thirsty animals attracted to its permanent river during the long dry season. Elephant herds number in the hundreds, buffalo congregate in the thousands among innumerable groups of eland, zebra, kongoni and gnu. Overnight at rustic Tarangire Lodge.

All Departures:

Day 16: Drive to Kenya and return to Norfolk Hotel in Nairobi. Evening departure on homeward-bound flights.

Day 17: Arrive home.

Dates: #1 Mar 7–Mar 23 (17 days)
#2 Jul 18–Aug 3
#3 Aug 15–Aug 31
#4 Sep 26–Oct 12
Leader: David Buitron
Grade: A-1
Land Cost: $3290 (10–15 members) +domestic flt. $100
Single Supplement: $450
IT5BA1YO49

Game viewing by landrover/*Allen Bechky*

Courting lions/*Allen Bechky*

Impala/*Allen Bechky*

Many companies offer tours to the parks of Kenya and Tanzania, but few offer the superlative experience of a camping safari in the style of Mountain Travel. The Great Parks trip combines the outdoor integrity of a real camping safari with some nights in scenic game lodges/Allen Bechky*

Mt. Kenya & Kilimanjaro Trek

Hiking to the top of Africa

The two highest peaks in Africa are Mt. Kenya (17,058') in Kenya, and Mt. Kilimanjaro (19,340'), in Tanzania. Both mountains rise in regal isolation from surrounding plateaus and plains. Hiking these equatorial giants takes one through three worlds of fascinating beauty: tropical forest, mist-shrouded moorlands, and high altitude alpine zone.

Our Mt. Kenya hike is a five-day traverse beginning in the forests of the little-known Sirimon Route. We ascend to the heights of Point Lenana and descend the other side through the splendid "tropical alpine" flora of the Teliki Valley. Point Lenana (16,355'), highest point that can be reached by hikers, has an astounding view of Mt. Kenya's two jagged summits, Batian and Nelion, surrounded by lesser needles and some fifteen glaciers.

Before leaving Kenya, we'll enjoy excellent game viewing in Amboseli National Park in the shadow of Mt. Kilimanjaro.

In Tanzania, our six-day Kilimanjaro trek takes us along the Machame Route, a remote trail skirting the southern glaciers of the mountain. Beginning in rain forest at 6,400 feet, we hike in isolation, enjoying fabulous alpine scenery as we make an altitude gain of nearly 13,000 feet on the way to the "snows of Kilimanjaro"—Uhuru Peak at 19,340 feet.

After the trip, we can arrange an optional seven-day safari in Tanzania's fantastic national parks.

Park headquarters, Kilimanjaro/ Leo Le Bon

Thorn tree/ Leo Le Bon

Itinerary: Day 1 to 3: Leave U.S. Arrive Nairobi. Transfer to Norfolk Hotel.

Day 4: Drive to Mt. Kenya and camp in the forest at Sirimon Camp (8,000').

Day 5: Drive to roadhead at 11,000 feet and hike for five miles to camp in Liki North Valley (13,000').

Day 6: Trek up Mackinder's Valley and camp at 14,500 feet.

Day 7: Making a pre-dawn start, we hike to Point Lenana from the north and descend to the south side of the mountain and camp at 13,600 feet.

Day 8: Descend the Teliki Valley and its infamous "vertical bog" to the forest clearing at 10,000 feet. Overnight at Aberdares Country Club.

Day 9: Drive to the Ark Lodge, which features nighttime viewing of such rare forest creatures as giant forest hog, bongo and rhino.

Day 10 and 11: Drive to our camp in Amboseli Game Reserve, which has fantastic game viewing with Mt. Kilimanjaro as a magnificent backdrop.

Day 12: Enter Tanzania and proceed to the Kibo Hotel.

Day 13: Drive to Machame Route and begin hiking at about 6,500 feet. Follow trails up through rain forest and heather to Uniport Hut (10,000').

Day 14: Cross the Shira Plateau to Shira Hut (12,600') with spectacular views of the glaciers of Kilimanjaro.

Day 15: Trek to Barranco Hut (13,500').

Chief Kilimanjaro guide/ Allen Bechky

Day 16: Trek beneath the wild south face of Kilimanjaro to the Barafu Hut (15,000').

Day 17: A long, memorable and very strenuous day: up at 1 a.m. and hike about five to nine hours (depending on your speed) to the crater rim, then along the rim to Uhuru Peak (19,340) and Gilman's Point. Descend to Horambu Hut (12,200'), reaching it by about 5 to 7 p.m.

Day 18: Pleasant descent on a good trail to Kibo Hotel.

Day 19: Depart Arusha and fly to London for overnight.

Day 20: Arrive home.

Dates: #1 Feb 15–Mar 6 (20 days)
#2 Jul 12–Jul 31
#3 Sep 6–Sep 25
Leader: #1 & #2: Iain Allan
#3 Jim Gardiner
Grade: C-3
Land Cost: $2895
(10–15 members)
Single Supplement: $330
IT5BA1YO51

Trekking up Mackinder's Valley on Mt. Kenya. Both Kilimanjaro and Kenya rise in regal isolation from surrounding plateaus and plains. Hiking these equatorial giants takes one through three worlds of fascinating beauty: tropical forest, mist-shrouded moorlands and high-altitude alpine zones/ Bruce Klepinger

Climb Kilimanjaro!

Africa's highest peak

Perhaps no other mountain on earth has the mystique and appeal of Kilimanjaro, the highest mountain in Africa. Rising in majestic isolation from game-covered plains to 19,340 feet, Kilimanjaro is an impressive sight, visible from vast distances away. When the morning haze obscures Kili's lower slopes, the mile-wide, ice-and-scree-covered summit dome, the "snows of Kilimanjaro," beckons dreamlike over the African landscape.

This trip centers around a six-day Kilimanjaro "climb," traveling on the Marangu Route. We begin hiking on trails through rain forest and heather, then up into open tussock grass and moorlands with weird tropical-alpine vegetation such as giant lobelias and groundsels. The final push goes up scree slopes to Gilman's Point at 18,635 feet (or further to Uhuru Peak at 19,340 feet, if you're up to it!). Porters carry all the gear, and nightly accommodations are in mountain huts.

Before the climb, we explore Africa with a three-day landrover safari in Ngorongoro Crater and Lake Manyara National Park, beautiful places to see the full panoply of African wildlife—lions, elephants, and a host of plains game.

Near the Shira Plateau on Kilimanjaro/ *Leo Le Bon*

Itinerary: Day 1 to 3: Leave New York. Arrive Nairobi, Kenya.

Day 4: Drive across the Tanzania border to Lake Manyara. Afternoon game drive and introduction to the wildlife of Africa in a breathtaking Rift Valley landscape.

Day 5: Morning game drive at Manyara observing elephants and possibly tree-climbing lions. Continue to the rim of Ngorongoro Crater.

Day 6: Fantastic game viewing on the Eden-like floor of Ngorongoro Crater. If you have only one day in your life to visit an African game park, this should be it!

Day 7: Drive to Kibo Hotel at the foot of Kilimanjaro.

Day 8: Hike from 6,000 feet to Mandara Hut at 9,000 feet.

Day 9: Hike across moorlands to Horombo Hut at 12,500 feet.

Day 10: Acclimatization day at Horombo (this rest day really boosts members chances for making it to the top!).

Day 11: Hike to Kibo Hut at 15,500 feet between the peaks of Kibo and Mawenzi.

Day 12: Pre-dawn start for the summit and late afternoon return to Horombo. A rewarding day!

Day 13: Descend to Kibo Hotel.

Day 14: Return to Nairobi. Depart on evening flight.

Day 15: Arrive New York.

Dates: #1 Jan 11–Jan 25 (15 days)
#2 Mar 8–Mar 22
#3 Jun 14–Jun 28
#4 Aug 2–Aug 16
#5 Oct 4–Oct 18
#6 Dec 6–Dec 20
Leader: local guides
Grade: C-3
*Tour Cost: *$3000 (10–15 members)*
$3490 (6–9)
*INCLUDING round trip economy-class airfare on British Airways from New York to Nairobi. *Tour Cost, based on British Air Apex fare, is subject to change).*
Single Supplement: $150
IT5BA1YO47

Special Note For All Trips Visiting Tanzania:

Land Cost of Tanzania trips may be subject to change. The government of Tanzania has imposed recent extreme increases on all national park fees, which may be raised (or lowered) again on short notice. Mountain Travel will adjust Land Costs accordingly.

"Just passing through..."

NAIROBI

City notes by Allen Bechky and Iain Allen

Jogging/walking tours:
Although Nairobi is basically a safe city, joggers and walkers are advised to stay in the town center and confine their excursions to daylight hours. The area around the Norfolk Hotel is good.

Shopping:
Walk down Biashara Street and try your hand at bargaining for discounts on curios. You might not get one but it's worth it for the fun! Buy hard-to-find books on Africa at Prestige Booksellers, the Book Corner or the Select Bookshop. Good quality Ethiopian and East African antiques are sometimes available at a store called African Heritage, and the Craft Market is a good place to buy locally produced clothing.

Museums:
Visit the excellent Kenya National Museum, within walking distance of the Norfolk Hotel. If you are interested in colonial history and the building of the famous "Lunatic Express" railway, visit the Railway Museum at Nairobi Railway Station.

Our six-day "climb" of Kilimanjaro begins with hiking on trails through rain forest and heather, then up into open tussock grass and moorlands with weird tropical-alpine vegetation such as giant lobelias and groundsels/ *Leo Le Bon*

Summit glaciers on Kibo/ *Leo Le Bon*

The subtropical forest/ *Leo Le Bon*

Tanzania Wildlife Safari

East Africa's finest game viewing: Serengeti, Ngorongoro, Mt. Meru, Lake Manyara

This is the Africa buff's "connoisseur" safari. By four-wheel-drive vehicle and on foot, we travel through some of the best landscapes the continent has to offer and visit the best gamelands on earth. This area, celebrated in Peter Matthiessen's *The Tree Where Man Was Born,* is truly "Old Africa" as we all have imagined it.

In Arusha National Park, we hike in the company of armed rangers, following game trails through Mt. Meru's lush cloud forest.

Leaving the cool highlands, we descend into the Great Rift Valley, land of wild animals and Masai herds, of baobab and whistling thorn.

We then enter the Serengeti ecosystem to witness the greatest wildlife spectacle on earth. Here vast herds of wildebeest, zebra and gazelle stretch to every horizon. On our extended camping safari, we may well witness the miracle of birth and the drama of predation and death. Our schedule is flexible, allowing us to follow the migration.

We also visit another natural wonder, the 100-square-mile expanse of Ngorongoro Crater, for a mind-boggling wildlife experience within the confines of the earth's largest relic caldera.

At Lake Manyara National Park, we enjoy unbelievable close-up observations of elephant family groups, marvel at massed flocks of waterbirds, and (with luck), find the celebrated tree-climbing lions.

This is a deluxe African camping safari. We travel four or five persons to a landrover, which gives us tremendous flexibility in catering to the personal interests and energies of trip members. We are supported by a full staff of experienced camp assistants. There are Tanzania safaris which are lower in cost, but if you compare, you'll find that Mountain Travel's safaris offer more time in the bush and fuller service, leading to a better wildlife experience.

After the safari, we can arrange a seven-day Kilimanjaro hike or a visit to the Selous for those who are interested.

Itinerary: Day 1 to 3: Leave U.S. Arrive Kilimanjaro Airport, Tanzania. Drive to Momella Lodge in Arusha National Park.

Day 4: With park rangers as escorts, we hike through the forests of Mt. Meru (14,990') to its beautiful volcanic crater.

Day 5: Drive into Rift Valley wilderness country.

Day 6: Camp in the shadow of the active volcano Ol Doinyo Lengai, the Masai "Mountain of God," and hike to the shores of Lake Natron to enjoy the hospitality of nearby Masai manyattas.

Day 7: Drive up the Rift Escarpment to the foot of the Gol Mountains. A day for Masai and wildlife.

Day 8: Hike into a spectacular gorge to view a large colony of griffon vultures, then drive across the short grass plains of the eastern Serengeti encountering large herds of wildebeest, zebra and gazelle.

Day 9 to 12: In the Serengeti, we stay in proximity to the migrating animals. Generally, from December to May, the great herds are on the short

The Tanzania Wildlife Safari ***is the Africa buff's connoisseur safari. By four-wheel-drive vehicle and on foot, we travel through some of the best landscapes the continent has to offer and visit the best gamelands on earth/***
Allen Bechky

grass plain of the southeast. Our June/July departures will catch migration moving through the western corridor. In addition to the spectacle of migration, Serengeti is "a kingdom of predators," and we shall see lion, cheetah, hyena, jackal, the elusive leopard and wide-ranging wild hunting dogs.

Day 13: Visit Leakey's archaeological site at Olduvai Gorge and drive to the Crater Highland massif. Descend and camp on the floor of Ngorongoro Crater.

Day 14: We have the Crater entirely to ourselves for our dawn game drive, on which we will see an incredible variety of wildlife in great abundance.

Day 15: After a morning game run, drive through fertile farmlands to Gibb's Farm to sample Tanzanian coffee, and continue to camp in Lake Manyara National Park.

Day 16: Our Manyara camp is situated in a lovely groundwater forest, alive with the calls of blue monkeys and silvery-cheeked hornbills.

Day 17: Stop at an African country market before moving to camp at Tarangire National Park.

Day 18: A final game drive in search of Tarangire specialities: leopard, kudu, and python. Afternoon return to Arusha for clean-up, then depart on homeward-bound flight.

Day 19: Arrive home.

Dates: #1 Jan 10–Jan 28 (19 days)
#2 Feb 14–Mar 4
#3 Feb 28–Mar 18
#4 Jun 6–Jun 24
#5 Jun 27–Jul 15
#6 Nov 28–Dec 16
#7 Dec 19, 1986–Jan 6, 1987
Leader: #1, #3, #6, #7 to be announced
#2 Allen Bechky
#4 & #5 Peter Ourusoff
Grade: B-2
Land Cost: $3290 (12–15 members)
$3390 (8–11)
Single Supplement: $300
IT4KL1000CKRB

In the Serengeti, we stay in proximity to migrating animals/Allen Bechky

Cheetah at a kill/Allen Bechky

Hippo pool, Manyara/Allen Bechky

Female elephants can be aggressive when defending their young/
Allen Bechky

The Tanzania Express

Best gamelands on earth

This short trip features the unexcelled game parks of Tanzania: Serengeti, Ngorongoro, Manyara and Tarangire. These are among Africa's best game parks, full of wild animals in settings of unimaginable natural splendor (see *Tanzania Wildlife Safari* for further description). To keep costs down, accommodations on this trip are in lodges and permanent camps, and we travel by roof-hatched mini-vans with expert driver-guides.

Note: Due to seasonal animal migration, Trip #2 will not visit Ndutu but instead will tour Tarangire, a fabulous dry-season park.

Itinerary: Day 1 to 3: Leave U.S. Arrive Arusha, Tanzania.

Day 4: Drive to Lake Manyara. Afternoon game drive.

Day 5 and 6: Explore the Ndutu area of the Serengeti, the great open plains which are seasonally filled with migrating animals.

Day 7 and 8: Cross the plains and explore the Serengeti woodlands around Seronera, where year-round resident animals abound.

Day 9 and 10: Ngorongoro Crater! We stay on the Crater rim and enjoy a full day of game viewing on the teeming crater floor.

Day 11: Return to Arusha. Late evening departure on homeward-bound flights.

Day 12: Arrive home.

Dates: #1 Mar 7–Mar 18 (12 days)
#2 Jul 11–Jul 22
Leader: local guide
Grade: A-1
Land Cost: $2290 (10–15 members)
Single Supplement: $150
IT4KL1000CKR9

Encountering wildebeests on the short grass plains of the Serengeti/
Allen Bechky

Private Trips

In addition to our regular programs, we can make arrangements for private groups or individuals in Kenya, Tanzania, Rwanda, Zambia, Botswana, Zimbabwe and Egypt.

Ideally, a group of four or more persons is the best number from a cost standpoint, but we will make arrangements for individuals and couples.

Let us know your travel dates, number in party, and lodging preferences about three months (or more) in advance of your proposed trip so we can plan an exact itinerary for you and quote a cost.

Kilimanjaro Hiking

Mt. Kilimanjaro, the "mountain of springs," is a challenge to strong hikers but those who have trekked to its summit know that the effort is well rewarded —to stand on its glaciers and look down over the hot African plains is an unforgettable thrill. We offer a six-day hike starting from the forests at 7,000 feet and pushing upward to Uhuru Peak (19,340′). Accommodations are in alpine huts and porters carry the gear. This is a great addition to our Tanzania Wildlife Safari and many other East Africa trips.

Time: Seven days. Season: Most of the year (avoid April/May and October/November).

Rwanda Tracking Optional Tour

Tracking the Great Apes through the misty forests of Virunga Volcanoes is one of the most unique wildlife experiences imaginable. We can arrange gorilla tracking options in conjunction with many of our regular East Africa trips.

Time: Four days or longer. Season: All year except November, April, May.

Zambia: The Luangwa Valley Foot Safari Optional Tour

Zambia's Luangwa Valley is one of Africa's premier national parks. Massive concentrations of wildlife inhabit its vast wooded plains. More than 60,000 elephants live here, and the park's 2000 rhinos are the last truly viable population of that endangered species. With an armed ranger and naturalist guide, one can take a marvelous five-day "foot safari" in the game-filled bushlands. This option works well with our Botswana and Zimbabwe safaris.

Party size: Four or more. Time: Eight days or longer. Season: June through November.

Our Man in Kenya

Iain Allan, managing director of Mountain Travel Kenya, was born in Scotland and educated in Kenya, where he has lived since he was nine. He worked for a time in London as a journalist and returned to Kenya to become a professional safari guide. Iain is very knowledgeable on African wildlife, speaks fluent Swahili and is deeply involved in Kenya's wildlife conservation problems. A mountaineer of note, he has pioneered new routes on both Mt. Kenya and Kilimanjaro and is author of the definitive trekking and climbing guidebook to both these peaks.

On the Machame Route, Kilimanjaro/ *Allen Bechky*

About Camping Safaris in Africa

Mountain Travel's Africa trips are deluxe camping experiences with such amenities as walk-in safari tents, bathroom tent and shower tent. We travel by "go anywhere" landrover (not minibus or truck), with four or five persons plus driver. A landrover is the classic safari vehicle, allowing maximum game viewing and photographic opportunities.

Our camp staff does all camp chores and prepares good meals from fresh local supplies. We maintain a very high standard of camp hygiene.

We are the leading operator of "special interest" tours such as camel treks, mountain hikes and wildlife safaris on foot. Our leaders have extensive experience in Africa and are there to instruct you in the "rules of the bush."

Our campsites are chosen for their scenic appeal and wilderness isolation. When safari lodges are required, we use deluxe facilities which combine charm and wilderness atmosphere.

Masai wanderer/ *Allen Bechky*

For private trips let us know your travel dates, number in party and lodging preferences about three months (or more) in advance of your proposed trip so we can plan an exact itinerary for you and quote a cost/ *Leo Le Bon*

Rwanda/Zaire Gorilla Expedition

In search of the Great Apes

This is an adventurous safari into the heart of Africa, that mysterious part of Africa first explored 100 years ago by H.M. Stanley, the continent's most celebrated explorer. Here tall tropical forests stand in sight of snow-capped peaks and the jungle floor still shakes from the upheavals of active volcanoes.

Our prime objective here will be to seek and observe mountain gorillas, the great apes protected in the lush parks of both Rwanda and Zaire.

In Rwanda, we first view the savannah wildlife of Akagera National Park, then move to the Virunga Volcanoes, prime gorilla country, a setting of lush, misty forests and giant vegetation.

Here several family groups of wild-living gorillas have become habituated to the presence of observers and can be approached quite closely in their natural habitat. In very small groups, we'll be able to sit down right in the middle of these gentle apes, observing them in their daily activities.

It is quite fair to say that no other wild animal has shown as much tolerance for quiet human observance. This is really a one-of-a-kind wildlife experience.

Crossing the border into Zaire, we visit Parc de Virunga for superb wildlife viewing, including elephants, hippos and buffalos.

In the forests around Mt. Hoyo, we take a dugout canoe ride down a forest river and hike for a day with Balese (Pygmy) hunters to observe their unique hunting techniques.

We shall then visit Zaire's Kahuzi-Biega National Park to track and watch another protected population of gorillas. The gorillas of Kahuzi-Biega are not as "tame" or accustomed to human observors as the Rwanda gorillas.

With our Batwa (Pygmy) guides, we walk through forests in search of the apes. Here we have better chances to witness such things as the hair-raising mock charges of unhabituated gorillas. We must be on our best behavior!

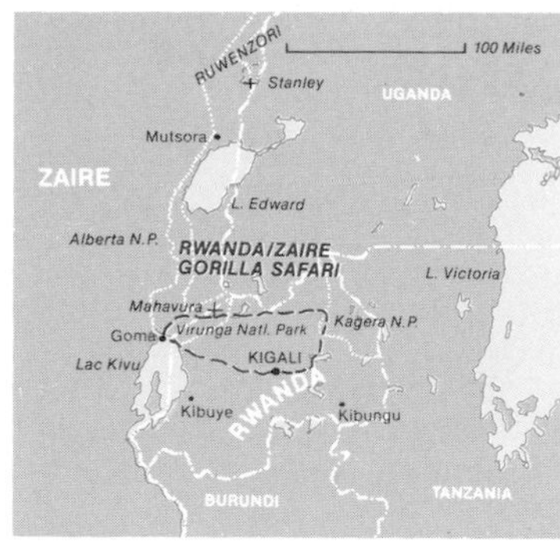

Itinerary: Day 1 and 2: Leave U.S.

Day 3 and 4: Arrive in Rwanda and proceed to Akagera National Park. Search for lion and roan antelope among herds of impala and topi.

Day 5: Drive to Virunga Volcanoes.

Day 6 to 8: Two days tracking gorillas. The third day, we can hike to the summit of Visoke Volcano (12,139') for fabulous mountain views (a third day of gorilla tracking is an optional alternative).

Day 9 and 10: Cross over to Zaire and visit Parc de Virunga.

Day 11: Scenic drive along the Lumbero Escarpment. The Virunga Volcanoes and Ruwenzori Range may be seen.

Day 12 and 13: With Balese (Pygmy) hunters in the forests of Mt. Hoyo.

Day 14 and 15: Drive through tropical forests en route to Goma on the shore of Lake Kivu.

Day 16 and 17: Gorilla tracking in Kahuzi-Biega Park with Batwa (Pygmy) guides.

Day 18: Return to Kigali, Rwanda. Depart on evening flights.

Day 19: Connect with homeward-bound flights.

Day 20: Arrive home.

Dates: #1 Jul 10–Jul 29 (20 days)
#2 Sep 4–Sep 23
Leader: to be announced
Grade: A-2
Land Cost: $3290
(10–11 members)
+domestic flts. $60
$3590 (6–9 members)
+domestic flts. $60
Single Supplement: $265
IT5SN1788

In the lush jungles of Virunga several family groups of wild-living gorillas have become habituated to the presence of observers and can be approached quite closely in their natural habitat. In very small groups, we'll be able to sit down right in the middle of these gentle apes, observing them in their daily activities/*Allen Bechky*

The Zimbabwe Expedition

Canoeing the Zambesi, game viewing at Hwange and Mana Pools

This special safari offers unique game viewing experiences: canoe, foot and landrover safaris.

Our first stop is Victoria Falls, the spectacular mile-wide cascade of the Zambesi River.

In Hwange National Park, we explore Zimbabwe's best known reserve. Located where the Kalahari sands meet the woodlands of central Africa, Hwange hosts what could be Africa's greatest variety of animals.

A four-day canoe safari on the Zambesi River gives a thrilling perspective on African bush game as we glide past hippo pools and sunning crocodiles, watching elephant and cape buffalo grazing along the banks. This historic river figured prominently in the epic explorations of Livingston and Stanley. We'll paddle down it in stable, easy-to-maneuver two-man canoes and camp under the stars at night.

At Mana Pools National Park, we explore an unvisited wilderness encompassing the vast game-filled flood plain of the Zambesi. Foot safaris with expert naturalists reveal the secrets of the African bush.

Note: At the end of the trip, we can arrange an optional five-day Luangwa Valley foot safari, an exciting walk to remote bush camps through a national park which is home to 60,000 elephant, 2,000 black rhino, and vast herds of buffalo. Hippos and crocodiles abound in the Luangwa River, and there are more than 400 species of birds in the park.

A four-day canoe safari on the Zambesi River gives a thrilling perspective on African bush game as we glide past hippo pools and sunning crocodiles, watching elephant and cape buffalo grazing along the banks/Dick McGowan

Itinerary: Day 1 to 3: Leave U.S. Arrive Victoria Falls, Zimbabwe.

Day 4: Tour Victoria Falls.

Day 5 and 6: Game viewing in Hwange National Park. Its dry semi-desert landscape teems with a fantastic variety of wildlife. Everything from aardvark to zebra may be found, including both black and white rhino.

Day 7: Fly to Kariba.

Day 8 to 11: Canoe safari on the Zambesi. We paddle through Kariba Gorge and out onto the broad floodplain of the great river, finishing at Rukomechi Camp at the Mana Pools National Park.

Day 12 and 13: Explorations by foot and by landrover of the undiscovered Rukomechi area. This is one of the wildest areas in Zimbabwe and promises especially exciting foot safaris, stalking elephant, buffalo, lion, waterbuck and kudu.

Day 14 and 15: Drive to Kariba and depart on homeward-bound flights.

Day 16: Arrive U.S.

Dates: #1 May 22–Jun 6 (16 days)
#2 Aug 7–Aug 22
#3 Oct 2–Oct 17
Leader: to be announced
Grade: B-1
Land Cost: $2150
(7–14 members)
+domestic flt. $100
Single Supplement: $250
IT5SA1NO40

Victoria Falls/Dick McGowan

Botswana Camping Safari

Kalahari bushmen, Okavango Delta landrover exploration

This is a true expedition, a journey into a very wild and remote land, traveling by four-wheel drive vehicle and carrying our own mobile camps.

An extended visit to Botswana's great wildlife areas allows for a special feature: a fascinating visit to the Tsodilo Hills to meet the legendary wanderers of the Kalahari, the !Kung bushmen. These self-sufficient hunter-gathers still practice the consumate bushcraft which enables them to master living in the harsh Kalahari thirstlands.

Our extensive wildlife observations take place in the celebrated Okavango Delta, where we travel by boat to get to the heart of this great marsh, a gentle wilderness where lechwe (antelope) stamp through the grassy shallows and hippo and crocs reside in the sparkling waters. The birdlife is spectacular.

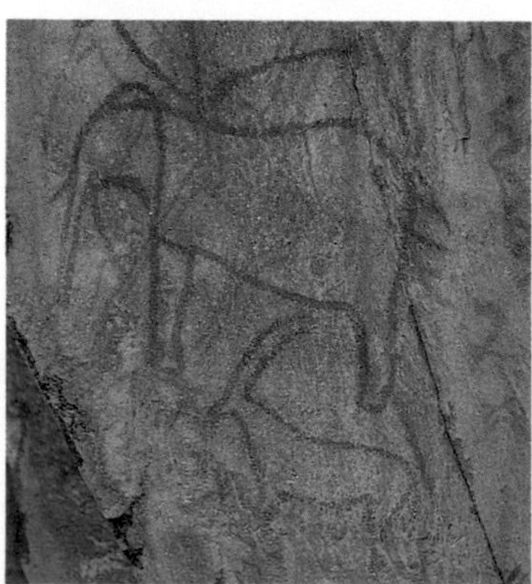

Bushmen paintings, Botswana/
Allen Bechky

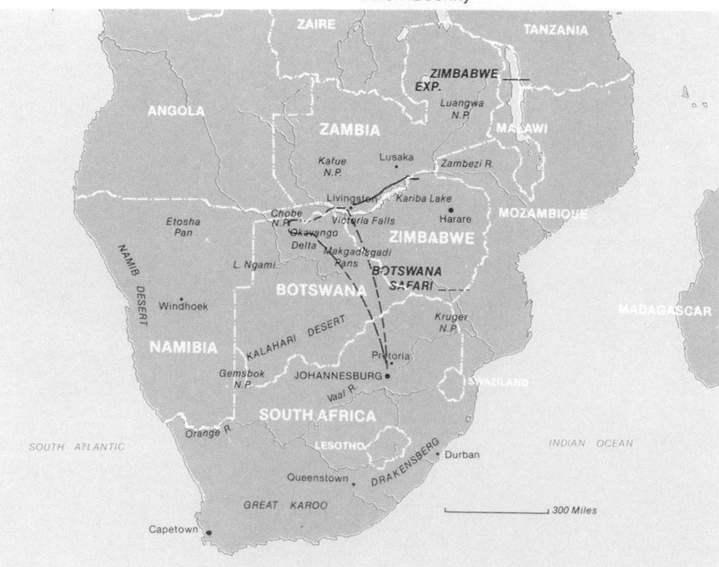

We also visit Moremi Wildlife Reserve and famed Chobe National Park (see *The Botswana Safari* for more details on Chobe and Moremi).

We end with a visit to Mosi-oa-Tunya ("the smoke that thunders"), better known as Victoria Falls.

Itinerary: Day 1 and 2: Leave U.S. Arrive Johannesburg, South Africa. Transfer to hotel.

Day 3 to 5: Fly to Maun, Botswana, for a charter flight into Xaxaba Camp in the Okavango Delta. After a night at Xaxaba, we board makoros, the traditional dugout canoes of the Delta natives, and paddle into the waterways of the Delta, for fishing, swimming and wildlife viewing. We camp on the larger Delta islands.

Day 6: We take a charter flight to the Tsodilo Hills. View ancient Bushman rock paintings and meet a group of !Kung hunters. Charter flight back to Maun.

Day 7 and 8: Drive to Moremi Game Reserve, one of the most interesting and beautiful reserves of southern Africa.

Day 9 to 13: We explore Chobe National Park, camping wherever game concentrations are thickest: Savuti, Tsinga, and Serondella camps.

Day 14 and 15: Drive across the Zimbabwe border to Victoria Falls. Check into the elegant Victoria Falls Hotel and visit this spectacular waterfall which has a flow of more than 120 million gallons per minute in flood!

Day 16: Fly to Johannesburg. Overnight in hotel.

Day 17: Tour Praetoria, historic capital of South Africa. Evening departure on homeward-bound flights.

Day 18: Arrive home.

Dates: #1 Aug 1–Aug 18 (18 days)
#2 Oct 3–Oct 20
Leader: Colin Bell
Grade: B-2
Land Cost: $1650
(5–15 members)
Single Supplement: $200
IT5SA1NO41

The Botswana Safari

Okavango Delta Park, Moremi Game Reserve, Savuti Channel

A visit to Botswana is always an adventure, but this trip features deluxe permanent camps which conform to the highest standards of safari accommodations.

The Okavango Delta, a huge expanse of wilderness wetlands, is a place of extraordinary beauty and tranquility. The crystal-clear waters of the "swamp" support a chain of life which finds its ultimate expression in the many thousands of water birds to be seen: a wide variety of storks, herons, ibises and other water birds including pygmy geese, malachite kingfishers and the magnificent African fish eagle. Larger wildlife includes abundant hippo and crocodile, and the unusual sitatunga and lechwe antelopes.

The Moremi Game Reserve is one of the most interesting and beautiful in southern Africa. Its mix of deciduous mopane woodlands and grasslands support antelope such as sassaby, kudu, impala and gnu as well as elephant, buffalo and the always-elusive predators: lion, leopard, cheetah and wild dog.

Chobe National Park features spectacular concentrations of elephant around its permanent water sources: the Savuti Channel, the marshes of the Mababe Depression, and the Chobe River. The trophy antelopes (sable, roan, and kudu) are all found here, while herds of zebra, giraffe and wildebeest support large prides of lions.

Itinerary: Day 1 and 2: Leave U.S. Arrive Johannesburg, South Africa.

Day 3: Fly to Victoria Falls, one of the most spectacular sights in Africa. Overnight at Victoria Falls Hotel.

Day 4 and 5: Drive into Botswana and explore the elephant country of Chobe National Park.

Day 6 and 7: Move to Savuti Channel, Botswana's finest wildlife area.

Day 8 and 9: We move to the Moremi Reserve, located on the eastern edge of the Okavango Delta, an ideal location from which to explore either the Delta swamps or the gamelands of Moremi.

Day 10 and 11: Move to Kubu Camp in the San-ta-wani area. Here we have a great choice of exploration activities: we explore Moremi on game drives, cruise the Delta channels on boats, and take walks through the bush in the company of rangers.

Day 12: Drive to Maun, fly to Johannesburg, depart on homeward-bound flights.

Day 13: Arrive home.

Dates: #1 Jun 9–Jun 21 (13 days)
#2 Jun 30–Jul 12
#3 Sep 15–Sep 27
Leader: to be announced
Grade: A-1
Land Cost: $1590
(8–15 members)
Single Supplement: $250
IT5SA1NO42

Special Departure:

Halley's Comet In Botswana

The South African skies promise to be an excellent viewing site for the arrival of Halley's comet. Join our special camping trip (in the company of an expert astronomer) to be part of this unique event.

Dates: Mar 28–Apr 14 (18 days)
Leader: to be announced
Grade: B-2
Land Cost: Approx. $1900
(5–15 members)
Single Supplement: $200
IT5SA1NO41

"Just passing through..."

ZIMBABWE
HARARE/ VICTORIA FALLS

City notes by Allen Bechky

In Harare (Zimbabwe's capital):

Day Trips:

Rent a car and visit Lake McIlwaine Game Park for hiking and birdwatching, where animals are in large natural enclosures. Or visit Ewinrigg Botanical Garden with its great native plant selection.

At Victoria Falls:

Take the "flight of angels," a charter flight with superb aerial views of Victoria Falls, or learn about the natural history and conservation of crocodiles while visiting a "crocodile farm," a commercial enterprise where crocs are raised for their skins.

Watch the nightly outdoor native dance displays at Victoria Falls Hotel, complete with traditional spirit costumes and the beat of native drums. Visit Falls Craft Village, where a 19th century Matabele village has been recreated and a witch doctor will cast the bones to foretell your future!

On the Zambesi itself, you can tour the falls by launch cruise or cross over to Zambia for an exciting one-day float through the dizzying gorge below Victoria Falls.

Lechwe antelopes. The Okavango Delta, a huge expanse of wilderness wetlands, is a place of extraordinary beauty and tranquility/*Allen Bechky*

Crocodiles in the Savuti Channel/*Allen Bechky*

Today, the Alps, stretching from the Mediterranean to the Adriatic, are rightly called "the playground of Europe," a haven for hikers, climbers and skiers/ *Susan Thiele*

SECTION IV
EUROPE & THE U.S.S.R.

"We returned to the southern end of the ridge to build a cairn, and then paid homage to the view. . . Ten thousand feet beneath us were the green fields of Zermatt, dotted with chalets, from which blue smoke rose lazily. Eight thousand feet below, on the other side, were the passes of Breuil. There were forests black and gloomy, meadows bright and lively; bounding waterfalls and tranquil lakes; fertile lands and savage wastes; sunny plains and frigid plateaus. There were the most rugged forms and the most graceful outlines—bold, perpendicular cliffs and gentle, undulating slopes; rocky mountains and snowy mountains, sombre and solemn or glittering and white, with walls, turrets, pinnacles, pyramids, domes, cones and spires! There was every combination that the world can give, and every contrast that the heart could desire."

Edward Whymper, on conquering the Matterhorn in 1865
from *Scrambles In The Alps*

200 years ago, the summits of the Alps were untouched by man. There were a few Roman trade routes pushed across the high passes, and Hannibal somehow managed to get his army on elephants across an alpine pass, but the peaks themselves remained mysterious and rather frightening.

Up until 1835, the only men who climbed above snowline were scientists like de Saussure and Agassiz, who struggled up with their instruments.

Then between 1855 and 1865 came the "Golden Age of Mountaineering." During this decade, every important peak in the Alps was climbed (24 of the 33 peaks over 12,000 feet were climbed by British). The men who climbed did so for the sheer joy of it, for the physical and emotional challenge. The sport of mountaineering was born.

After the climbers came the hikers, people who wanted to venture high enough to see the views they'd heard about and breathe the cool mountain air during hot summers. And by 1870, alpine enthusiasts even began to appear in the winter, principally the wealthy, who began "taking the waters" at new health spas high in the Swiss Alps.

By 1880, the Swiss Alpine Club had erected no less than 34 "huts" to shelter mountain travelers.

About this time came the ski-mountaineers, importing an ancient form of "adventure travel" which existed in Scandinavia as early as the 13th century.

By 1898, the little town of Chamonix, birthplace of mountaineering, was open for a "winter season," becoming the world's first four-season resort.

Today the Alps, stretching from the Mediterranean to the Adriatic, are rightly called "the playround of Europe," a haven for hikers, climbers and skiers.

Hikers on the Haute Route, Switzerland/ *Susan Thiele*

In what other great mountain range can you spend the day hiking across glaciers, toiling up ridges for hours on end and then descend to the valley on the other side for a big bowl of fresh pasta, a glass of red wine and a hot bath?/ *Susan Thiele*

Whymper praised the Alps for containing "every contrast that the heart could desire." And indeed they do. In what other great mountain range can you spend the day hiking across glaciers, toiling up ridges for hours and then descend to the valley on the other side for a big bowl of fresh pasta, a glass of red wine and a hot bath?

Despite the encroachment of man on the Alps, and despite the fact that every face has been climbed and every trail has been walked, these mountains retain a mystery and excitement like no other place on earth.

In Europe, the possibilities for adventure travel extend far and wide from the Alps . . . to Iceland, to camp in Skaftafell National park surrounded by Europe's largest glaciers, to Mt. Ararat in Turkey to look for the resting place of Noah's Ark, to Mother Russia, where American backpackers can now travel mountain passes from the Caucasus into Georgia.

Europe's season for hikers and climbers is generally May through October, at its peak in July.

Adventure Travel in Europe

Mountain pension in the Dolomites/ Dick McGowan

"Il Duomo," cathedral of Orvieto, Italy/ Leo Le Bon

Britain & Ireland:

If you want to climb or hike, don't miss Snowdonia National park, in the craggy wilds of Wales, where many a British Everest expedition trained. In England's Lake District, where some claim that the sport of rock climbing originated, there are unforgettable hill walks in an exquisite pastoral land which inspired Wordsworth, Ruskin, Shelley, Tennyson and others. Further north, the Scotland Highlands preserve Western Europe's greatest wilderness, and the Isle of Skye contains "the far Cuillins," limestone peaks rising above ancient clan castles. Wildlife enthusiasts will want to visit the Orkney Isles in the far north, with their great bird colonies.

Italy:

The Dolomites, with their sheer red-rock pinnacles, are the most famous hiking/climbing region in northeast Italy. In the northwest, hikers in nearby Val D'Aosta and Gran Paradiso National Park are rewarded with some of the best views of the Matterhorn and Mont Blanc. The Lombardia region is less known and less traveled, yet offers some of the best alpine scenery in Italy. In Piemonte, the mountains are literally "foothills" and the cultural encounters with local Ousitanes are unique.

The Dolomites, with their sheer red-rock pinnacles, are the most famous hiking/climbing region in northeast Italy/ *Dick McGowan*

Mountain Travel's 'Trekking in the Pyrenees' group/*Pierre Jamet*

Switzerland, France:

In the Pennine Alps, greatest concentration of high mountains in Europe, the ice-bound frontiers of Switzerland, Italy and France come together. On a hiking circuit around Mont Blanc, one can pass through all three countries. In the Bernese Alps, entirely within Switzerland, there are hikes with views of the famous "North Wall of the Alps:" the Eiger, the Monch and Jungfrau. In the gentler Jura Mountains along the Swiss/French border, a winter visit is a chance to experience cross-country skiing at its best.

Germany/Austria:

The hut system of these countries allows visits to the Tyrolian and Bavarian Alps, with their pastoral setting of orchards, hayfields, meadows and the snowy summits of the Ortler Alps and the Wetterstein Alps. In the winter, this region is a paradise for ski touring.

Czechoslovakia & Poland:

The adventurer will be principally attracted to the High Tatras, a mountain range on the Czech-Polish frontier. With many 8,000-foot peaks, it is fine terrain for hut-to-hut hikes.

Greece & Crete:

Hut-to-hut hiking in the mountains above Sparta is one way to visit rural Greece; another might be to charter a *kaiki* with captain and crew and sail to little-visited islands where the old Greek way of life can be found. In Crete, a classic two-day hike follows the rugged Gorge of Samaria from the mountains to the sea.

Spain, Portugal:

In Spain, hike the Pyrenees, with their Yosemite-like canyons or the Sierra de Guara, a desert landscape much like the U.S.'s southwest. The "Picos de Europa" range offers hikes in dramatic alpine gorges. In Portugal, walks in rural wine country are always rewarding, as is a trip out to the lush isle of Madeira, with its well-maintained hiking paths and ocean views.

San Jean Pied-de-Port, a Basque village/*Martin Zabaleta*

Seritos Island. Hiking in the mountains above Sparta is one way to visit rural Greece; another might be to charter a kaiki, shown above, with captain and crew and sail to little-visited islands where the old Greek way of life can be found/*Allen Steck*

Cappadocia, with its rock-hewn chapels, cave dwellings and monasteries is a fascinating trip/*Leo Le Bon*

Norway, Iceland:

Norway's national parks in winter are the place to experience the best cross-country skiing in the world, in the land in which the sport originated. In the summer, the Jotunheimen Mountains offer great hut-to-hut hikes in craggy fjord-country which was the setting for Ibsen's *Peer Gynt.* Iceland's national parks offer geology-buffs a look at a new land which is still growing and changing—as witnessed in its creaking glaciers, smoking volcanoes, and bubbling geysers. Ornithologists will find that Iceland's wildlife is primarily winged—with more than 240 species of migrant birds visiting annually, and 76 species nesting regularly.

Turkey:

Any time spent in Turkey, heart of historic Asia Minor, is an adventure! The attractions here are non-technical climbs of Mt. Ararat, Biblical resting place of Noah's Ark, where summit views extend into Soviet Armenia and Iran (special permits are required for this climb). Week-long treks in the limestone Taurus Mountains on the southern coast and the Kachkar Range along the Black Sea allow the visitor an unusual look into village life.

U.S.S.R.

The U.S.S.R.'s International Mountaineering Camps, in operation since the early 1970's, take place in the most remote and scenic mountain areas of the Soviet Union: the Caucasus of Eastern Europe, the Pamirs, the Tien Shan and Kazakhstan regions of Central Asia. The camps are very moderately priced and geared to self-sufficient hikers, climbers and backpackers. This is the only permitted way to explore mountian regions in the U.S.S.R.

Backpacking in the Caucasus. The U.S.S.R.'s International Mountaineering Camps take place in the most remote and scenic areas of the Soviet Union: the Caucasus of Eastern Europe, the Pamirs, the Tien Shan and Kazakhstan in Central Asia/*Louise McGowan*

Europe Bibliography

ITALIAN ALPS
Douglas Freshfield, Basil R. Blackwell, 1937. A classic.

HUTS AND HIKES IN THE DOLOMITES
Ruth Rudner, Sierra Club, 1974.

FOOTLOOSE IN THE SWISS ALPS
William E. Reifsnyder, Sierra Club, 1979.

HUT HOPPING IN THE AUSTRIAN ALPS
William E. Reifsnyder, Sierra Club, 1973.

100 HIKES IN THE ALPS
Ira Spring and Harvey Edwards, Mountaineers, 1979.

WALKING IN THE ALPS
Brian Spencer, Moorland Publishing, 1981.

WANDERING: A WALKER'S GUIDE TO THE MOUNTAIN TRAILS OF EUROPE
Ruth Rudner, Dial, 1972.

SCRAMBLES IN THE ALPS
Edward Whymper, Ten Speed Press, 1981. Reprint of a classic.

THE NATIONAL TRUST BOOK OF LONG WALKS
Adam Nicolson, Weidenfeld & Nicolson, 1981. Walking in Britain.

CLASSIC WALKS
Ken Wilson and Richard Gilbert, Diadem, 1982. Mountain and moorland walks in Britain and Ireland.

STORM AND SORROW IN THE HIGH PAMIRS
Robert W. Craig, Mountaineers, 1977. Mountaineering expedition in the Pamirs.

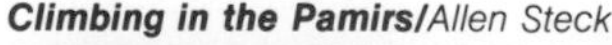

Climbing in the Pamirs/*Allen Steck*

Ascending Noah's Mountain

by Richard McMahon

I watched anxiously as the drivers urged their horses and mules upward, struggling and stumbling in the steep scree. Soon they began cursing and shouting among themselves. it seemed the exhausted animals could go no further.

Our climbing party had reached the high camp location by another route, taking us over huge boulders which the animals could not negotiate. Observing the baggage party far below us in distress, I had descended to their position. I stood there now, beside Ray Jewell, our leader from Mountain Travel, who was discussing the situation with Fehmi Hasanoglu, our Turkish guide.

"Maybe the drivers will have to carry the gear the rest of the way," said Ray.

"The Kurds will rent you their horses, but never themselves," answered Fehmi. "They will not carry a burden that they feel should be borne by an animal."

The drivers began unloading our baggage, still arguing with each other and bellowing at the defeated animals. "Then how will we get our supplies to the high camp?"

Fehmi turned toward me. *"Allah Karim,"* he smiled. God will provide.

We had begun our journey to Noah's mountain from various points in the United States, a party of seven men and three women, under Ray Jewell's informal and delightful leadership. At our rendezvous point in Istanbul, we were met by Mr. Fikret Gurbuz, who had secured the necessary permits for the climb. I arrived a day earlier than the rest of the group, and Fikret met me at the airport.

"Agri Dagi (Ah-ree Dah-uh), is what we Turks call Mount Ararat," he informed me, as we enjoyed a magnificent seafood dinner on the shores of the Bosporus. "Few people realize it is so high." Ararat soars thirteen thousand feet from the alluvial plain of the Aras River, which is

The food in Turkey is delicious!/ *Leo Le Bon*

itself nearly four thousand feet above sea level. Reaching a total elevation of 16,945 feet, it is visible from as far as 100 miles away. An extinct volcano, Ararat stands in majestic isolation in easternmost Turkey, less than twenty miles from the Russian and Iranian borders.

"That is why it was 'off limits' to foreigners for so long," Fikret told me. "The Russians accused us of allowing spying from the top." He shrugged. "Since our government opened the mountain again, there has been much interest in climbing."

I thought of some earlier climbs: the monk, Aftonomov, in 1834, who wanted to see if the stars could be seen from the highest mountains; the geologist Abich, in 1845; and General Chodzko's party in 1850, while making a topographic survey of the Caucasus. And I had recently read James Bryce's account of his climb in 1876.

The town of Dogubayazit, our starting point for the Ararat climb, lies astride the main road to Iran. "There used to be much traffic on this road," said Fehmi. "Trucks bringing goods all the way from Europe. But since the war between Iran and Iraq . . ." He shrugged.

From our hotel window, a vast arid plain stretched for miles. But the dominant feature was Ararat, its massive bulk less than twenty miles away. Starting out from our hotel early in the morning, we had crowded into the bed of a large pick-up truck for a two hour ride to the small village

Mountain Travel trip leader Ray Jewell, with Turkish farmers/*Leo Le Bon*

of Eli. Here, the mountain looming above us, we transferred our baggage to the animal team, and started out on foot.

The walk was leisurely and scenic, traversing the broad grasslands that were summer pasture for the Kurds, occasionally passing through their encampments. They greeted us with pitchers of *ayran,* a popular drink made by mixing yoghurt and water. Recalling Bryce's record of his 1876 climb, I was reminded how some things never change, for he had written, "They brought us bowls of sourish milk mixed with water, a frequent drink in these countries, and we found it refreshing." Although it was only mid-August, pasturage was becoming sparse, and some of the rock-walled enclosures that housed the tents were already empty, the inhabitants departed to their winter settlements.

Some five hours later we had arrived at our base camp. Located at the high end of a green meadow, we found tents already pitched, a lamb slaughtered, and our cook busily preparing supper. Fehmi noticed that one of our party had left his Swiss Army knife lying on a rock. He picked it up. "You should not do this," he said, looking at me.

"The Kurds would steal it?"

"Perhaps they would be tempted to take it. But they would not consider it stealing. Your packs or other things lying beside your tents, are perfectly safe. But if you leave something like this on the ground," he said, holding up the knife, "and then walk away, they conclude that you have no respect for it, or that it is not important to you. It is very important to them." But despite Fehmi's warning, with our usual carelessness, we continued to leave our things around the campsite. Yet nothing ever turned up missing.

As the lamb sizzled over a roaring fire, my thoughts had turned to these hardy, tribal people who, although mostly Muslims, often display the aquiline features and fair coloring which suggests descent from Nordic stock.

The next day's climb was rugged. A full day of rock hopping proved tiring, but not nearly as difficult as the trail up through the scree that the animals had been forced to use. I was only too familiar with that type of climbing: an exhausting process of two steps forward then one lost as sliding gravel gave way beneath boots. I did not envy the Kurdish drivers who had to follow their animals, urging them upward.

Ray, Fehmi and the Kurdish drivers were huddled in a small circle. The shouting had finally stopped and the conversation was subdued and serious. The rest of us, since we did not speak the language of these proud mountain people could only watch and wait. At last the group dispersed. The drivers returned to their animals and Ray came over, smiling.

"The drivers will leave our baggage here," he announced, "and return to base camp with the animals. The young boys who work at the camp will come up and carry the baggage the rest of the way. Because they haven't reached manhood yet, Fehmi says it's not undignified for them to do it." The problem was solved and the expedition saved. *Allah Karim.* God had provided.

The high camp was now established on a small, rocky plateau, just beneath the snow line, at 13,700 feet. Miles distant, and nine thousand feet below, we could just make out the town of Dogubayazit, our starting point two days earlier. Above, huge volcanic rocks stretched an almost endless distance to the massive summit glacier, an icy cap which never melted. The following morning, we would

Leo Le Bon

"the mountain loomed above us. We transferred our baggage to the animal team and started on foot...."/
Ray Jewell

The Turkish countryside/Leo Le Bon

begin our attempt on the peak, only flashlights to guide us over the great blocks of black basalt.

August 14th, 2 A.M.—a cold, but crystal clear sky. We stumbled about in our parkas like great shaggy bears, gathering around the small stove as if it could actually provide some warmth. An early start was essential if we were to arrive on the summit before noon, when the weather would be at its best.

Halis Ceven, a resident of the area, would lead the way to the summit. Dressed to the teeth and still shivering, we marveled at Halis, who wore only a light jacket over his coveralls, and a pair of tennis shoes. He seemed quite comfortable.

While we labored in the thinning air, Halis sang and danced his way up the slope, starlight his only illumination. He stopped frequently, waiting for us to catch up, never letting us out of his sight.

At dawn, we crossed several tongues of ice and snow, outriders of the great summit glacier. Halis stamped footsteps in the crust with his smooth soles, and we, in our sturdy mountain boots with their cleated bottoms, followed somewhat ignominiously in the path made by his humble tennis shoes.

The rising sun brought a welcome warmth, but an unwelcome increase in wind velocity as well. We found ourselves now more frequently on ice and snow, and less on the black rock, until, cresting a small ridge, we saw the icy white world of the summit glacier stretching before us. Halis stopped and replaced his tennis shoes with a pair of boots.

"Aha, I see he is human after all," commented Eve Bruenger, one of our two women climbers who had come this far.

We began roping up. "There are a few crevasses," explained Fehmi, as he checked the knots. "They are not wide, but it is best to be safe."

We were all feeling the effects of the altitude. The long saddle between the knoll where we had donned our crampons and the dome-shaped peak ahead was a relatively gentle slope, yet our breath came in labored gasps. Crampons came loose, simply because freezing hands and oxygen-starved minds had been too clumsy to strap them on properly. We reached the base of the dome and the climb became steeper. Ice now replaced the hard snow crust of the saddle and we were forced to chop steps. Painfully, we struggled upward. Almost abruptly, we crested a wide rise. Aghast,I saw another long saddle stretching before us, leading to a high distant peak. It seemed at least half a mile away. My heart sank. I was not sure that I could go that far. But Halis was jumping up and down, embracing the other members of the party, who were untying ropes, shaking hands and fumbling for their cameras. Fehmi came up from the rear and clapped me on the back. Mutely, I pointed to the distant peak. He shook his head.

"That is the eastern summit," he yelled in my ear. "We are standing on the western one, which is the highest."

Halis grabbed my arm and pointed to the northeast. "Erevan," he shouted. Far below, we could see that Russian city, capital of Soviet Armenia, glinting in the sunlight across the Aras valley. And, on the northern horizon, we could barely make out the peaks of the Caucasus Mountains, well over a hundred miles away.

In the elation of attaining the peak, we had forgotten the cold, but it was quick to reassert itself. The wind had not diminished and it tore viciously at our parka hoods and other loose items of clothing. It was ten A.M.; time to descend.

We roped again and started down. We had a long way to go, by-passing the plateau where we had spent the night and descending all the way to the main camp. But the wind was at our backs, and the view, which we could now enjoy, was magnificent. Mercifully, tired as we were, the altitude did not interfere with our downhill efforts. Far below, in the distance, the town of Dogubayazit beckoned. It was two days away, but hot showers, good food and warm beds awaited. It seemed a sufficient reward.

Mr. McMahon was a member of our MT. ARARAT & THE TAURUS MOUNTAINS trek in Turkey.

Turkish family/Leo Le Bon

Our exceptionally talented staff of European trip leaders have skills, enthusiasm and an understanding of the local culture which adds immeasurably to the success of each trip.

MIKE BANKS, 59, is one of Britains's leading polar explorers and mountaineers. He was awarded the Polar Medal by Queen Elizabeth for his epic 800-mile crossing of the Greenland icecap, and received the M.B.E. (Member of the British Empire) for climbing Rakaposhi (25,550′) without oxygen. His wife, Pat, is a radio-TV journalist.

HELGI BENEDIKTSSON, 28, is a mountaineer, skier, and founding member of the Icelandic Alpine Club with many first ascents in the Icelandic Mountains. He is a professional mountain guide, mountain rescue instructor and has also climbed in the Alps and on Mt. McKinley.

ROD BUNTZ, 64, is a retired colonel in the French Marine Corps and a world traveler who with his wife, Maryvonne, leads the "Other France" walking tours.

SILVANA CAMUS, 37, is a skier and mountaineer who lives in the mountains of Italy. She has led trekking expeditions in Nepal, Ethiopia, Bhutan, Canada (with huskies) and New Guinea.

ANGUS ERSKINE regularly takes visitors around the Scottish Highlands (in between his Arctic expeditions). He is an experienced mountain guide well versed in the history, folklore and natural history of North Britain.

PIETRO GIGLIO, 41, is one of the best known mountaineer-guides in the Val D'Aosta region of Italy. He has climbed many of the most difficult rock and ice routes in the European Alps and has led treks in Morocco, northern Europe and Greenland.

AVNER GOREN, 38, born in Jerusalem, has a B.A. in archaeology and Jewish history and is completing his thesis in archaeology. He has worked for 13 years as a resident archaeologist in Greece, Turkey, the Sinai and Israel.

MAKI IDOSIDIS, 39, is a Greek mountaineer who divides his time between living in Greece and the U.S. He knows Greece well, is a fine Greek dancer and leads our Greek sailing journeys.

Wolfgang Koch

Rodolphe and Maryvonne Buntz

Paddy O'Leary

PIERRE JAMET, 52, of France, leads mountain treks and ski tours in France, Switzerland, Italy and Austria. A mathematics professor turned trekking guide, he has been a member of several climbing expeditions in Nepal and India.

WOLFGANG KOCH, 33, of Stuttgart, is a chemist by profession and has been hiking, skiing and climbing in Europe for many years. He knows the German and Tyrolean Alps and along with his wife, Renate, leads Bavarian hiking tours.

SHANAN MILLER, an Australian and now resident of Britain, has traveled extensively in Africa, Asia and South America and leads treks full-time in the Alps and mountains of Asia.

Maki Idosidis *on left*

Mike and Pat Banks

Pierre Jamet

Angus Erskine

Shanan Miller

Silvana Camus

Helgi Benediktsson

PADDY O'LEARY, 49, director of Ireland's National Association for Adventure Sports, has 25 years of mountaineering experience in Britain and the Alps and has led expeditions in the Karakorum, Himalayas and Andes.

MARTIN ZABALETA, 35, is a Basque mountaineer who in 1981 became the first Spaniard to climb to the summit of Mt. Everest. He has worked professionally as both a safari leader and climbing guide and has a passion for nature photography and Basque cuisine.

Martin Zabaleta

The Other Britain

Walking tour from Cornwall to Yorkshire

This tour reveals Britain from a totally fresh viewpoint, striking a balance between sightseeing and day hiking, finding Britain's favorite walks among tranquil hills and along windswept cliff paths from Cornwall to Wales to Yorkshire. With Mike Banks, British author and mountaineer, and his wife Pat, we will discover the lovely unspoiled rural England that the English themselves enjoy.

Starting in legend-laden Cornwall, we shall hike its spectacular coastline, explore hidden fishing coves, and ramble over lonely Dartmoor in Devon.

We'll enjoy the elegance of Georgian Bath and visit medieval Cotswolds villages before crossing the border to spend three days in Wales, land of song, castles and mountains.

In the Lake District, we will hike its fells and follow its becks to the famous waters that inspired Beatrix Potter to weave her fairytale world, and by which still stands Dove Cottage, where Wordsworth lived and wrote.

Coastal paths of Cornwall/*Mike Banks*

In Yorkshire we hike through "James Herriot country" and visit the ancient walled city of York, one of Britain's historical treasures, still entered by its medieval gates.

Best of all, we will constantly be meeting friendly British people, in their own homes and in their equally friendly pubs.

The tour finishes with a night's stay in Dallington Hall, an elegant country castle, where we will be the welcome guests of the owner, Robert Spencer, cousin of Princess Diana, future Queen of England.

Travel is by two comfortable minibuses. Accommodations are in small country hotels of character.

Itinerary: Day 1 and 2: Leave U.S. Arrive London, and enjoy a relaxed drive to the West-country, calling at mystic Stonehenge. Overnight at an ancient coaching inn in the historic town of Wells, Somerset.

Day 3: Continue west to Devon to hike Dartmoor's haunted wilderness and glimpse its wild ponies. Stroll the cobbled streets of historic Plymouth.

Day 4 to 6: To Celtic Cornwall, land of King Arthur, to enjoy its rugged coastline, old smugglers' coves and taverns. Then on to Bath, the elegant Georgian spa built over an ancient Roman city.

Day 7: Drive through the Cotswolds, villages of honey-colored stone cottages and 14th century wool merchant's houses with flower-filled gardens.

Day 8 to 10: Over the border into Wales, we hike along Offa's Dyke, the great entrenchment built on the frontier in A.D. 785, then explore Snowdonia National Park, visit a woolen mill and a massive medieval castle. Evening banquet in ancient Ruthin Castle.

Day 11 and 12: Walks in the Lake District.

Day 13 to 15: Driving east to Yorkshire, we explore narrow cobbled streets, museums and colorful taverns.

Day 16: Drive south to Northhampton and stay in Dallington, a magnificent private home.

Day 17: Drive to London with afternoon at leisure.

Day 18: Depart London and connect with homeward-bound flights.

Dates: #1 Jun 12–Jun 29
(18 days)
#2 Aug 14–Aug 31
Leader: Mike & Pat Banks
Grade: A-1
Land Cost: $1790
(10–12 members)
$1990 (8–9)
Single Supplement: $175
IT5BA1YO55

"Just passing through..."

LONDON

City notes by Mike Banks and John Cleare

Local walking/jogging routes:

Try a walk from the West End (say Picadilly Circus) to the city via Covent Garden, Lincolns Inn Fields, Lincolns Inn, Chancery Lane, Fleet Street, Ludgate Hill and St. Paul's Cathedral. The "London Walks" program is highly recommended: skilled guides takes you on special interest walks (i.e., Sherlock Holmes or Dickens' London). Pick up the leaflet at any London tourist office. Joggers will delight in London's parks—a run from Hyde Park to Green Park to St. James Park can be linked, and there is good jogging also in Regent's Park and Hampstead Heath.

Day trips:

Visit Kew Gardens, about 15 miles out of town, one of the world's finest botanical gardens. Take a day trip by river boat to Greenwich to visit the Maritine Museum, clipper "Cutty Sark," and Greenwich's Royal Observatory. The nearest rock climbing center to London is Turnbridge Wells, 30 miles away.

Special shops:

Visit Stanfords Map Shop (south side of Long Acre in Covent Garden), full of every map published in the world and all sorts of guidebooks.

Museums:

London is famous for them! If you've seen all the big ones, try little ones such as the Wallace Collection in Manchester Square.

Cornish garden/*Mike Banks*

Stonehenge/*Mike Banks*

Britain & Ireland trips include: twin accommodations in hotels, breakfasts (lunches and dinners on your own), ground transportation by mini-bus, entrance fees, airport transfers, leadership.

Highland Hikes Of North Britain

The Lake District and Scottish Highlands

The aim of this hiking trip is to venture over the peaks, passes and valleys of north England's "Lake District" and the famous Highlands of Scotland.

In the Lake District, all that is needed, said the poet Wordsworth, is "an eye to perceive and a heart to enjoy." Here in the land of Wordsworth and Coleridge, we hike up Scafell Pikes, Great Gable and Helvellyn, some of the most scenic corners of this "miniature Switzerland." There will also be time to visit the Lake District's beautiful villages, farms and tarns, some of which were the locations of Beatrix Potter's books for children.

Moving north to the Scottish Highlands, hills of purple heather, rock and rowan tree, we will hike Britain's highest mountain, Ben Nevis (4,406'), and view the wooded slopes around the Trossaches, scene of Sir Walter Scott's poems and novels. We also hike over such craggy summits as Ben Lawers, Cairngorm and Glas Maol, and have plenty of time to see the banks of Loch Lomond, visit ancient castles and watch the local whisky being distilled (perhaps sample some). Accommodations are in small hotels.

Itinerary: Day 1 and 2: Leave U.S. and arrive Prestwick, Ayrshire. Drive to Carlisle, visit Hadrian's Wall, continue to Lake District. Overnight at hotel.

Day 3 and 4: Hike up Great Gable, Scafell Pikes, Helvellyn (3,116') and visit Dove Cottage, the Wordsworth Museum.

Day 5 to 7: Drive north to Aberfoyle and hike up Ben Venue (2,393') and Ben Ledi (2,873'), which has a superb view from its summit. Overnights at hotel.

Day 8: Drive to Loch Tay and climb Ben Lawers (3,984').

Day 9: Drive to Cairnwell Pass and walk to the summit of Glas Maol (3,502').

Day 10: Sightseeing drive into the Dee Valley for a distant view of Balmoral, the Queen's highland residence. Visit Craigievar Castle and a whisky distillery to see the intricacies of whisky-making.

Day 11 and 12: The mountain range called "The Cairngorms" is the largest area of wilderness in Britain. Hike up Cairngorm, Ben Macdui (4,296'), and Braeriach (4,248').

Day 13: Drive to Inverness, "capital" of the Highlands, and then proceed to Loch Ness, keeping a sharp eye for "Nessie," the monster. Visit Castle Urquhart and continue down the Great Glen to Fort William.

Day 14: Weather permitting, make a long climb up a well-marked trail to the summit of Ben Nevis (4,406').

Day 15: Drive south to Glencoe, Scotland's most dramatic glen, and along a road which winds down the west side of Loch Lomond.

Day 16: Hike up Ben Lomond (3,192').

Day 17: Drive to Prestwick and connect with homeward-bound flights.

Dates: #1 Jun 15–Jul 1 (17 days)
#2 Sep 7–Sep 23
Leader: Angus Erskine
Grade: B-2
Land Cost: $1190
(10–12 members)
$1290 (6–9)
Single Supplement: $125
IT5BA1YO54

Ireland & Britain Walking

This tour combines walks in Ireland, Wales, England and Scotland all in one trip.

A week-long Irish ramble will take us through the lake-dotted territory of "the Ferocious O'Flaherty's," and the Atlantic-washed haunts of the great pirate queen, Grace O'Malley. We'll visit the fabled "Mountains of Mourne" overlooking the Irish Sea, and walk in a lovely green landscape filled with Ireland's storied past, including 4000-year-old dolmens, early Christian settlements and Norman castles.

Crossing by ferry to Scotland, we hike in the Border country and visit Edinburgh, Scotland's elegant capital city.

Journeying south, we walk Hadrian's Wall, the greatest military artifact of the Roman Empire. South again, via Durham's majestic Norman cathedral, we explore the hills and dales of Yorkshire, then drive to Chester, an ancient city still with medieval walls.

Driving southwest into Somerset, we spend a memorable night as private guests at Forde Abbey, a country castle founded in 1141 A.D. as a Cistercian monastery. The trip ends with a day in London to enjoy its famous museums and theatres.

Itinerary: Day 1 and 2: Leave U.S. Arrive Shannon. Meet trip leader and drive to County Clare. Walk along the 700-foot Cliffs of Moher.

Day 3: Hike in the Burren and drive around Galway Bay, a Gaelic-speaking area.

Day 4: Drive north to Westport, County Mayo, and hike on Achill Island.

Day 5: Travel through County Mayo and Sligo, visiting the haunts of poet W.B. Yeats, then through lake country to Enniskillen in Northern Ireland.

Day 6: Visit the cathedral city of Armagh and hike the famous Mountains of Mourne along the Brandy Pad, an old smugglers' trail.

Day 7: Drive to Dublin. Visit the favorite pubs of playwrights Behan and O'Casey, and enjoy Irish music in the Abbey Tavern.

Day 8: Visit County Wicklow, walk in the valley of Glendalough, and continue to Wexford.

Day 9 and 10: Depart Ireland on a two-hour ferry crossing to Scotland, and meet our British leaders. Enroute to Edinburgh, stop to visit the house of Robert Burns, Scotland's national poet.

Day 11 and 12: Riverside walk at Peebles and cross into Northumberland in England. Walk Hadrian's Wall.

Day 13 and 14: South to Durham Cathedral and walk in Swaledale, Yorkshire.

Day 15 and 16: Drive to the walled city of Chester. Day at leisure.

Day 17 and 18: To South Wales to walk in the valley of the River Wye.

Day 19: Drive to Somerset for a candle-lit dinner and overnight at Forde Abbey.

Day 20: In London.

Day 21: Depart on homeward-bound flights.

Dates: #1 Jun 29–Jul 19 (21 days)
#2 Jul 20–Aug 9
Leader: Mike Banks &
Paddy O'Leary
Land Cost: $1890
(10–12 members)
$2160 (7–9)
Single Supplement: $260
IT5BA1YO56

Hadrian's Wall/ *Mike Banks*

Gloucester. With Mike Banks, British author and mountaineer, and his wife Pat, we will discover the lovely unspoiled England that the English themselves enjoy/ *Mike Banks*

The Irish Countryside

Walking tour from Kerry to Connemara to Wicklow

This easy walking tour is a relaxed and low-key look at little-known areas and aspects of Ireland, conducted by mountaineer Paddy O'Leary. It's an unusual chance to see "an Irishman's Ireland," with its quiet country towns, wild moors, and lonely coastal cliffs.

We begin with a visit to Clare, "Land of Castles," and the peculiar landscape of the Burren country, where mild weather and the proximity of the sea have led to exquisite flora.

We take a ferry to the Aran Islands, then return to Galway and visit the lake-dotted wilds of Connemara, one of Ireland's most beautiful regions.

Driving south, we tackle the rough mountain and coastal country of South West Kerry, staying in a secluded cove on the Ring of Kerry.

Heading through a region steeped in the lore of the Norman Conquest, we tour Kinsale with its sheltered harbor then walk in St. Mullins, an unspoiled river village and burial place of the Kings of Leinster.

Our last lap takes us through the prosperous farms of County Wexford and the Wicklow Hills, where we'll walk in wooded and historic valleys and glens, including Glendalough, with its 6th century monastery founded by St. Kevin.

Travel will be by minibus; accommodations are in small hotels.

Itinerary: Day 1 and 2: Leave U.S. Arrive Shannon, Ireland. Drive to the Burren. Afternoon stroll on the Cliffs of Moher.

Day 3: Walk in Burren country and enjoy a session of Irish traditional music in a pub at Doolin.

Day 4: By ferry to the Aran Islands, where islanders proudly foster the Gaelic language and traditions. Evening banquet at Knappogue Castle, 15th century home of the McNamara clan.

Day 5: Drive around Galway Bay to Galway and Connemara.

Day 6: Drive through Limerick to Adare, with its thatched cottages, and ruins dating from the 13th to 15th century, and on to Tralee, county town of Kerry.

Day 7: Walk in the vicinity of Carrauntoohil (3,414′), Ireland's highest mountain, and drive around the shores of the glorious Ring of Kerry.

Day 8: By fishing boat to Skellig Michael, a dramatic rock pinnacle with an old church clinging to its 700-foot-high summit.

Day 9: Drive the lovely shoreline of Lamb's Head, Afternoon visit to the home of Daniel O'Connell, the Liberator.

Day 10: Drive to Kinsale, stopping at Staigue Fort.

Day 11: Day in Kinsale.

Day 12: Drive to Waterford, with its famous glass factory. Continue to a secluded guest house on the banks of the peaceful River Barrow.

Day 13: Stroll through the little hamlet of St. Mullins, with its fine example of early Norman fortification.

Day 14: Drive to Kilkenny.

Day 15 and 16: Drive through farm country to the Wicklow Hills.

Day 17: Drive to Dublin. Evening at the Abbey Tavern to enjoy traditional music and dancing.

Day 18: Depart Dublin and connect with homeward-bound flights.

Dates: #1 May 17–Jun 3 (18 days)
#2 Aug 24–Sep 10
Leader: Paddy O'Leary
Grade: A-1
Land Cost: $1490
(7–12 members)
Single Supplement: $160
ITE112000

Exploring Iceland

Camping, hiking, travel by jeep

Iceland, that peculiar environment of fire and ice, is a living laboratory for geologists. Natural cataclysms are constantly shaping and reshaping the land with major volcanic eruptions on the average of every five years.

We will travel in southern Iceland by four-wheel drive vehicle, camping enroute and visiting some of its most interesting spots, including Great Geyser (a famous thermal spout from which the international word geyser was derived) and Gullfoss, one of Europe's highest waterfalls. We'll hike up Mt. Hekla (4,927′), Iceland's best known volcano, and (for those who are fit) climb Iceland's highest peak, Mt. Oraefajokull (6,952′).

In contrast to the creaking glaciers, spouting geysers and steaming lava fields, we'll find that Iceland's landscape can also be very serene. In midsummer (the time of our visit), there will be almost continuous daylight illuminating a pleasant and pristine landscape of deep fjords and coastal farm country which has been inhabited by Icelanders for more than 1100 years. The climate is mild (tempered by the Gulf Stream) and the air is probably the clearest and cleanest in the inhabited world.

Itinerary: Day 1 and 2: Leave U.S. Arrive Reykjavik, Iceland. Drive to Pingvellir National Park. Short hike in the area and overnight at hotel.

Day 3: Drive to Pjorsardalur at the foot of Mt. Hekla and camp.

Day 4: Easy hike up Mt. Hekla, then drive to Thorsmork, a beautiful valley surrounded by glaciers, mountains and glacial rivers on all sides. Camp.

Day 5: Hiking in Thorsmork area.

Day 6: Hike down to Skogar and drive to Hjorleifshofoi. Good birdwatching opportunities from our campsite.

Day 7: Drive to Skaftafell National Park and camp.

Day 8: Optional hike up Mt. Oraefajokull, third largest volcano in Europe. This is a strenuous hike, and those not wishing to participate can take other local walks.

Day 9: Visit Breioamerkurlon, an iceberg-strewn glacial lake. Afternoon hike.

Day 10: Drive to Eldgja.

Day 11: Drive to Landmannalaugar and soak in a natural hot spring.

Day 12: Drive to Reykjavik. Overnight in hotel.

Day 13: Free day in Reykjavik.

Day 14: Depart Reykjavik and connect with homeward-bound flights.

Greenland Option:

After the trip, we can arrange an optional four day tour to Angmagssalik, an Eskimo fishing and seal-hunting settlement on the eastern coast of Greenland. Advance booking is necessary.

Dates: Jul 8–Jul 21 (14 days)
Leader: Filippus Petursson
Grade: B-2
Land Cost: $1490
(8–12 members)
Single Supplement: to be paid locally
IT86FIREK/MT

Iceland, that peculiar environment of fire and ice, is a living laboratory for geologists. Natural cataclysms are constantly shaping and reshaping the land/
Phillipe Patay

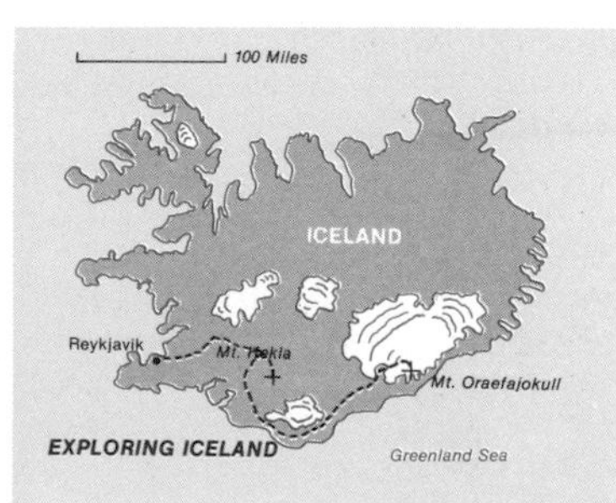

Natural History Of Norway

10-day walk in forests and glens

The rolling forests and fells of eastern Norway are a wonderland for summer hiking. The sun is up almost round the clock, the meadows are filled with wildflowers, reindeer are seen grazing on hillsides, and the birds are nesting in remote lakes and marshes. Things have changed little here since Swedish botanist Linneaus walked these wildlife-rich hills in the 18th century, developing his famous system for the classification of plants and animals.

Our summer ramble begins with a scenic train ride along the Norway/Sweden border, taking us deep into old Norwegian farm country. From here we follow a well-planned trail and hut system through forests and glens which conjure up images of trolls, mythical creatures of Nordic folklore.

The hiking time per day is about five hours and the terrain is moderate and varied. Enroute, we pass Stone Age settlements, Lapp reindeer herders, and numerous active summer farms.

The Norwegian hut system is the best in Europe: immaculate wooden cabins complete with food, bunks and everything needed for a pleasant stay. The huts are staffed by Norwegian students who enjoy spending the long, light summer evenings sharing their knowledge of the local wildlife and folklore.

Only a small daypack need be carried while walking This is an excellent tour for families who want to enjoy a European hike together.

Itinerary: Day 1 and 2: Leave U.S. Arrive Oslo. Transfer to hotel.

Day 3: By train to Tynset and continue by bus to Rausjodalseter. Overnight at an old "seter" (summer farm) that serves as a hikers' lodge.

Day 4 and 5: Hike up to Rausjo Peak (4,281'), then down into the forest past tarns and becks to the old summer farm at Saether.

Day 6 and 7: A three-hour walk, then a boat journey across Lake Femund into Femund National Park, ending with a one-hour stroll to Svukurset Lodge. Layover day to look for reindeer and perhaps meet some Sami people, the Lapps who herd reindeer in the borderlands.

In Norway, we follow a well-planned trail and hut system through forests and glens which conjure up images of trolls, mythical creatures of Nordic folklore/*Helge Sunde*

Day 8 and 9: Hike along cairned paths to the barren and boulder-strewn country around Roveltjorn Lakes. There is time here for an easy ascent of Mt. Svuken (4,400') for panoramic views of the Norwegian/Swedish border country.

Day 10 and 11: Easy hike through the forest to the village of Langen. Layover day.

Day 12 and 13: Scenic walk to Marenvollen Hut, followed by an easy walk to Roros, a small mining town with a long history. Overnight at hotel in Roros.

Day 14: By train to Oslo. Afternoon sightseeing. Overnight in hotel.

Day 15: Depart Oslo and connect with homeward-bound flights.

Dates: Jun 27–Jul 11 (15 days)
Leader: to be announced
Grade: B-2
Land Cost: $1290
(6–15 members)
Single Supplement: $150
IT1SK1MOUN

Basque sheepdog contests/ *Martin Zabaleta*

The Other Spain

Walks in Basque Country, Pyrenees, Catalonia

Exploring the mountains, villages and coasts of Northern Spain, this tour is a combination of hikes in completely untouristed areas and visits to the ancient towns in Aragon, Catalonia, and Euskadi (Pays Basque).

We meet our trip leader (a Basque mountaineer and Everest summiteer), in Madrid. After a stop in Avila, holy city of St. Teresa, we begin our walk along the green meadows, aquamarine lakes and splendid granite cirques of the Sierra de Gredos. Then we'll see the Gothic and Romanesque art treasures in medieval Leon and the golden university town of Salamanca before roaming into the Picos de Europa, a *cordillera* (mountain range) with a mysterious labyrinth of gorges and valleys cut by streams alive with fish.

The next few days are spent exploring along the verdant Basque Coast, with its caves, sheltered bays, and charming fishing villages, including San Sebastian, where we dine on amazing seafood and hike along the fertile Cantabrian coast and Bay of Biscay.

Driving through Huesca, ancient capital of Aragon, to Catalonia, we hike into the Sierra de Guara, fantastically carved and colored canyons reminiscent of our own southwestern desert.

After a final walk in the Monserrat Massif, we end the trip with a stay in the magnificent city of Barcelona, capital of Catalonia.

Southern Spain in November:

Write for details of our newest Spain trip with Martin Zabaleta, an 18-day walking tour of the medieval cities of Toledo, Seville and Cordoba, the green setting of Moorish Grenada and the footpaths of the Sierra Nevada and Sierra de Cazorla. Day-by-day itinerary for 1986 is availabl

The Picos de Europe, Spain/ *Martin Zabaleta*

"The Other Spain" is a combination of hikes in completely untouristed areas and visits to ancient towns in Aragon, Catalonia and Euskadi/*Martin Zabaleta*

Leader of our Spain & Portugal trips, Basque mountaineer Martin Zabaleta

Itinerary: Day 1 and 2: leave U.S. Arrive Madrid Overnight at hotel.

Day 3: Drive to Avila. Afternoon hike in the Sierra de Gredos and night in a lakeside refuge.

Day 4: Easy hike along the trails of the Sierra de Gredos then drive to Salamanca.

Day 5: Drive to Zamora and Leon for a stay in that medieval city's old quarter.

Day 6 and 7: Hikes in the Picos de Europa, highest range in the Cantabrian Cordillera. Overnight at local village hotels.

Day 8: Beautiful drive along the indented Santander coastline to Santillana del Mar.

Day 9: Morning hike in the Sierra de Hornijo. Overnight in the fishing village of Lequeitio.

Day 10: Drive along the steep-cliffed beaches of the Basque Coast. Dinner at Gastronomique Society (a private eating club) and overnight in San Sebastian.

Day 11: Free day to enjoy the beach, the tapa bars and shops in the heart of Basque country.

Day 12: Roam through villages of the Baztan Valley. Lunch in a caserio (farm) then on to spend the night in a splendidly refurbished parador in Sos de Rey Catolico.

Day 13: Visit a 9th century monastery and hike in Sierra de San Juan de la Pena.

Day 14: A whole day to hike in Ordesa National Park.

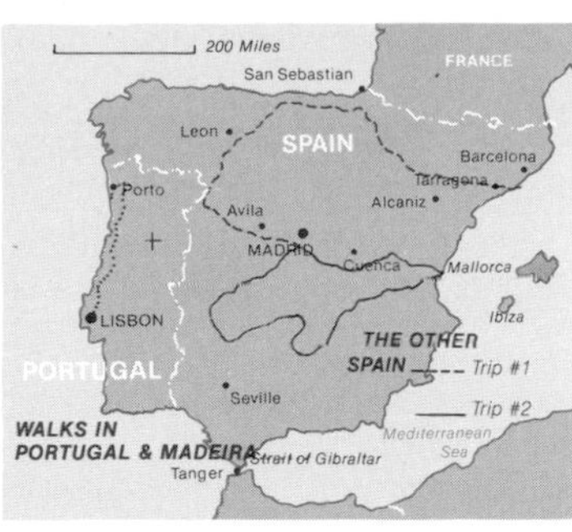

Day 15: Hiking in the Sierra de Guara, a fantastic "badlands" in the foothills of the Aragonese Pyrenees.

Day 16: Drive to Catalonia and walk in the grand Sierra de Montserrat.

Day 17: Short drive to Barcelona.

Day 18: Transfer to the airport and connect with homeward-bound flights.

Dates: #1 Jun 8–Jun 25 (18 days)
#2 Sep 21–Oct 8
Leader: Martin Zabaleta
Grade: A-2
Land Cost: $1490
(9–12 members)
$1675 (6–8)
Single Supplement: $150
IT6TW15641

Spain & Portugal trips include: twin accommodations in hotels, breakfasts (lunches and dinners on your own), ground transportation, admission charges, leadership.

Walks In Portugal & Madeira

Wine country and island walks

Hill hikes and coastal walks are the focus of this journey to Portugal and the island of Madeira.

After touring Lisbon, we drive along the Costa do Sol, with its resort towns and traditional fishing villages. Our walks take us through Bucaco National Park and Peneda Geres National Park, and colorful Minho province, the heart of Portuguese wine country. All week, we'll sample the astounding array of wines and enjoy our share of renowned Portuguese cuisine.

Our second week is in Madeira, an island known for its roller-coaster hills and charming medieval towns. Madeira is lush with orchids, bougainvillaea, birds of paradise, calla lillies, willows and sugar cane. Hiking is taken seriously by the locals, and there's no such thing as a dull walk. 1,300 miles of *levadas,* (water channels which make up a sophisticated irrigation system) and well-maintained paths open up the beautiful interior of the island to walkers. One of our walks takes us easily up Pico Ruivo (6,144'), the island's highest peak, and we'll also spend a day deep-sea fishing by private boat.

Travel is by mini-van and accommodations are in small hotels and interesting guest houses.

Itinerary: Day 1 and 2: Leave U.S. Arrive Lisbon.

Day 3: Tour Lisbon.

Day 4: Drive to Guincho, a wild windswept beach near the westernmost edge of Europe. Afternoon walk in the Sierra da Sintra.

Day 5: Boat trip to Belenga Islands, seven miles out into the Atlantic. Overnight in a 16th century castle.

Day 6: Morning walk in the old town of Obidos and afternoon visit to Batalha Monastery, a Gothic ediface with unparalleled limestone carvings. Overnight in the Royal Hunting Lodge in Bucaco.

Day 7: Morning hike in Bucaco National Park, where Wellington defeated the French during the Napoleonic Wars. Afternoon in Guimaraes, a town with a delightful blend of medieval and Renaissance architecture.

Day 8: Walk in Peneda-Geres National Park along the mossy track of an old Roman road.

Day 9: Explore the heart of Portuguese wine country.

Day 10: Fly to Madeira's capital, Funchal (cost not included).

Day 11: Hike 12 level miles through gardens of orchids, roses and hydrangeas, with magnificent sea views.

Day 12: Drive through the Jardin da Serra and hike four hours with spectacular views of the island's jagged and lush interior.

Day 13: By private boat for deep-sea fishing for barracuda, swordfish and tuna. Anchor for barbeque on the Desertas, small desert islands off the coast of Madeira.

Day 14: Four-hour hike along the North Coast path. Afternoon drive around Madeira's west coast by private coach or taxi.

Day 15: Hike up Pico Ruivo and descend into Quemados, a rain-forest paradise. Return to Funchal for evening flight to Lisbon (cost not included).

Day 16: Depart Lisbon on homeward-bound flights.

Dates: #1 Jun 22–Jul 7 (16 days)
#2 Oct 5–Oct 20
Leader: Martin Zabaleta
Grade: A-2
Land Cost: $1390
(9–12 members)
$1590 (6–8)
Single Supplement: to be paid locally
IT6TW15642

Madeira is lush with orchids, bougainvillae, birds of paradise, calla lillies, willows and sugar cane/
Martin Zabaleta

The Hills Of Czechoslovakia

Walks in the High Tatras and northern Bohemia

This walking tour encompasses Czechoslovakian hill country at its finest—both in the alpine High Tatras and the romantic valleys of northern Bohemia.

The peaks of the High Tatras, astride the Polish-Czech border, are a compact and spectacular mountain range, somewhat like a scaled-down version of the Alps, with granite pinnacles, aretes and rock walls rising as much as 4,000 feet above timberline. The highest peak in the Tatras is Gerlach (8,710′). The region's residents are farmers and shepherds who are far removed from the mainstream of modern Czechoslovakian life and still retain their traditional costumes in everyday life.

This is fine hiking country, with its gentle meadows and beech forests, and we'll spend four days based in a mountain lodge with time for a variety of hikes to suit individual tastes.

Before visiting the Tatras, we journey to northern Bohemia, another area where ancient dress is still worn and folk traditions are cherished. The history of Bohemia dates to medieval times when the Hussites defeated the 70,000-strong armies of the Crusaders. Today it is a land of rich orchards and cultivated fields, a rural landscape dotted with castles and churches of Gothic and Baroque architecture.

In Bohemia, we will make a leisurely three-day trek in the Krkonose Mountains (rugged hills known as the "Giant Mountains"), hiking from village to village and spending nights in small hotels.

The trip begins and ends in Prague, the graceful capital city built on the sores of the Vltava River, and full of well-preserved buildings and monuments dating from the 13th to 19th century.

Itinerary: Day 1 and 2: Leave U.S. Arrive Prague and transfer to hotel. Afternoon free.

Day 3: Half-day sightseeing in Prague.

Day 4: Full-day excursion visiting Karlstejn Castle, Koneprusy Caves, and Konopiste Castle.

Day 5: By bus to Harrachov in Krkonose, north of Prague. Afternoon hike. Overnight at inn.

Day 6: A whole day of hiking (about 12 miles) through the western part of Giant Mountains National Park. Overnight at hotel.

Day 7 and 8: Hike about 11 miles to the village of Pec Pod Snezkou. Layover day for hikes. Overnight at hotel.

Day 9: Morning free. Afternoon drive to Prague and overnight train to Poprad in the High Tatras.

Day 10: Arrive and take the electric train to Strbske Pleso (4,455′). Afternoon hike. Overnight at hotel.

Day 11: Drive to Sliezky Dom Mountain Hotel (6,560′). Overnight in hotel.

Day 12 and 13: Optional hikes

Day 14: Morning return to Poprad. Board the overnight train to Prague.

Day 15: Arrive in Prague. Morning free. Transfer to airport and connect with homeward-bound flights.

Dates: Jun 14–Jun 28 (15 days)
Leader: to be announced
Grade: A-2
Land Cost: $1190
(7–15 members)
Single Supplement: not available
IT5LH16011

Alpine hut in Bavaria/Wolfgang Koch

The Other Bavaria

Touring and easy day hikes

This is an insider's look at the ancient culture of Bavaria and the Tyrol, as experienced in its rural villages and on easy day walks among high alpine valleys.

The places trip leaders Renate and Wolfgang Koch have chosen to show us in Bavaria and Tyrol are unique, varied and filled with much history. The pace of the trip is busy, but not rushed, and there is always time to take advantage of spur-of-the moment opportunities that present themselves (perhaps a town fair in Zweisel, or a lunchtime organ concert in Passau).

We first visit the alpine ski resort of Garmisch and the mountain village of Berchtesgaden, with its classic Bavarian architecture. Near Garmisch, we ride up Zugspitze (10,000′), Germany's highest peak, by cable car, and take excursions by boat on to Konigsee, the most beautiful alpine lake in Germany.

Several pleasant walks are planned in two national parks (Bayerischer Wals and Altmuhltal) which show Bavaria's gentle yet spectacular alpine country at its best. Also included is a visit to charming Salzburg, city of Mozart, and a final farewell dinner at one of the most famous restaurants in the world, Munich's Hofbrauhas.

Accommodations will be in small hotels and inns of character. There will be many chances to sample fine Bavarian *bier* and the justly-famed cuisine of the region.

Itinerary: Day 1 and 2: Leave U.S. Arrive Munich. Continue to Garmisch.

Our pension at Berchtesgaden/ Wolfgang Koch

Day 3: Ride up Zugspitze by cable car. Return to hotel.

Day 4: Day hike to Hollental Hut with wonderful views of the Wetterstein peaks. Return to hotel.

Day 5: Travel to Berchtesgaden along lovely Bavarian lakes and visit Herren-Chiemsee Castle enroute. Overnight at hotel.

Day 6: Day hike to Kuhroint Hut with great views of Watzmann Peak. Descend to St. Bartholoma Monastery. Boat to Berchtesgaden across Konigsee Lake.

Day 7: Hike to Blaueis Hut and Schartenspitze Peak, with views of the Blaueis Glacier. Return to Berchtesgaden.

Day 8: Day tour of Salzburg. Return to Berchtesgaden.

Day 9: Drive to the town of Passau. Overnight in hotel.

Day 10: Tour Passau and environs. Overnight at hotel.

Day 11: Afternoon hike in Bayerischer Wals National Park. Overnight in hotel.

Day 12: Drive to Racheldienst Hut via Rachelsee, a pretty alpine lake. Overnight at pension.

Day 13: Day hike to Falkenstein Peak. Return to pension.

Day 14: Drive to Kelheim (Altmuhltal National Park), visiting Walhalla and Regensburg. Overnight at hotel.

Day 15: Day hike to Befreiungshalle and the monastery at Weltenburg. Return to hotel in Kelheim via boat on the Danube.

Day 16: Day hike from a stalactite cavern with prehistoric wall paintings to the castle of Prunn. Return to hotel in Kelheim.

Day 17: Drive to Munich. Farewell dinner at the Hofbrauhaus. Overnight at hotel.

Day 18: Depart Munich on homeward-bound flights.

Dates: #1 Jun 6–Jun 23 (18 days)
#2 Sep 4–Sep 21
Leader: Wolfgang Koch
Grade: A-2
Land Cost: $1650
(8–14 members)
Single Supplement: $100
IT6PA1SFMT20

The pace of The Other Bavaria trip is busy, but not rushed, and there is always time to take advantage of spur-of-the moment opportunities that present themselves (perhaps a town fair in Zweisel or a lunchtime organ concert in Passau)/Wolfgang Koch

Alpine Hikes In Bavaria & Tyrol

Hut to hut in the mountains of Berchtesgaden and Tyrol

This journey centers around two multi-day alpine hikes in the alps of Germany and Austria.

From Innsbruck, a 700-year-old university town which is Austria's most famous alpine center, we hike from hut to hut for five days through the Karwendel Mountains of the Tyrolean Alps, a region with lovely alpine flora and fine peaks.

Driving through green alpine valleys to Berchtesgaden, famed for its landscape and romantic Bavarian architecture, we make a four-day hut-to-hut trek which takes us over Watzmann Peak and to St. Bartholoma, a monastery and down to Lake Konigsee, from where we boat back to Berchtesgaden.

The trip ends with a visit to Salzburg. Hiking accommodations will be in well-maintained alpine mountain huts.

Itinerary: Day 1 and 2: Leave U.S. Arrive Munich. Drive to Innsbruck. Overnight at hotel.

Day 3: Tour Innsbruck, including the site of the Olympic winter games. Overnight at hotel.

Day 4: Ride by cog railway to Hungerburg. Continue to Halleranger Hut for overnight.

Day 5: A long hike and climb up Birkarspitze (9,100′), descending to the Karwendel Hut for overnight.

Day 6: Hike through lovely alpine country to Falken Hut, with views of the Lalliderer Walls, a famous rock climbing area.

Day 7: Hike over the peak of Lamsenspitze. Overnight at Lamsenjoch Hut.

Day 8: Descend to the lake at Achensee and enjoy a refreshing swim. Overnight at hotel.

Day 9: Drive to Berchtesgaden via Kitzbuhl, one of the most famous ski resorts in Europe. Overnight in hotel.

Day 10: Tour Berchtesgaden.

Day 11: Hike up Watzmann Peak. Overnight at Watzmann Hut.

Day 12: Day hike around the Watzmann area with breathtaking views down the steep rock faces of the Eastern Alps. Overnight at Wimbachgries Hut.

Day 13: Short Hike to Karlinger Hut.

Day 14: Hike to St. Bartholoma Monastery at Konigsee, then boat across to Berchtesgaden.

Day 15: Tour Salzburg then proceed to Munich for dinner in the Hofbrauhaus. Overnight in hotel.

Day 16: Depart Munich on homeward-bound flights.

Dates: Jul 6–Jul 21 (16 days)
Leader: Wolfgang & Renate Koch
Grade: B-2
Land Cost: $1350 (12–14 members)
$1560 (8–11)
Single Supplement: $60
IT6PA1SFMT21

Eastern Alps Climbing Circuit

This trip includes hiking and non-technical ascents of the three highest points within Germany, Austria and Italy.

Above the German mountain town of Garmisch, we hike for five days in the Wetterstein Mountains, with an ascent of the Zugspitze (10,000′), Germany's highest peak.

Traveling to Vent, a highland village in Austria, we hike for four days in the Otztaler Alps, climbing Wildspitze (12,850′).

Crossing the border into Italy, we hike in famed Dolomites and climb Italy's highest peak, Ortler (13,016′).

This circuit is for strong hikers or mountaineers (it is not a technical mountaineering trip). Transport will be by van, with accommodations in pensions and mountain huts.

Itinerary: Day 1 and 2: Leave U.S. Arrive Munich. Continue to Garmisch.

Day 3 to 7: Hikes and climbs in the Wetterstein peaks

Day 8 to 12: Hikes and climbs in Austria's Otztaler Alps.

Day 13 to 16: Drive to Grodner Joch in Italy. Hikes and climbs in the Dolomites.

Day 17 to 20: Drive to Bozen. Hikes and climbs in the Eastern Alps, including Ortler (13,016′).

Day 21: Drive to Milan. Overnight at hotel.

Day 22: Depart Milan on homeward-bound flights.

Dates: Aug 3–Aug 24 (22 days)
Leader: Wolfgang Koch
Grade: B-3/D-1
Land Cost: $1575 (12–14 members)
$1830 (8–11)
Single Supplement: $75
ITPA1SFMT22

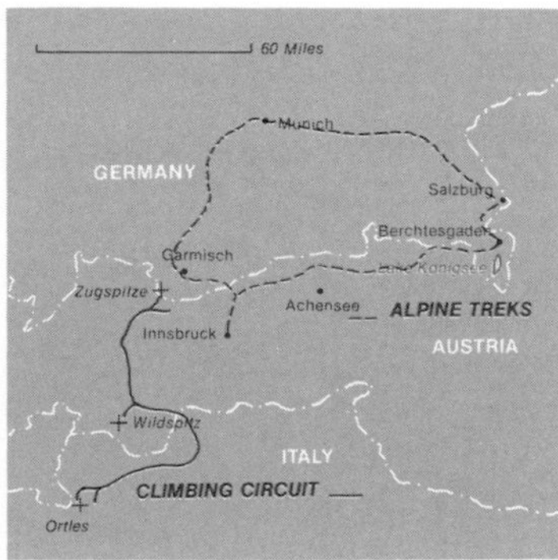

After driving through green alpine valleys to Berchtesgaden, famed for its landscape and romantic Bavarian architecture, we make a four-day hut-to-hut hike which takes us over Watzmann Peak/*Wolfgang Koch*

"Just passing through..."

MUNICH

City notes by Wolfgang Koch

Walking/jogging routes:

Visit Haidhausen, the student quarter, with its little beer halls, restaurants and theatres. Walk around Bogenhausen and Naihausan (many old-style houses and villas, parks and cafes). Jog in city parks like English Garden, Nymphenburg Park (botanical garden and castle) and West Park.

Day trips:

South of Munich, day trips are possible to lakes like Staruberg, Chiemsee and Ammersee for sailing and swimming, or to the mountains (Berchtesgaden, Garmisch) for hikes.

Museums:

Munich has unusual museums: the BMW Museum (more than just cars) and the City Museum, within which is a puppet museum and a beer museum!

Restaurants:

Don't miss the unique experience of Munich's huge beer halls like the Hofbrauhaus, Lowenbraukeller and Augustinerkeller, where thousands of people gather nightly for singing and celebrating.

The Eastern Alps Climbing Circuit is for strong hikers (it is not a technical mountaineering trip)/*Wolfgang Koch*

Germany & Austria trips include: twin accommodations in hotels, dorm accommodations with meals in mountain huts (if applicable), breakfasts at hotels, 2 dinners, ground transportation, airport transfers, leadership.

The Other Italy

Touring the northern Alps

This trip is a chance to appreciate the scenery, culture and cuisine of two of Italy's most beautiful mountain regions: Val D'Aosta and the Dolomites.

While this is a touring trip rather than a hiking trip, we plan several wonderful optional day hikes with some of the best views in the Alps—including Mont Blanc and Monte Rosa, the Alps' two highest peaks.

From a hotel in the Gressoney Valley, nestled in the foothills below the massif of Monte Rosa, we ride to the upper valleys by tram and chairlift for views of the shining glaciers on the Italian side of Monte Rosa.

From the resort town of Courmayeur, we take a scenic tram ride up to Refuge Torino, with its views of the great snow dome of Mont Blanc, surrounded by avenues of spectacular lesser peaks.

Our next two days are spent around Maggiore Lake and Como, the two most beautiful lakes in Italy, where we visit classic gardens and villas.

Driving over the very steep Stelvio Pass (highest road pass in Europe) with its dozens of switchbacks and views of the ice-covered Ortler Mountains, we descend into the South Tyrol, part of Austria until World War II, which is apparent in its Austrian architecture and customs.

To enjoy the Dolomites, one of the most famous rock climbing centers in Europe, we stay at the deluxe Prato Piazza, a hotel spectacularly situated in green alpine pastures with exceptional views. Our optional walks take us very close to the jagged spire of Croda Rossa, the spectacular pinnacles of Tre Cime de Laverado, the most famous rock faces in the Dolomites.

The trip ends with visits to Cortina, the major winter sports center situated in a cirque of magnificent mountains, and Venice, with a brief stop in Verona.

Travel will be by mini-bus or van, with accommodations in small hotels.

Itinerary: Day 1 and 2: leave U.S. Arrive Milan. Overnight at hotel.

Day 3: Drive to Gressoney Valley. Overnight at hotel.

Val D'Aosta is a spectacular valley in the heart of the highest Alps of Europe, where the mountainous borders of Italy, Switzerland and France meet/ *Leo Le Bon*

Day 4 and 5: Excursions by tram and chairlift to Refugio Quintana Sella. Return to hotel.

Day 6: Drive to Courmayeur for overnight.

Day 7: Excursion by tram to Refuge Torino for views of Mont Blanc. Return to hotel.

Day 8: Drive to Stresa on Maggiore Lake. Overnight in hotel.

Day 9: Visit the gardens of Villa Taranto and drive through Laveno to a village on Lake Como.

Day 10: Drive over Stelvio Pass to Merano. Overnight in hotel.

Day 11: Day excursion in the surroundings of Merano. Afternoon drive to Hotel Prato Piazza.

Day 12: Optional day hike from hotel.

Day 13: Optional hike. Drive to Cortina for overnight.

Day 14: In Cortina.

Day 15: Morning drive to Venice.

Day 16: Afternoon drive to Milan with stop in Verona. Overnight in Milan.

Day 17: Depart on homeward-bound flights.

Dates: #1 May 25–Jun 10 (17 days)
#2 Sep 7–Sep 23
Leader: to be announced
Grade: A-2
Land Cost: $2190 (11–15 members)
$2390 (7–10)
Single Supplement: available on request
IT5LH16011

Leo Le Bon at rifugio gabiet (mountain hotel) in the Val D'Aosta/*Nadia Le Bon*

Val D'Aosta Trek

11-day hike in highest Italian Alps

Val d'Aosta is a long and narrow valley in the heart of the highest Alps of Europe, where the mountainous borders of Italy, Switzerland and France meet.

Surrounding Val d'Aosta are some of the most magnificent and well-known peaks in the Alps: the Mont Blanc massif, whose 15,771-foot summit is the highest point in Europe west of the Caucasus and the great peaks of the Pennine Alps, including the Matterhorn (14,692′), Monte Rosa (15,203′) and Gran Combin (14,154′).

The first 8 days of our 11-day hike will take us along miles and miles of ancient footpaths connecting valleys, villages and alpine meadows surrounding the Aosta Valley, all with views extending from Monte Rosa to the Matterhorn to Mont Blanc.

The last three days of hiking take us through Gran Paradiso National Park, where the delicate mountain environment remains unspoiled and we may see a graceful ibex or chamois poised among the rocks. In the summer, a profusion of wildflowers add brilliant color to every vista. The climate here is generally fair and dry, since the massive flanks of Mont Blanc shelter the valley from wet weather and storms.

At night we will stay in small inns in mountain refuges.

Itinerary: Day 1 and 2: Leave U.S. Arrive Milan. Transfer to hotel.

Day 3: Drive to Aosta, main town of the Aosta Valley. Afternoon free to explore the city.

Day 4: Drive to St. Jacques. Begin 11-day hike with a walk to Refuge Casole. Good views of Monte Rosa.

Day 5: Cross the Col de Nana (9,100′) to Cheneil (6,975′). Views of the Matterhorn (14,492′) will be spectacular today.

Day 6: Descend to Valtournanche (5,000′), with its ancient houses and church, then up to Cignana Lake (7,086′). Overnight at Refuge Barmasse.

Day 7 to 9: Hike to Torgnon (5,577′), passing by alpine houses and open meadows, over Col Fenetre (7,246′) to Oratoire de Cuney (8,700′).

Day 10 and 11: Cross over Col Vessona, with its views of Monte Rosa (and our first views of Mont Blanc and Gran Combin), and reach Aosta. Overnight at hotel.

Day 12: Visit Aosta and nearby Roman ruins, then hike up to Refuge Vittorio Sella (8,477′).

Day 13 and 14: Hike in the heart of Gran Paradiso National Park. Cross Col Lauson (10,813′) and Col de Entrebor (10,120′) to the village of Rhemes Notre Dame.

Day 15: We cross from one valley into another, over Col Fenetre (9,317′) and end our trek at Valgrisenche.

Day 16: Drive to Milan. Afternoon sightseeing. Overnight at hotel.

Day 17: Depart Milan and connect with homeward-bound flights.

Dates: #1 Jul 6–Jul 22 (17 days)
#2 Aug 10–Aug 26
Leader: Pietro Giglio
Grade: B-3
Land Cost: $1560 (10–12 members)
$1680 (8–9)
Single Supplement: available on request
IT5LH16011

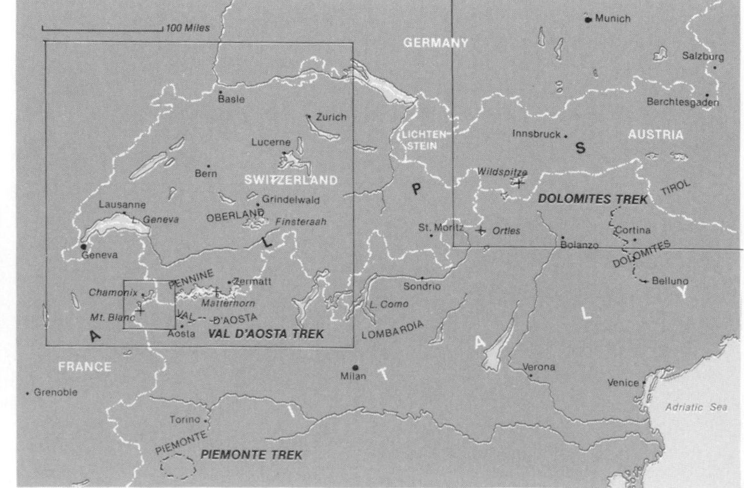

The Dolomites Trek

11-day hike in the spectacular South Tyrol

This trip centers around an 11-day hut-to-hut hike through the heart of the Dolomites.

Although the mountains of the Dolomites are not exceptionally high (the highest peak is 10,965-foot Mt. Marmolada), they are among the most striking mountains in Europe, steep spires of fantastic form colored in weathered hues of rose, yellow and grey.

Below the "fairytale" spires and dramatic walls lie bright green meadows alive with wildflowers all summer. In the lower valleys, there are orchards, vineyards and a checkerboard of cultivated fields.

Continuously sheer cliffs flank most of the Dolomite's peaks. The great mountaineers of the 1920's and 1930's practiced the emerging sport of rock climbing on these cliffs, forging routes which remain classics to this day.

The name Dolomites is generally considered to include all the limestone mountains of the Alto Adige, Trentino and Vento, a region favored with sunny, dry weather.

Up until Word War I, this was part of the Austrian South Tyrol. The present-day people of the Dolomites speak their own special patois (Ladin) as well as Italian and German.

Our nights will be in traditional mountain "refuges," often spectacularly situated and offering rustic dorm-style accommodations.

Visits are also included to Verona (city of Romeo and Juliet) and Milan.

Itinerary: Day 1 and 2: Leave U.S. Arrive Milan. Overnight at hotel.

Day 3: Drive to Cornuda. Overnight at Hotel San Sebastiano.

Day 4: Begin 11-day hike starting at Duran Pass and reaching Refuge Vazzoler (5,623'). The walk takes us along the base of the huge rock faces of the 10,500-foot Civetta Range, known by rock climbers all over the world.

Day 5 to 7: Hike to Refuge Sonnino at Coldai (7,979'), to Refuge Palmieri (6,692') and walk through woods and meadows of the Ampezzo Valley to Refuge San Marco (4,855').

Day 8: Early start to hike up Forcella Grande for views of Torre Dei Sabbioni, Sorapis (10,515'), Marmarole (9,714'), and Antelao (10,705'). Descend to Hotel Palus San Marco (3,608').

Day 9: Rest day.

Day 10: Hike to Refuge Fonda Savio (7,775'), crossing an 8,500-foot pass with wide-ranging views of the Dolomites.

Day 11: Hike to Refuge Locatelli (7,972'), following a trail to Refuge Lavaredo at the base of the three summits called Tre Cime De Lavaredo (9,842'), the most famous rock trinity in the Alps.

Day 12: Rest day.

Day 13: Descend to Lake Landro and drive to Cortina. Overnight in hotel.

Day 14: Drive to Milan, stopping for lunch at historic Verona. Overnight at hotel.

Day 15: Depart Milan and connect with homeward-bound flights.

Dates: #1 Jul 20–Aug 3 (15 days)
#2 Aug 24–Sep 7
Leader: #1 Enrico Bertolini
#2 to be announced
Grade: B-3
Land Cost: $1450
(8–12 members)
$1560 (5–7)
Single Supplement: available on request
IT5LH16011

A Walk Through Piemonte

Foothills of the Italian Alps

In the western part of the Italian Alps, near the Maritime Alps, lies Piemonte (literally "foothills") an area of green and gently rolling hills at altitudes of 5,000 to 7,000 feet.

Piemonte traces its human history back to medieval times. The oldest existing historical documents on this area date to 1200 A.D., as do many of its fine old churches.

With a geography which has left it relatively isolated from the mainstream of modern Italy, the pastoral villages of Piemonte have maintained a traditional way of life ruled by the passing seasons. Farming and cattle raising are the summer activities, and the making of handicrafts (particularly wood carving) fills the winter.

To walk these valleys is to wander back in time, strolling on stone-paved paths, exploring ancient churches with historic wall paintings, meeting shepherds and enjoying old-style Italian country life.

The people of Piemonte descend from an ethnic group which still speaks an ancient dialect of French called "provencal." They are proud of their heritage and celebrate it often in their dances and festivals.

Worth a special mention for this trip (and trips in the Dolomites and Val D'Aosta) is the fantastic food at the small mountain inns and refuges we stay in. Lunches and dinners are typical three-course Italian classics: a hearty soup course followed by a wonderful pasta course and then a meat and/or vegetable course (sometimes a casserole), with plentiful quantities of fresh bread, wine, beer and soft drinks. After a morning or afternoon's hike in the mountains, it's a treat to look forward to a delicious meal!

Visits are also included to Torino, 19th century capital of Italy, and Milan.

Itinerary: Day 1 and 2: Leave U.S. Arrive Milan. Transfer to hotel.

Below the "fairytale" spires and dramatic walls of the Dolomites lie bright green meadows alive with wildflowers all summer. In the lower valleys, there are orchards, vineyards and a checkerboard of cultivated fields/ Dick McGowan

Day 3: Drive to Rore. Overnight in hotel.

Day 4: Begin 11-day walk. Hike to Pagliero through woods and pastures. Lunch stop at Birrone Pass (5,577').

Day 5: Walk to Cella Macra (4,169'), with its typical ancient architecture.

Day 6: Cross the Maira Valley with its cobbled pathways, small chapels and old houses and reach Stroppo.

Day 7: Climb up to Col Bettone and descend to the town of Elva, where we admire the paintings of the "Maestro d'Elva" dated 1504 in the local church.

Day 8: Walk through pastures and pine woods to the Blins Valley, the heart of the "Ousitanes" culture

Day 9 and 10: Hike to Pontechianala and walk along the Fintursa Valley, then follow a hillside path to Chinale one of the best preserved villages in the region.

Day 11: Follow a path through gentle pastures and farms where local cheeses are made.

Day 12: Today we cross the largest "cembri" pine forest in Italy. Overnight at Ciampanesio.

Day 13: Walk to Colle de Luca, closest view of the southeast face of Monviso.

Day 14: Hike up to Colle Cervetto (7,385'), walk down to Dragoniere for lunch and end in Rore, where we started our hike. Overnight at hotel.

Day 15: Drive to Milan, with a sightseeing stop in Torino. Overnight in hotel.

Day 16: Depart Milan and connect with homeward-bound flights.

Dates: #1 Jul 13–Jul 28 (16 days)
#2 Aug 10–Aug 25
#3 Sep 14–Sep 29
Leader: Silvana Camus
Grade: B-2
Land Cost: $1495
(10–12 members)
$1590 (8–9)
Single Supplement: available on request
IT5LH16011

Italy trips include: twin accommodations at hotels (meals on your own in cities and towns), dorm accommodations with meals in mountain huts, ground transportation, leadership.

The Other France

Walks in Basque hills, Loire Valley, Bordeaux

In the style of our popular "Other Britain" walking tours, we will tour rural western France, immersing ourselves in French country life as we visit the Basque hills, the Pyrenees, the coastal plains of Aquitaine, the vineyards of Bordeaux, and the Loire countryside with its famed chateaux.

We begin with a swift train ride from Paris south to the French Pyrenees. Here we tour Basque villages and hike in the beautiful high altitude mountain pastures of the Ossau and Aspe valleys of the Pyrenees.

Driving north through the largest conifer forest in Europe, we discover the medieval city of St. Emilion, known for its wines. We hike its vineyards, sample its wine, then stop in Cognac and visit the Martell cellars.

At La Rochelle, we stroll the streets along this 17th century city's fortified harbor and enjoy delicious fresh seafood.

Heading for the Loire Valley and the heart of France, we visit the famous chateaux of Usse-Villandry and Chenonceaux and take walks in the Fontainebleu forest.

Travel will be by comfortable minibus, with accommodations in hotels and inns.

Day hike in the Pyrenees/Rodolphe Buntz

Country beehives/Rodolphe Buntz

Itinerary: Day 1 and 2: Leave U.S. Arrive Paris. Continue by train to Dax in the south of France. Overnight in hotel.

Day 3: Morning visit to a spa. Afternoon boat ride on the "courant d'Huchet" through an almost tropical underwood.

Day 4: Morning visit to a typical duck market of this region then hike along the river Adour, to the trip leaders' 17th century country house, where we'll have dinner. Overnight at hotel in Dax.

Day 5: Drive to Bayonne, Biarritz, and St. Jean de Luz. Picnic in a private summer house with time to enjoy the wonderful scenery of the bay at St. Jean de Luz. Afternoon drive through the Basque hills. Overnight at St. Jean-Pied-De-Port.

Day 6: An entire day's hike in the beautiful "foret des Arbailles," then drive to Oloron-Ste. Marie.

Day 7: Full day or half-day walk in one of the wildest valleys in the Pyrenees, the Ossau Valley.

Day 8: Full day's hike in the Aspe Valley to meet shepherds.

Day 9: Drive to St. Emilion, the world-famous wine-making city. Overnight at St. Emilion.

Day 10: Morning walk in the vineyards. Visit the wine cellar at Chateau Lignac, owned by friends of the trip leaders.

Day 11: Drive to La Rochelle through the Cognac vineyards.

Day 12: Day at leisure in La Rochelle, strolling along the harbor.

Day 13: Drive to Montreuil Bellay, a little town surrounded by the Anjou vineyards. Overnight at medieval Chinon, Joan of Arc's town.

Day 14: Drive to Candes. Morning walk on the hills above the Loire and Vienne rivers.

Day 15: Visit the Loire Valley, and the chateaux of Usse-Villandry and Chenonceaux.

Day 16: Drive to the Fontainebleu forest for a walk and picnic, arrive in Paris in the evening.

Day 17: Free day in Paris.

Day 18: Depart Paris and connect with homeward-bound flights.

Dates: #1 Jun 8–Jun 25 (18 days)
#2 Sep 7–Sep 24
Leader: Rod & Maryvonne Buntz
Grade: A-1
Land Cost: $2090
(10–12 members)
$2270 (7–9)
Single Supplement: $225
IT6PA1SFMT17

In the style of our popular "Other Britain" walking tours, we will tour rural western France, immersing ourselves in French country life as we visit the Basque hills, the Pyrenees, the coastal plains of Aquitaine, the vineyards of Bordeaux and the Loire countryside with its famed chateaux/Rodolphe Buntz

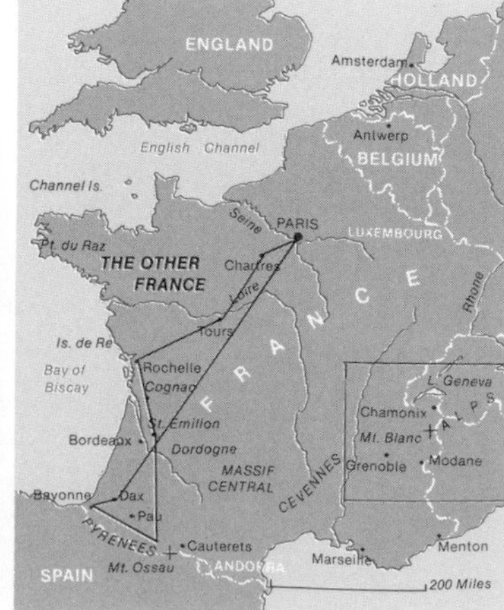

Hiking In The Pyrenees

Alpine scrambles on the French/Spanish border

This 11-day hike offers challenging hiking in the beautiful Vallee d'Aspe of the western Pyrenees, part of the French national park system.

One of the great attractions of the Pyrenees, besides the peaks themselves (50 over 10,000 feet), is the large alpine area between timberline and the summits. Timberline is about 6,800 feet and snowline is about 9,000 feet. For those who love to wander through alpine high country at its finest, this is one of the most appealing regions in Europe. The climate favors a wide-ranging and lovely flora, including daffodils and alpine roses.

We'll hike about eight hours a day, carrying 20 to 25 lb. rucksacks. Accommodations and meals will be in mountain huts maintained by the French Alpine Club.

The route is almost all on the French side of the frontier, except for two brief crossings into Spain. No climbing skills are necessary, but we will cross some snowfields on the passes.

Itinerary: Day 1 and 2: Leave U.S. Arrive Paris. Continue by train to Pau. Transfer to hotel.

Day 3: Travel to Urdos by train and bus. Overnight at hotel.

Day 4: Drive down the Valley d'Aspe, hike over Col d'Ayous (7,168') and descend to the Refuge d'Ayous.

Day 5: Descend into the Bious Valley (4,900') and climb steeply to Lac de Peyreget. Cross Col de Peyreget (6,804') and descend to Refuge de Pombie, with views of Pic du Midi d'Ossau, one of the classic climbs of the Pyrenees.

Day 6: Rest day.

Day 7: Descend to the Brousett Valley (4,600'), then climb steeply to the Col d'Arrious (7,411') overlooking Lac d'Artouste.

Day 8: Hike over Col du Palas (8,257'), where we cross into Spain and traverse back into France and the Refuge de Larribet (6,758').

Day 9: Descend to the Azun Valley (5,100'), then up to Col de la Fache (8,740'). Overnight at Refuge Wallon.

Day 10: Rest day.

Day 11: Cimb to the Col d'Arratille, where we enter Spain, then into the Ara Valley entering France at the Col des Mulets (8,500'). Continue down to Refuge Oulettes with its inspiring view of the Vignemale (10,820'), a sheer-walled limestone peak.

Day 12: Ascend a pass at 8,969 feet, and descend to Refuge Bayssellance (8,401').

Day 13: Take a short trail into the Lutour Valley to the town of Cauterets. Overnight in hotel.

Day 14: Afternoon train to Pau. Overnight at hotel.

Day 15: Fly to Paris and connect with homeward-bound flights.

Dates: #1 Jun 29–Jul 13 (15 days)
#2 Aug 30–Sep 13
Leader: Pierre Jamet
Grade: B-3
Land Cost: $1050
(6–10 members)
Single Supplement: to be paid locally
IT6PA1SFMT18

For those who love to wander through alpine country at its finest, this is one of the most appealing regions in Europe. The climate favors a wide-ranging and lovely flora, including daffodils and alpine roses/*Pierre Jamet*

"Just passing through..."

PARIS

City notes by Pierre Jamet

Walking/jogging routes:

Paris is one of the most walkable cities there is! Walks along the Seine are always nice, especially where you can walk close to the water, such as along the left bank near the Ile Sainte Louis and Ile de la Cite. Go for a jog in the Bois de Vincennes or the Bois de Boulogne, all easily accessible by the metro.

Day trips:

40 miles from Paris, you can hike (and climb on big sandstone boulders) in the forests around Fontainbleau. If you go by train, get off at the town of Bois-le-Roi and hike to Fontainbleau (and visit Fontainbleau castle).

Special shops:

Visit Au Vieux Campeur (48 Rue des Ecoles), largest sporting goods store in France, for its great array of top quality, sensibly-priced European hiking and climbing gear.

Museums:

If you finish the Louvre and Jeu de Paume still in one piece, try a museum called Musee de l'Homme, just across from the Eiffel Tower, with its fine ethnographic collection.

Pic du Midi d'Ossau, one of the classic climbs of the Pyrenees/*Pierre Jamet*

"The Other France" includes: twin accommodations in hotels, breakfasts, 2 dinners, ground transportation, admission charges, airport transfers, leadership.

The Mont Blanc Circuit

12-day walk in French, Swiss and Italian Alps

This is one of the world's great walks, a complete circuit around Mont Blanc, highest peak in Europe west of the Caucasus.

The classic *tour du Mont Blanc* takes about twelve days. The trail passes in and out of France, Italy and Switzerland. Views enroute make it a photographer's dream, with a background of tumbling glaciers and famous peaks like the Aiguille du Midi, Les Grandes Jorasses, and Mont Dolanot.

Mont Blanc (15,771′) presents an 11,000-foot flank of Himalayan scale and grandeur on the Italian side; the French flank is less steep but higher still. From this massif, seven valleys extend into France, Italy and Switzerland. Each of these alpine countries has its own unique culture, architecture and landscape. In circling Mont Blanc, we pass from one to the other and take time to enjoy their individual delights amidst alpine scenery which has few equals in the world.

This is a vehicle-supported hike so we only need to carry small daypacks. We'll camp each night, either in our own camps or at organized camping areas with shower facilities. This makes us independent of local mountain refuges, which can be crowded. Daily hiking time is about five hours. The guides prepare and cook all the camp meals.

Itinerary: Day 1 and 2: Leave U.S. Arrive Geneva, take the train to Martigny and camp.

Day 3: Short bus ride to Champex. Camp beneath the Trient Glacier at La Peuty, Switzerland.

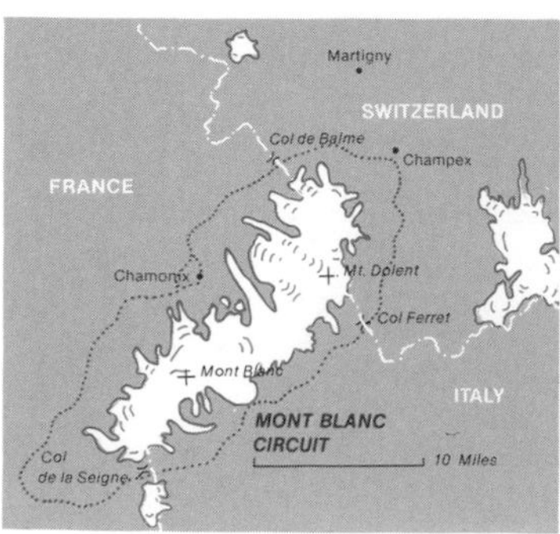

Day 4: Hike into France via the Col de Balme (7,188′), with first views of the entire Mont Blanc massif and the Glacier du Tour. Visit Argentiere in the afternoon.

Day 5: Rejoin the Grand Balcon route, which looks across the Chamonix Valley toward Mont Blanc. Descend via cable car to Les Plaz de Chamonix and camp.

Day 6: Rest day in Chamonix.

Day 7: We rejoin the trail at La Flegere, using the cable car, and continue along the Grand Balcon to the Col de Brevent (8,284′), one of the high points of the tour with face-to-face views of the Mer de Glace and Bossons glaciers. Descend to Les Houches where there are excellent camping facilities.

Day 8: By cable car to Hotel Bellevue (5,906′), then walk by the snout of the Bionassey Glacier to Col Tricot (6,955′), and descend through forest to the charming town of Les Contamines. Camp near the old chapel of Notre Dame De La Gorge.

Day 9: Make a long ascent to Col du Bonhomme (7,641′), stop at a refuge for tea, then descend to Chapieux, one of the most attractive campsites of the trek.

Day 10: Over Col de la Seigne (8,245′) into Italy, and drive to camp in the Val Veni, east of Courmayeur.

Day 11: Rest day in Courmayeur.

Day 12: By van to road's end and walk up a track past the classic Glacier de Pre de Bar which spills down from Mont Dolent. Proceed to the excellent Swiss campsite of La Fouly (5,230′) beneath the Glacier de l'A Neuve.

Day 13: Rest day.

Day 14: Hike the Swiss Val Ferret, one of the loveliest hikes of the trip, through forests and fields alive with wildflowers, through the charming villages of Praz de Fost and Les Arlaches. Overnight at hotel in Martigny.

Day 15: Train to Geneva and connect with homeward-bound flights.

Dates: #1 Jun 21–Jul 5 (15 days)
#2 Jul 5–Jul 19
#3 Aug 16–Aug 30
#4 Aug 30–Sep 13
Leader: #1 Shanan Miller
#2 to be announced
Grade: B-2
Land Cost: $1090
(6–12 members)
Single Supplement: to be paid locally
IT5SR1MT03

"The Mont Blanc Circuit" includes: twin accommodations in hotels, dorm accommodations in mountain huts, camping equipment, meals (except 6 restaurant meals), ground transportation, leadership.

Unterengaden, Switzerland/Susan Thiele

Swiss villager/Susan Thiele

The classic Tour du Mont Blanc takes about twelve days. The trail passes in and out of France, Italy and Switzerland. Views enroute make it a photographer's dream, with a background of tumbling glaciers and famous peaks/ Susan Thiele

Hiking The Haute Route

Backpacking traverse from Chamonix to Zermatt

No region is more steeped in mountaineering lore than the "Haute Route," a high-level traverse which crosses the Alps between Chamonix, France, and Zermatt, Switzerland. Along this route rise ten of the twelve highest peaks in the Alps, including the Matterhorn and Monte Rosa. It was here that the sport of mountaineering, a phenomenon of 19th century Europe, was born.

In the winter, the "Haute Route" is the finest ski mountaineering tour in Europe; in summer it presents one of the most spectacular hikes in all the Alps.

Besides traveling much of the famed Haute Route, our hiking route covers some rarely-visited parts of the Swiss Valais, crossing high passes of true alpine character and meandering into charming villages where the style of farming has remained unchanged for centuries. Most of the trails are relatively untrodden, giving excellent opportunity to see a variety of alpine flowers and wildlife.

From the Chamonix Valley, we cross the northern part of the French side of the Mont Blanc Massif via the Col de Balme into Switzerland. The remainder of our trek will be in Switzerland, concluding at the famous alpine resort of Zermatt, where we spend a few days enjoying outstanding day walks.

Wherever possible, accommodations will be in mountain refuges, to maintain the high mountain ambiance. There is one three-day section of self-contained backpacking, and on most other hiking days, we carry rucksacks weighing perhaps 20–25 lbs. (depending on personal gear).

Itinerary: Day 1 and 2: Leave U.S. Arrive Geneva and continue by train to Chamonix. Overnight in hotel.

Day 3: Day free in Chamonix.

Day 4: Train to Argentiere and hike over Col de Balme (7,230') with panoramic views of the Mont Blanc massif. Descend to hut at Trient.

Day 5: Steep hike to the Fenetre d'Arpette (8,743'), and long descent to the resort of Realis d'Arpette.

Day 6: Descend to Champex and organize for three-day backpacking trip. Hike to the hut at Cabane Mt. Fort (8,061').

Day 7: Steep, cross-country hike across the Col de Gele (9,200'), one of the most remote areas of the Alps. Descend to Refuge St. Laurent.

Day 8: Steep ascent over Col de Prafleuri (9,728'), a remote area with panoramic views of Mont Blanc de Cheelon and Pigne d'Arolla. Overnight at the hut at Cabane Prafleuri.

Day 9: Descend to Lac des Dix then ascend the long route over Col de Riedmatten (9,577') for the first view of the Matterhorn before Zermatt. Overnight in hotel.

Day 10: Free day in Arolla.

Day 11: Drive to Villa, seeing local Valais women still wearing traditional dress as they tend their fields. Hike up Col de Torrent (9,574'), and descend to Grimentz, an extremely charming old Valais town. Overnight at pension.

Day 12: Walk to Cabane de Weisshorn, superbly located hut with panoramic views.

Day 13: Walk over Meidpass (9,154'), then enter German-speaking Switzerland. Long descent to Gruben. Overnight at pension.

Day 14: Climb up to Augstbordpass (9,495'), descend to Jungu and take the cable car to St. Niklaus and train to Zermatt. overnight in hotel.

Day 15: Day free in Zermatt.

Day 16: Morning train to Geneva and connect with homeward-bound flights.

Dates: #1 Jul 5–Jul 20 (16 days)
#2 Aug 4–Aug 19
Leader: to be announced
Grade: B-3
Land Cost: $1090
(6–12 members)
Single Supplement: locally paid
IT5SR1MT01

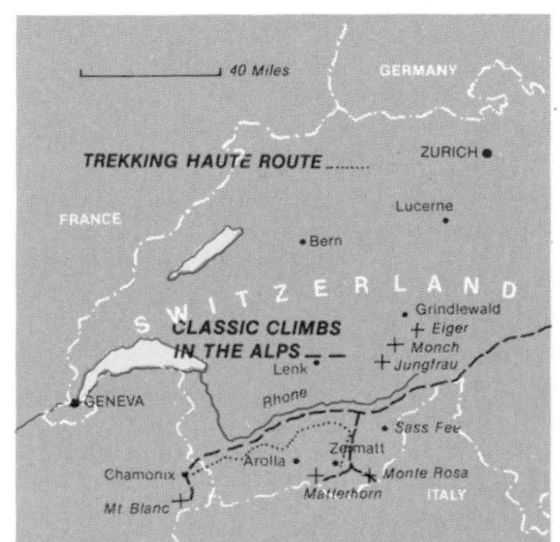

Classic Climbs In The Alps

Matterhorn, Mont Blanc, Monte Rosa, Gross Glockner

On this mountaineering journey, we will attempt some of the most famous peaks of the Swiss, French and Austrian Alps.

In Austria, we climb magnificent Gross Glockner (12,461'), whose icy cone is Austria's highest summit.

From Chamonix, birthplace of mountaineering, we attempt Mont Blanc (15,771'), highest point in Europe west of the Caucasus.

From Zermatt, the best known mountain resort in the world, we climb Monte Rosa (15,208'), 2nd highest peak in the Alps, and the Matterhorn (14,962'), the beautiful spire whose classic shape is familiar to everyone.

Itinerary: Day 1 and 2: Leave U.S. Arrive Munich. Travel to Mittersill.

Day 3: Organization and practice.

Day 4 to 6: Hike to hut, ascend Gross Glockner and return to hut.

Day 7: Descend and transfer to Innsbruck. Overnight at hotel.

Day 8: By train to Chamonix. Overnight in hotel.

Day 9 to 11: Hike to hut, ascend Mont Blanc and descend to Chamonix.

Day 12: Train to Zermatt. Overnight at hotel.

Day 13 to 15: Hike to hut, ascend Monte Rosa and descend to Zermatt.

Day 16 to 18: Hike to hut, ascend Matterhorn, descend to Zermatt.

Day 19: Travel to Geneva. Overnight at hotel.

Day 20: Depart and connect with homeward-bound flights.

Dates: #1 Jul 12–Jul 31 (20 days)
#2 Aug 1–Aug 20
Leader: to be announced
Grade: D-2
Land Cost: $1890
(6–10 members)
Single Supplement: to be paid locally
IT5SR1MT02

The Matterhorn/Susan Thiele

"Just passing through..."

GENEVA

City notes by Leo Le Bon

Jogging/walking routes:

Geneva's botanical gardens house a very unique rock garden of alpine flora. Walk along the Quai du Mont Blanc, a broad sidewalk on the north side of Lake Geneva, for a great distant view of the Alps (in clear weather). Beyond the sidewalk are three connecting lakeside parks well worth visiting: Parc Mon Repos, La Perle du Lac and Villa Barton.

Day trips:

Not far from Geneva is the Saleve, a small mountain visible from downtown and a popular hangout for rock climbers and day hikers. There's a good view of the city from here, and on the top of Saleve are several small inns serving delicious country food. Be sure to sample the famous "tome de Savoie" cheese here!

Shopping:

Geneva is a good place to buy outdoor and mountain clothes at many excellent camping and climbing shops. Ski equipment in particular is readily available. There is also good shopping at the Place du Molard quarter.

Besides traveling much of the famed Haute Route, our hiking route covers some rarely visited parts of the Swiss Valais, crossing high passes of true alpine character and meandering into charming villages where the style of farming has remained unchanged for centuries/*Susan Thiele*

The Greek Islands

Exploring by boat in the Western Cyclades

For this free-form journey, we charter a *kaiki* and cruise to several of the most interesting and remote islands in the western Cyclades.

We travel island to island, avoiding the tourist areas, to explore remote fishing villages where the old Greek way of life still exists. This trip will have a very flexible itinerary and a few surprises.

We also plan to do some beach hiking, swimming, snorkeling and spend many evenings dancing in small *tavernas.*

Our boat will be a motor-sailer, called a *kaiki,* a term which refers to a variety of hull shapes and boat designs. It will be a very comfortable and livable boat. There will be a crew of two.

A typical day on the boat may go like this: up early for a light breakfast on board, then leave port (usually my motor) for the next island. We stop around noon on most days for a swim at a secluded beach followed by a Greek salad-style lunch on board. Continuing to the next port, we might go ashore for coffee (perhaps some ouzo and octopus!) then walk to a nearby village. The evening meal will be taken in a *taverna,* where those who wish can do some Greek dancing.

Much of the emphasis of the trip is on enjoying the scene in the local *tavernas* and outdoor cafes, where we spend a lot of our time. Greece is one of the few places where the national dances are not just relegated to the performing stage, but are part of everyday life. Every joyous occasion calls for music and dancing, and we will dance with the Greeks in their *tavernas*

and cafes, or sometimes by ourselves on isolated beaches . . . wherever the spirit moves us! Nightly accommodations will be four-bunk cabins on the boat.

Itinerary: Day 1 and 2: Leave U.S. Arrive Athens. Transfer to hotel.

Day 3: Day free in Athens. Evening visit to our favorite dancing spot in the Plaka.

Day 4: Drive to Pireaus or Porto Rafti and board the boat.

Day 5 to 13: For the next nine days, we will motor (or occasionally sail when winds and currents are favorable) among the following islands: Kithnos, Sifnos, Sikinos, Thera, Skinoussa, Antiparos, Tinos, Delos, Kea and back to Pireaus and Athens. We will keep the sea itinerary flexible according to weather conditions.

Day 14: Depart Athens and connect with homeward-bound flights.

Dates: Jul 5–Jul 18 (14 days)
Leader: Maki Idosidis or Allen Steck
Grade: A-1
Land Cost: $1890 (9–10 members) $1990 (7–8)
Single Supplement: not available
IT6TW15644

Hiking In Greece & Crete

3-day Pelopponesos walk, 3-day Gorge of Samaria hike

This hiking journey ventures into the back-country to come into close contact with the hospitable mountain villagers of Greece and Crete.

These rugged hills and coasts are an exquisite place for hiking, a Mediterranean panorama of wooded mountains, barren rock summits, silver-green olive groves, golden beaches and a wide blue sea.

Our first hike takes us for three days through the Taiyetos Mountains which rise above Sparta, and our journey follows Spartan warrior paths through forests of chestnut and oak.

On Crete, largest and most mountainous of the Greek islands, a second three-day hike takes us into the Levka Ori ("White Mountains"), a tremendous range from whose peaks we can see almost the entire western half of Crete. Besides meeting local villagers, we visit some of the most famous Mycenean and classic sites of Greece, and the mysterious sites of the Minoan civilization on Santorini, the most beautiful island in the Cyclades.

Gorge of Somaria/ *Allen Steck*

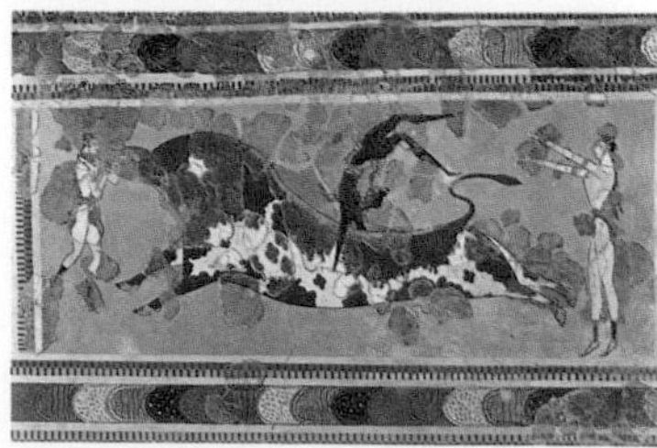

Frieze at Knossos, Crete/ *Allen Steck*

We travel island to island, avoiding the tourist areas, to explore remote fishing villages where the old Greek way of life still exists. This trip will have a very flexible itinerary and a few surprises/ *Ken Scott*

Our camp gear is transferred by vehicle while we walk, so we only need to carry day packs. Accommodations are in mountain huts, tents and in very simple pensions.

Itinerary: Day 1 and 2: Leave U.S. Arrive Athens. Continue by ferry to Hydra. Overnight in the fishing village of Kaminia.

Day 3: By ferry to Hermione and continue to Epidavros, site of the temple of Aesclepius. Drive to Nafplion. Camp nearby.

Day 4: Drive to Mycene, Agamemnon's capital, and continue across the Tayetos Range to Sparta. Camp near the beautiful monastery of Phaneronamy.

Day 5: Hike to the village of Parury with excellent views of the valley of Sparta, the Parnon Range and the Aegean Sea. Continue by bus and tractor to Krionerion. Hike to a mountain hut maintained by the Greek Alpine Club.

Day 6: Hike over Pilgrim's Pass and descend and camp by a shepherds' colony.

Day 7: Descend on an ancient Spartan path along a spectacular canyon to the village of Exochorion. Drive to the seaside village of Kardamili. Overnight at pension.

Day 8: Rest day.

Day 9: Drive to Githion and board overnight ferry to Crete.

Day 10: Morning arrival in Kastely in northwestern Crete. Drive to Hania. Overnight in hotel.

Day 11: Drive southward across the western part of Crete and hike to the alpine hut of Kalergy atop a cliff which dominates the Gorge of Samaria.

Day 12: Rest day.

Day 13: Descend the Gorge of Samaria, one of the largest canyons in Europe.

Day 14: Drive along the coast toward central northern Crete, where most of the Minoan sites are found. Visit Knossos and Fesstos and continue to Heraklion. Overnight in hotel.

Day 15: Free day in Heraklion. Overnight ferry to Athens.

Day 16: Arrive in Athens. Afternoon, depart Athens and connect with homeward-bound flights.

Dates: Sep 6–Sep 21 (16 days)
Leader: Avner Goren
Grade: B-2
Land Cost: $1790 (11–12 members) $1890 (8–10)
Single Supplement: available on request
IT6TW15643

Turkey: Mt. Ararat & The Taurus Mountains

In search of Noah's Ark

When Mt. Ararat was opened to foreign travelers in 1983, Mountain Travlers were there, standing on its summit, looking out over northern Turkey, Soviet Armenia and the plains of northern Iran.

Mt. Ararat is a magnificent sprawling dome whose snow-covered summit is 16,945 feet above sea level. Many Armenians revere this peak as "Mother of the World" and most Christians believe it is the site where Noah's Ark came to rest after the Great Flood.

A climb of Ararat is really just a tough walk (non-technical but requiring a good deal of stamina). The upper third of the volcano is covered in snow and the last hundred meters to the summit is icy. (The actual climb to the summit from Camp II at 14,760 feet is optional).

The drive to Ararat is through the dusty and colorful frontier town of Dogu Beyazit, with its cobblestone streets and horse carts.

Before hiking on Ararat, we'll warm up with a six-day trek in the Taurus Range, a limestone group on the southern coast with a complex system of spires, peaks, and ridges of almost mystical beauty. On trek, we cross a high plateau beneath the rocky 12,000-foot summits of the Aladag group, highest portion of the Taurus Mountains.

Turkey has many of the world's most famous sites of antiquity, and we will be sure to see Cappadocia, with its rock-hewn chapels and the remarkable underground cities of Derinkuyu and Kaymakli.

Itinerary: Day 1 and 2: Leave U.S. Arrive Istanbul and fly to Ankara. Transfer to hotel.

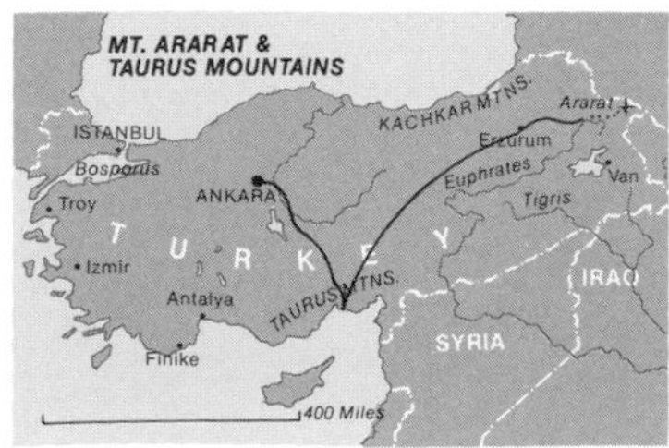

Turkey has many of the world's most famous sites of antiquity/Leo Le Bon

Day 3: Morning tour of Ankara and drive to Cappadocia. Visit rock churches, monasteries, cave dwellings.

Day 4: Sightseeing in Cappadocia.

Day 5: Drive to Nigde, visiting the "underground cities" of Derinkuyu and Kaymakli. Walk to the foot of Mt. Demirkazik.

Day 6: Hike to Cimbar Valley with impressive views of Mt. Demirkazak (12,322').

Day 7: Trek to Seven Lakes Valley. Optional hike up Mt. Embler (11,886').

Day 8 and 9: Trek to Sogukpunar and visit some spectacular waterfalls.

Day 10: Trek to the Aciman highlands at 7,000 feet and jeep to Karsanti over a rough road with panoramic views of the Taurus Mountains.

Day 11: Drive to the seaside town of Mersin.

Day 12: Free day for ocean swimming and resting.

Day 13: Fly to Erzurum, tour the city and drive to Dogu Beyazit.

Day 14: Drive to Eli, where Kurdish shepherds graze their sheep and cattle, and trek to a main camp at 10,500 feet.

Day 15 and 16: Trek to Camp I (13,780') and Camp II (14,760').

Day 17: Optional climb up to the summit. Descend to Camp II.

Day 18: Descend and drive back to the town of Dogu Beyazit.

Day 19: Drive to Lake Van. Sunset visit to the great citadel of Van.

Day 20: Afternoon flight to Istanbul.

Day 21: Tour Istanbul.

Day 22: Depart Istanbul and connect with homeward-bound flights.

Dates: Jul 27–Aug 17 (22 days)
Leader: to be announced
Grade: B-2/C-3
Land Cost: $1875 (10–15 members)
$1990 (6–9)
+ $100 domestic flights within Turkey
Single Supplement: $110
IT6PA1SFMT23

On our six-day trek in the Taurus Mountains, we'll get a glimpse into life in the remote mountain villages of Turkey's southern coast/Leo Le Bon

Travels In Kazakhstan

The Western Tien Shan Range

The mountainous backdrop of the Kazakh S.S.R. is formed by the western Tien Shan, one of the five great mountain chains which radiate out from high central Asia where the frontiers of Russia, China, Pakistan and Afghanistan meet.

The peaks of the western Tien Shan are jagged, icy and alpine in character. Although the Tien Shan Mountains rise from extremely arid country, they receive heavy snowfall and as a result the slopes below snowline are clothed with flowery meadows and fine forests of juniper and spruce, while massive glaciers gather on the upper slopes.

This is an exploratory trip focusing around backpacking and non-technical climbs of several peaks in the 12,000 to 14,000-foot range. The trip operates from a climbers hotel in the Chimbulak Valley near Alma Ata, capital of Kazakh S.S.R.

Itinerary: Day 1 and 2: Leave U.S. Arrive Moscow. Overnight at hotel.

Day 3: In Moscow.

Day 4 to 16: Hikes and easy climbs from a base in the Chimbulak Valley.

Day 17: Fly to Moscow.

Day 18: Sightseeing in Moscow.

Day 19: Depart Moscow on homeward-bound flights.

Dates: Aug 20–Sep 7 (19 days)
Leader: Dick & Louise McGowan
Grade: B-3/D-2
Land Cost: $1890 (6–15 members)
Single Supplement: not available
IT5AF155UH

Kazakh horseman/John B. Thune

Travels In Armenia

Hikes on Mt. Alagaz and Mt. Gora Azhrak

Armenia is the oldest Christian country in the world, converted by St. Gregory the Illuminator in 301 A.D. It's an ancient land whose long and turbulent history is well known.

During our visit to Soviet Armenia, we travel "Mountain-Travel style," camping, hiking and exploring out-of-the-way places.

One of our hikes is a three-day traverse of Mt. Gora Azhrak (11,788′) through arid country with wide-ranging views of Lake Sevan, the hills of Azerbaijman, Mt. Alagaz, and famed Mt. Ararat, just over the Turkish border, whose northern slopes drain onto the plains of the River Araxes.

Later on, we hike up the extinct volcano of Mt. Alagaz, which rises from the Araxes Valley to a height of 13,410 feet and forms a distant and snowy backdrop for the capital city of Yerevan.

We also visit Lake Sevan (6,340′), a mountain lake confined by the long ridge of mountains which divides Armenia and Georgia, and tour many churches and monasteries which are masterpieces of medieval Armenian architecture, dating from the 4th to 13th centuries.

Itinerary: Day 1 and 2: Leave U.S. Arrive Moscow.

Day 3: Sightseeing in Moscow.

Day 4: Fly to Yerevan, Armenia.

Day 5: Tour Yerevan, one of the oldest cities in the world, founded in 782 B.C.

Day 6: Drive south to camp in the Yechednazor District.

Day 7 and 8: Hikes in a nature preserve of woodlands with interesting wildlife.

Day 9: Hike to Garni, visit its beautiful 1st century Hellenistic temple, and drive to camp on Mt. Gora Azhrak, visiting 12th century Gegard Monastery enroute.

Day 10 and 11: Hiking traverse of Mt. Gora Azhrak (11,788′).

Day 12: Hike to Lake Sevan and overnight at hotel.

Day 13: Drive to Dilizhan, a high altitude health resort surrounded by coniferous and broad-leafed forests and orchards. Camp.

Day 14: Drive to Kirovakan and camp, with visits enroute to several sites of antiquity.

Day 15: Drive to camp on the eastern slopes of Mt. Alagaz.

Day 16: Hike to Mt. Alagaz and camp at a lake.

Day 17: Descend to the fortress-ruins at Amberd with views of Mt. Ararat and the Araxes Valley. Drive to Yerevan for overnight at hotel.

Day 18: Afternoon flight to Moscow.

Day 19: In Moscow.

Day 20: Depart on homeward-bound flights.

Day 21: Arrive home.

Dates: Oct 1–Oct 21 (21 days)
Leader: Peter Ourusoff
Grade: A-2/B-2
Land Cost: $1925 (12–15 members) $2090 (8–11)
Single Supplement: not available
IT5AF155UL

The Caucasus & Mt. Elbrus

Backpacking and optional climbing

Out itinerary focuses around the Central Caucasus, with its mountain scenery as beautiful as any in the heart of the Swiss and French Alps. There are deep forests of poplar and beech, high thickets of stunted birch and rhododendron and alpine meadows carpeted with wildflowers. The highest peak in Europe is located here—Mt. Elbrus (18,841′). Around it are other major peaks such as Shikhra (16,529′), Katyntau (16,355′), Jangitau, (16,571′), and Ushba (15,453′), the "Matterhorn of the Caucasus."

Our base will be a hotel in the Baksan Valley below Mt. Elbrus. From this central location, we'll make a variety of excursions, including a seven-day backpacking trip across the major passes of the Caucasus into Svanetia, a Georgian mountain region with 1000 years of history dating back to the Crusades.

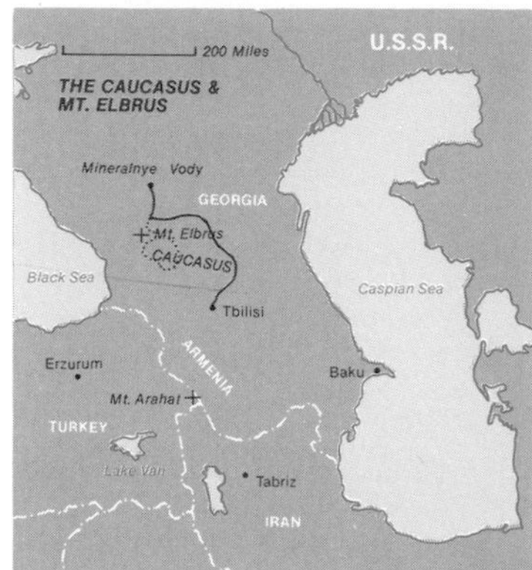

The medieval town of Mestia, Georgia/ Louise McGowan

We tour many churches and monasteries which are masterpieces of medieval Armenian architecture, dating from the 4th to the 13th centuries/ *Bruce Klepinger*

We'll make a variety of excursions, including a seven-day backpacking trip across the major passes of the Caucasus into Svanetia, a Georgian mountain region/ *Dick McGowan*

Returning to the Baksan Valley, climbers in the group will have a chance to ascend Mt. Elbrus, a challenging (but not technically difficult) high altitude climb. During the two-day climb, others in the group can hike up to the Priutt Refuge on Mt. Elbrus for great mountain views.

Itinerary: Day 1 and 2: Leave U.S. Arrive Moscow. Transfer to hotel.

Day 3: Fly to Mineralnye Vody and bus to Baksan Valley. Overnight at hotel.

Day 4 and 5: Day hikes on Cheget and Mt. Elbrus for acclimatization.

Day 6 to 12: Backpacking across the passes of the Caucasus into Svanetia, Georgia. Cross Betcho Pass (10,580′), visit villages of Masery and Mestia, hike across Dongus-Orun Pass (12,795′) and return hike to Baksan Valley.

Day 13: Rest day, optional local walks.

Day 14 to 16: For mountaineers, non-technical climb of Mt. Elbrus; for others, hike to refuge on Elbrus for overnight.

The group will have a chance to ascend Mt. Elbrus, a challenging but not technically difficult high-altitude climb/ *Louise McGowan*

Day 17: Descend to the Baksan Valley. Overnight at hotel.

Day 18: Rest day at hotel.

Day 19 to 21: Three-day excursion by road to Georgia, including visits to Kasbegi and Tbilissi.

Day 22: Fly to Moscow. Transfer to hotel.

Day 23: Day free in Moscow for sightseeing.

Day 24: Depart Moscow and connect with homeward-bound flights.

Dates: Sep 7–Sep 30 (24 days)
Leader: Peter Ourusoff
Grade: B-3/D-2
Land Cost: $1890
(8–15 members)
Single Supplement: not available
IT5AF155UI

Plaques commemorating Russian war heroes/Dick McGowan

Soviet mountain guides/Louise McGowan

Mountain camp in the Pamirs. The U.S.S.R. Sports Committee hosts an important series of International Mountaineering Camps open to climbers, skiers and hikers. The camps are truly international and are attended by people from dozens of nations/ *Allen Steck*

The Pamirs & Peak Lenin

Within the U.S.S.R., four peaks rise to over 7,000 meters. Three of these lie in the Pamirs, a unique cluster of mountains in the southeast corner of the Tadzhik S.S.R., where China, the Soviet Union, Pakistan and Afghanistan meet.

The goal of our expedition is an ascent of Peak Lenin (23,406′), the most frequently climbed high peak in the world. While the climb is not technically difficult, extreme altitude and potentially severe weather conditions on the mountain make it a demanding ascent.

From Moscow, we fly to Osh, capital of the Kirghiz S.S.R., and Daraut Kurgan, an old fortress city dating from the Silk Route, and drive by truck to our base camp at Achik-Tash at 11,700 feet. Sixteen days are allotted for the climb via the Lipkin Route on the northeast ridge of Peak Lenin.

Itinerary: Day 1 and 2: Leave U.S. Arrive Moscow. Overnight at hotel.

Day 3: Fly to Osh and Daraut Kurgan and drive to base camp.

Day 4 to 10: Acclimatization hikes and ascents.

Day 11 to 26: On the mountain.

Day 27: Fly to Moscow.

Day 28 and 29: Sightseeing in Moscow.

Day 30: Depart Moscow and connect with homeward-bound flights.

Dates: Jul 27–Aug 25 (30 days)
Leader: Bruce Klepinger
Grade: E-2
Land Cost: $2875
(8–12 members)
Single Supplement: not available
ITAF155UJ

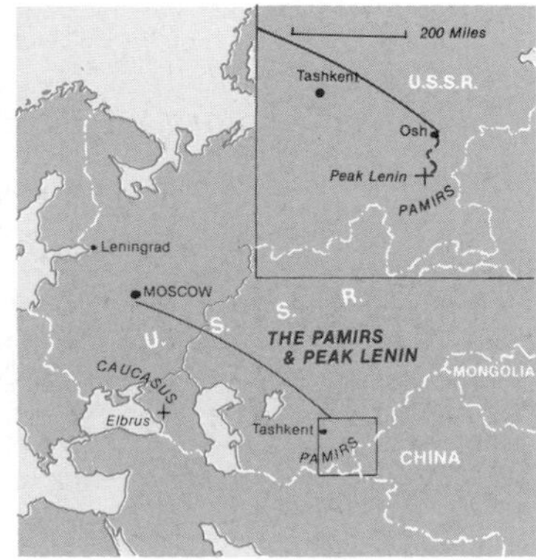

U.S.S.R. International Mountaineering Camps

The U.S.S.R. Sports Committee hosts an important series of International Mountaineering Camps open to climbers, skiers and hikers. The camps are truly international and are attended by people from dozens of nations. This program has been on-going since 1974.

Participants must supply their own personal camping, climbing and/or skiing equipment. Cost includes all expenses within the U.S.S.R. The Soviet staff provides assistance in planning your activities at the camps, but there is no pre-planned itinerary; each individual must arrange his/her own activities. No change is allowed from the set program dates. Mountain Travel will provide some written material and maps.

At the time of writing, the exact dates and prices for 1986 are not known. As soon as they are, we will print an Information Sheet on the 1986 U.S.S.R. International Mountaineering Camps. Send for a copy.

For 1986, the programs will take place in four mountain regions:

The Caucasus:
24-day climbing/hiking program in the Mt. Elbrus region (two July camps); 17-day alpine skiing program (camps in February, March and May).

The Pamirs:
30-day program of expedition mountaineering with climbs in the Pamir Range. Five July camps. Minmum four in party.

The Western Tien Shan:
15-day program of skiing and climbing in the Chimgan region. One camp is offered in February.

The Altai:
24-day climbing/hiking program with an ascent of Mt. Belukha (14,800′), highest peak in the Altai. One July camp is planned.

U.S.S.R. trips include: air transportation within the U.S.S.R., ground transportation, twin accommodations in hotels, all meals, interpreter services, visas, transfers, sightseeing, group camping and commissary equipment, supplementary food.

For 400 years, Machu Picchu remained a mystery, sealed off from the world. The conquering Spaniards combed Peru, but they never found it, nor did others who searched. Many doubted that such a "lost city" existed until July 24, 1911, when Hiram Bingham of Yale University came upon this place/*Bruce Klepinger*

Section V
South America & Mexico

"Then the boy urged us to climb up a steep hill over what seemed to be a flight of stone steps. Surprise followed surprise in bewildering succession. We came to a great stairway of large granite blocks. Then we walked along a path to a clearing where the Indians had planted a small vegetable garden. Suddenly we found ourselves standing in front of the ruins of two of the finest and most interesting structures in ancient America. Made of beautiful white granite, the walls contained blocks of Cyclopean size, higher than a man. The sight held me spellbound."

In the inner sanctum of the Cordillera Urubamba, below ice-covered peaks and within jungled canyons, the Inca king, Manco Capac II, found a safe hiding place from the conquering Spaniards.

He took with him his priests and his court, and created a hilltop citadel which for 40 years was the focus of Indian resistance to the conquerors of Peru.

For 400 years, the city remained a mystery, sealed off from the world. The conquering Spaniards combed Peru, but they never found it, nor did others who searched. Many doubted that such a "lost city" ever existed. Until July 24, 1911, when Hiram Bingham of Yale University came upon this place.

Bingham's discovery was not an accident—it was the result of a long, diligent and sometimes-painful search on foot across ice-covered passes, through steaming orchid-laden jungles and alongside raging rivers which had cut canyons through rock to a depth of 2,000 feet.

Today, of course, thousands of people every year "discover" Machu Picchu, arriving heavy-laden with cameras, fresh from a swift 60-mile train ride from Cuzco!

But the real feeling of the "discovery" can be recaptured by visitors who choose to *walk* to Machu Picchu as Bingham did, on Inca pathways from ruin to ruin along the ridges and valleys of the Cordillera Urubamba.

There is nothing to equal the feeling one gets from "earning" one's view of this sanctuary at the finish of a three-to-six-day hike. That's what adventure travel is all about.

Inca trail in the Cordillera Urubamba/ *Leo Le Bon*

Part of the enjoyment of trekking in Peru is meeting the people who have inhabited these highlands for centuries and through whose villages and lives we will pass/*Bruce Klepinger*

Any continent which boasts both the Andes and the Amazon, two of the natural wonders of the world, is bound to attract adventurers, treasure-hunters and naturalists.

The Andes are the longest continuous mountain range in the world, extending the entire 4,500-mile length of the continent from Colombia to Cape Horn.

On the western side of the Andes, there are deserts where rain hasn't fallen for 20 years. On the eastern side, the landscape forms the deep Amazon Basin, an area twice as large as India and the world's most extensive equatorial rain forest.

To the south lie Patagonia's continental ice sheets, deep fjords and golden pampas where *gauchos* tend to their flocks of sheep.

Beyond, the continent narrows and the Andes plunge into the sea, only 600 miles north of Antarctica.

As varied as this continent's landscape is its mixture of Spanish and indigenous cultures, found in colonial cities and roadless Indian villages.

Adventure Travel In South America

The Cordillera Carabaya of Peru show the Andes at their most exquisite: immense altiplano, high rolling plains dotted with isolated, iceberg-like massifs/*Bruce Klepinger*

Porters at top of Warmiwanusqa Pass, Inca Trail/*Sara Steck*

Peru:

Peru is one of those rare countries which offers everything: mountains (20 ranges), deserts, jungles, ancient ruins and a rich heritage. Trekking to Machu Picchu can take three to six days, depending on where you start.

In the northern ranges, a variety of trekking routes cross the Cordillera Blanca and Cordillera Huayhuash, highest tropical mountain ranges in the world, ideally suited for shirt-sleeve hiking.

For riding enthusiast, horseback treks can be arranged in the Cordillera Negra. Scenic whitewater trips are possible on the upper Urubama and several other Peruvian rivers. Manu National Park, largest in the Amazon, is the best place for exploration by dugout canoe in an untouched area which was declared in 1977 a Biosphere Reserve of major scientific value by the U.N.

For trekking, March through October is the best season. For sightseeing and touring, just about any time of the year is good (one just experiences a little more rain in Machu Picchu and sun in Lima from November to February).

Setting out across the altiplano enroute to trails of Cordillera Real, Bolivia/*Sara Steck*

Villagers from the Santa Valley carry goods and serve as cooks for trekking parties in the Cordillera Blanca/ *Sara Steck*

Bolivia:

The little-traveled Bolivian Andes offer exceptional trekking, particularly in the Cordillera Real. Several 20,000-foot volcanoes on the *altiplano* offer challenging non-technical climbs. Lake Titicaca, the "inland sea" shared by both Bolivia and Peru, can be visited by boat from either country. Of particular interest are the Indian communities living on "floating" reed islands on the lake.

In Bolivia, the Indian communities that live on "floating" reed islands on Lake Titicaca, are of particular interest/ *Bruce Klepinger*

Marine iguana. The reptile-inhabited archipelago called the Galapagos, "Darwin's Island," provided the setting for one of the most significant chapters in science history/ *Sara Steck*

Ecuador:

The reptile-inhabited archipelago called the Galapagos provided the setting for one of the most significant chapters in science history. The islands, now a national park, can be visited by small yacht, with a Galapagos-trained naturalist guide. Ecuador's green highland plateau contains beautiful 20,000-foot volcanoes; to camp and hike at their bases on the "Avenue of the Volcanoes" is a wonderful adventure, as is non-technical climbing to reach their snow-capped summits. Jungle excursions to the Ecuadorian Amazon attract birding enthusiasts from around the world.

Hiking and touring season lasts virtually all year in Ecuador. For climbing, November to March is best. For a wildlife cruise in the Galapagos, December through April is the warm, rainy season, May to November is the cool season.

Ecuador's green highland plateau contains beautiful 20,000-foot volcanoes: to camp and hike at their bases on the "Avenue of the Volcanoes" is an adventure, as is a non-technical climb to their snow-capped summits/ *Sergio Fitch-Watkins*

Sea lion/ *Alla Schmitz*

Frigate bird, displaying/ *Alla Schmitz*

Trekkers find a challenge walking around the rock cuernos and granite slabs of Torres del Paine/ *Bruce Klepinger*

South America Bibliography

Chile & Argentina:

"The uttermost end of the earth," that's what the wilds of Patagonia have been called. Shared by Chile and Argentina, this is a remarkable landscape at the southernmost tip of South America where the Andes are 11,000-foot granite spires rising from dense forests of Magellan beech trees.

Climbers find challenge on the rock *cuernos* (horns) and granite slabs of Paine and Fitzroy, and wildlife enthusiasts marvel at the site of wild herds of vicuna, cousin to Peru's llama. Further north is Aconcagua (22,834'), highest mountain in the Western Hemisphere.

On the east coast of Argentina at Peninsula Valdez, one can visit the world's largest penguin rookery. Northern Chile has one of the world's most unusual deserts: the Atacama, a vast waterless expanse at 12,000 feet which is sprinkled with huge 20,000-foot volcanoes, some of them active.

The best season for Chile and Argentina is our winter (their summer)—December to March.

Colombia & Venezuela:

Colombia has two interesting mountain ranges: the best known is the Nevada de Santa Marta, highest coastal mountain range on earth, where 18,000-foot peaks rise just 30 miles from the Caribbean shore. On the Venezuelan border is the Sierra Nevada de Cocoy, most heavily glaciated range in Colombia. Both ranges offer challenging non-technical climbs. Venezuela boasts Angel Falls, the world's longest waterfall at 3,200 feet, which can only be reached by a three-day dugout canoe journey, and the *Gran Sabana,* where the adventurous can backpack to 9,000-foot Mt. Roraima, setting for Sir Arthur Conan Doyle's *Lost World.*

Patagonia is a land of Alaskan-size fjords and of glaciers which fall into the sea/*Len Chatwin*

A TRAVELER'S GUIDE TO EL DORADO AND THE INCA EMPIRE
Lynn Meisch, Viking Press, 1984. Colombia, Ecuador, Peru and Bolivia.

ADVENTURING IN THE ANDES
Charles Frazier, Sierra Club, 1985.

SOUTH AMERICA AND CENTRAL AMERICA: A NATURAL HISTORY
Jean Dorst, Random House, 1967.

FLIGHT OF THE CONDOR
Michael A. Andrews, Collins, 1982. Wildlife exploration of the Andes.

LOST CITY OF THE INCAS
Hiram Bingham, Librerias, 1975. Machu Picchu discoveries. Reprint.

CONQUEST OF THE INCAS
John Hemming, Harcourt, Brace, Jovanovich, 1970. History.

MONUMENTS OF THE INCAS
John Hemming, Little, Brown, 1982. Archaeology.

THE ANCIENT CIVILIZATIONS OF PERU
J. Alden Mason, Penguin, 1968.

EXPLORING CUZCO
Peter Frost, Bradt, 1984. A guide to the city and its surrounding areas.

THE OLD PATAGONIAN EXPRESS
Paul Theroux, Houghton Mifflin, 1979. Railway journey through Central and South America.

THE OTHER SIDE OF THE MOUNTAIN
James Ramsey Ullman, Carrick & Evans, 1938. An escape to the Amazon

CORDILLERA BLANCA (PERU)
Hans Kinzl and Erwin Schneider, Universitats-Verlag Wagner, 1950. General information and photos.

TRAILS OF THE CORDILLERA BLANCA AND HUAYHUASH, PERU
Jim Bartle, 1981. Trail guide and general information.

YURAQ JANKA: CORDILLERA BLANCA AND ROSKO
John F. Ricker, American Alpine Club, 1981. The mountains of Peru with maps.

THE ASCENT OF YERUPAJA
John Sack, Jenkins, 1954. Mountaineering in Huayhuash, Peru.

RONDOY
David Wall, John Murray, 1965. Expedition to the Huayhuash.

TRAVELS AMONGST THE GREAT ANDES OF THE EQUATOR
Edward Whymper, various editions, 1891. A classic.

CLIMBING AND EXPLORATION IN THE BOLIVIAN ANDES
William Martin Conway, various editions, 1894. A classic.

THE HIGHEST ANDES
E.A. Fitzgerald, Methuen, 1899. First ascent of Aconcagua.

ACONCAGUA: SOUTH FACE
Rene Ferlet and Guy Poulet, Constable, 1956. Argentina.

LAND OF TEMPEST
Eric Shipton, Dutton, 1963. Travels in Patagonia.

IN PATAGONIA
Bruce Chatwin, Summit, 1977.

MISCHIEF IN PATAGONIA
H.W. Tilman, Travel Book Club, 1956.

CONQUEST OF FITZROY.
M.A. Azema, Andre Deutsch, 1957. Mountaineering, Patagonia.

TIERRA DEL FUEGO: THE FATAL LODESTONE
Eric Shipton, Knight, 1973.

THE NATIONAL PARKS OF COSTA RICA
Maria A. Boza and Rolando Mendoza, INCAFO, 1981.

A NATURALIST IN COSTA RICA
Alexander F. Skutch, University of Florida Press, 1971.

BIRDS OF VENEZUELA
Rudolph de Schauensee, Princeton University Press.

GALAPAGOS, ISLANDS LOST IN TIME
Tui de Roy Moore, Viking, 1980.

GALAPAGOS
Bryan Nelson, Morrow, 1968.

THE CROSSING OF ANTARCTICA
Vivian Fuchs, Little, Brown, 1958.

BEYOND CAPE HORN: TRAVELS IN THE ANTARCTIC
Charles Neider, Sierra Club, 1980.

ENDURANCE: SHACKLETON'S INCREDIBLE VOYAGE
Alfred Lansing, McGraw-Hill, 1959. Shackleton's third expedition to the Antarctic.

Trekking . . . Reminiscences And Rewards

by Barbara Bowden

I hadn't really thought too much about it before, of trekking being something akin to eating peanuts or potato chips. It is really not possible to stop at one.

I had made a trek to Nepal at a time of year when my husband was unable to go along. It was such a remarkable experience for me, that I was eager for him to share a similar adventure.

We decided upon a trip to the Andes. A trek to Machu Picchu along the old Inca trail was something that was especially interesting to us. We were intrigued with the idea of visiting the ancient city of the Incas, and getting an opportunity to see first hand and learn more about that ancient culture.

As we walked the Inca trail to Machu Picchu, we saw the evidence of these ancient people along the way. Some of the ruins were far below us near the banks of the Urubamba River, while others were right along the trail.

One afternoon, after a particularly long day, we proceeded finally up an ancient Inca staircase, carved right out of the mountain. We found ourselves among some old Incan walls on a piece of real estate that was barely large enough to accommodate our tents. It was not large enough for our mess tent, and dinner would be served in that valley—way down there!! There was a bit of grumbling from the weary group, but most of us pulled ourselves together for one last "hike" of the day in order to have our dinner. That campsite may not have been too convenient, but the view was spectacular.

Machu Picchu/*Bruce Klepinger*

The following day we were to arrive at Machu Picchu. It was rather warm, and another good day of hiking. We came upon a small cabin situated on a sunny hillside. Much to our amazement, we discovered that the people who lived there had beer for sale. How astounding!! Sales were brisk, needless to say. The group was revived sufficiently to attack the last leg of the journey to Machu Picchu.

Will we ever forget rounding that bend, and seeing for the first time that scene before us? The classical picture so familiar to all was there in front of us. There was Huayna Picchu standing almost as a sentinal, high above the magnificent ruins of that once lost city.

Rima Rima, Portachuelo, Cordillera Blanca/*Sara Steck*

Indian woman with weavings for sale/
Sara Steck

I had that same sense of wonder and satisfaction that I'd experienced in Nepal, after rounding a similar bend in the trail and having my first glimpse of Everest. I cannot explain that feeling of accomplishment, after days on the trail to see at last that your goal is nearly at hand. How often I have thought that people who come to Machu Picchu on the train really miss a lot. The first view of the ruins from the "top" of the Inca trail could not possibly be duplicated by coming up from the train station below on the bus. The days spent on the trail, retracing the steps of the Inca people, all became especially worthwhile, when the Machu Picchu panorama spread out before me in the late afternoon sun.

During my trip to Nepal, I had been intrigued by the notion of seeing Mt. Everest with my own eyes. I had not realized that "ordinary" people could actually walk in to the very base camp of that fabled mountain. That in itself was really the main goal I'd had in mind as the trip began. As the days on the trail proceeded, I began to realize that the goal of seeing the *mountain* became less important to me. Seeing how the *people* lived in the Himalaya became the real focal point of that trip.

That too was one of the main points of trekking in Peru. You can go to a developing country, visit the major cities, stay in the local "Holiday Inn", but never really see or understand about the kind of living that is going on in small villages throughout that country. As a trekker you observe people as they really live in remote areas of the country.

We were able to witness the day to day activities of the local people . . . tilling their fields with wooden plows. Many of these fields were so steep, I wondered how they even managed the job at all.

I was equally fascinated to see the smallest of children taking an active part in family life. How often I saw even the youngest of children herding a few small pigs or taking care of their smaller brothers and sisters.

Porters on the Inca Trail/*Sara Steck*

The women too, were remarkable to see. They were never idle. Whether walking through village or market place, their hands were always busy spinning yarn. Most of us had never seen "portable" spinning before.

Several times we camped in school yards. We looked into the school rooms themselves, certainly an interesting comparison to the schools in the United States, and of special interest to the teachers in our group to see the very primitive conditions in

"One afternoon, after a particularly long day, we proceeded up an ancient Inca staircase carved right out of the mountain. We found ourselves among some old Incan walls on a piece of real estate that was barely large enough to accommodate our tents...."/*Sara Steck*

which the children of the Andes did their school work.

One school yard that we stayed in was right near a fair sized village. A group of local people came to visit us late in the afternoon, after we had set up the camp. Among them were a group of young boys. There was a young fellow in our group about 16 years old. He had brought along a frisbee, and started up a game with the visiting youngsters. It didn't take them long to catch on to how it was done. It turned out to be quite an afternoon, with everyone joining in the game. Although there were only a few on either "side" who could actually speak the others' language, the frisbee game seemed to eliminate that barrier. We were simply all human beings, friends for that fleeting moment in time.

It is moments such as this that make this type of trip so worthwhile. The scenery is always magnificent, and making it over the pass is such a moment of exhilaration. But the times of joining in the culture of a people who appear to be living so far in the past are more often the moments that you take home with you and remember long after the blistered feet have healed.

"The times of joining in the culture of a people who appear to be living so far in the past are more often the moments that you take home with you and remember long after the blistered feet have healed...."/*Bruce Klepinger*

To me a trekking trip goes far beyond being a mere physical experience. One comes home a changed person. Not only having gained insight into the land that you have traveled through, but with a renewed sense of all that is good about the United States, and indeed, what could be improved about our country as well.

The pleasure of making new friends among your fellow trekkers is another joy of this kind of adventure. Living in close proximity with ten or twelve people for three weeks gives ample opportunity for the exchange of ideas and chances to learn from one another.

Certainly I learn to be more tolerant on this type of a trip. Living so closely with "strangers" for several weeks, I quickly overlook things I might not overlook at home. I can always hope that my own foibles will be forgiven in return.

A trekking trip may not be for everyone, but it seems to me that the effort expended in getting to your destination somehow makes it far more worthwhile than passively sitting in a tour bus or train and just being an observer. A trek provides the opportunity to become a participant in your own adventure.

Ms. Bowden was a member of our INCA-BLANCA Trek in Peru.

Chincheros/*Bruce Klepinger*

Our South American trip leaders have unique backgrounds, an individual blend of cultural expertise and wilderness knowledge. They are capable guides whose experience will enhance the special delights of South American travel.

TERRY BRIAN, 33, is an experienced wilderness guide with expertise in the ethnology and natural history of South America. An avid river-runner, he is a senior guide on the Colorado River and has made many first descents of South American rivers. Fluent in Spanish, with a knowledge of various Indian dialects, he has explored most of South America and has led Mountain Travel treks for nine years.

JAMES DIRKS, 38, a Canadian, was born in Peru and raised in the Peruvian jungle among the Campa Indians. He has traveled throughout South America (and once walked from Bolivia to Chile for three months, crossing much of the Atacama Desert). He lives on a farm in Curahuasi, Peru.

RONALD ESQUIVEL, 33, is a Costa Rican architect whose interest in ecological concepts in architecture led to his professional interest in the ecology of Costa Rica. He has many years of outdoor experience in his native Costa Rica.

LINDY FARLEY, 35, was raised in the Canadian Rockies, which she explored on foot and by cross-country skis for years. She spent a year traveling in South America, including an expedition by balsa raft on Peru's Tambo River. She is interested in Peru's native crafts and is studying knitting designs in the Cuzco area, where she lives on an anise farm with her husband, Mountain Travel leader James Dirks, and their two children.

SERGIO FITCH-WATKINS, 34, of Mexico, is a professional climbing guide with experience in the U.S., the Alps, Spain and the Himalayas. he leads our climbing expeditions on the volcanoes of Mexico, Bolivia, Colombia and Ecuador as well as on Aconcagua, highest peak in the Western Hemisphere.

BRUCE KLEPINGER, 44, has led more than 80 Mountain Travel treks in Asia and South America.

Terry Brian

Carlos Velaochaga

His mountaineering background includes over 1,000 climbs, and he has led numerous expeditions on Aconcagua (highest peak in the Western Hemisphere), Huascaran (highest peak in Peru), and peaks in Nepal and India. Bruce also has 11 years experience as a boatman on the Grand Canyon of the Colorado River and on several South American rivers. He speaks fluent Spanish.

JOSE "PEPE" NORIEGA, 31, of Cuzco, Peru, spent most of his younger years living in Europe and the U.S. with his father, a member of Peru's diplomatic corps, and it was in Europe that he developed his love of the mountains. Settling in Cuzco after his schooling, he has spent the last three years leading hiking and rafting expeditions.

ESMERALDA PONCE DE LEON, 28, is a sociologist, born in Mexico City. She has traveled extensively in her native country with her husband, Sergio Fitch-Watkins (leader of our South American climbing trips). She co-led our Tarahumara Easter Fiesta trip in 1985.

Lindy Farley

James Dirks

Sara Steck

Bruce Klepinger

Jose "Pepe" Noriega

Sergio Fitch-Watkins *(2nd from left) with expedition porters*

SARA STECK, 31, is Mountain Travel's South American operations manager. She has lived in Central America, speaks fluent Spanish, and spends six months of each year leading treks in Peru, Ecuador and the Galapagos.

CARLOS VELOACHAGA, 45, has a degree in cultural anthropology. A native of Peru, he has lived in Cuzco for the last eight years, where he leads trekking expeditions and continues his studies of both Quechua and Inca cultures.

15,000 feet on Aconcagua/ Sergio Fitch-Watkins

The Aconcagua Expedition

Highest peak in Western Hemisphere

At 22,834 feet, Aconcagua is the highest mountain in the Western Hemisphere and the highest outside Asia.

Aconcagua lies entirely within Argentina, just across the border from Chile. It rises some 4,000 feet above neighboring peaks and is easily visible from the Pacific on a clear day.

While not a technically difficult mountain to climb, weather and altitude make this peak a true mountaineering challenge requiring a range of skills.

We will attempt the Polish Route, first climbed in 1934, which involves some 1800 feet of technical ice climbing which, although low angle, can often present difficulties depending on weather and acclimatization of the party.

Members must be very fit and capable of carrying loads of up to 75 lbs. at high altitudes. All members will be expected to assist with expedition chores (load carrying, setting up tents, cooking, etc). All community climbing equipment will be provided.

Itinerary: Day 1: Leave U.S. Arrive Buenos Aires, Argentina.

Day 2 and 3: Fly to Mendoza. Two days for organizing gear.

Day 4: Bus to Punta de Vaca (7,500') and camp.

Day 5 to 7: Approach hike to Aconcagua base camp at 13,500 feet.

Day 8: At base camp.

Day 9 to 24: Sixteen days will be devoted to the climb and descent to base camp.

Day 25 and 26: Hike out to roadhead.

Day 27: Bus ride back to Mendoza.

Day 28: Free day in Mendoza.

Day 29: Depart Mendoza and connect with homeward-bound flights.

Dates: Jan 25–Feb 22 (29 days)
1987: Jan 24–Feb 21
Leader: Sergio Fitch-Watkins
Grade: E-2
Land Cost: $2190
(9–10 members)
$2390 (6–8)
Single Supplement: $75
IT5AR10369

King Penguin/Bruce Klepinger

The approach to Aconcagua. While not a technically difficult mountain to climb, weather and altitude make Aconcagua a true mountaineering challenge/ Sergio Fitch-Watkins

Volcanoes Of Chile

Climb South America's second highest peak

The objective of this trip is a non-technical climb of Ojos del Salado (22,583'), second highest peak in South America and one of the world's highest volcanoes.

Ojos del Salado is on the Puna de Atacama, a vast high altitude plateau in northern Chile which in height and extent has no equivalent outside Tibet. The floor of the Atacama averages 12,000 feet and is a barren, almost waterless desert covered by salt flats. Snowline here is almost 20,000 feet!

A motorable road will take us as high as 17,000 feet, from which we hike to a refuge at 19,000 and a high camp at 20,000 feet enroute to the summit.

The climb is physically (not technically) demanding and participants must be in top shape with previous experience at altitude.

Itinerary: Day 1 and 2: Leave U.S. Arrive Santiago.

Day 3: All-day drive to Copiapo, a city in north central Chile.

Day 4 and 5: Drive to Copiapo Valley and camp.

Day 6: Drive to Quebrada Colorado and camp at 13,000 feet.

Day 7 to 9: Acclimatization hikes around Ojos del Salado.

Day 10: Drive to a refuge at 17,000 feet.

Day 11: Hike to a refuge at 19,350 feet.

Day 12: Hike to a high camp at 20,000 feet.

Day 13: Summit attempt.

Day 14: Spare day for bad weather.

Day 15: Descend and drive to Copiapo.

Day 16: Fly to Santiago. Depart on homeward-bound flights.

Day 17: Arrive Miami.

Dates: Mar 1–Mar 17 (17 days)
1987: Feb 28–Mar 16
Leader: Bruce Klepinger
Grade: C-2/D-1
Land Cost: $1590
(10–12 members)
$1990 (7–9)
Single Supplement: $75
IT6PA1SFMT16

Antarctica: Journey To The Bottom Of The World

Touring the continent that is an international scientific preserve

This is a very special visit to the land of icebergs, penguins and an international community of scientists.

By special arrangement, we charter a Chilean Air Force C-30 transport and take a two-hour flight from Punta Arenas in Patagonia, on the southernmost tip of the South American continent, to the Chilean scientific base on King George Island, Antarctica.

Here we spend seven days at the base's guest house, choosing from optional daily activities. Possibilities include a field trip to Ardley Island for an inspection of the penguin rookery with a biologist who specializes in Antarctic wildlife, a visit to the Drake Passage to see an elephant seal colony and other Antarctic fauna, and a visit to the Meteorological Center and to the Soviet Union's Bellinghausen Scientific Station.

Other optional activities are cross-country skiing and helicopter rides for spectacular views by air (all activities subject to permission and weather).

Itinerary: Day 1 and 2: Leave U.S. Arrive Santiago, Chile.

Day 3: Fly to Punta Arenas.

Day 4: Two-hour flight to Teniente Marsh Air Force Base in Antarctica, King George Island. Overnight at guest house, our lodging for the next 7 days.

Day 5 to 11: Optional activities depending on weather and availability of personnel and equipment.

Day 12: Afternoon flight to Punta Arenas, Chile.

Day 13: Fly to Santiago. Late afternoon departure on homeward-bound flights.

Day 14: Arrive U.S.

Dates: #1 March (14 days)
#2 November
1987: March
Leader: #1 Leo Le Bon
#2 Bruce Klepinger
Grade: A-1
Land Cost: $2875
(10–20 members)
Single Supplement: $95
IT6PA1SFMT24

Patagonia Overland

26-day trip to Fitzroy, Paine, Tierra Del Fuego

"All the attending marvels of a thousand Patagonian sights and sounds. . ."—Herman Melville, *Moby Dick*

Shared by Argentina and Chile on the southernmost tip of South America is a wild land called Patagonia, the "uttermost end of the earth."

Patagonia is a land of Alaskan-sized fjords, of glaciers which fall into the sea, of red and yellow Magellan beech trees with parrots nestling in their branches and penguins pacing the ice beneath.

On the Argentine side of Patagonia, there are great lakes and forests, and to the east lie the great rolling *pampas,* where millions of sheep roam, tended by *gaucho* shepherds, wild characters who live on meat and *mate* tea and ride down ostriches with whirling boas.

In Patagonia, the spine of the Andes tapers into the sea, and although the Patagonian Andes are not extremely high, they are among the most spectacular in the world. The fantastic spires of Fitzroy (11,073′), Cerro Torre (10,280′) and the great granite "towers" of Paine are sought-after prizes by mountaineers the world over.

Our journey through this wild place will be over rough roads, traveling in our own "expedition" bus, camping and occasionally staying in simple inns.

The trip begins with a visit to Peninsula Valdez to view its renowned penguin colony, the world's largest.

Driving across the plains to Glacier National Park, we establish a camp right at the bases of the jagged spires of Fitzroy and Cerro Torre. We have three full days to explore the park, walking through beech forests and hiking up Cerro Pliegue Tumbado for fantastic views extending out onto the Patagonian icecap.

Driving out of the park and around the eastern end of ice-blue Lago Argentino, we establish our next central three-day camp in a meadow on the shores of Laguna Roca. From here, we can hike up Cerro Cristal or take excursions onto Lago Argentino and the Moreno Glacier, whose 100-foot headwall constantly calves massive blocks of ice into the lake.

Continuing over rolling pampas into Chile, we approach Paine National Park, and have our first sight of the spectacular granite towers and black slate *cuernos* (horns) of the Cordillera del Paine, whose compelling grandeur is an unmistakable landmark of Patagonia.

In three days at Paine, we take day hikes around the northern flanks of Paine Grande (10,600′) for the most sensational views in all Patagonia. Large herds of *guanacos* (cousins of alpacas and llamas) roam Paine National Park and the birdwatching is incredible.

Leaving Paine for Puerto Natales, we drive along the Strait of Magellan and take a motor launch ride on the Last Hope Sound to view the glaciers of Cerro Balmaceda and the rugged peaks at the southern end of the Great Patagonian icecap.

We end the trip with a visit to Ushuaia, southernmost town in the world, situated on the island archipelago of Tierra del Fuego. Here, our activities will be day excursions to Lapataia National Park, landscape of fjords and beech forests on the shores of the Beagle Channel.

Itinerary: Day 1: Leave U.S. Arrive Buenos Aires.

Day 2: Fly to Puerto Madryn, Peninsula Valdez.

Day 3: Visit penguin colony.

Day 4: Drive to camp at Lago Buenos Aires.

Day 5: Arrive at Glacier National Park.

Day 6 and 7: Excursions from camp for views of Fitzroy, the Patagonia icecap and Viedma Glaciers.

Day 8: Drive to camp at Laguna Roca.

Day 9 to 11: Daily excursions to Moreno Glacier, Lago Argentino, or hike up Cerro Cristal for views extending from the Paine Towers to the main body of Lago Argentino. Good fishing here!

Day 12: Cross into Chile and camp within sight of Last Hope Sound and the Darwin Cordillera.

Day 13: Drive to Parque Nacional de Paine and set up central camp with fantastic views of Paine Towers.

Day 14 to 16: Day hikes or fishing.

Day 17 to 19: Excursions from Puerto Natales including boating on Last Hope Sound to view Balmaceda Glacier.

Day 20: Drive to Punta Arenas.

Day 21: Drive along Strait of Magellan and cross border into to Argentina and camp.

Day 22: Drive to Ushuaia.

Day 23: Visit Lapataia National Park.

Day 24: Fly to Buenos Aires.

Day 25: Day free and evening departure on homeward-bound flights.

Day 26: Arrive home.

Dates: #1 Jan 10–Feb 4 (26 days)
1987: Jan 9–Feb 3
Leaders: Bruce Klepinger & Sara Steck
Grade: A-2
Land Cost: $1890 (10–16 members) $2190 (7–9)
Single Supplement: $200
IT5AR10397

Leaving Paine for Puerto Natales, we drive along the Strait of Magellan and take a motor launch ride on the Last Hope Sound to view the glaciers of Cerro Balmaceda/*Sara Steck*

"Cappachito"/Norma Chatwin

Patagonia Overland

16-day trip to Fitzroy and Paine

This 16-day Patagonia journey focuses on the major sights of Glacier (Fitzroy) National Park and Paine National Park (see 26-day itinerary for fuller description of these parks).

Itinerary: Day 1: Leave U.S. Arrive Buenos Aires.

Day 2: Tour Buenos Aires.

Day 3: Fly to Rio Gallegos, drive towards Glacier National Park and camp.

Day 4 and 5: Arrive Glacier National Park. Day hikes for views of jagged Cerro Fitzroy, Cerro Torre and Torre Egger.

Day 6 to 8: Drive to camp at Laguna Roca. Excursions to Moreno Glacier and Lago Argentina.

Day 9: Drive into Chile and camp near Last Hope Sound.

Day 10 and 11: Drive to Paine National Park. Excursions from camp.

Day 12: Drive to Puerto Natales.

Day 13: Drive to Punta Arenas.

Day 14: Afternoon flight to Santiago, Chile, passing above the Patagonian icefields enroute.

Day 15: Tour Santiago. Evening departure on homeward-bound fights.

Day 16: Arrive U.S.

Easter Island Option:

Trips #2 & #3 allow an optional three or five-day visit to isolated Easter Island, with its hundreds of 60-foot-tall stone-carved monoliths which have intrigued archaeologists for centuries. Contact us for details.

Dates: #2 Feb 6–Feb 21 (16 days)
#3 Dec 18, 1986–Jan 2, 1987
1987: Feb 5–Feb 19
Leaders: Bruce Klepinger & Sara Steck
Grade: A-2
Land Cost: $1490 (10–16 members)
Single Supplement: $125
IT5AR10397

Paine National Park/Bruce Klepinger

Sea lions, Last Hope Sound/Norma Chatwin

Easter Island/Sara Steck

Bolivia 21,000

Mountaineering in the Cordillera Real

Our main objective on this climbing expedition is the ascent of two glaciated and spectacular tropical mountains in the Cordillera Real: Illimani (21,201′), just southeast of the capital city of La Paz, and Huayna Potosi (19,992′).

The ascents of both Illimani and Huayna Potosi are non-technical, but very physically demanding due to the extreme altitude. This expedition is designed for mountaineers with several years of snow and ice-climbing experience.

Itinerary: Day 1 and 2: Leave U.S. Arrive La Paz, Bolivia.

Day 3: In La Paz.

Day 4: Acclimatization hike.

Day 5: Drive to camp below Huayna Potosi at approximately 15,400 feet.

Day 6: Carry loads to Camp I and Campamento Argentina ("Argentina Camp") at about 17,700 feet. Return to base camp.

Day 7 to 9: Move up to Camp I. Summit attempt and return to Camp.

Day 10: Return drive to La Paz.

Day 11: In La Paz.

Day 12: 8-hour drive to camp at Illimani at about 16,400 feet.

Day 13 to 15: Summit attempt and return to Camp I.

Day 16 and 17: Spare days for inclement weather.

Day 18: Hike down to roadhead.

Day 19: Drive to La Paz.

Day 20: Depart on homeward-bound flights.

Dates: Jul 19–Aug 7 (20 days)
Leader: Sergio Fitch-Watkins
Grade: E-1
Land Cost: $1690
(6–12 members)
Single Supplement: $125
IT6EA1MT05

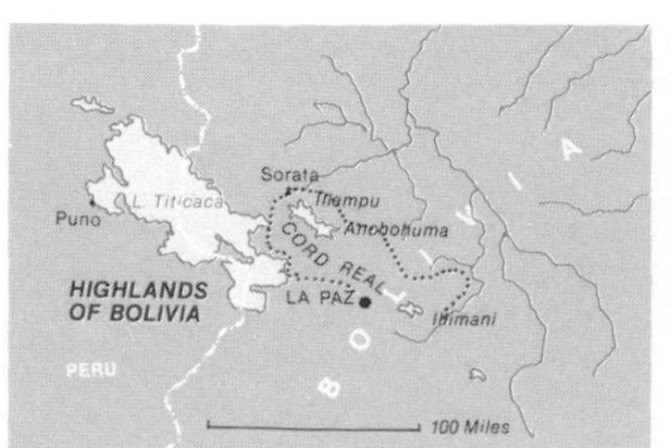

Highlands Of Bolivia

16-day trek in remote Andes

The main range of the Bolivian Andes is the Cordillera Real ("Royal Mountains"), a superb wilderness where massive blue-white glaciers tumble from 20,000-foot peaks. The high valleys of the Cordillera Real descend thousands of feet into the cloudy forests of the upper Amazon.

Our 16-day trek begins at Sorata, in the shadows of some of the highest peaks in of the Cordillera Real, including Ancohuma (21,082′) and Illampu (20,873′).

Our 100-mile trek crosses several 14,000-foot passes and visits villages where we'll meet Indian descendants of the Incas and Aymaras who seldom see "outsiders."

Visits are also included to the high city of La Paz (12,000′) and enormous Lake Titicaca (12,500′), legend-filled birthplace of the first Inca king.

Itinerary: Day 1: Leave U.S. Arrive La Paz, Bolivia.

Day 2: Morning city tour of La Paz.

Day 3: Drive to Lake Titicaca (12,500′), and camp on the shores.

Day 4: By motor launch, visit Inca tombs and monuments on the island of Kalahuta. Continue to eastern side of the lake and drive to Sorata over San Francisco Pass (14,200′) where the snow peak of Illampu comes into view.

Day 5: Drive by truck to the picturesque village of Oncoma.

Day 6: Trek to Cocoo (12,250′) over Kalamutuni Pass (14,600′), passing silver mines enroute.

Day 7: Rest day and optional hikes.

Day 8: Hike past numerous waterfalls and the hanging glaciers on Chearoco. Cross Sarani Pass (15,050′) and descend to the valley of Chacolpaya.

Day 9 and 10: Trek past the flanks of the Chacocomanis massif. Splendid views of glaciers and ice-covered peaks.

Day 11 and 12: Cross Taipipata Pass (16,100′) with its stunning mountain views.

Our Bolivian chefs/*Sara Steck*

Day 13 and 14: Ascend the Ancolacaya Valley to a 15,650-foot pass. Great views across the entire width of the altiplano as far as Sajama, 150 miles away.

Day 15: Walk to roadhead and drive to Lago Tuni (14,050′).

Day 16: Walk to a lake at the base of Cerro Condiriri.

Day 17 and 18: Explore around Cerro Condiriri, then cross two passes and continue down to camp at Chacapampa (12,800′). Return to La Paz by bus.

Day 19 to 21: Drive to San Francisco mine and walk across the southern Cordillera Real on an old, well-preserved Inca highway. Arrive at the roadhead and drive to Chiquilini. Drive to La Paz by bus, crossing valleys with impressive tropical canyons.

Day 22: Day for shopping then evening transfer to airport; depart La Paz.

Day 23: Arrive Miami and connect with homeward-bound flights.

Dates: May 24–Jun 15 (23 days)
Leader: Terry Brian
Grade: C-2
Land Cost: $1590
(11–15 members)
$1690 (6–10)
Single Supplement: $115
IT6EA1MT05

On Lake Titicaca, we visit Inca tombs and monuments on the island of Kalahuta and continue to the eastern side of the lake to drive over San Francisco Pass (14,200′), where the snow peak of Illampu comes into view/
Bruce Klepinger

Discover Peru

Ancient cultures and remarkable wildlife

This is both a cultural and natural history journey, exploring archaeological sites, mountain sites and wildlife environments.

There is no trekking or camping on this trip and all the walks are non-strenuous.

After visiting Lima's famed museums, we drive south along the Pacific Coast to Paracas, visiting the Pachacamac ruins (circa 500 B.C.). We also boat out to Islas Ballestas, islands off the shores of Paracas Wildlife Park with large colonies of flamingos and sea lions.

Driving further along the coast, we make a tour and scenic overflight of the famous archaeological site of the Nazca Lines, enormous mysterious markings cut into the coastal desert during Nazca Civilization (800 B.C.). Maria Reiche, the German expert who has studied the lines for over 25 years, maintains that the lines represent a vast astronomical pre-Inca calendar.

Indian from Chincheros/S.M. Estanvik

Turning inland and heading into the highlands, we arrive at Arequipa (8,000′), a lovely white stone city built in the colonial era and set in an arid highland environment. The big peaks of the Cordillera Volcanica can be seen from town—snow-capped El Misti (19,200′) and Chachani (20,000′).

We then fly to Juliaca and continue across the *altiplano* ("high plains") to Puno, a town on the shores of Lake Titicaca (12,500′), a huge "inland sea," the highest navigable body of water on earth.

Orchid on the Inca Trail/Sara Steck

On the lake, we visit Takili Island, with its population of Aymara Indians, and we pass the floating reed islands of the Uros Indians, with their hand-made reed boats, still the main form of transport on the lake.

A train ride across the Andes takes us to Cuzco (11,300′), the Inca's "navel of the universe." Here we round out the trip with visits to the Inca sites at Pisac and Ollantaytambo, then finally, to Machu Picchu, where we spend the night and have ample time to explore the vine-covered stone buildings of the "lost city" of the Incas.

Itinerary: Day 1: Leave U.S. Arrive Lima. Visit museums.

Day 2 and 3: Drive to Paracas Wildlife Park and visit Islas Ballestas.

Day 4: Tour Nazca Lines.

Day 5: Drive to Arequipa.

Day 6: Tour Arequipa.

Day 7: Fly to Juliaca and drive to Puno on Lake Titicaca.

Day 8: Excursion on the lake.

Day 9: By train from Puno to Cuzco (11,200′).

Day 10: Visit beautiful Inca ruins at Pisaç and Ollantaytambo. Overnight at Urubamba.

Day 11: By train to Machu Picchu. Overnight at hotel.

Day 12: More exploration at Machu Picchu. Late afternoon train to Urubamba. Overnight at inn.

Day 13: In Cuzco.

Day 14: Fly to Lima. Day free in Lima. Depart on evening flight.

Day 15: Arrive Miami and connect with homeward-bound flights.

Dates: #1 Jan 24–Feb 7 (15 days)
#2 Mar 28–Apr 11
#3 Sep 19–Oct 3
#4 Nov 14–Nov 28
#5 Dec 19, 1986–Jan 2 1987
1987: Jan 23–Feb 6, Mar 27–Apr 10
Leader: Carlos Velaochaga
Grade: A-2
Land Cost: $1590 (10–16 members) $1690 (7–9)
Single Supplement: $265
IT5AR10360

On our Discover Peru trip a train ride across the Andes takes us to Cuzco then on to Machu Picchu Station. We have all afternoon and most of the next day to walk among the vine-covered stone buildings/Ann M. Swartwout

"Just passing through..."

LIMA

City notes by Sara Steck and Alfredo Ferreyros

Walking routes:
Walk around Miraflores, a pretty residential part of Lima with excellent shops, galleries and restaurants. In downtown Lima, however, walk only in the central part of town (Plaza San Martin or Plaza de Armas). Since there are world-class pickpockets in Lima, walk only in the daytime and never alone. Lima's not a great place for jogging because it's smoggy and foggy, but in Miraflores, you might enjoy a run along the beach and along the road which runs above it.

Shopping:
The above-mentioned Miraflores district is full of boutiques and shops.

Museums:
The best of the Inca legacy can be seen in Lima's famous museums: the Gold Museum is a must, plus The Larco-Herrera for pre-Inca pottery and The Amano Museum for Textiles.

Restaurants:
La Rosa Nautica, on the ocean, for afternoon drinks, *bocas* or dinner. Good fancy seafood.

About Trekking in the Andes

To make your Peru trek as comfortable as possible, all camping gear is carried by pack animals and/or porters. You will only need to carry a light day-pack for your jacket, camera and water bottle.

In addition to the Mountain Travel leader, there will be a camp manager, camp staff and cook. Breakfast and dinner are hot meals served in a dining tent; a plentiful lunch is served picnic-style each day at a scenic spot on the trail.

All water used for drinking and cooking is filtered and boiled; we maintain a high standard of camp hygiene. The staff does all camp chores.

Most of our Peru treks take place in sparsely populated highland regions, often at 10,000 feet or higher. Campsites are chosen for their scenic beauty and proximity to sources of water and fodder for the pack animals.

The Peru Adventure

Trekking, rafting, jungle wildlife

Our popular Peru Adventure begins with an easy two-day float trip through the "Sacred Valley of the Incas," a green mountain valley dotted with Inca ruins and highland Indian villages.

Leaving our rafts and donning our hiking boots, we then take a five-day trek along the Inca Trail, the ancient ridgetop route taken by the elect of Inca society on their pilgrimages to the important mountain citadel at Machu Picchu.

As we trek, often walking over the original Inca paving stones still lining the trail, we visit four major Inca ruins enroute. The trek ends with the exhilarating experience of walking through the portals of the "Door of the Sun" into Machu Picchu itself.

After a day to explore the ruins, we fly to the Amazon Basin and spend two days at a comfortable jungle lodge taking nature walks along a tributary of the Amazon River.

Itinerary: Day 1: Leave U.S. Arrive Lima.

Day 2: Fly to Cuzco.

Day 3 and 4: Leisurely two-day raft trip on the Urubamba River, floating through the beautiful Urubamba Valley, "sacred Valley of the Incas." Visit Inca ruins at Pisac and Ollantaytambo. Overnight at inn.

Day 5 to 8: Trek the Inca Trail on Inca-built steep stone stairs. Begin at Chilca (8,000'), cross Warmiwanusqa Pass ("Pass of the Dead Woman"—13,776'), steepest part of the trek, continue past Phuyupatamarca ("town in the clouds") at 11,906 feet to Intipunku at 8,900 feet, where we enter the ruins of Machu Picchu.

Day 9: All day at the ruins. Late afternoon train to Cuzco.

Day 10: Touring Cuzco and environs.

Day 11: Fly to Puerto Maldonado, and proceed by motorized dugout canoe to a lodge on the tributary of the Amazon River.

Day 12: Nature walks, bird viewing by boat.

Day 13: Fly to Lima. Overnight in hotel.

Day 14: All day in Lima. Late evening transfer to airport.

Day 15: Arrive Miami and continue on homeward-bound flights.

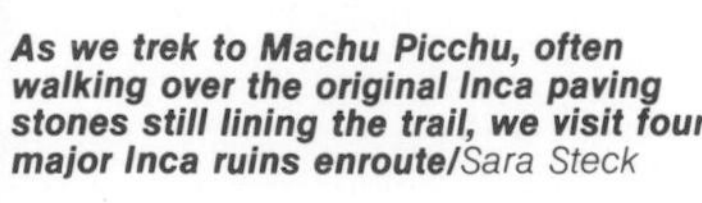

As we trek to Machu Picchu, often walking over the original Inca paving stones still lining the trail, we visit four major Inca ruins enroute/*Sara Steck*

Dates: #1 Mar 22–Apr 5 (15 days)
#2 Apr 12–Apr 26
#3 May 31–Jun 14
**#4 Jun 15–Jun 29*
***#5 Jun 28–Jul 12*
#6 Jul 5–Jul 19
#7 Jul 19–Aug 2
#8 Aug 2–Aug 16
#9 Aug 16–Aug 30
#10 Sep 6–Sep 20
1987: Mar 21–Apr 4

Leader: #1, #6, #8 & #10 Pepe Noriega
#2 & #3 James Dirks
#4 Carlos Veloachaga
#5, #7 & #9 Lindy Farley

Grade: B-2

Tour Cost: including round trip economy-class air fare from Miami on Aeroperu.
$1890 (13–16 members)
$1990 (10–12
$2150 (7–9)

Single Supplement: $195

IT5PL1M1051

**Jun 15 departure coincides with Cuzco's Inti-Raymi celebration, Inca "festival of the sun."*

***Jun 28 departure is set aside as a "Family Trek in Peru"—special rates for children available on request.*

Rafting on the Urubamba River/ *Sara Steck*

Corn drying at Ollantaytambo, Urubamba Valley/*Bruce Klepinger*

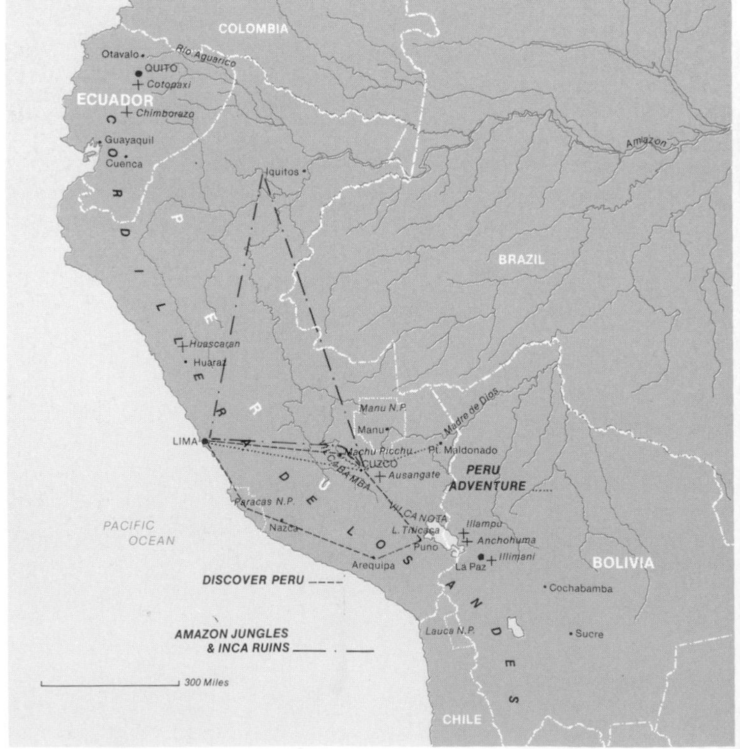

Our six-day foot journey to Machu Picchu follows a little-traveled route over two 15,000-foot passes with astounding views of Salcantay (20,574') in distance/*Sara Steck*

The Peruvian Highlands

Trek to Machu Picchu and around Mt. Ausangate

A Peru classic: this trip combines a trek to Machu Picchu on an off-the-beaten-path route plus an alpine trek in the Cordillera Vilcanota, a superb Andean wilderness where we cross glaciated passes in a wonderland of 20,000-foot ice peaks.

Our six-day foot journey to Machu Picchu follows a little-traveled route over two 15,000-foot passes with astounding views of Salcantay (20,574′) and Palcay (18,645′), ice peaks whose glaciers feed the Amazon. We have beautiful, remote Inca paths all to ourselves for the first three days, then join the popular Inca Trail leading to Machu Picchu for the last three days.

The Machu Picchu trek culminates with the spine-tingling experience of walking through the "gate of the sun," original entrance to mist-shrouded Machu Picchu, reclaimed by the jungle for centuries and only rediscovered in 1911.

After a day at a beautiful country inn in Urubamba for showers and cleanup, we begin our second trek, a seven-day circle around the big massif of Mt. Ausangate (20,945′) in the Cordillera Vilcanota.

Here the Andes are at their most exquisite: immense *altiplano,* high rolling plains dotted with isolated, iceberg-like massifs such as icy-walled Mariposa (19,117′), Cayangate (19,718′) and Colque Cruz (20,049′).

Our Vilcanota campsites are set next to turquoise lakes where we can actually hear and see Ausangate's glaciers "calving" huge chunks of ice with a thunderous roar. Our trailside companions are highland Indians and their herds of colorfully-tasseled llamas and alpacas. A trek through this Vilcanota wilderness is an unforgettable Andean experience.

Itinerary: Day 1: Leave U.S. Arrive Lima and fly to Cuzco.

Day 2: Visit weekly Indian market at Chincheros.

Day 3: Visit the beautifully situated Inca site at Pisac in the Urubamba Valley.

Day 4: Drive to a rustic hacienda at Mollepata (8,500′).

Day 5: Trek to a high meadow at Soray (10,000′), just beneath the spectacular southwest face of Salcantay.

Day 6 to 8: Over Incachilaska Pass (about 15,000′), then follow the remnants of Inca terraces and irrigation canals.

Day 9 and 10: Join the Inca Trail, crossing Warmiwanusqa Pass (13,776′) to Machu Picchu.

Day 11: All day at Machu Picchu. Afternoon train to a beautiful inn in Urubamba.

Day 12: Visit Ollantaytambo's Inca ruins.

Day 13: Drive to highland village of Tinki (13,000′).

Day 14: Trek across an expanse of golden pampas dominated by Mt. Ausangate. Camp at Upis (13,500′) hot springs.

Day 15: Hike over the sand-colored slopes of the Incapampa Pass (15,400′) and then alongside a deep glacial lake called Pucacocha.

Day 16: Down to Lake Ausangatecocha, then over Palomani Pass (16,900′) with views of Ausangate and the "butterfly" peak called Mariposa (19,800′).

Day 17 and 18: Trek above Lake Ticllacocha, with views of the 19,000-foot ice peaks of Jatunjampa and Collque Cruz, enroute to Pacchanta hot springs.

Day 19: Hike to Tinki and drive to Cuzco.

Day 20: In Cuzco.

Day 21: Fly to Lima. Day free. Evening transfer to airport.

Day 22: Depart Lima, arrive Miami and connect with homeward-bound flights.

Dates: #1 Jul 5–Jul 26 (22 days)
#2 Aug 9–Aug 30
Leader: #1 Sara Steck
#2 James Dirks
Grade: C-2
Land Cost: $1850
(13–16 members)
$2075 (10–12)
$2150 (7–9)
Single Supplement: $185
IT5AR10360

Cuzco, the Inca's "navel of the universe."/*Bruce Klepinger*

A visit to the weekly Indian market at Chincheros is an opportunity to bargain for hand-woven wool mantas (shawls)/*Bruce Klepinger*

Our Man in Peru

Alfredo Ferreyros, director of trekking operations in Peru, was raised in Peru's northern mountains and educated in Europe and the U.S. (at Cornell University). He knows the Andes intimately and makes trekking logistics run smoothly, even in the most remote places. He has traveled to Nepal to compare the fine points of Andean versus Himalayan trekking, and he organizes, without a doubt, the very best treks in Peru. During off-season, he is an environmental activist, consultant to Peru's newly developing national park system (his special interest is the new Machu Picchu National Park), and is spearheading an effort to maintain the environmental integrity of Manu National Park, one of his favorite places and one of the Amazon's most pristine wilderness regions.

Trekking trips in Peru include: twin accommodations in hotels and 2-person tents, breakfasts (lunches and dinners on your own in cities and towns), camp meals, group camping gear, porters and/or pack animals, ground transportation, airport transfers for designated group flights, sightseeing, leadership.

Non-Trekking trips in Peru include: twin accommodations in hotels, breakfasts (lunches and dinners on your own in cities and towns where there is a choice of restaurants), ground transportation, airport transfers for designated group flights, sightseeing, leadership.

Trekking In The Carabaya

From Lake Titicaca to the Cordillera Carabaya

One of our favorite new treks in Peru and destined to become a classic is this 14-day trek across the wild Carabaya.

The Carabaya, a mountain range in the easternmost reaches of Peru's *altiplano,* just north of Lake Titicaca, is little traveled by outsiders and has fantastic mountain scenery, colonial-era Inca ruins and some of the most beautiful pampas in the Andes. It also has a fine share of Andean wildlife, including condor, vicuna and flamingos. At its western end, it links with the impressive Cordillera Vilcanota, and both ranges together stretch nearly 100 miles across the highlands from Lake Titicaca to Cuzco.

Bruce Klepinger

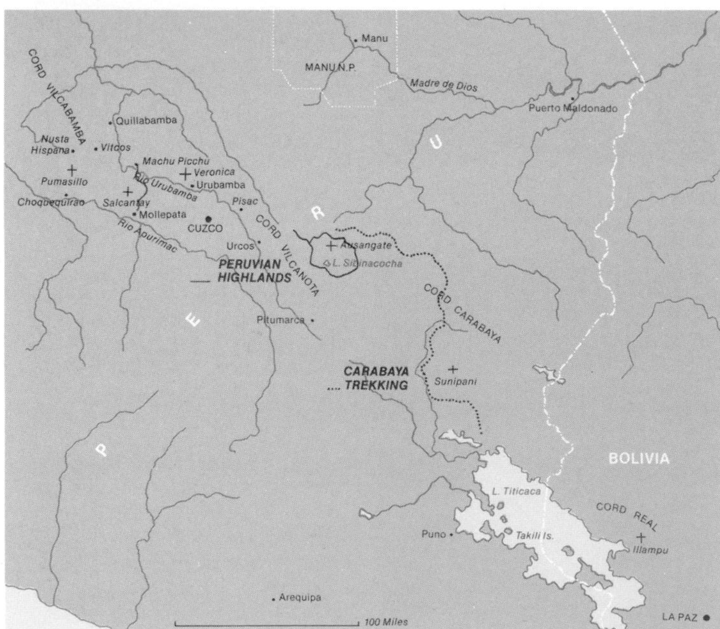

Before beginning the Carabaya trek, we visit the remote Indian village of Ayapata, where few Westerners have ever been/*Bruce Klepinger*

Our 14-day Cordillera Carabaya trek begins near Lake Titicaca's northern shore, following trails with surprising subtropical vegetation, hot springs and waterfalls. Views extend upwards to the Carabaya's carved and fluted 18,000-foot ice peaks and down thousands of feet to the mists of the Amazon Basin

At mid-point in the trek, we cross a 16,500-foot pass with views of the Andean ice cap and a 360-degree panorama of ice peaks. This pass is the line where the Carabaya changes names and becomes the Cordillera Vilcanota (see *Peruvian Highlands* trek for description). From here we descend to Lake Sibinacocha (15,000′), where we might see flocks of pink flamingos. Finally, we pass along the ramparts of Mt. Ausangate (20,945′) and end the trek at the highland village of Tinki (13,000′).

Before the trek, we'll visit Lake Titicaca and at the end of the trip we enjoy the markets of Cuzco and museums of Lima.

Itinerary: Day 1: Leave U.S.

Day 2: Arrive Lima and fly to Juliaca. Drive to Puno on the shores of Lake Titicaca (12,500′), visiting pre-Inca tomb towers at Sillustani enroute.

Day 3: By boat across the lake, passing the floating island-villages of the Uros Indians. Camp at Taraco.

Day 4 and 5: Drive to Macusani and camp. Hike around Lake Chungara and visit remote village of Ayapata.

Day 6 and 7: Cross a 13,500-foot pass with extensive views north toward deep valleys which lead to the Amazon.

Day 8 and 9: Ascend from Olleachea, past the town of Asiento, over two passes with splendid views of open pampas, flanks of steep carved mountains and the deep gorge of the Rio Corani.

Day 10 to 12: Trek west through immense pampas, approaching snow-capped peaks. Rest day and optional hike to the head of the Rio Corani valley, where the peaks of the western Carabaya are at their most magnificent.

Day 13 and 14: Cross a 17,000-foot pass, entering the "Departmento de Cuzco" and the mountain range called the Cordillera Vilcanota. Descend past a large cirque of 20,000-foot peaks and camp at the pueblo of Finaya.

Day 15 and 16: Trek along the banks of Lake Sibinacocha with incredible views of lakes and towering ice peaks and cross a 17,500-foot pass to Jampa.

Day 17 and 18: Descend toward Lake Ticllacocha, cross Pacchanta Pass (16,900′) and camp near hot springs.

Day 19: Walk to Tinki, drive to Cuzco.

Day 20: Free day in Cuzco.

Day 21: Fly to Lima. Day free.

Day 22: Depart Lima, arrive Miami and connect with homeward-bound flights.

Dates: May 17–Jun 7 (22 days)
Leader: Sara Steck
Grade: C-3
Land Cost: $1990
(13–16 members)
$2275 (10–12)
$2375 (7–9)
Single Supplement: $190
IT5AR10360

Amazon Jungles & Inca Ruins

From the rain forests to the Andean highlands

Our tour of the natural and archaeological wonders of Peru begins on the Amazon River, which meanders through cloud forests and rich jungle habitat where one encounters animal and plant life found nowhere else on earth.

Based in a comfortable jungle lodge for two days, we take excursions by trail or dugout canoe through quiet Amazon waterways with overhanging canopies of greenery.

Moving to the Pacific Coast, we tour the seaside Paracas Wildlife Park, with its marine mammals and sea-bird colonies, and visit the famed Nazca Lines, a pre-Incan archaeological enigma (see *Discover Peru* trip for more description).

From Cuzco our excursions take us to the magnificent Inca ruins at Pisac and Ollantaytambo and lastly to the greatest monument of Inca civilization, Machu Picchu.

There is no hiking or camping on this trip.

Itinerary: Day 1 and 2: Leave U.S. Arrive Lima and fly to Iquitos. Transfer to jungle lodge on the Amazon.

Day 3 and 4: Excursions from the lodge.

Day 5: Drive to Paracas Wildlife Park.

Day 6: Visit Islas Ballestas, then drive to Nazca.

Day 7: Scenic overflight of Nazca. Return to Lima.

Day 8: Fly to Cuzco.

Day 9: Explore ruins in the "sacred valley of the Incas."

Day 10: All-day excursion by train to Machu Picchu.

Day 11: Fly to Lima. Day free and evening transfer to airport.

Day 12: Arrive U.S.

Dates: #1 Mar 8–Mar 19
(12 days)
#2 May 3–May 14
#3 Aug 16–Aug 27
#4 Oct 4–Oct 15
1987: Mar 7–Mar 18
Leader: #1 & #4 Lindy Farley
#2 Sara Steck
#3 Carlos Veloachaga
Grade: A-1
Land Cost: $1290
(4–16 members)
Single Supplement: $65
IT5AR10360

Halley's Comet Tour

A once-in-a-lifetime spectacle

Halley's comet, last seen in 1910, will be making its next swing by the earth in early April, 1986. According to astronomers, the best place in the Western Hemisphere to view Halley's comet is in the pre-dawn skies over Peru.

The trip's "resident scientist" will be David Dearborn, Ph.D., an astrophysicist with a special interest in archaeo-astronomy (the rising and setting positions of the sun, moon and stars in relation to archaeological sites.)

We first visit the planetarium in Lima for a lecture and introduction to the Southern Hemisphere sky. Other stops include the seaside wildlife colonies at Paracas Wildlife Park and the mysterious Nazca Lines (a giant pre-Inca astronomical calendar), which the group will "flightsee" by small plane. To assure maximum comet-viewing, four days will be spent in the colonial highland town of Arequipa, the best place in Peru for celestial observation, with its 8,000-foot elevation and usually clear skies.

There is no hiking or camping on this trip.

Itinerary: Day 1: Leave U.S. Arrive Lima. Briefing at the planetarium.

Day 2: Tour Lima.

Day 3: Drive to Paracas for boat trip to Islas Ballestas.

Day 4: Drive to Nazca for tour and scenic overflight.

Day 5: Drive inland to colonial Arequipa, nestled between two giant volcanoes.

Day 6 and 7: Arequipa has been singled out as a very good location from which to view the comet, which will be visible in the sky just before sunrise.

Day 8: Day excursion to one of Arequipa's nearby volcanoes.

Day 9: Fly to Lima. Day free. Evening transfer to the airport for homeward-bound flights.

Day 10: Arrive U.S.

Dates: Apr 2–Apr 11 (10 days)
Leader: Sara Steck
Special Guest:
David Dearborn, Ph.D.
Grade: A-1
Land Cost: $1390
(10–25 members)
Single Supplement: $165
IT5AR10360

Walking Inca Trails

Treks in both northern and southern Peru

This trip features not only the classic four-day Inca Trail trek to Machu Picchu, but also a four-day trek in the snow-capped Cordillera Blanca, the world's highest tropical mountain range.

Our Inca Trail walk begins near the Urubamba River in the "sacred valley of the Incas," where we meet the porters who carry our gear as we hike from one Inca ruin to the next along the ancient trail to Machu Picchu. Arriving at Machu Picchu, we have a day to climb around in the ruins and imagine how Yale professor Hiram Bingham must have felt when he first came upon this amazing place in 1911.

Driving on the Pan American Highway to northern Peru, we begin to see the great white peaks of the Cordillera Blanca as we arrive in the mountain town of Huaraz at 10,200 feet.

Our four-day Cordillera Blanca trek is on the paths of Huascaran National Park, where there are 11 peaks over 20,000 feet, including Huascaran (22,204'), highest in Peru. As we hike on trails once followed by the Incas, we cross flower-filled valleys, pastures cultivated with potatoes, small azure lakes and glacier-fed tarns. Gazing upward, we'll feast our eyes on the delicate corniced snow ridges and fluted ice faces which make the Cordillera Blanca the most beautiful mountains in Peru . . . and in all South America.

Itinerary: Day 1 and 2: Leave Miami. Arrive Lima, fly to Cuzco (11,200').

Day 3: Train or bus to Chillca and begin trek to camp at the ruins of Patallacta.

Day 4: Trek to the town of Huayllabamba. Spectacular views of Mt. Huayanay.

Day 5: Hike over the Warmiwanusqa Pass (13,776'), down into the Pacamayo River Valley. Continue to camp at the ruins of Sayacmarca via the ruins at Runkuraqay.

Day 6: Visit ruins of Phuyupatamarca, descend to the ruins of Winay Wayna, walk through Intipunku, "door of the sun," the original entrance to Machu Picchu. Camp on the river below Machu Picchu.

Day 7: Morning at ruins. Late afternoon train to Cuzco.

Day 8: Fly to Lima and drive to Huaraz in northern Peru.

Day 9: Drive over Llanganuco Pass and camp at Vaqueria.

Day 10: Hike up the Huaripampa Valley and camp at Paria.

Day 11: Cross Punta Union Pass (15,580') and camp at Taullipampa.

Day 12: Descend Santa Cruz valley past lake Jatuncocha, camp at Llamacorral.

Day 13: Meet vehicles for drive to Huaraz.

Day 14: Drive to Lima.

Day 15: Day free in Lima. Late night transfer to airport.

Day 16: Arrive Miami and continue on homeward-bound flights.

Dates: #1 May 24–Jun 8
(16 days)
#2 Jun 14–Jun 29
#3 Jul 12–Jul 27
#4 Aug 9–Aug 24
Leaders: #1 Pepe Noriega
#2 Terry Brian
#3 James Dirks
#4 Sara Steck
Grade: C-2
Land Cost: $1290
(7–16 members)
$1390 (4–6)
Single Supplement: $80
IT5AR10360

As we hike on trails once followed by the Incas, we cross flower-filled valleys. Gazing upward, we'll view the delicate corniced snow ridges and fluted ice faces which make the Cordillera Blanca the most beautiful mountains in Peru/Bruce Klepinger

Inti Watani, "stone of the sun," Machu Picchu/Bruce Klepinger

Cultural Expedition:

Peru: The Inca Legacy

Civilizations of ancient America

We begin our tour in Peru's northern highlands with a visit to the Chavin ruins, Peru's oldest, dating back to 1,000 years B.C.

Our next stop is Trujillo, center of ancient Mochica-Chimu culture, where we see a distinct style of art developed in yet another of Peru's early civilizations. The Mochica culture flourished in the first few centuries A.D. and produced the exquisite gold art of Lima's famed Gold Museum.

At Cuzco, we acquaint ourselves with the realm of Inca civilization and make a five-day trek on the Inca Trail to Machu Picchu, sometimes walking on stone roads built by the Incas themselves. Our trek repeats a pilgrimage which once only the elect were allowed to undertake. We pass four major ruins which served as preparation (ritual bathing and other ceremonies) for initiates enroute to this important Inca citadel.

Near Cuzco, we attend the one-day festival of the "lord of Huanca," which reveals the complex blend of Spanish and Inca culture that makes up the culture of today's Andean highlanders.

Lecturer/Leader: Carlos Velaochaga, from Peru, has a degree in cultural anthropology and continues his studies of both Quechua and Inca cultures in Cuzco, Peru.

Itinerary: Day 1 and 2: Leave U.S. arrive Lima.
Day 3: Drive to Huaraz.
Day 4: Drive to Chavin and tour ruins.
Day 5: Return to Huaraz.
Day 6: Drive to Trujillo.
Day 7: Tour ruins at Trujillo.
Day 8: Fly to Lima.
Day 9: Fly to Cuzco.
Day 10: In Cuzco.
Day 11 to 15: Five-day trek on the Inca Trail from Chilca to Machu Picchu.
Day 16: Afternoon train to Cuzco.
Day 17: Attend the Festival of the Lord of Huanca.
Day 18: Tour ruins of Pisac in the Urubamba valley.
Day 19: Visit weekly Indian market at Chincheros.
Day 20: Train to Puno at Lake Titicaca
Day 21: Tour the lake and environs.
Day 22: Fly to Lima.
Day 23: Depart Lima and board homeward-bound flights.

Dates: Aug 27–Sep 18 (23 days)
Grade: B-2
Land Cost: $2050 (10–15 members) $2150 (7–9)
Single Supplement: $225
IT5AR10360

There are 11 major summits topping 20,000 feet and more than 70 peaks higher than 18,000 feet. These mountains rival the Himalayas in their alpine grandeur and are much frequented by mountaineers and trekkers/Sara Steck

The Trans Andean: Trekking The Cordilleras Blanca And Huayhuash

19-day high altitude adventure

In the great ice range of the Cordillera Blanca, an exquisite mountain environment now protected within "Huascaran National Park," there are eleven major summits topping 20,000 feet and more than 70 peaks higher than 18,000 feet. These mountains rival the Himalayas in their alpine grandeur and are much frequented by the world's mountaineers and trekking enthusiasts.

We spend our first 10 days walking a classic circuit through the heart of the Cordillera Blanca, viewing its famed northern massifs such as the "perfect" pyramid of Alpamayo (19,511′).

As we walk, often along neatly cultivated fields, and deep blue lakes with hidden waterfalls, we also see the high peaks much farther south, as a network of trails takes us on a circle around the 19,000-foot massifs of Contrahierbas, Hualcan and Copa.

At the end of the first trek we drive back to Huaraz for showers and clean-up, then make a second trek, this one eight days long, in the Cordillera Huayhuash, second highest of Peru's great ice ranges. Views throughout the Huayhuash trekking circuit include the imposing ice fang of Jirishanca (20,099′) and Yerupaja (21,759′), 2nd highest peak in Peru.

Itinerary: Day 1 and 2: Leave U.S. Arrive Lima. Transfer to hotel. Visit archaeological museums.
Day 3: 8-hour bus ride to the northern highland town of Huaraz at 10,200 feet. First views of the southern Cordillera Blanca.
Day 4: Acclimatization hike in Rio Santa Valley.
Day 5: Drive over Llanganuco Pass at 15,740 feet to roadhead camp at Vaqueria.
Day 6 to 9: Hike up Huaripampa Valley, passing small settlements and farmlands, cross Pucaraju Pass (15,345′) and continue to Tingopampa (14,380′). Incredible views of the major Cordillera Blanca peaks.
Day 10 to 13: Climb steeply through woods, grassy meadows and over glacially polished cliffs. Beautiful views of Alpamayo.
Day 14: Hike past a large Inca ruin and meet vehicles for the drive to Huaraz. Overnight at hotel. Prepare for second trek.
Day 15: Drive to Chiquian, main village of the Cordillera Huayhuash. Camp nearby.
Day 16 to 19: Trek to Punta Llamac Pass (13,860′) and beautiful lake Jahuacocha (13,200′) with first major views of the Cordillera Huayhuash. Hike a wide trail and scree slope to Cacanampunta Pass (14,890′) on the Continental Divide of the Andes.
Day 20 to 23: Ascend a side valley to the pass of Punta Carhuac (14,950′), reach the superb lakeside setting of Carhuacocha, cross a river on horseback, and enter the Carnicero Valley, with its small glacial lakes. End trek at Cajatampo.
Day 24: Drive to Lima. Overnight at hotel.
Day 25: Evening transfer to airport for homeward-bound flights.
Day 26: Arrive U.S.

Dates: Jun 8–Jul 3 (26 days)
Leader: Sara Steck
Grade: C-3
Land Cost: $2075 (13–16 members) $2290 (10–12)
Single Supplement: $90
IT5AR10360

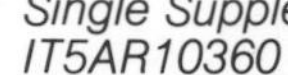

Highland porters/Bruce Klepinger

Andean Climbing Seminar

Learn mountaineering techniques in a spectacular setting

Our climbing seminar takes place in the high altitude valleys of the Cordillera Raura, a beautiful range with a multitude of gentle peaks. These mountains offer a great variety of high altitude terrain on which to learn and practice snow and ice climbing techniques.

To get to our Cordillera Raura base camp, we hike up and over the eastern flanks of the stunningly beautiful Cordillera Huayhuash, a compact range with six summits topping 20,000 feet.

Crossing the Continental Divide into the Cordillera Raura, we establish a camp at about 15,000 feet and spend three days in an intensive climbing course given by skilled teacher and climber, Sergio Fitch-Watkins. We review rope handling, snow and glacier travel, ice climbing and crevasse rescue. We spend four more days on ascents of two or more moderate 18,000 to 19,000-foot peaks in the region.

Itinerary: Day 1: leave U.S. Arrive Lima. Transfer to hotel.

Day 2: Drive to Cajatambo (11,100′) and camp.

Day 3: Trek up a gentle valley to Laguna Viconga (14,200′).

Day 4: Establish base camp at Aguascocha (14,200′).

Day 5 to 7: Instruction and practice.

Day 8 to 11: Proposed ascents of Nevado Leon Yuaccanan (about 16,500′) and Quesillojanca (17,500′), a slightly more difficult peak.

Day 12: Hike out to roadhead and drive to Lima. Overnight in hotel.

Day 13: Day free in Lima, evening transfer to the airport and depart Lima.

Day 14: Arrive Miami and connect with homeward-bound flights.

Dates: Jun 8–Jun 21 (14 days)
Leader: Sergio Fitch-Watkins
Grade: C-3/D-1
Land Cost: $1450 (10–12 members) $1650 (7–9)
Single Supplement: $100
IT5AR10360

Cordillera Blanca Expedition: Huascaran

Climb Peru's highest peak

The goal of this expedition is an ascent of Huascaran (22,204′), highest peak in the Peruvian Andes and one of the highest in the Americas.

Huascaran was first climbed in 1932 (Huascaran Sur, the highest of its twin summits) by the landmark Austrian-German expedition of Kinzl and Schneider, who also made the first survey of the Cordillera Blanca.

Snow conditions have changed on Huascaran in the last few years, increasing the technical difficulties of an ascent. Participants should be experienced in snow and ice climbing.

Before the ascent, we will freshen up our climbing and glacier travel techniques with climbs in the vicinity of Nevado Kayesh (18,800′) and Nevado Chinchey (20,532′). Visits are included to Huaraz and Lima.

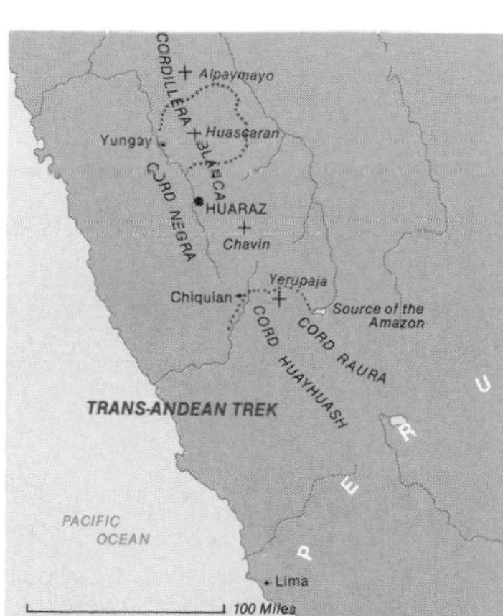

Llanganuco Pass, Cordillera Blanca/ Sara Steck

Itinerary: Day 1: Leave U.S. Arrive Lima. Transfer to hotel.

Day 2: All day drive to Huaraz (10,200′), the main town in northern Peru.

Day 3 and 4: Acclimatization hikes along the crest of the Cordillera Negra.

Day 5: Drive to Pitec and hike to Quebrada Quelquehuanca. Establish base camp at about 13,500 feet.

Day 6: Practice and review climbing techniques.

Day 7 to 10: Ascents in the area of Nevado Kayesh.

Day 11 to 14: Climb Nevado Chinchey (20,532′)

Day 15: Hike out and truck back to Huaraz.

Day 16: By truck down the Rio Santa Valley to lower base camp of Huascaran.

Day 17 to 19: Shuttle loads to higher camps on Huascaran.

Day 20 to 22: Summit attempts on Huascaran Sur (22,204′).

Day 23 and 24: Return to lower camps and return to Huaraz.

Day 25: Drive to Lima.

Day 26: Day free in Lima.

Day 27: Depart Lima, arrive Miami and connect with homeward-bound fights.

Dates: Jun 22–Jul 18 (27 days)
Leader: Sergio Fitch-Watkins
Grade: E-1
Land Cost: $2390 (7–12 members)
Single Supplement: $145
IT5AR10360

Peru Options

Whether you plan to visit Peru on one of our trips or on your own, we can arrange a variety of outdoor adventures for you, on foot, on horseback, by raft or dugout canoe.

For private treks, we can provide a full range of services such as bilingual guides, pack animals, camp staff and cooks, camp equipment and transport. Contact Mountain Travel for rates and further details.

Among our most popular "after the trek" excursions are:

Iquitos Amazon Exploration

From a remote lodge on the banks of the Amazon River, hike the trails of the jungle, swim in secluded lagoons, and explore the Amazon's tributaries by boat. *Time: Three days.*

Urubamba River Rafting

Whitewater rafting on the lively Urubamba River as it tumbles through the "sacred valley of the Incas." Also visit the fine Inca sites at Pisac or Ollantaytambo. *Time: One or two days.*

Puno/Lake Titicaca Excursion

From the red-roofed village of Puno on the shores of Lake Titicaca, journey by boat to visit Indian weavers on Takili Island and watch the sunset over the highest navigable body of water on earth. *Time: Three days.*

Our goal is an ascent of Huascaran (22,204′), highest peak in the Peruvian Andes and one of the highest in the Americas/Leo Le Bon

The Galapagos Islands

Wildlife journey to "Darwin's Islands"

"Considering the small size of these islands, we feel the more astonished at the number of their aboriginal beings, and at their confined range . . . Hence, both in space and time, we seem to be brought somewhat nearer to that great fact—that mystery of mysteries—the first appearance of new beings on earth."—Charles Darwin. 1860, *Voyage of the Beagle.*

The Galapagos Islands, situated in quiet isolation some 600 miles off Ecuador's coast, were the focal point for one of the most dramatic chapters in science history. It was here, in 1835, that Charles Darwin observed and cataloged the evidence that led him to formulate his theory of evolution through natural selection.

Galapagos plants and animals vary from island to island; climatological influences, soil textures and different altitudes have given rise to specific plants on specific islands, which in turn has influenced differential evolution of wildlife.

The processes of natural selection that inspired Darwin are still at work in the islands today; the islands are a living laboratory and the subject of constant scientific study.

In the 400 years since their discovery, the Galapagos have been sorely affected by the influence of man. Pirates, whalers and sporadic settlers killed many of the tame indigenous animals and introduced domestic animals and plants. In 1934, these practices were stopped when Ecuador set aside the islands as a sanctuary for native flora and fauna. In 1959, the Galapagos became a fully protected national park and tourism on the islands is strictly regulated.

Galapagos wildlife has no fear of human presence and can be approached closely, making this place a photographer's dream!

Our explorations here are eight-day yacht cruises, sailing or motoring island to island with an experienced Galapagos-trained naturalist guide and skilled crew.

Itinerary: Day 1: Leave U.S. Arrive Quito. Transfer to hotel.

Day 2: Fly to Guayaquil. Continue by charter flight to Baltra in the Galapagos Islands. Board yacht.

Day 3 to 8: The cruise itinerary varies according to weather, but most trips will visit Plazas Island, Academy Bay and highlands of Santa Cruz Island, Caleta Tortuga, James Island, Bartolome Island, Hood Island and either Tower Island or Floreana Island.

Day 9: Motor to Baltra. Fly to Guayaquil and continue by air to Quito. Overnight in hotel.

Day 10: Depart Quito and connect with homeward-bound flights.

Dates: #1 Mar 31–Apr 9 (10 days)
#2 May 19–May 28
#3 Dec 22–Dec 31
1987: Feb 17–Feb 24
Leader: On-board naturalist
Grade: A-1
Land Cost: $1390 + chtr. $325 (8–10 members)
$1590 + chtr. $325 (6–7)
Single Supplement: $40
IT6EA1MT08

In 1959, the Galapagos became a fully protected national park and tourism on the islands is strictly regulated/ *Sara Steck*

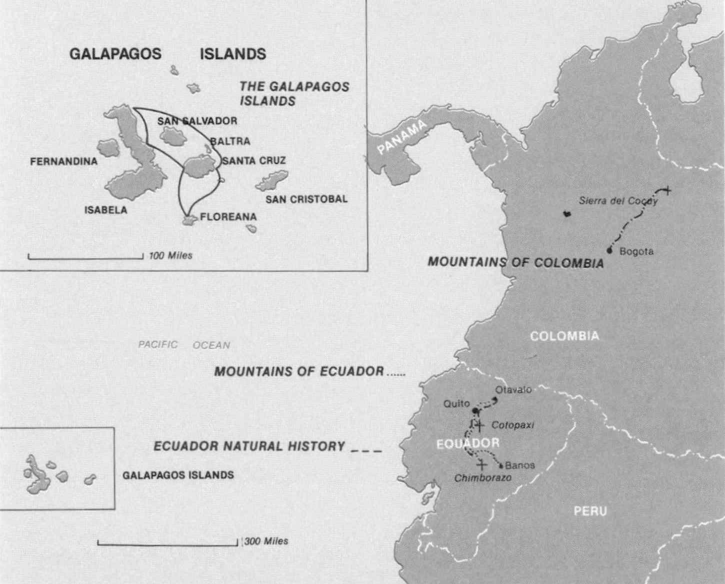

White-face boobies/*Sara Steck*

Galapagos wildlife has no fear of human presence and can be approached quite closely, making this place a photographer's dream!/*Sara Steck*

Ecuador Natural History

Amazon jungles and snow-capped volcanoes

Straddling the Equator for which it is named, Ecuador includes thousands of square miles of tropical rainforest as well as a magnificent highland plateau dotted with 20,000-foot volcanoes. Our trip here takes in both of these contrasting zones.

In the misty, fragrant tropics of the Amazon Basin, we travel by dugout canoe on the Rio Aguarico and Rio Aguanegro, visiting Secoya and Sinoa Indian villages, and spending lots of the time birdwatching, fishing and swimming. This is a very "untouristed" part of the Amazon and our accommodations will be in an isolated and rustic jungle camp. We sleep outside in hammocks.

Moving up to the cool, dry air of the Andes, we camp at about 13,000 feet in a national park in the sparkling green highlands and take an optional hike on Chimborazo (20,561′), one of the world's most famous mountains.

Until the beginning of the 19th century, when Himalayan exploration began in earnest, Chimborazo was thought to be the highest mountain on earth. In one sense, it is the highest, because its elevation combined with the "bulge" of the earth at the equator makes the summit the farthest point in the world from the center of the earth!

Chimborazo was first climbed in 1880 by the indefatigable Englishman Edward Whymper, first conqueror of the Matterhorn. Whymper wrote books on both these climbs which are classics of mountaineering literature.

Our day hike on Chimborazo gets us high enough for a good look at the volcano's glaciers and icecap.

We also spend a day camping at the base of beautiful Cotopaxi (19,347′), one of the highest active volcanoes on earth, admired for its Fuji-like symmetry.

Time is also set aside for visits to the capital city, Quito (9,350′), and to the great Indian markets at Otavalo and Ambato.

Itinerary: Day 1: Leave U.S. Arrive Quito, Ecuador. Transfer to hotel.

Day 2: Morning tour of Quito. Afternoon free.

Day 3: Drive to Taraboa, swim in hot springs and continue to Rio Agua Negra and camp.

Day 4: Paddle by dugout canoe down the Rio Agua Negra. Camp near a village of Siona Indians.

Day 5 and 6: By motorized boat upstream to the Lagunas of Cuyabeno and camp.

Day 7: Drive to the rough and tumble "frontier" jungle town of Lago Agrio.

Day 8: Fly to Quito. Drive to Otavalo. Overnight at hacienda.

Day 9: Visit the Otavalo market and drive through the "Avenue of the Volcanoes" to Cotopaxi National Park and camp at 13,000 feet.

Day 10: Hike and optional climb.

Day 11: Drive to Ambato. Overnight in hotel.

Day 12: Drive to the base of Chimborazo (20,561′). Camp at about 13,500 feet. Optional hike up to the climbers' hut at 16,000 feet.

Day 13: Drive back to Quito.

Day 14: Depart Quito and connect with homeward-bound flights.

*Dates: *May 6–May 19 (14 days)*
Leader: Terry Brian
Grade: B-2
Land Cost: $1550 (10–16 members)
$1750 (5–9)
Single Supplement: $130
IT6EA1MT07

**This trip can be taken in conjunction with the Galapagos cruise.*

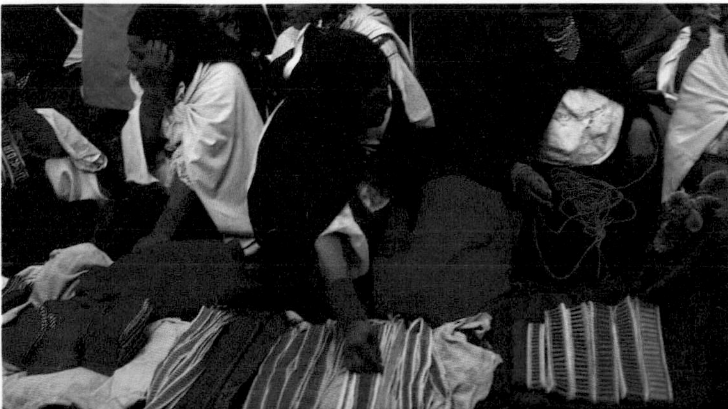

Mountains Of Ecuador

Climb high-altitude tropical volcanoes

The Andes of Ecuador are actually two separate ranges, the Eastern and Western Cordillera. Running between these ranges for over 200 miles is a central valley lined with more than 30 volcanoes. On this mountaineering journey, we will attempt two of these volcanoes: majestic Cotopaxi (19,347′), one of the highest active volcanoes on earth, and Chimborazo (20,561′) (see *Ecuador Natural History* trip for more information on Chimborazo.)

While not technically difficult, these climbs are physically demanding due to the altitude and snow conditions. Ample time is allowed for inclement weather and acclimatization. Basic mountaineering experience is required.

The trip begins with a visit to the capital city of Quito and ends with a relaxing visit to the Banos hot springs.

Itinerary: Day 1: Leave U.S. Arrive Quito, drive to the village of Otavalo. Overnight at hotel.

Day 2: Visit the Otavalo market, one of South America's oldest Indian markets.

Day 3: Drive to Imbabura; afternoon fitness and acclimatization hike. Camp nearby.

Day 4 to 6: Hiking, climbing and glacier practice on Nevado Cayambe (18,991′).

Day 7: Return to Quito.

Day 8: In Quito.

Day 9 to 11: Climb and descend Cotopaxi.

Day 12: Drive to Ambato, "the city of flowers."

Day 13 to 15: Climb and descend Chimborazo.

Day 16: In Banos, a town on the edge of the jungle.

Day 17: Drive to Quito, arriving in the afternoon.

Day 18: Depart Quito and connect with homeward-bound flights.

Dates: Nov 28–Dec 15 (18 days)
Leader: Sergio Fitch-Watkins
Grade: D-2
Land Cost: $1590 (10–12 members)
$1750 (7–9)
Single Supplement: $60
IT6EA1MT07

In Ecuador, time is set aside for visits to the great markets at Otavalo and Ambato/Bruce Klepinger

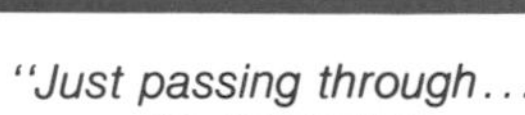

"Just passing through..."

QUITO

City notes by Sara Steck

Walking/jogging;
The best walking tour would be through the old part of Quito, with its narrow cobblestone streets, colonial buildings and churches. There is a big park in the center of town off Avenida Amazonas for jogging. You can also try various routes just outside the city, notably a hill out of town called Cerro Panicillo.

Day trips:
Visit various highland markets including the famous one at Otavalo, which although a bit "touristy", is still the best place to buy Otavalo Indian weavings.

Restaurants
Try Casa De Me Abuela ("grandma's house"), for family-style dinners and huge Argentine-style steaks.

On Chimborazo/Sergio Fitch-Watkins

On Cotopaxi/Sergio Fitch-Watkins

Approaching Cotopaxi/
Sergio Fitch-Watkins

The Mountains Of Colombia

Climbing in the Sierra Nevada de Cocuy

Just south of the Venezuelan border is the Sierra Nevada de Cocuy, the most heavily glaciated range in Colombia, with its misty, icy summits rising directly above the steaming jungles of the Orinoco basin. There are 15 summits here topping 16,500 feet.

Our expedition will make non-technical climbs of four peaks in this range, finishing up with the highest and most difficult of the four, Ritacuba Blanco (17,490′).

The climbs, though not technically difficult, are physically demanding due to altitude and snow conditions.

Itinerary: Day 1: Leave U.S. Arrive Bogota, Colombia.

Day 2: Day free in Bogota.

Day 3: 10-hour, 250-mile drive to Hacienda El Cocuy.

Day 4: Four-hour hike to Laguna Del Pichacho and camp.

Day 5 and 6: Acclimatizing hikes and practice on the Pichacho Glacier.

Day 7: Climb El Pichacho (approx. 17,000′).

Day 8: Summit attempt on Puntiagudo Peak (approx. 16,900′).

Day 9: Set up camp on the glaciers of Ritacuba Negro at about 16,600 feet.

Day 10 to 12: Summit attempts on Ritacuba Negro and Ritacuba Blanco.

Day 13: Hike down and drive to the town of Suata.

Day 14: Drive to Bogota.

Day 15: Depart on homeward-bound flights.

Dates: Jan 5–Jan 19 (15 days)
1987: Jan 4–Jan 18
Leader: Sergio Fitch-Watkins
Grade: D-2
Land Cost: $1290
(6–12 members)
Single Supplement: $95
IT6EA1MT03

Glacier camp in Sierra Nevado de Cocuy/*Sergio Fitch-Watkins*

The Sierra Nevado de Cocuy is the most heavily glaciated range in Colombia, with its misty, icy summits rising directly above the steaming jungle lowlands of the Orinoco basin/ *Sergio Fitch-Watkins*

Natural History Of Costa Rica

Rainforests, wilderness beaches, still-active volcanoes

The tiny country of Costa Rica has exceptional birdlife and unmatched flora that includes over 1,000 species of orchids alone. Its national park system is known throughout the world.

Our first stop is the orchid-laden Monteverde Cloud Forest, an environment composed of six different ecological communities of plants and animals, with over 2,000 active plant species, more than 320 bird species and 100 mammal species. This is probably the best place in the world for viewing the rare Quetzal, the beautiful, long-plumed bird which was sacred to both the Aztec and Mayan Indians.

Driving to the Pacific Coast, we visit Santa Rosa National Park, a beautiful beach wilderness. At Tamarindo Beach on the Peninsula of Nicoya, we'll do some night game viewing to see Giant Leatherback Sea Turtles as they come up on the beach at night to lay eggs, and we'll travel by small boat along estuaries to view the many water birds that inhabit this area.

We round out the trip with an exciting day of whitewater rafting on the Pacuare River, a visit to the moonscape of the still-active Poas volcano, and a classic train ride from Costa Rica's central highlands to the Caribbean Coast at Limon.

Itinerary: Day 1: Leave U.S. Arrive San Jose. Transfer to hotel.

Day 2: Morning city tour including archaeological museum, then continue to Monteverde Cloud Forest. Overnight at lodge.

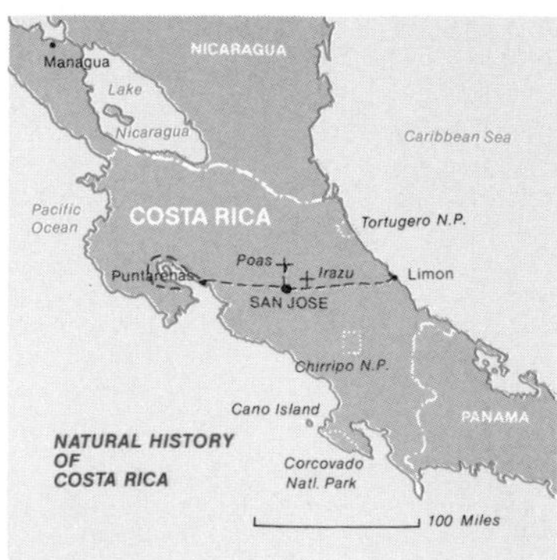

We'll do some night game viewing to see Giant Leatherback Sea Turtles as they come up on the beach at night to lay their eggs, and possibly view hatched baby turtles/Sara Steck

Day 3: All day to enjoy hiking and bird-watching in the cloud forest. Overnight at lodge.

Day 4: Drive to Hacienda La Pacifica in Guanacaste Province for lunch (and a swim in a pool), then continue to the town of Liberia for overnight.

Day 5: Enter Santa Rosa National Park, with time for hiking and birdwatching, then continue to Tamarindo Beach on the Peninsula of Nicoya. Night viewing of Giant Leatherback Sea Turtles as they come up on the beach to lay their eggs, and possible viewing of the hatched baby turtles as they return to the sea. Overnight at hotel.

Day 6: Tour the estuary by boat, viewing water birds, and probably seeing some monkeys and crocodiles. Afternoon free to enjoy the beach, or take wildlife walks. Overnight at hotel.

Day 7: Drive to San Jose. Overnight at hotel.

Day 8: All-day raft trip on the Pacuare River. Return to hotel in San Jose.

Day 9: By train across Costa Rica from the central highlands to near the eastern Caribbean coast, arriving late afternoon. Dinner in Turrialba and drive by bus back to San Jose.

Day 10: Visit a small coffee plantation.

Day 11: Day trip to Poas (or Irazu) volcano. Farewell dinner in the evening.

Day 12: Depart San Jose on homeward-bound flights.

Dates: #1 Jan 11–Jan 22 (12 days)
#2 Jan 22–Feb 2
#3 Feb 8–Feb 19
#4 Dec 22–Dec 31
Leader: Ronald Esquivel
Grade: A-2
Land Cost: $1350 (10–15 members)
$1450 (7–9)
Single Supplement: $195

The Other Mexico

Archaeological sites, colonial towns, highland country

This trip explores Mexico's past, both colonial and Aztec, with visits to archaeological ruins, beautiful colonial towns and a short camping sojourn in the Mexican highlands, with its active volcanoes and snow-capped peaks.

Travel is by mini-bus, accommodations are in haciendas and classic colonial inns, and there are three nights of camping.

We begin in Mexico City, staying at the historic 300-year-old Hotel Cortes. We visit the great museum which houses the major Aztec and Mayan treasures, and drive out to the famous Aztec pyramids of the sun and moon at Teotihuacan ("the place where men become gods").

Continuing into the countryside, we take a day's hike near El Chico, a mining town lost in the *sierras,* and drive to our first colonial-era town, San Miguel de Allende, one of the most beautiful in Mexico. We'll appreciate its classic colonial architecture, cobblestone streets, fountains and parks, and perhaps browse in some of the town's art galleries.

At another colonial town, Uruapan, we enjoy an evening walk in the town's downtown park, a national park complete with streams, fountains and waterfalls.

Our next stop is Volcano Paricutin, one of the newest volcanoes on earth. Driving up to its lava fields, we hike to the top for a picnic lunch, then return on foot via the ruins of the town of San Juan Parangaricutiro, which was partially buried by the lava flow when Volcano Paricutin was born with a fiery eruption on February 20, 1943.

Circling around to Nevado de Toluca, a snow-capped 14,800-foot highland peak, we camp on its forested slopes, drive to its summit the next day and fish in its crater lake or hike to the top.

At the town of Almealco, we make a day's hike into Michautlaco Canyon to visit the lovely Pozas De Las Culebras ("snake pools"), where legend has it that Ceacatl Tipltzin, King of the Toltecs, was baptized and became Quetzalcoatl, the plumed serpent diety of the Mayans.

The trip ends with a visit to the pretty hill town of Taxco, known for its silver handicrafts.

Itinerary: Day 1: Fly to Mexico City. Overnight at Hotel Cortes.

Day 2: Visit museum, attend performance of Ballet Folkorico National.

Day 3: Drive to Teotihuacan, continue to Huasca and stay at a 200-year-old hacienda.

Day 4: Day hike to El Circo del Creston, then camp at the mining town of El Chico.

Day 5: Drive to San Miguel de Allende. Overnight at colonial inn.

Day 6: In San Miguel de Allende.

The Other Mexico explores Mexico's past, both colonial and Aztec, with visits to archaeological ruins and beautiful colonial towns/Leo Le Bon

Day 7: Drive to Uruapan. Overnight at hotel.

Day 8: Drive to the colonial town of Morelia. Overnight at hotel.

Day 9: Drive to camp at base of Nevado de Toluca.

Day 10: Drive up to Toluca's crater. Time for fishing or hiking. Return to camp.

Day 11: Drive to Cocoyoc and stay at a hotel on a very old hacienda.

Day 12: Drive to Taxco. Overnight at hotel.

Day 13: Morning in Taxco, afternoon drive to Mexico City. Overnight at Hotel Cortes.

Day 14: Depart on homeward-bound flights.

Dates: #1 Apr 19–May 2 (14 days)
#2 Sep 27–Oct 10
Leader: Sergio Fitch-Watkins
Grade: A-1
Land Cost: $975 (5–15 members)
Single Supplement: $75
IT5AM1MTN01

Volcanoes Of Mexico

Learn basic mountaineering skills

On this trip we climb Orizaba (18,851′) and Popocatepetl (17,887′), the third and fifth highest mountains in North America, plus a third peak, Ixtaccihuatl (17,343′).

Many now-famous mountaineers started their careers on these snowy peaks, which provide a good introduction to climbing. We've been operating successful Mexican volcano climbs for 15 years.

The climbs require the use of ice axe and crampons and are not technically difficult. The real criteria for reaching these high altitude summits are desire and stamina.

Itinerary: Day 1: Leave U.S. Arrive Mexico City. Overnight at hotel.

Day 2: Free day in Mexico City (7,000′).

Day 3: Drive to base camp on Ixtaccihuatl at Alcalican Canyon at 11,000 feet.

Day 4 to 6: Climb and descend Ixta, and drive to Tlamacaz.

Day 7: Day free in Tlamacaz.

Day 8: Early morning start for the climb of Popocatepetl, via the Ventorrillo Route.

Day 9: Drive to the pretty colonial town of Puebla.

Day 10: Drive to Piedra Grande Hut (13,776′) on the north side of Pico de Orizaba.

Day 11: Early morning start to cimb and descend Orizaba via the Glacier de Jamapa.

Day 12: In Puebla.

Day 13: Drive to Mexico City.

Day 14: Depart Mexico City and connect on homeward-bound fights.

Dates: #1 Feb 24–Mar 9 (14 days)
#2 Mar 10–Mar 23
#3 Oct 27–Nov 9
#4 Dec 22, 1986–Jan 4, 1987
1987: Feb 23–Mar 8, Mar 9–Mar 22
Leader: Sergio Fitch-Watkins
Grade: C-3/D-2
Land Cost: $890 (5–15 members)
Single Supplement: $75
IT5AM1MTN01

On Pico de Orizaba/*Sergio Fitch-Watkins*

Climbing on Ixtaccihuatl/ *Sergio Fitch-Watkins*

Approaching Ixtaccihuatal. Many now-famous mountaineers started their careers on these snowy peaks, which provide a good introduction to climbing. We've been operating successful Mexican volcano climbs for years/ *Sergio Fitch-Watkins*

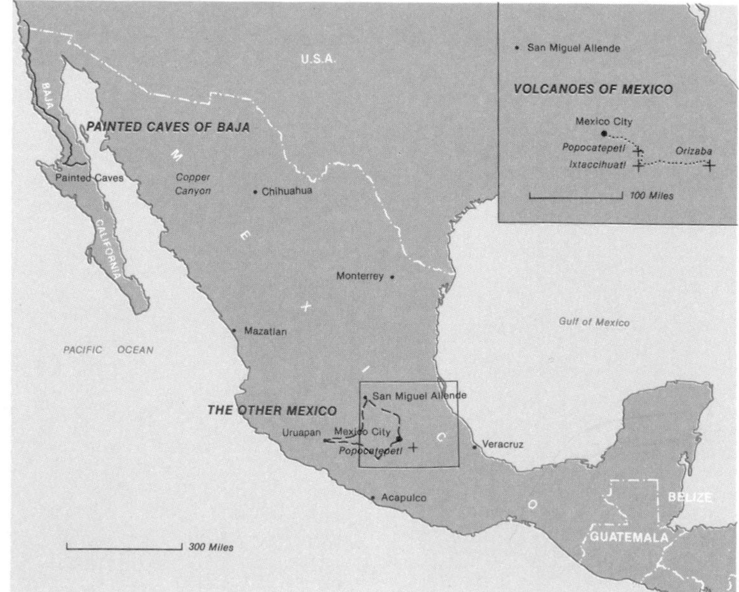

Tarahumara Easter Fiesta

A glimpse of a vanishing culture

This is a very special opportunity to witness the Tarahumara Indian Easter Fiesta, which takes place within the maze of peaks and canyons of the Sierra Madre Oriental of central Mexico.

We fly by private charter to a very remote canyon of the Barranca del Cobre ("copper canyon"), landing on a dirt airstrip within the inner canyons where there are several communities of Tarahumara Indians who have little contact with the outside world.

The exact place names of the communities on our seven-day trekking itinerary will not be disclosed to protect the privacy of our Tarahumara friends. On trek, all our baggage will be carried by mules.

This is not tourist country, and fiesta activities are staged according to ancient traditions.

The fiesta includes candle processions at dark, a drummer who signals the beginnings of

Tarahumara Easter Fiesta/Leo Le Bon

Holy Week, colorful ceremonies like the dance of the Pharisee, played by men with mud-painted bodies and feathered headdresses, and other men who carry wooden lances and bows and arrows. Then comes the great procession which stages the Way of the Cross and ends in the local church. Informal wrestling matches between Tarahumara men and a night-long *tesquinada* (drinking festivity) will follow.

After the two-day Easter fiesta, we trek out for four days and fly by charter to a hotel on the rim of scenic Copper Canyon, from where we return to Chihuahua on a scenic eight-hour train ride.

Itinerary: Day 1: Fly to Chihuahua, Mexico.

Day 2: Sightseeing in Chihuahua.

Day 3: By private charter flight to remote canyon. Overnight at village inn.

Day 4 and 5: With mules carrying the gear, trek to the site of the Easter Fiesta. Camp nearby.

Day 6 and 7: Easter Fiesta.

Day 8 to 12: Trek to other small Tarahumara settlements, eventually returning to the Mestizo village where we started.

Day 13: By charter flight to Divisadero. Overnight at Hotel Cabanas.

Day 14: Eight-hour train journey through "Copper Canyon" to Chihuahua.

Day 15: Depart Chihuahua on homeward-bound flights.

Dates: Mar 31–Apr 14 (15 days)
1987: Mar 30–Apr 13
Leader:
Esmeralda Ponce de Leon
Grade: B-1
Land Cost: $975
(10–14 members)
$1175 (7–9)
Single Supplement: $75
IT5AM1MTN01

This is not tourist country, and fiesta activities are staged according to ancient traditions. Despite our presence, the Indians go on about having their fiesta, a very important cultural event/ *Leo Le Bon*

The Painted Caves Of Baja

Hiking to neolithic art sites

In the hidden inner canyons of Baja California, there is a wealth of prehistoric cave art. In fact, the largest painted cave in the world is here, a site with 500 feet of drawings of human and animal forms, some of them 10 feet high and 20 feet above the ground.

Although little known, the painted caves of Baja are larger and more numerous than their counterparts in celebrated European sites such as Lascaux and Altamira.

To approach the major caves, we hike across desert mesas of the "Sierra de San Francisco," traveling along the banks of palm-fringed streams which flow through vertical-walled canyons.

Our accommodations will be in campsites near various *ranchos,* which are scattered here and there near the precious water sources. The longest hike is about five hours. Mules will carry all our gear.

Itinerary: Day 1: Drive from San Diego, California, to Guerrero Negro, Baja.

Day 2: Drive to camp at Rancho Santa Martha.

Day 3 to 8: Hike with mule train, visiting caves and camping at ranchos enroute.

Day 9: Drive back to Guerrero Negro.

Day 10: Drive to Tijuana. Overnight at hotel.

Day 11: Return drive to San Diego.

Dates: #1 Oct 13—Oct 23
(11 days)
#2 Nov 10–Nov 20
Leader: Sergio Fitch-Watkins
Grade: B-1
Land Cost: $590
(6–15 members)
Single Supplement: $60
IT5AM1MTN01

Tarahumara women/Nadia Le Bon

One of John Muir's lifelong passions was the study of glaciers, and his fondest memories of Alaska were of Glacier Bay, which he discovered, and to which he returned again and again/ *Pam Shandrick*

SECTION VI
NORTH AMERICA & HAWAII

"The white, rayless light of the morning, seen when I was alone amid the peaks of the California Sierra, had always seemed to me the most telling of all the terrestrial manifestations of God. But here, the mountains themselves were made divine, and declared His glory in terms still more impressive. How long we gazed I never knew. The glorious vision passed away in a gradual, fading change through a thousand tones of color to pale yellow and white, and then the work of the ice-world went on in everyday beauty. The green waters of the fjord were filled with sun-spangles; the fleet of icebergs set forth on their voyages with the upspringing breeze; and on the innumerable mirrors and prisms of these bergs, and on those of the shattered crystal walls of the glaciers common white light and rainbow light began to burn, while the mountains shone in their frosty jewelry, and loomed again in the thin azure in serene terrestrial majesty."

John Muir in Glacier Bay,
1879,
Travels In Alaska

John Muir, Scottish-born naturalist and founder of the Sierra Club, visited Alaska in 1879, just 12 days after the United States purchased it from Russia.

One of his lifelong passions was the study of glaciers, and his fondest memories of Alaska were of the exquisite setting of Glacier Bay, which he discovered, and to which he returned again and again.

When Muir set out on his frequent trips into the wilderness, almost always alone, he carried little more with him than tea and dry bread in a small sack thrown over his shoulder. So great was his absorption with the wilderness environment that he needed little else. He would be bewildered to see the elaborate "creature comforts" today's backpackers bring with them!

Chuck Horner

Chuck Horner

Why is Alaska so important? Because it is a symbol of wilderness, of freedom, of renewal of the spirit.

It is America's final frontier, last stronghold of precious wilderness on our continent. Since its statehood in 1959, the pressure has been on to exploit Alaska's natural resources. Perhaps the environmental lessons sadly learned in the Lower 48 will help us to treat Alaska's wild places with more respect.

Chuck Horner

Adventure Travel In North America

Camp life on McKinley/Gary Bocarde

Alaska:

Hiking in Alaska is very different than in the Lower 48. Access to the wilderness is often by chartered bushplane and, once the hiker is deposited in a remote region, there are few marked trails.

Southeast Alaska features water-bound wilderness journeys by canoe, kayak or raft, and by small boat to remote glacier-lined inlets such as Glacier Bay.

In the grand volcanic Valley of Ten Thousand Smokes in Katmai National Monument, backpackers can cross the ash-covered floor of a huge extinct volcano and hike up to Katmai's 2-mile-wide crater rim.

In central Alaska, the focus is on Mt. McKinley, highest peak on the continent, centerpiece of the Alaska Range.

In the jagged Brooks Range south of the Arctic Slope, there is unlimited hiking, rafting, kayaking, cross-country skiing and dogsledding in a primal wilderness aglow with the luminescent Northern Lights.

During summer in the high arctic, wildlife enthusiasts can search for the caribou migration in William O. Douglas National Wildlife Range at a time when there is almost 24-hour daylight.

The Pribilof Islands in the Bering Sea are home to some of the world's great seabird colonies and breeding ground for the largest fur seal herd in the world.

Canada:

Canada boasts the Yukon, the Klondike, the coastal St. Elias Range, the fjords of British Columbia, the rock monoliths of Baffin Island, the northern woodlands of Ontario, and of course, some of the most spectacular scenery in the entire Rockies. For sailing, canoeing, snowshoeing, bicycling, and horsepack trips, the adventure possibilities in this great land are almost too numerous to list!

Hawaii:

Classic Hawaiian adventures include backpacking the Na Pali Coast or Waimea Canyon on Kauai, summit hikes on the great 13,000-foot Pacific volcanoes of Mauna Kea and Mauna Loa (on Hawaii) and Haleakala (on Maui).

New England:

The Appalachian Mountain Club maintains a fine series of huts in the White Mountains of New Hampshire, making a 6-day traverse a pleasure for hikers.

Pacific Northwest:

In Oregon and Washington, the wooded islands of the Puget Sound and Olympic Peninsula are a naturalist's delight and great volcanoes such as Rainier and Hood present a range of hiking and climbing adventures.

The Rockies & Sierra Nevada:

It would take a lifetime to exhaust the possiblities in western national parks. To name but a few major attractions: Rocky Mountain National Park, The Grand Tetons, Yellowstone, Yosemite, Death Valley, the Grand Canyon, and world-class rivers such as the Colorado! This is the American wilderness at its best for hiking, whitewater, skiing and climbing.

Alaska /Hayden Kaden

Gathering At The River

by Beverly Fraknoi

Rafting on the Tatshenshini River/
Bruce Klepinger

Few people I know have heard of this river—the rolling, gray-green Tatshenshini. It begins as a riffle of glaciermelt, high in the Canadian Yukon. Some dozens of miles to the north the Alsek River rises from a similar origin in southeastern Alaska. At the mountainous seam where Alaska and Canada join, the two watercourses come together and tumble to meet the sea at Dry Bay on the Gulf of Alaska. Altogether, a trip down the Tatshenshini comprises 140 river miles through wilderness more pristine than most people ever experience.

At the moment, the promise of that experience is beginning to tingle in my skull. Along with ten others, including two doctors from New York, an Australian scoutmaster, a schoolteacher and a geologist, I have been lured to a tip of sandy gravel called Dalton Post, a wide place in the riverine road where a crystalline Yukon stream flushes itself into the silted water of the Tatshenshini. To the north and west lie the sharp peaks of Alaska's St. Elias Mountains. At eleven-thirty in the morning their permanent frosting of snow and ice is baking like the rest of us in 75-degree heat.

On the cobbled riverbank, three cheerful, brawny men are loading ammo boxes and heaps of duffels into three gray neoprene rafts. All are professional wilderness guides; the leader for this trip is Dick Rice; his associates are Larry Derby and Mike Braal.

Shadows flicker fifty yards upstream, and the boatmen stop work; there is the faint crunch of weight dislodging loose gravel. Now I see what they see: a large brown ovoid with a rolling gait has emerged from a willow thicket and is making its way toward the water. *Ursus horribilis,* the Alaskan grizzly bear, has come to fish in the river for its lunch. In a moment a great shaggy arm the color of brown sugar slaps the water; a luckless sockeye, its rosy belly now red and gaping, rockets up in a plume of foam and disappears down the grizzly's gullet. Another swipe procures another fish. Then, as suddenly as it came, the bear hoists its body onto an upstream bank and slips into the forest.

It is time now for the river, for the journey to begin. We clients assort ourselves into the three rafts, two of which have been named in honor of Edward Abbey's Monkey Wrench Gang. Dick's boat is "Seldom Seen," while Mike is at the helm of "Hayduke." Larry pilots "Strider," provenance unknown. I choose: Strider it is. We shove off into an eddy, neoprene grinding against the pebbled streambed. Larry grimaces as his muscles begin to work, powering the raft across the rippling eddy line and into the main current of the Tatshenshini.

Camp tonight is a rocky outwash, one of hundreds of small deltas along the river where glacial streams deposit bits of the Yukon that are slowly being tranported, grain by grain, to the sea. We assiduously observe the practices of no-trace camping: fires in a fire box, garbage burned or carried out, human wastes buried six inches deep. Dick Rice is a stickler for detail in this regard—not even tent circles, the unnatural rings of stones used by campers to keep their lodgings from becoming airborne in the subarctic breeze, will be here to mark our passage when we leave.

Supper is opulent: grilled salmon, salad, wine, thick chocolate brownies that emerge from a cast iron pot in steaming four-inch slabs. Later, people fall away from the fire and amble through the mauve twilight to their tents. In the distance the angular, frosted peaks of the Noisey Range—thrusting upward like huge bicuspids—are turning purple.

We are now five days in and the inevitable has happened: the Tatshenshini has converged with the mighty Alsek, we are officially in Alaska, and it has begun to rain. I have spent the afternoon peering out from under a rubber visor and calculating our EPH—eagles per hour. The rate seems to be about one bald eagle every five to ten minutes, each holding court on the naked tip of a hemlock spar.

The terrain and the riverscape are changing. Our present goal, a layover camp at Walker Glacier, lies in an elbow of the Alsek Range, among uncouth mountains that are still largely in the grasp of 20,000-year old ice. The nearer foothills have been freed of the glacial embrace between six and eight decades ago. That has been enough time for liberated spurs, conical kames, gravelly eskers, sheer-walled escarpments, scoured domes— the mystical vocabulary of glacial conversation—to acquire what appears from the shining, pewter river to be a coat of many colors, all of them green.

As the river surges and arches toward the south, the Walker comes plunging into view. The scene is almost appallingly beautiful, and it takes an effort of will to realize that this flowing mass of ice has existed, more or less intact, for two thousand centuries.

Our penultimate river day dawns chilly and damp, but upriver the overcast is breaking, impaling black peaks to the east and north on pikes of silvery light. We are headed downriver, however, toward berg-choked Alsek Bay. In that direction the sky is Wagnerian, a celestial oration on the mutability of the color gray. Once more we lash gear to rafts and set out, wistfully watching Walker Glacier as it recedes, nearly eclipsed now by its own vapor.

A few days earlier we had edied out in similar terrain, in the concavity of a shrubby gravel bar where Dick had seen wolf cubs on a previous trip. Larry had begun to howl, a falsetto peal in honor of wolves.

We waited.

Nothing.

It was only later, when we turned to leave, that the high, sad, ancient reply floated up so lightly that no one could say, for sure, from which direction it had come.

Now, the mist ahead is beginning to lift, revealing the rounded pate of Gateway Knob, several million tons of granite set square in the center of the Alsek.

Skirting the knob's southern rim, we enter the bay. A sea of icebergs appear; some are tiny, fist-sized translucent baubles, others have fat Volkswagen bodies and long swan necks, still others are magnificent floating mesas as big as houses. Sizzling, like frying bacon, as the atomizing crystals liberate gases trapped—free at last!—from a Pleistocene atmosphere. Later someone picks bits of ice from a cruising floe and adds it to the Kool-Aid.

In the wee hours last night the wind blew fiercely, and this morning the boatmen are patching a gaping hole in Strider's bow, the result of a wrenching collision between raft and rock. Tonight we will camp just short of the Pacific Ocean in Dry Bay, then head by bush plane tomorrow to Gustavus, to Juneau, to miscellaneous points south and east. After that will be re-entry—the skewed time between realities that overtake returnees from trips like this. Goodbye river, goodbye glaciers, goodbye grizzly, wherever you are.

Strider is finally ready to go. It is late. I notice that the moon is already rising. Perhaps, if the sky stays clear, that moon will shine its platinum light on the rivers and the ice. I would like to see that.

Ms. Fraknoi was a member of our TATSHENSHINI-ALSEK RAFTING trip in Alaska.

All our North American trip leaders are adept at making your outdoor journey agreeable and memorable. The Alaskan leaders are experienced members of the Alaska Wilderness Guides Association.

GARY BOCARDE, 38, in his 17 years of climbing, has been involved in many difficult ascents, including the first ascent of the Shield on El Capitan, the first big wall route in Alaska (Moose's Tooth), first winter ascent of Mt. Hunter, and many other ascents throughout the Alaska Range. He has guided for ten years on Mt. McKinley, Mt. Foraker, Mt. Hunter, and Mt. Sanford and was a member of two mountaineering expeditions in China: 1980 Gongga Shan and 1981 Everest East Face.

JOHN & IDA BURROUGHS lead our White Mountains hiking trip in New Hampshire. They have spent considerable time exploring the mountains of New England as well as climbing in the American West, Alaska and Mexico. Jon is a former White Mountain hutman and guide.

FRED FAYE-HILTNER, 31, spends his winters as a ski patrolman and his summers as a river guide. He has taught rock and ice climbing, whitewater kayaking, canoeing and has worked as a wildlife biologist for the U.S. Forest Service.

DAVE KETSCHER, 35, is an Alaskan river runner, bush pilot, dog team guide and wilderness enthusiast who resides in the bush community of Bettles, Alaska.

CHUCK HORNER, 55, is Chief Ranger for the Southeast District of the Alaska Division of Parks and is an active canoeist, kayaker and cross-country skier.

HAYDEN KADEN, 41, is an outdoorsman and naturalist with 15 years' experience in kayaking and camping in southeast Alaska. A lawyer turned wilderness guide, he lives on a homestead at the mouth of Glacier Bay.

RICHARD McMAHON, 57, a resident of Hawaii for the last 12 years, retired from the U.S. Army as a colonel. His avocations center around hiking, backpacking, skiing, scuba and non-technical mountain climbing. He has hiked extensively in Hawaii and is very familiar with all the main islands of the Hawaiian chain and their history, geology, flora and fauna.

Hayden Kayden

Mike & Debbie O'Connor

MIKE & DEBBIE O'CONNOR are professional wilderness guides. A high school counselor in Angoon during the school year, Mike guides backpacking and kayak trips in the summer. Debbie teaches special education and also spends the summers guiding wilderness trips.

PETER OURUSOFF, 45, is an inveterate nature enthusiast and trekker. A former school teacher (science), counselor, park naturalist and landscape gardener, he has led adventure trips for 20 years and for the last five years with Mountain Travel in Mexico, Hawaii and Africa.

NIC PARKER, 36, is a lifetime Alaskan climber and explorer with over fifty first (and first winter) ascents in the ranges of Alaska. He has twenty years of alpine experience and has been a professional mountain guide for ten years. He has extensive mountain rescue training and is qualified as a medic-EMT. He lives in the village of Talkeetna, near the foothills of the Alaska Range.

Nic Parker and Gary Bocarde

Chuck Horner

Dave Ketscher

ERIC SANFORD, 33, has been climbing, skiing and guiding for more than 16 years in the U.S. Canada, Alaska and Europe. He has many major climbs and first ascents to his credit and has worked with Colorado Mountain Rescue and the Yosemite Rescue Team.

RON STORRO-PATTERSON, 44, is a naturalist and marine biologist. He has led natural history trips for 20 years to numerous places including Africa, the Amazon, the Galapagos and Alaska. Since 1975, he has spent his summers observing the wildlife of Southeast Alaska. He helped found the Whale Center, an international non-profit organization dealing with the conservation of whales.

Ron Storro-Patterson

Fred Faye-Hiltner

Peter Ourusoff

Eric Sanford

The Other Hawaii

Camping, hiking, natural history

During our sojourn in the "other" Hawaii we will hike, camp and explore the exotic natural beauty of the Hawaii of old, as it still exists on the outer islands.

With ten days on the "big island" of Hawaii, we will hike the Waipio Valley, swim and snorkel in the warm waters of Hapuna Beach, and hike on Mauna Kea (13,796′), highest peak in the Pacific.

Driving down the beautiful Kona Coast, we stop at Hawaii Volcanoes National Park to hike across the still-steaming Kilauea Caldera to explore Mauna Ulu, a very active volcano.

Our five-day sojourn on Maui includes a memorable sunrise from the summit of Haleakala (10,023′), followed by a two-day backpack trip across the moonscape of craters which form the volcano's floor. Our accommodations will be in beach camps and state park cabins, with our last night spent at an inn in the picturesque whaling port of Lahaina.

Itinerary: Day 1: leave hometown. Arrive Hilo, Hawaii. Transfer to hotel.

Day 2: Walk in the Waipio Valley, a six-mile long valley bounded by 2,000-foot high walls. Camp at Keokea.

Day 3: A day's hike on the Pololu Trail, with its fantastic seascapes and profusion of native plants. Overnight at Hapuna Beach.

Day 4: Morning swimming at Hapuna, best beach on the island of Hawaii. Afternoon drive to cabins at 6,000 feet in the saddle between Mauna Kea and Mauna Loa.

Day 5: Drive to the trailhead and begin hiking, reaching the summit of Mauna Kea (13,796′) by noon. Return hike to cabins.

Day 6: Morning visit to the town of Kamuela, afternoon at Hapuna Beach. Sunset barbecue.

Day 7: Drive along the Kona Coast and camp at a beach park.

Day 8: Drive around the southernmost point on the island. Overnight at cabins.

Day 9: Spend the day hiking at Hawaii Volcanoes National Park.

Day 10: Visit the bird park and hike to Mauna Ulu, a recently active volcano. Drive down the rugged southern coast for a short walk.

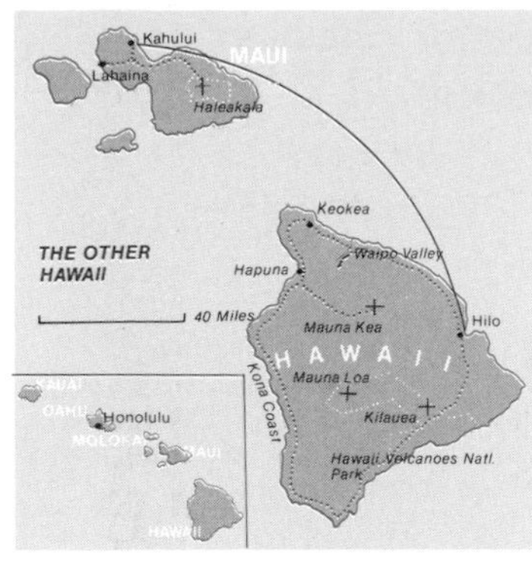
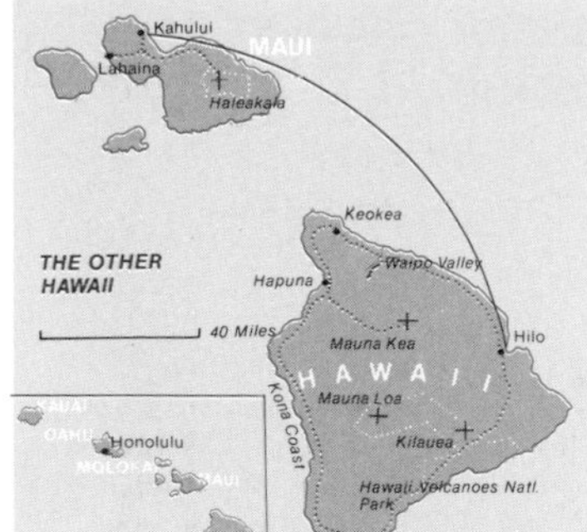

Day 11: Drive to Hilo and fly to Kahului on the island of Maui. Drive to Haleakala Volcano and camp at Hosmer Grove at 8,000 feet.

Day 12: Drive to the top of Haleakala to view sunrise from the summit, then don 25–35 lb. backpacks for a day's hike across the seven-mile-long crater on Sliding Sands Trail. Overnight at cabins or in camp.

Day 13: Hike the Halemauu Trail back through the crater to camp at Hosmer Grove.

Day 14: Last morning on the beach, then drive to Lahaina. Overnight at Pioneer Inn.

Day 15: Transfer to airport to connect with homeward-bound flights.

Dates: #1 Jan 4–Jan 18 (15 days)
#2 Apr 5–Apr 19
#3 Oct 4–Oct 18
#4 Dec 18, 1986–Jan 1, 1987
Leader: #1 & #2 Peter Ourusoff
#3 & #4 to be announced
Grade: B-2
Land Cost: $1150
(11–14 members)
$1250 (6–10)
Single Supplement: $75

Hawaii Outer Island Adventure

Backpacking on Kauai and Hawaii

This trip visits the islands of Hawaii and Kauai, eastern and westernmost of the main island chain.

On Hawaii, we explore Hawaii Volcanoes National Park, including a hike to the currently active East Rift Zone. We also climb Mauna Loa (13,677′), an active volcano and the world's largest mountain (when measured from the floor of the ocean!). Mauna Loa is an active volcano, accessible only by trail, and a very interesting climb.

On Kauai, we hike in Kokee State Park where we enjoy magnificent views into some of Hawaii's most inaccessible "hanging" valleys, then descend into Waimea Canyon ("Grand Canyon of the Pacific") and hike an 11-mile-long ancient Hawaiian trail along the spectacular Na Pali Coast, arriving at the isolated and historic Kalalau Valley.

While there is some strenuous hiking on this trip, we will devote plenty of time to relaxing, swimming, and snorkeling on some of Hawaii's most splendid beaches.

Itinerary: Day 1: Leave hometown. Fly to Hilo, Hawaii. Transfer to hotel.

Day 2: Hiking in Hawaii Volcanoes National Park.

Day 3: Eight-hour hike over moonscape lava formations to scene of current eruption in East Rift Zone.

Day 4: Drive to 6,600 feet on Mauna Loa and hike for six hours to cabin at 9,000 feet.

Day 5: Eight-hour hike to Summit Cabin at 13,000 feet.

Day 6: Descend via the Observatory Trail. Drive to Kona and camp.

Day 7: Day free in Kona.

Day 8: Fly to Kauai. Overnight at hotel or camp.

Day 9: Six-hour hike on the Awaawapui-Nualolo Trail Loop for one of the most beautiful vistas in all the Hawaiian Islands. Camp.

Day 10: Hike down into Waimea Canyon via the Kukui Trail and camp.

Day 11: Ascend out of Waimea Canyon (about 3,000 feet) and drive to Haena Beach Park.

Day 12: Hike eight hours to Kalalau Valley, accessible only by an ancient Hawaiian trail along the spectacular Na Pali Coast.

Day 13: Day to explore Kalalau Valley.

Day 14: Hike out of Kalalau Valley. Overnight at hotel.

Day 15: Depart Kauai on homewardbound flights.

Dates: Jun 27–Jul 11 (15 days)
Leader: Richard McMahon
Grade: B-3
Land Cost: $950
(10–12 members)
$1050 (8–9)
Single Supplement: $100

Kilauea Caldera/Sara Steck

With ten days on the "big island" of Hawaii, we will hike the Waipio Valley, swim and snorkel in the warm waters of Hapuna Beach, and hike on Mauna Kea, highest peak in the Pacific/ Sara Steck

Mauna Kea/Sara Steck

White Mountains Of New Hampshire

60-mile New England walk

This is one of New England's classic adventures—a nine-day, 60-mile "range walk" from Franconia Notch to Pinkham Notch by way of Mt. Washington (6,288′), highest peak in the northeastern U.S.

Although these mountains are not high, they are extremely rugged and demand a high level of fitness, as one must carry a pack weighing from 15–20 lbs. (for clothing only; no sleeping bag, food or tent need be carried). Despite the many steep "ups and downs" of this walk, it is a popular one for its scenic beauty.

The White Mountains have a system of well organized huts, maintained by the Appalachian Mountain Club. Bunks and blankets are provided, as are home-style breakfasts and dinners. Each hut has a distinctive New England ambience—rustic, friendly, alpine and wholesome. The Hutmasters and their assistants are generally young men and women from eastern colleges who are energetic and more than willing to share their knowledge of these mountains.

Itinerary: Day 1: Leave hometown. Arrive Boston. Bus to Franconia, New Hampshire. Hike six miles to Lonesome Lake Hut.

Day 2: Hike to Greenleaf Hut (4,200′). 7 miles.

Day 3: Ascend over the summits of Mt. Lafayette and Mt. Garfield (4,488′) to Galehead Hut (3,800′), a strenuous 7.6 miles.

Day 4: Steep ascent of Mt. South Twin (4,926′) and descend to Zealand Falls Hut. 7 miles.

Day 5: Either a spectacular 14.2-mile hike up to Mt. Webster

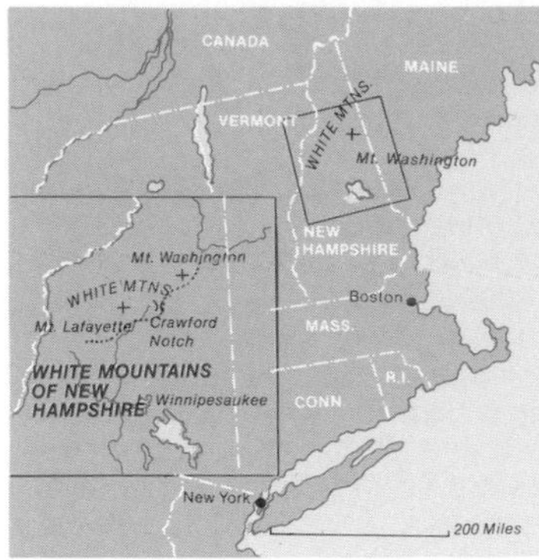

(3,910′), with views into Crawford Notch, site of the Willey House (immortalized by Nathaniel Hawthorne) or take the moderate trail to Mizpah Spring Hut, an easier 7.7 miles.

Day 6: An easier but no less spectacular day over the Southern Presidential Range to Lake Of The Clouds Hut. 5 miles.

Day 7: Along famed Crawford Path to the summit of Mt. Washington (6,288′), highest peak east of the Mississippi and north of the Carolinas. From here, we descend to Madison Spring Hut (4,825′). 7.7 miles.

Day 8: Down the precipitous Madison Gulf Trail and up to Carter Notch Hut. 8 miles.

Day 9: A rugged 6.8 miles over Wildcat Ridge, with its views of the Northern Presidential Range and Mt. Washington. Down to Pinkham Notch Camp.

Day 10: Return by bus to Boston to connect with homeward-bound flights.

Dates: Aug 29–Sep 7 (10 days)
Leader: Jon or Ida Burroughs
Grade: B-3
Land Cost: $635 (10–15 members) $750 (7–9)
Single Supplement: not available

The North Cascades Seminar instructs in belaying, knots and rope work, rock, snow and ice climbing techniques, route selection, crevasse rescue, glacier travel and more/Eric Sanford

North Cascades Seminar & Climb

Pacific Northwest mountaineering

This two-week course is designed to teach all the basics for safe and efficient mountain travel. While little or no previous mountaineering experience is required, it is advised that members be in top physical shape as backpacking is required on the approach.

Trip members will learn belaying, knots and rope work, rock, snow and ice climbing techniques, route selection and safety, crevasse rescue and glacier travel, mountain first aid, safety and rescue, and use of ice axe and crampons. Several major Cascades peaks, including Mt. Baker (10,750′), will be climbed during the course.

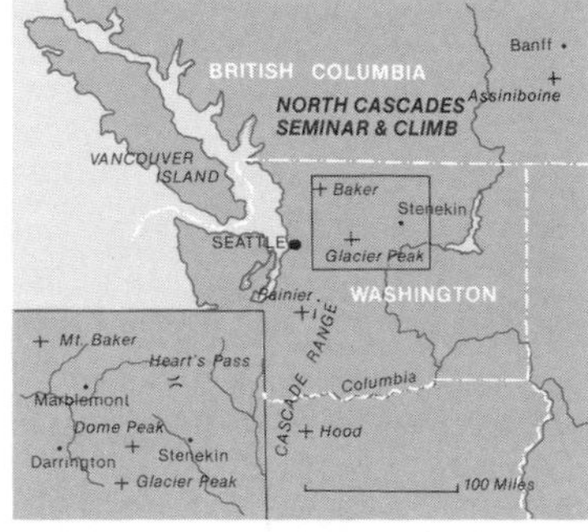

Itinerary: Day 1: Meet group and leader in Seattle. Drive to Mazama and camp.

Day 2 to 4: Hike into Wing Lake (5 miles) and camp. Instruction and climb of Black Peak (8,970′).

Day 5: Hike out from Wing Lake, drive back to Mazama and camp nearby. Afternoon rock climbing practice.

Day 6 to 8: Climbs from a high camp in the Liberty Bell basin.

Day 9: Drive to Mt. Baker and hike into Kulshan Cabin

Day 10 to 12: Establish a high camp on the Coleman Glacier and practice snow and ice climbing and crevasse rescue.

Day 13: Climb Mt. Baker and Return to high camp.

Day 14: Hike out, drive to Seattle and connect with homeward-bound flights.

Dates: Jul 6–Jul 19 (14 days)
Leader: Eric Sanford
Grade: B-3
Land Cost: $1190 (5–10 members)
Single Supplement: not available

The Inland Passage

Beach combing and whale watching

The waterways of Southeast Alaska are among the most fascinating and beautiful "ocean passages" on earth.

Numerous islands support sea bird and marine mammal colonies; the waters team with fish, dolphins, porpoises and whales. The most intensive summer feeding areas for humpback whales in the entire eastern Pacific are located here. In addition to superb wildlife attractions, the Inland Passage has a unique blend of native American culture, Russian heritage and a frontier spirit.

We will explore these reaches aboard the *Delphinus,* a custom-built 50-foot natural history cruising ship which accommodates ten passengers and a crew of three, including a naturalist guide.

The small size of the boat allows travel into the most remote coves, a far different experience than that offered by larger boats. We will also explore in the small skiffs which the *Delphinus* carries and go ashore for hikes, berry-picking, "botanizing," and beachcombing.

The *Delphinus* has windows throughout the galley, salon and pilot house which allow uninterrupted visibility from inside. She provides three double cabins and a four-bunk cabin, two bathrooms with shower facilities and a full galley which serves excellent meals.

Cruise #1 begins in Ketchikan and explores Misty Fjords National Monument, one of the newest and most spectacular national monuments, notable for deep fjords and 3,000-foot-high granite cliffs rising straight up from the waters' edge. Many have called it "a Yosemite to explore by boat." Shore trails make it convenient to explore on foot along the edges of this two-million-acre wilderness. We arrive in Petersburg via the Wrangell Narrows, one of the most amazing navigational features in southeast Alaska.

Itinerary: Day 1: Fly to Ketchikan.

Day 2 to 8: On cruise. Day 9: Arrive Petersburg. Day 10: Depart Petersburg on homeward-bound flights.

Cruise #2 begins in Petersburg, a town aptly called "Little Norway." From Petersburg, we travel to the LeConte Glacier to witness a thunderously calving tidewater glacier, then move to Frederick Sound for some of the most spectacular whale watching in the world. The sights and sounds of leaping humpback whales will probably cause us to linger here a few days. Continuing up Stephens Passage, we have fine views of a series of active glaciers: the Dawes, Sawyer, Sumdum and Taku. The cruise ends in Juneau.

Itinerary: Day 1: Fly to Petersburg. Day 2 to 8: On cruise. Day 9: Arrive Juneau. Day 10: Depart Juneau on homeward-bound flights.

Hayden Kadon

Ronn Storro-Patterson

Cruise #3 begins and ends in Juneau, heading up the Lynn Canal and Icy Strait to magnificent Glacier Bay for three days exploring and viewing active glaciers. We also visit the important Indian settlement of Hoonah and visit the fishing outpost of Elfin Cove. Much of our time will be spent exploring coves, whale watching, visiting dense rainforests, fishing and relaxing.

Itinerary: Day 1: Fly to Juneau. Day 2 to 8: On cruise. Day 9: Return to Juneau. Day 10: Depart Juneau on homeward-bound flights.

Cruise #4 begins in Juneau and emphasizes the wildlife found on Admiralty and adjoining islands, along with the culture and flavor of native American villages and Alaskan outposts. We first travel to Glacier Bay for an overnight visit, then stop in at Angoon, one of the most important native American settlements in Alaska. Across Chatham Strait are the remote outposts of Tenakee and Baranoff Hot Springs. A further highlight of this cruise is Frederick Sound, with its abandoned whaling stations, sea lion rookeries and outstanding population of humpback whales.

Itinerary: Day 1: Fly to Juneau. Day 2 to 8: On cruise. Day 9: Arrive Petersburg. Day 10: Depart Petersburg on homeward-bound flights.

Dates: #1 Jun 29–Jul 8 (10 days)
#2 Jul 8–Jul 17
#3 Jul 19–Jul 28
#4 Jul 31–Aug 9
Leader: Ronn Storro-Patterson
Grade: A-1
Land Cost: $1490
(8–10 members)
$1790 (6–7)
Single Supplement: not available

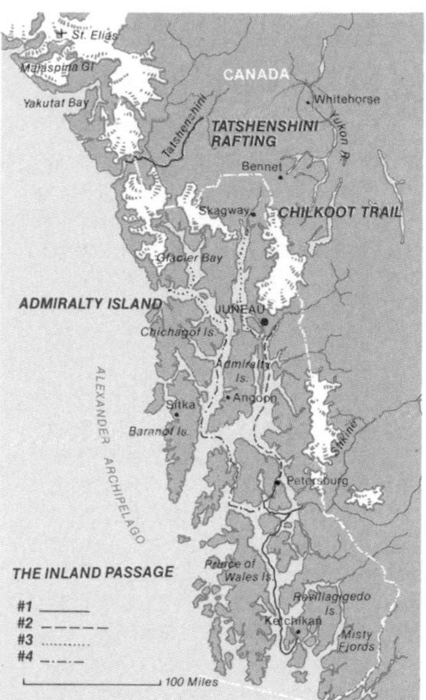

About Raft, Kayak & Canoe Trips

Our adventures on the wilderness waterways of Alaska are conducted by professional guides, each of whom is an expert in making a wilderness experience a pleasant and safe one. Previous camping experience is recommended, but certainly not required. No previous experience with kayaks, canoes or rafts is needed. Trip members are expected to pitch in and help with camp chores such as packing and unpacking group gear from the boats, pitching tents, etc. Breakfast and dinner will be hot, hearty meals served in camp; lunch will be picnic-style. All boat gear (including life jackets) is provided, and the boats are stable, easy-to-handle and fun to use. Camp supplies are transported from place to place by raft, canoe or kayak (depending on the particular trip). Mountain Travel's Alaska leaders are all members of the Alaska Wilderness Guides Association.

Government Permits:

We work with outfitters or agents properly licensed for the government areas in which the trips operate. Appropriate federal and state governments may contact Mountain Travel for further information.

Glacier Bay. We will explore the Inland Passage aboard the Delphinus, a custom built, 50-foot natural history cruising ship which accommodates ten passengers and a crew of three including a naturalist guide. We will go ashore for hikes, berry-picking botanizing and beach combing/*Pam Shandrick*

Tatshenshini/ Alsek Rafting

9-day journey from mountains to the sea

Known by seasoned river runners the world over, the Tatshenshini/Alsek is one of the world's premier wilderness raft trips. From the lush green hills at the start to the glaciated mountains near the end, this journey reveals nature in its most pristine state.

As we approach the coast, the horizon seems to shrink as the great St. Elias Mountains, highest coastal range in the world, rise from the river's edge. Wildlife abounds, including grizzlies, bighorn, Dall sheep and bald eagles.

Perhaps the single most impressive thing about this river trip is the immense blue-white glaciers we'll see.

Once the Tatshenshini joins the Alsek, glaciers flow right down to the river banks. The sights and sounds of the seven-mile-wide Alsek Glacier are an experience not to be missed.

We travel five to a raft with an experienced oarsman. No previous rafting experience is necessary.

Itinerary: Day 1: Leave hometown. Arrive Juneau. Continue by ferry or air taxi (cost not included) to Haines.

Day 2: Drive about 100 miles to the put-in point near Dalton Post, Canada. On the upper Tatshenshini, we enjoy exhilarating rapids in the Tatshenshini Gorge. Emerge from the gorge into more placid waters.

Day 3 and 4: The river slowly builds momentum as we wind our way towards the beautiful Alsek and Noisy Ranges.

Day 5 and 6: The river gets increasingly broad as hugh unnamed tributary creeks add their silted water to the Tatshenshini. This is prime country for moose, bear and wolf.

Day 7 and 8: The Alsek quickly carries us through terrain where high peaks rise steeply from the river. This is ice age country and dozens of large and small glaciers fill every vista around our tiny rafts.

Day 9: Enter the grandeur of Alsek Bay, a spectacular place. Mt. Fairweather looms 15,000 feet above us across the bay. Hike up to an overlook on Gateway Knob, then paddle the rafts quietly among the icy giants of Alsek Bay

Day 10: Leaving high country, we will begin to smell and feel the salt air of the ocean, as the Tatshenshini/Alsek system empties into Alaska's coast on the boundary of Glacier Bay National Park.

Day 11: Fly by float plane to Gustavus. Continue by commercial flight to Juneau (cost not included). Overnight at hotel.

Day 12: Connect with homeward-bound flights or Alaska State Ferry.

Dates: Aug 2–Aug 13 (12 days)
Leader: Fred Faye-Hiltner
Grade: A-3
Land Cost: $1590 incl. chtrs. (8–15) members)
Single Supplement: to be paid locally

Once the Tatshenshini joins the Alsek, glaciers flow right down to the river banks. The sights and sounds of seven-mile-wide Alsek Glacier are an experience not to be missed/*Fred Fay-Hiltner*

Backpacking The Chilkoot Trail

In Gold Rush country

A four-day backpack trip across the historic Chilkoot Trail of the 1898 Gold Rush crosses from the little town of Skagway to Lake Bennett over the Chilkoot Trail, "the meanest 32 miles in history," or so the gold stampeders called it, since they were required to carry a year's worth of supplies over it in the dead of winter. Our baggage will be considerably lighter! Our backpacks should weigh 25 to 30 lbs. (depending on personal gear).

Chuck Horner

Chuck Horner

We start with a floatplane ride to Skagway. From here, we hike through deep forest, exploring old gold mining camps and venturing up into alpine country. Enroute, we pass ruins of former gold miners' weighing stations and cross the Chilkoot Pass itself. Descent takes us along a series of lakes in alpine country to camp at historic Lake Lindeman. The hike ends by the shores of Lake Bennett.

Itinerary: Day 1: Leave hometown. Arrive Juneau.

Day 2: Fly by floatplane to Skagway and begin backpack trip.

Day 3 to 7: Chilkoot Trail backpacking, ending with a flight by charter from Skagway to Juneau.

Day 8: Depart Juneau on homeward bound flights.

Dates: #1 Jul 11–Jul 18 (8 days)
#2 Jul 29–Aug 5
Leader: to be announced.
Grade: B-2
Land Cost: $995 incl. chtr. (10–12 members)
$1050 incl. chtr. (6–9)
Single supplement: $50

Note: This trip can be taken in combination with Kayaking In Glacier Bay *or* Canoeing Admiralty Island.

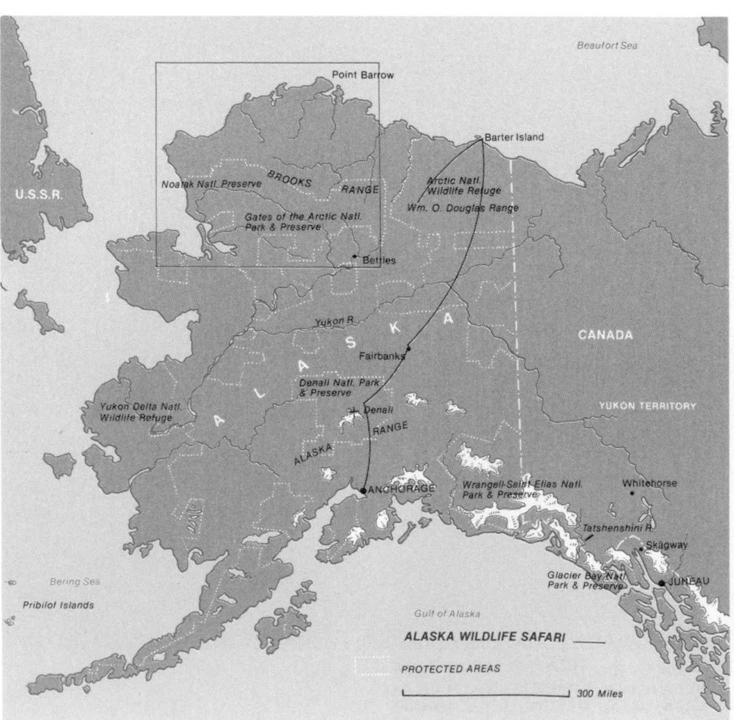

Kayaking In Glacier Bay

Exploring a fjord wilderness

A week-long kayaking and camping adventure in the water wilderness of Southeast Alaska is a wonderful way to see Glacier Bay National Park.

We fly by scenic floatplane to a remote section of John Muir's beloved Glacier Bay, where snow-covered 15,000-foot mountains rise above ice-choked fjords.

From a very remote inlet, we'll have five days of easy kayaking in turquoise waters amidst sculpture-like ice floes. There will be time for hiking on shore to explore several glaciers. Our stable two-man Klepper kayaks are simple and fun to use, allowing easy access to remote coves and inlets.

Glacier Bay's mountains are habitat for brown and black bear, wolves, coyotes, and mountain goats; the waters are home to seal, sea lion, humpback and killer whales, salmon and trout. There is an abundance of waterfowl, including guillemots, puffins, murrelets, cormorants and kittiwakes.

Itinerary: Day 1: Leave hometown. Arrive Juneau.

Day 2 to 6: Fly to the tiny town of Gustavus by scheduled flight and continue by charter flight directly to Reid Inlet, a remote region of Glacier Bay. We have five full days here to explore the Glacier Bay wilderness. Different campsites each night enable us to travel to inlets and nearby glaciers by kayak and on foot.

Day 7: Pack up camp gear and fly by charter flight to Gustavus. Overnight in cabins.

Day 8: Fly to Juneau and continue on homeward-bound flights.

Dates: #1 Jul 4–Jul 11 (8 days)
#2 Jul 17–Jul 24
#3 Jul 29–Aug 5
#4 Aug 4–Aug 11
#5 Aug 16–Aug 23
#6 Aug 22–Aug 29
Leader: to be announced
Grade: A-3
Land Cost: $1090 incl. chtrs. (10–12 members)
$1190 (6–9)
Single Supplement: $25

Note: This trip can be taken in combination with Backpacking The Chilkoot Trail *or* Canoeing Admiralty Island.

From a very remote inlet, we'll have five days of easy kayaking on the turquoise waters amidst ice floes and tiny coves/*Hayden Kaden*

Canoeing Admiralty Island

Forested wilderness of the Inland Passage

This trip centers around a six-day canoe traverse of heavily forested Admiralty Island, the "fortress of the bears," where brown bears outnumber people.

We start on the east shore of Admiralty Island National Monument, connecting five blue wilderness lakes by canoe with short portages.

There is great fishing here, so those who want can try angling for trout along the way. The trip ends at the native American village of Angoon, where hunting and fishing are still the main occupations.

No previous canoe experience is necessary. There are occasional short canoe "portages" between lakes.

Itinerary: Day 1: Leave hometown. Arrive Juneau.

Day 2: Charter flight to Mole Harbor on the east side of Admiralty Island. Hike 2.5 miles to camp at Alexander Lake.

Day 3 to 6: Paddling the lakes of Admiralty, with a layover day at camp for fishing, wildlife viewing, laying about or all three.

Day 7: Paddle through Mitchell Bay to Angoon. Charter flight to Juneau. Overnight at hotel.

Day 8: Depart Juneau on homeward-bound flights.

Dates: #1 Jun 27–Jul 4 (8 days)
#2 Jul 23–Jul 30
#3 Aug 28–Sep 4
Leader: #1 Hayden Kaden
#2 & #3 to be announced
Land Cost: $990 incl. chtr. (10–12 members)
$1090 incl. chtr. (6–9)
Single Supplement: $50

Note: This trip can be taken in combination with Backpacking The Chilkoot Trail *or* Kayaking In Glacier Bay.

Alaska trips include: twin accommodations in hotels, camp meals (meals on your own in cities and towns), air charters (but not scheduled flights, which will be written into your overall air ticket), ground transportation, leadership, group commissary and comping gear, group boat equipment (if applicable), group climbing equipment (if applicable).

We start on the east shore of Admiralty Island National Monument, connecting five blue wilderness lakes by canoe with short portages/*Leo Le Bon*

Kobuk River Kayaking

7-day river journey in the arctic summer

This trip features a week-long journey down the swift Kobuk River through a scenic region recently designated as Kobuk Valley National Park. Enroute, we stop often to enjoy the sunny, sandy beaches and try our hand at fishing for migratory salmon and sheefish. We'll also visit some Eskimo fishing camps and see remnants of abandoned gold mining operations. The beaches are a rock hound's paradise since the area is highly mineralized—jasper and jade are especially common.

The Kobuk is one of the richest rivers in all the arctic for fish and supports an amazing abundance of birdlife, including bald and golden eagles, osprey, kingfishers, ravens, arctic terns, and many varieties of gulls and predatory birds. Grizzly and black bears, moose, fox and wolves are common.

No previous kayaking experience is necessary. We paddle stable, easy to use, two-person Folboat kayaks.

Itinerary: Day 1: Leave hometown. Arrive Fairbanks.

Day 2: Fly to Bettles, continue by chartered floatplane to Walker Lake.

Day 3: Free day for exploring around Walker Lake or fishing.

Kayaking on the Kobuk/Dave Ketscher

Day 4: Begin kayak trip with a short paddle through some easy and fun rapids.

Day 5: Continue float trip through prime arctic wildlife habitat. The river picks up speed as we pass through the upper Kobuk Canyon, with its 200-foot rock bluffs.

Day 6: Enter lower Kobuk Canyon, with its exciting but safe whitewater, the last rapids on the Kobuk.

Day 7 to 12: Continue float trip on the now-placid Kobuk. Salmon will be spawning up small creeks and bears are commonly seen. At the Pah River confluence, we spend half a day trying our luck at catching arctic sheefish, a tarpon-like fish distantly related to salmon and whitefish. Arrive on Day 12 at the village of Kobuk.

Day 13: Visit Eskimos at Kobuk, watching them cutting and drying fish. Fly by scheduled charter to Kotzebue.

Day 14: Fly to Anchorage and connect with homeward-bound flights.

Dates: Aug 10–Aug 23 (14 days)
Leader: to be announced
Grade: B-2
Land Cost: $1775 inc. chtr. (8–10 members)
$1890 (5–7)
Single Supplement: $75

Noatak Kayaking

15 days on a high arctic river

In a fascinating geological display, the Noatak River pours from the jagged Brooks Range, over broad tundra plains, between steep, carved canyon walls and finally through deep spruce forest and out into the Bering Sea. There is only one permanent human settlement on its entire 400-mile length. Otherwise its inhabitants are moose, bear, caribou, wolves, hawks and eagles.

Using stable, two-person "Folboat" kayaks, we will journey for fifteen days on the Noatak from its headwaters all the way to the Eskimo village of Noatak near Kotzebue Sound. Along the way, we stop to hike, photograph and fish for delicious arctic char, grayling and salmon.

No previous kayak experience is necessary.

Itinerary: Day 1: Leave hometown. Arrive Fairbanks.

Day 2: Fly to Bettles, continue by a spectacular floatplane ride to the headwaters of the Noatak.

Day 3: Hike to look for Dall sheep and caribou.

Day 4: Portage to the Noatak River and float to the confluence of the Noatak and Kugruk Creeks.

Day 5: Hike up Kugruk Creek and visit hot springs.

Day 6 and 7: Continue float to Lake Matcharak. Layover day for exploring Lake Matcharak.

Day 8 and 9: Float past rapids below Douglas Creek. Caribou are commonly seen in the Aniuk Lowland area. The Noatak waters pick up speed here. This is a good opportunity to learn the art of "reading the water."

Day 10 and 11: Float to Aniuk Creek where the river becomes at least 100 yards wide, and beyond Okak Bend, where there are several Eskimo archaeological sites.

Day 12: Rolling terrain gives way to rugged hills. Small groves of cottonwood trees appear along the river—the first trees we've seen since Bettles.

Day 13 to 16: Enter the "Grand Canyon of the Noatak," a beautiful broad valley where vertical-walled cliffs rise from either side of the river.

Day 17 and 18: To the Kelly River and Noatak Village. Visit Eskimo settlement.

Day 19: Fly by charter to Kotzebue. Overnight in hotel.

Day 20: Fly by commercial flight to Anchorage and connect with homeward-bound flights.

Dates: Jul 29–Aug 17 (20 days)
Leader: Mike & Debbie O'Connor
Grade: B-3
Land Cost: $1965 incl. chtrs. (8–12 members)
$2115 incl. chtrs. (5–7)
Single Supplement: $75

Canoeing the Noatak/Dave Ketscher

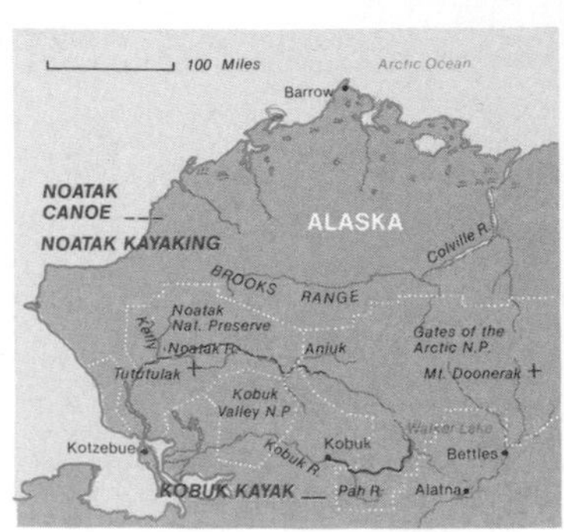

River camp/William C. Kronholm

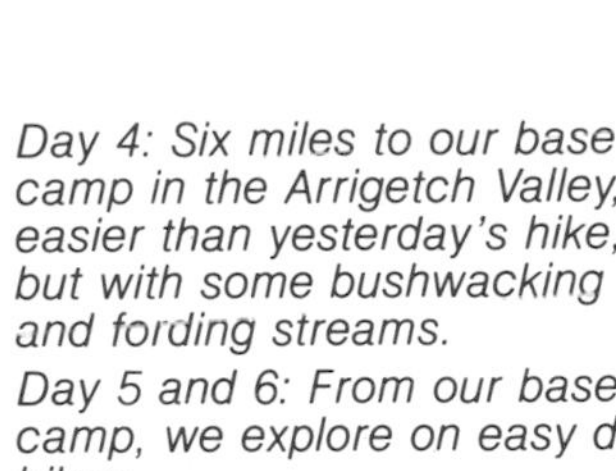

Rafting the Alatna/William C. Kronholm

Noatak River By Canoe

Float trip in the Brooks Range

Born in the melting snows of the Brooks Range and emptying 400 miles later into Kotzebue Sound, the Noatak is a majestic wilderness river, all of it above the Arctic Circle. It is now protected as a national park called Noatak National Preserve.

This trip features a leisurely week-long float trip by canoe on the Noatak's headwaters where the peaks of the Brooks Range rise on both sides of the river.

There will be time for fishing and day hikes on tributary creeks. Wildlife is abundant here: we'll see caribou, Dall sheep, grizzly bear and possibly bald eagles.

No previous canoe experience is necessary.

Itinerary: Day 1: Leave hometown. Arrive Fairbanks.

Day 2: Fly to Bettles, continue by chartered float plane to the headwaters of the Noatak. Land at the farthest upstream lake where the river is still navigable and camp on smooth tundra.

Day 3: Today we'll hike most of the day, looking for Dall sheep and caribou.

Day 4: Portage gear and canoes to the Noatak and begin float by canoe.

Day 5: Hike up the gravel beaches along Kugruk Creek to visit secluded hot springs. Excellent fishing for grayling and arctic char.

Day 6 and 7: By canoe to camp at Igning Creek confluence. Free day to fish, hike or look over old gold mining claims.

Day 8 to 11: We pass by a denning area for wolves, which are easily seen by the careful observer. Numerous ground squirrels live here, too, unwilling food for the growing wolf families. Our last two days will be spent canoeing and exploring Matcharak Lake.

Day 12: Charter flight back to Bettles.

Day 13: Commercial flight to Fairbanks.

Day 14: Leave Fairbanks and connect with homeward-bound flights.

Dates: Jun 15–Jun 28 (14 days)
Leader: Tamara Ketscher
Grade: A-2
Land Cost: $1575 incl. chtrs. (8–12 members)
Land Cost: $1690 (5–7)
Single Supplement: $75

The Arrigetch Wilderness

6-day Brooks Range backpacking trip

The impressive granite spires of the Arrigetch Peaks, now part of "Gates of the Arctic National Park," are perhaps the most spectacular part of the entire Brooks Range. The name Arrigetch in the native language means "fingers of the hand outstretched," and these peaks seem to reach up toward the sky, rising out of delicate alpine valleys.

To reach the Arrigetch wilderness, we fly to Bettles (above the Arctic Circle) and continue by floatplane to Circle Lake. From here, a two-day backpack trip takes us to our base camp in the heart of the Arrigetch Peaks, where we'll spend a few days hiking and photographing among the peaks. Dall sheep, black and grizzly bears are often found in the remote valleys. The hike into the Arrigetch is strenuous but the spectacular scenery makes it worth the effort. Depending on personal gear, backpacks will weigh 30–35 lbs.

We then hike out to the Alatna River for a float trip on a gentle arctic river which meanders through scenic bluffs and mountains. Moose, wolves, beaver and waterfowl are seen along the river. We will set aside ample time for hiking to nearby lakes to fish for lake trout and northern pike.

Itinerary: Day 1: Leave hometown. Arrive Fairbanks.

Day 2: Fly to Bettles. Continue by chartered floatplane to Circle Lake and camp.

Day 3: Today's hike, although only about 3 miles, is a strenuous one through bogs and terrain with tricky footing. Camp overlooking Arrigetch Creek in Gates of the Arctic National Park.

Day 4: Six miles to our base camp in the Arrigetch Valley, easier than yesterday's hike, but with some bushwacking and fording streams.

Day 5 and 6: From our base camp, we explore on easy day hikes.

Day 7: Break camp and retrace our route back to Arrigetch Creek.

Day 8: Hike to the Alatna River.

Day 9: Begin float trip on the gentle Alatna, a nice change of pace after our backpack trip.

Day 10: Continue float trip and arrive at Takahula Lake. Camp on the lakeshore.

Day 11: Free day at Takahula.

Day 12: Afternoon charter flight back to Bettles.

Day 13: Fly to Fairbanks.

Day 14: Depart Fairbanks on homeward-bound flights.

Dates: #1 Jul 14–Jul 27 (14 days)
#2 Jul 26–Aug 8
Leader: #1 Mike & Debbie O'Connor
#2 Dave Ketscher
Grade: B-3
Land Cost: $1575 incl. chtr. (8–12 members)
Single Supplement: $75

A two-day backpack trip takes us to our base camp in the heart of the Arrigetch Peaks, where we'll spend a few days hiking and photographing among the peaks/William C. Kronholm

Alaska Wildlife Safari

5-day high arctic camp, 4-day Denali cabin camp

This safari begins in the "ultimate wilderness park" in the northernmost reaches of the North American continent—the 8.9-million acre William O. Douglas Wildlife Range (formerly the Arctic National Wildlife Range).

Here, in the luxury of almost 24 hours of daylight, we spend five days experiencing the high arctic in summer, making optional day hikes in a land where caribou, moose, and wolves roam. Our trip takes advantage of the best season for viewing the caribou migration.

From Fairbanks, we take the train to the sub-arctic splendor of Denali (McKinley) National Park, home to 37 species of mammals and 132 species of birds. With five days in comfortable cabins at Camp Denali, we have an unregimented schedule during which we can hike, fish, photograph, or just relax and enjoy the beauty of the alpine tundra world.

At the end of the trip, we can arrange an optional visit to the Pribilof Islands in the Bering Sea, renowned as the breeding ground of the largest fur seal herd in the world and of literally millions of birds.

Itinerary: Day 1: Leave hometown. Arrive Fairbanks.

Day 2: Fly to Barter Island in the Beaufort Sea.

Day 3 to 7: By charter flight from Barter Island to a very remote part of the William O. Douglas National Wildlife Range. Here in America's largest wildlife refuge, the great caribou herds will migrate from near Barter Island southeastward toward the Yukon.

Day 8: Return by charter flight to Barter Island

Day 9: Fly to Fairbanks.

Day 10: Day free in Fairbanks, or to adjust itinerary if weather has delayed flights.

Day 11 to 15: By train to Denali, then continue by bus about 90 miles to Camp Denali, set in tundra and spruce woods with splendid views of Mt. McKinley (20,320').

Day 16: By bus and train to Anchorage.

Day 17: Depart Anchorage on homeward-bound flights.

Dates: Jun 19–Jul 5 (17 days)
Leader: Chuck Horner
Grade: A-2
Land Cost: $2390 + $395 chtr. (10–12 members)
Single Supplement: available on request

Nature walk in Denali N.P./*Chuck Horner*

Backpacking On McKinley

8-day hike onto McKinley's glaciers

This is a fantastic backpack journey which takes advantage of McKinley's full 17,000-foot rise above the Alaskan plains. It leads right up onto the glaciers of Mt. McKinley, North America's highest peak, known in the native language as Denali—"the great one."

Starting near Wonder Lake in Denali National Park, we ford the mile-wide McKinley River and hike up Cache Creek to the alpine meadows of McGonagall Canyon. Crossing McGonagall Pass, we'll stop for a day of instruction on safe glacier travel and the use of ice axe and crampons.

We then ascend the Muldrow Glacier (from which the pioneer ascent was made in 1913) to a point near the lower icefall beneath McKinley's great northern flanks. From a central camp, we'll make day hikes near the Tralieka and Brooks glaciers.

This will be a very spectacular trip involving simple glacier travel, vigorous hiking and a few difficult river crossings. No mountaineering experience is required, but members will carry backpacks weighing 30 to 35 lbs., depending on personal gear. Some group supplies will have been carried in ahead of the group, in order to keep the packs lighter.

Itinerary: Day 1: Leave hometown. Arrive Anchorage.

Day 2: By Alaska Railroad to Denali National Park. Camp at Park Headquarters.

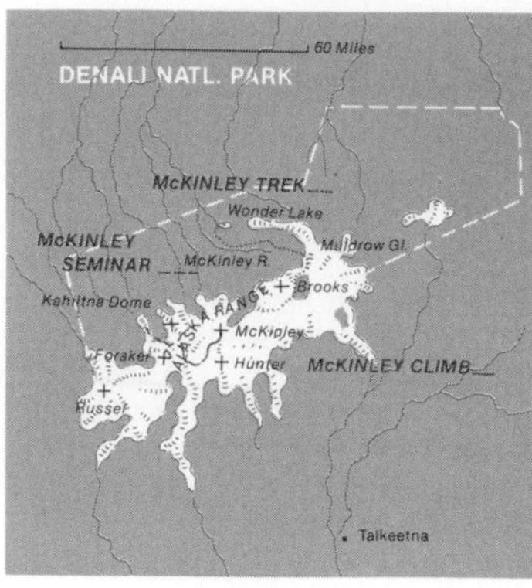

Day 3: Scenic bus ride to Wonder Lake. Camp.

Day 4: An exciting fording of the mile-wide McKinley River, then hike to Clearwater Creek.

Day 5 and 6: Hike up to Cache Creek drainage, McGonagall Canyon and cross McGonagall Pass.

Day 7: Ascend the Muldrow Glacier to the base of the Lower Icefall and Gunsight Pass.

Day 8 and 9: Ascend Gunsight Mountain; spectacular views of the north side of McKinley.

Day 10 and 11: Walk out to Clearwater Creek.

Day 12: Bus to Park Headquarters.

Day 13: Train to Anchorage.

Day 14: Leave Anchorage and connect with homeward-bound flights.

Dates: Aug 8–Aug 21 (14 days)
Leader: to be announced
Grade: B-3
Land Cost: $1490 (5–10 members)
Single Supplement: $75

Our Wildlife Safari takes advantage of the caribou migration and best wildlife viewing season/*Chuck Horner*

In the luxury of almost 24 hours of daylight, we spend five days experiencing the high arctic in summer, William O. Douglas Wildlife Range/*Anne Millet*

McKinley Climbing Seminar

Learn mountaineering in the Alaska Range

This climbing seminar takes place in a spectacular mountain setting surrounded by the big peaks of the Alaska Range including McKinley (20,320′), Foraker (17,402′) and Hunter (14,573′). We will fly to the southeast fork of the Kahiltna Glacier, the starting point for most McKinley ascents. From here, we ski or snowshoe to the base of Control Tower Peak (8,060′).

After a few days of instruction, we make an ascent of Control Tower Peak. The seminar continues with instruction in technical rock and ice climbing techniques, and the final few days are spent climbing Radar Peak (8,670′) and Mt. Francis (10,450′).

The seminar is suitable for strong backpackers (capable of heavy load-carrying) who want to learn a full range of mountaineering techniques.

Itinerary: Day 1: Leave hometown. Arrive Anchorage.

Day 2: Drive or take the train to Talkeetna. Continue by spectacular charter to the Kahiltna Glacier at the base of Mt. McKinley.

Day 3: By ski or snowshoe to the base of Peak 8060 (Control Tower Peak). Establish a base camp, learning winter camping techniques.

Day 4 to 6: Begin the seminar: basic knots, belaying, self arrest, glissading, snow climbing, rappelling, use of ice axe and crampons, glacier travel, crevasse rescue, avalanche rescue procedures, mountain safety and first aid.

Day 7 and 8: Technical ice climbing instruction and practice.

Day 9 and 10: Basic rock climbing instructions.

Day 11 and 12: Ascend Mt. Francis and Radar Peak.

Day 13: Fly out to Talkeetna and return to Anchorage.

Day 14: Depart Anchorage and connect with homeward-bound flights.

Dates: Jun 13–Jun 26 (14 days)
Leader: Nic Parker
Grade: B-3/D-1
Land Cost: $1590 incl. chtr. (5–12 members)
Single Supplement: to be paid locally

Mt. McKinley Expedition

Climb North America's highest peak

Mt. McKinley (20,320′) is the highest point on the North American continent. It is a beautiful and impressive mountain by any standards, soaring a dazzling 17,000 feet above the plains—one of the greatest base-to-summit rises of any mountain on earth. It was first climbed in 1913; subsequent ascents were few until the 1950's.

The West Buttress route, first climbed in 1951, has become the standard approach to the summit. This will be our route of ascent, beginning at a base camp on the Kahiltna Glacier at 7,000 feet.

A climb of McKinley is physically demanding and requires a range of mountaineering skills. Technically, it is of moderate difficulty. Weather and altitude make it a true mountaineering challenge. The duration of the ascent can take as little as ten days, but can require 15 or more because of frequent and prolonged storms which hit the peak.

Members must be very fit, and capable of carrying loads of 75 lbs. or more at high altitudes and assisting with expedition chores. All community equipment will be provided. The party will be flown in by charter from Talkeetna.

Itinerary: Day 1: Leave hometown. Arrive Anchorage.

Day 2: Drive to Talkeetna. Prepare expedition gear.

Day 3: By charter flight to the 7,000-foot level on the Kahiltna Glacier.

Day 4 to 7: Carry loads from 7,000 feet to 10,000 feet at Kahiltna Pass.

Day 8 to 10: Move camp from 11,000 feet to 14,200 feet in a basin below the West Buttress.

Day 11 to 14: Load carrying up fixed lines to 16,400 feet on the West Buttress. Establish high camp.

Day 15 and 16: Move to high camp at 17,200 feet.

Day 17 and 18: Summit attempts, depending on weather conditions.

Day 19 and 20: Descend and return to Kahiltna Glacier.

Day 21 and 22: Charter flight to Talkeetna. Return to Anchorage by bus or train and connect with homeward-bound flights.

Dates: May 2–May 23 (22 days)
Leader: Gary Bocarde
Grade: E-2
Land Cost: $2390 incl. chtr. (5–10 members)
Single Supplement: to be paid locally

The West Buttress route, first climbed in 1951, has become the standard approach to the summit/*Gary Bocarde*

On McKinley, members must be fit, capable of carrying loads of 60 lbs. or more at high altitudes and assisting with expedition chores. All community equipment will be provided/*Gary Bocarde*

Section VII
Ski Adventures

Skiing the Haute Route (summit of Pina Arolla)/Lanny Johnson

Every skier dreams of a winter adventure to some place far away where the snow is perfect, the air is crystal clear and each morning brings an exciting new possibility.

After scouting the world, we have come up with the following ski holidays that we consider real "dream tours" in the Mountain Travel tradition. We selected destinations with outstanding skiing, interesting culture, and expert guides to help you get the most out of your trip.

These are "complete" ski vacations that include the details other tours leave out. In some cases even ski equipment is included.

Day-by-day itineraries with full details on each of these tours are available from our office.

DOWNHILL CLASSICS

These are tours to world-class resorts for downhill skiers. Guides take you on the best marked runs and out into the backcountry for exciting skiing away from crowds. Included are lift passes, transfers to the slopes, most meals, excellent lodging, daily guide service, and helicopter or ski plane travel when indicated in the itinerary.

Guides take you on the best marked runs and out into the back country for exciting skiing away from the crowds/
Lanny Johnson

France: Chamonix Ski Week

Chamonix, the most famous mountain resort in the world, is known for long ski runs with spectacular views of Mt. Blanc and a lively atmosphere rich in the history of alpinism. The skiing is nearly unlimited and your guide will help you find the best skiing, whether it's on a groomed slope at a resort or down the glaciers of Valle Blanche. Ski equipment shops are numerous in Chamonix, and you can rent or buy at a fraction of U.S. prices.

Maximum of 7 persons per guide. Groups are arranged by ski ability.

Dates: 9-day trips
#1 Jan 25–Feb 2
#2 Feb 8–Feb 16
#3 Feb 15–Feb 23
#4 Mar 1–Mar 9
#5 Mar 15–Mar 23
#6 Mar 29–Apr 6
Land Cost: $940
(4–16 members)

Val D'isere-Tignes

This is perhaps the best downhill ski area in the world. Ski with a guide who can pick the very best places to go—a choice of ultra-long runs, 116 lifts, and unlimited backcountry skiing. You'll stay at a charming 4-star hotel known for its cuisine and atmosphere.

Dates: 11-day trips
#1 Jan 16–Jan 26
#2 Mar 13–Mar 23
Land Cost: $1060
(6–15 members)

Italy: Monte Rosa

The northern Italian Alps offer a paradise of intermediate skiing and quiet winter culture. Our lodging is in a quaint hotel nestled below the massif of Monte Rosa (15,203′). Lifts connect Monte Rosa with the slopes at Zermatt, Switzerland, and you can ski beneath the Matterhorn!

Dates: 11 day trips
#1 Jan 9–Jan 19
#2 Feb 13–Feb 23
#3 Mar 6–Mar 16
Land Cost: $990
(6–15 members)

Argentina: Ski The Andes!

From a hotel at the sophisticated Argentine ski resort of Bariloche, spend days skiing on runs up to eight miles long and spend evenings sampling Argentina's delicious wines and cuisine. Visit Buenos Aires enroute.

Dates: 10-day trips
#1 Jul 18–Jul 27
#2 Aug 1–Aug 10
Land Cost: $1290
(9–12 members)

Washington: Powder Skiing in the North Cascades

Learn to ski deep powder during a seminar that includes powder skis, guides, up to 65,000 vertical feet of helicopter skiing, videotapes of your skiing, and a guide-to-skier ratio of 1 to 4.

Dates: Jan 19–Jan 25 (7 days)
Land Cost: $1680

DOWNHILL TOURING: RANDONEE

Downhill touring, called randonee in Europe, offers the thrill of breathtaking descents on untracked slopes plus the freedom of roaming terrain far from resorts. It's a form of ski mountaineering that lets you ski across the mountains to a new destination each day, and stay in comfortable mountain huts or hotels along the way. Special lightweight alpine touring skis and bindings allow you to ski up slopes in regions where there are no lifts.

The Haute Route

This is the classic alpine tour from Chamonix to Zermatt. Spend a few days in Chamonix polishing your ski technique (and perhaps buying bargain-priced, top-of-the-line ski equipment), then tour across the Alps to Zermatt via Verbier and Arolla. Lodging alternates between first-class hotels and simple mountain refuges. Extra days are included so you can ski the slopes at Verbier and Zermatt. Enroute, carry only a daypack with extra clothes. The Haute Route tour is for strong alpine skiers.

Dates: April 11–Apr 24 (14 days)
Land Cost: $1240
(6–10 members)

Introduction to Randonee at Monte Rosa and Gran Paradiso

Learn and practice *randonee* skills at the Monte Rosa downhill resort in the heart of the Italian Alps, then make a three-day wilderness tour to Paradiso Peak (13,323′). For intermediate skiers in good physical shape.

Dates: Apr 3–Apr 13 (11 days)
Land Cost: $990
(6–12 members)

New Zealand Alps

Fly by skiplane to the comfortable Murchison Hut on the Tasman Glacier in Mount Cook National Park for a week of glacier ski tours. This is more than just a ski trip: it also includes hiking the trails of the Milford Track. For intermediate downhill skiers.

Dates: 21-day trips
#1 Oct 9–Oct 29
#2 Nov 21–Dec 18
Land Cost: $1990
(9–12 members)

USSR: Ski the Caucasus & Mt. Elbrus

Skiing Europe's highest peak, Mt. Elbrus (18,510′), is a unique cultural encounter with Eastern European skiers. Lodging is in a mountain hotel and also in huts on Mt. Elbrus. Open to intermediate skiers and above. Three nights in Moscow with sightseeing are included.

Dates: Feb 16–Mar 5 (18 days)
Land Cost: $1640

Himalayan Ski Expedition: Kedarnath Dome

This expedition for expert ski mountaineers will attempt an ascent of Kedarnath Dome (22,410′) in India's Garhwal Himal. This is a classic Himalayan expedition complete with porters.

Dates: Sep 21–Oct 23 (33 days)
Land Cost: $2290
(9–10 members)

CROSS-COUNTRY TOURING

These trips go to outstanding backcountry: forests, national parks, and glaciers with magnificent scenery and ski touring. Despite the remote locations, very comfortable accommodations are available at wilderness lodges with delicious food.

Norway: The National Parks

Explore wide open slopes and valleys in Norway's spectacular Jotunheimen and Rondane national parks. Accommodations are in cozy ski lodges. This is ideal terrain on which to perfect your telemark turns.

Dates: Feb 21–Mar 3 (11 days)
Land Cost: $995
(9–14 members)

Ski Lappland

In the arctic homeland of the Lapps and their migrating reindeer herds, take day tours from lodges at Lake Kilpisjarvi, Finland, and ski on an overnight tour across the border into Norway. Accommodations at modern Finnish lodging with saunas and exotic Lapp food. Travel is via Oslo and Tromso, Norway.

Dates: Apr 4–Apr 13 (10 days)
Land Cost: $1090
(9–12 members)

Alaska: Spring Tour In the Brooks Range

With dog teams carrying the gear, ski the spectacular arctic wilderness environment of the Brooks Range. Spend two nights in cabins and camp in heated-wall tents. Access is from Bettles, Alaska, located north of the Arctic Circle.

Dates: Apr 4–Apr 13 (10 days)
Land Cost: $1350
(8–10 members)

New Zealand Alps

Same dates and itinerary as *New Zealand Alps* trip listed in *Randonee* section, but geared for cross country skiers.

Despite the remote locations, very comfortable accommodations are available at wilderness lodges with delicious food/Dave Parker

Some cross-country skiers seek the quiet exhilaration of exploring untracked wilderness; others prefer the athletic thrill of prepared tracks and ultra-light equipment/Dave Parker

CROSS-COUNTRY TRAIL SKIING

This type of trip takes advantage of the well-prepared and well-marked trails in Europe. The trail systems are exclusively for cross-country skiers and connect small villages and nordic ski centers. Lodging ranges from quaint country inns to modern hotels.

Ski Holiday in Switzerland

Ski all day on the fine tracks in the rolling Jura Mountains along the Swiss-French border, then enjoy a gourmet meal in a country inn. Baggage is transported separately. This is the best tour for skiers with a taste for scenic trails and French food.

Dates: 10-day trips
#1 Jan 17–Jan 26
#2 Jan 31–Feb 9
Land Cost: $990
(8–12 members)

Engadin Ski Marathon

Ski the best tracks in Switzerland and compete in an exciting 42 km. citizen's race! Warm up on the trails of the Jura Mountains, then travel to the Engadin Valley for final training and participation in the ski race, a fun event for both spectators and racers.

Dates: Feb 28–Mar 10 (11 days)
Land Cost: $1190
(8–12 members)

Norway:: Villages and Trails

From a hotel at a forest trailhead, ski scenic parkland tracks with views of Oslo Fjord, then travel to Lillehammer to enjoy the trail network that connects outlying villages and farms. Accommodations at Sjusjoen village are in a converted dairy farm.

Dates: Feb 13–Feb 23 (11 days)
Land Cost: $995
(8–12 members)

Czechoslovakia: the High Tatras Mountains

This is an old-world tour to the mountains of Bohemia. Start with a visit to ancient Prague, then take the overnight train to the alpine High Tatras and ski the trails along the Czech-Polish border. Lodging is in hotels.

Dates: Mar 14–Mar 23 (10 days)
Land Cost: $890
(8–12 members)

SECTION VIII
TRAVEL GALLERY
THE PEOPLE & ART OF TIBET

The following selection of photos was taken in 1981 during the first Mountain Travel trek in Tibet, home of Tantric Buddhism, one of the world's oldest and largest religions.

Lhasa, capital of Tibet, is the religious and political center of the "roof of the world." Just outside the center of Lhasa stands the Potala Palace, once the traditional seat of the line of 13 Dalai Lamas, spiritual leaders of Tibet. In the old section of town, visitors can admire the Lakhang "cathedral," spiritual apex of Tibetan Buddhism, with its magnificent chapels and wall paintings.

The Tibetans, a tough, resiliant and friendly people with great national pride, have a cultural heritage steeped in the lore and mythology of an ancient and complex religion.

After Lhasa, our group visited Shigatse, Tibet's second largest city, and the famous Tashilumpo Monastery, home of another spiritual leader, the venerable Panchen Lama, and now once again an active monastery with over 300 monks. The culmination of our trip was a visit to Rongbuk Monastery, once the highest inhabited site in the world (16,500′), from which we trekked to Mt. Chomolongma (the Tibetan name for Mt. Everest), Mother Goddess of the Earth.

Leo Le Bon

Sakyamuni Buddha

This huge relief image of Sakyamuni Buddha has been carved out of a rocky cliff along the Kyichu River. A pile of mani (prayer) stones given individually as offerings by pilgrims has accumulated in the center.

Lhasa Valley

The Potala Palace (south side)

The Potala is home of the Dalai Lama, spiritual leader and "God-King" of Tibet. With construction begun in the 7th century A.D., this monumental thousand-room palace—now a museum—was extensively rebuilt to its present form in the 17th century by the fifth Dalai Lama. The Potala contains a vast array of treasures, from subterranean vaults filled with paintings and sculptures to its gold-leaf rooftops, decorated with statues and bells.

Lhasa

Wheel of Existence

The wheel of existence explains the Buddhist theory of reincarnation: all beings are trapped in a cycle of death and rebirth from which they can be liberated only by reaching spiritual enlightenment. The life and teachings of Buddha indicate the path. Clutched by Yama, Lord of Death, the wheel shows in the center, the pig, cock and snake, symbolizing the three main human vices: ignorance, desire and hatred. The six sections show realms of rebirth: gods, demi-gods, tortured spirits, hell dwellers, animals and humans. The symbols shown in the outer ring illustrate the twelve conditions that bind people to rebirth.
Potala Palace

Golok Pilgrims

Golok pilgrims have come many hundreds of miles from northeastern Tibet, a region once called Amdo, to worship the sacred sites of the Lhasa Valley, much as devout Catholics would journey to Rome and the Vatican. Golok women braid their hair in 108 strands, a holy number, taken from the 108 books of the Kanjur, the Tibetan Buddhist canon which contains the translated words of Buddha.
Potala Palace

Jokhang Roof

The Wheel of the Dharma with the Potala Palace in the distance. The adoring deer commemorate Gautama Buddha's preachings at Varanasi, India, where according to legend the deer came and listened as Buddha delivered his first sermon.

Jokhang

King Songtsen Gampo's Shrine
First historical king of Tibet, Songtsen Gampo unified the country in the 7th century. Here he is shown with his two wives, one Chinese and one Nepalese, who have become the goddesses called White Tara and Green Tara in Tibetan Buddhism.
Jokhang

Kamba La Pass (16,200′)

This is the view from the Kamba La Pass, looking southward to the Himalayas. Passes in Tibet are traditionally festooned with prayer flags, cloth imprinted with sacred mantras *(mystic prayers) to protect travelers against evil spirits.*
Enroute

Lamas

Lamas (Buddhist priests) guard the entrance to Chamba Hall, the largest and most important chapel of the Tashilumpo Monastery. Inside is an 87-foot-tall copper statue of Maitreya, the Buddha of the Future.
Shigatse

Devout Tibetans

With prayer beads in hand, the devout circumambulate the Tashilumpo Monastery in order to gain spiritual merit. The traditional Tibetan greeting is the phrase "tashi dele" accompanied by a joining of hands.
Shigatse

Vajrapani

Vajrapani is the guardian diety who holds power over evil. In his right hand, he wields a Vajra, a ritual tantric object symbolized by a thunderbolt. As with all wrathful dieties, his hair is red.
Shigatse

This center of heaven
This core of earth
This heart of the world
Fenced round with snow
6th Century Tibetan Poem

Rongbuk Monastery

Rongbuk was once covered with extraordinary murals but few have survived the destruction caused during China's Cultural Revolution, and the subsequent ravages of wind, snow and solar radiation. This Buddha image was found on a west facing wall in one of the side chapels, reflecting the rays of the setting sun.
Rongbuk Valley

Mani Stones

Mani *stones, so named for the prayers which are carved on them, are found along the Rongbuk Valley leading towards Mt. Everest (29,028'), which towers here 10,000 feet above the Rongbuk Glacier. The inscription on the* mani *stone reads Om Mani Padme Hum Om Ah Hum Vajra Guru Padma Siddhi Hum. Translation: Ode to the jewel in the lotus, conveying the power and energy of Guru Padma's wisdom.*
Rongbuk Valley

SECTION IX
PRACTICAL INFORMATION

Mountain Travel Medical Kit enroute. The job of the trip physician is to provide necessary minor medical care to our trip members and to be prepared for major problems, should they occur/ *Charles Gay*

Immunizations

Only a few immunizations are LEGALLY REQUIRED for entry to certain countries, but it is very unwise to take only those shots needed to travel legally. Mountain Travel trips are by definition designed to get you away from the "usual tourist routes" and into what U.S. Public Health Service calls "rural or remote sections." While every effort is made to ensure proper sanitation, there is always the chance of disease exposure.

These suggestions should be used *only as a guideline.* Requirements are subject to change and travelers should check with their local Health Department, the Center for Disease Control and/or your personal physician.

YOU MUST START EARLY (at least two months before leaving) so that the shots can be sensibly spaced for maximum protection and minimum discomfort. All immunizations must be entered on your yellow "International Certificate of Vaccination" form which you should keep with your passport while traveling.

Diptheria-Tetanus Booster

Normally needed every 8 years, unless you are injured. BUT almost everyone on a walking trip will get a minor scrape or cut and we do often share trails with the local livestock. Get a booster!

Oral Polio

Regulations change periodically; check with your Health Department. If you have had the original 3 doses, a single oral booster is all that is needed. This is still a real disease in much of the world. Get a booster!

Smallpox

The disease no longer exists and vaccine is no longer available or required.

Typhoid

This is desirable for anyone traveling and camping in rural areas—even in the U.S. It is essential for Mexico, South America, Asia, Africa and the Middle East. A booster is good for 3 years and gives about 60% protection. The Typhoid-Paratyphoid combination is no longer recommended since paratyphoid protection is minimal and the combination often causes reactions (i.e. fever, aches).

Gamma Globulin

An injection of 2 cc. (varies with weight) given as close to departure time as possible is for protection against hepatitis. The immunity is passive and does subside within a few months.

Some trip members report their physicians are reluctant to give Gamma Globulin, but it is no longer controversial. The U.S. Public Health Service recommends it for travelers to "tropical areas," "developing countries," and those who "bypass the ordinary tourist routes." Get it.

Typhus

Its value is debatable and it is generally not recommended.

Yellow Fever

This is a legal requirement for travel to many countries that either have the disease or fear its introduction. The yellow fever zone covers the central and northern half of South America and a band across Africa. Yellow fever immunization is mandatory for travel in the areas above, and is strongly recommended for all travel in Africa or South America. A few Asian countries fear its introduction and MAY require it.

Cholera

Often required by local authorities and subject to change on short notice. All travelers to Africa, the Middle East and Asia should have a current cholera shot. This immunization is only valid for 6 months, but a booster is all that is ever needed once the primary series has been completed. Get it even though its value is questionable, since at least you'll get it with a clean needle in the U.S.

Malaria

Malaria pills (Chloroquine Phosphate) are recommended for anyone traveling and camping in tropical areas. In some areas where malaria is prevalent and exposure cannot be avoided, some physicians recommend taking Primaquine during the six-week follow-up. In addition some areas require other medication for Chloroquine-resistant strains. *Consult your physician in this matter.*

Water Purification

For purifying questionable water sources, we recommend iodine tablets (available from camping stores) or iodine crystal solution (available by prescription from your physician. Iodine in crystal form should be used with care, as it is poisonous if ingested). Consult your physician and/or druggist.

Personal First Aid Supplies

The following suggestions are based on past traveling and trekking experience. Your own experience and preferences will, of course, influence your choice. Do not forget to bring medications used for individual conditions, since these are not generally available overseas. *This list is a guideline only, to be used as a basis for discussion with your physician.*

Mild Pain, Headache, Fever

Aspirin, 5 gr. or Tylenol, if allergic to Aspirin.

Pain, Cough, Diarrhea

Aspirin w/Codeine 1/2 gr. (Ascodeen-30), or Tylenol w/Codeine, 1/2 gr.

Antacid, Upset Stomach, Ulcers

Maalox, Gelusil M, or Mylanta antacid tabs. Donnatal tabs are good for stomach cramps, mild diarrhea, and are a mild sedative.

On Mountain Travel trips, food is prepared by experienced cooks using the highest possible degree of sanitation. We have a very good record of health on our trips/Richard Irvin

Diarrhea *(symptomatic relief)*

Codeine compounds listed above. Avoid Lomotil which has been reported to prolong illness with some types of dysentery. Some people find Peptobismol effective.

Diarrhea *(prevention)*

Small daily doses of tetracycline, or its long-acting relative, doxycycline, or a sulfa combination drug (Septra or Bactrim) have been shown to decrease the incidence of "traveler's diarrhea." This is certainly desirable when one has limited time and has invested a lot of money in a trip. This treatment is still somewhat controversial. Some people become sun sensitized by the drugs and can acquire a truly disabling sunburn. Also there is at least theoretical reason to fear that these drugs, while protecting against minor (albeit annoying) diarrheas, may be limiting the normal flora in the intestine and making one more susceptible to the more virulent organisms responsible for truly life-threatening dysenteries. *Please discuss the pros and cons carefully with your own physician before taking these medications.*

Colds, Allergies
(symptomatic relief)

Chlorpheniramine Maleate tabs., 4 mg. Actifed tabs (good for 4 hours) or Tuss-Ornade Spansule caps. (12-hour relief).

Topical Antibiotic

Most antibiotic ointments contain one or more of the following in about the following proportions: Neomycin (3.5 mg.)/ Bacitracin (400 units)/Polymyxin (5,000 units). Neosporin is typical.

Sun Protection

The sun can be fierce! PABA preparations such as Pre Sun (applied often because of perspiration) are usually okay to about 10,000 feet. At higher altitudes, the only sun protection that works for many of us is a total mechanical blocking agent—a hat, bandana around the back of the neck, etc. Don't forget reflected sun on areas such as under the chin and nose—especially when on snow. A-Fil Sun Sticks (Texas Pharmaceutical) are good for lips, and inside of nose.

Skin

Mycolog ointment is very useful for itching, chafing and irritation in moist areas (especially after diarrhea).

Miscellaneous

Band-Aids, Moleskin, foot powder, spare glasses, personal drugs, etc.

Food on the trek will be plentiful. Fresh vegetables, eggs, chickens and other foodstuffs are purchased as available. Meals are supplemented with tinned foods, such as peanut butter, fruit, coffee and fish/Richard Irvin

Trip Physicians

Mountain Travel seeks the services of a physician on trips to areas remote from medical care, such as the Himalayas and Andes. Physicians who undertake this job are given a reduction in Land Cost of up to 50%, depending on the trip (for specific information on discounts, write for our "List of Trips Requiring Physicians").

Applicants are considered on an individual basis: flexibility, a broad background, the ability to improvise and a sense of humor are important prerequisites. Our preference is for general surgeons, internists, well-qualified G.P.'s, full-time emergency physicians, orthopedists and other subspecialties that are not too far removed from care of the total body.

The job of the trip physician is to provide necessary minor medical care to our trip members and to be prepared for major problems should they occur. Mountain Travel provides well-stocked field medical kits. Trip physicians assemble their own small medical trail kit to carry with them each day on the trail.

Prior to the trip, trip members must complete our Medical Certificate and have it signed by their personal physician. We then send the Medical Certificates to the trip physician for his/her review and use.

Mountain Travel enjoys an enviable record of health and safety in the field and we want to keep it that way.

Trip physicians often find that caring for the local people is a trip highlight. Those of us on the Mountain Travel staff who have come to know and care about the people of these remote areas feel an obligation to do what we can, and it seems only fair to share the benefits of some of the technology we are attempting to escape momentarily when we choose to spend our vacations in underdeveloped areas. Trip physicians often find that a little effort, concern and medicine can do wonders, particularly with infants and children, and the gratitude is overwhelming. Acting as a health educator is important, too, encouraging local people to take advantage of any nearby dispensaries and facilities which can deliver continuing care.

Equipment Checklist

For each trip, we make up a specific list of recommended clothing and equipment, based on our 18 years of experience. Items are selected from the complete list below, tailored to the conditions of each particular trip. Many trips involve the logistical support of small aircraft, boats, porters or pack animals, so try to keep your baggage as light as possible. On most trips, a suitcase of your "city clothes" can be stored in a hotel while you are on trek.

Taking proper clothing and equipment for your trek is an important ingredient to enjoying your adventure. Take time to look at what's on the market, don't underestimate the unpredictability of weather, and let your own experience guide you.

☐ Casual Clothes for Travel in Cities

Shirt
- ☐ Wool, long-sleeved.
- ☐ Cotton, long-sleeved.
- ☐ Cotton, short-sleeved, or T-shirt.
- ☐ Windshirt.

Sweater
- ☐ Heavy wool or pile/bunting jacket.
- ☐ Light wool or synthetic.

Trousers
- ☐ Full length trousers, wool or blend.
- ☐ Pile or bunting pants coupled with windpants & polypropylene underwear.
- ☐ Cotton hiking trousers (khakis, Levis).
- ☐ Windpants (Gore-tex) with side zipper, large enough to go over boots (and crampons) for wind, rain or snow.
- ☐ Hiking shorts.

Underwear
- ☐ Thermal, polypropylene.
- ☐ Regular, everyday type.

Headwear
- ☐ Silk or nylon face mask.
- ☐ Bandana.
- ☐ Balaclava, wool.
- ☐ Light hat with wide brim or visor for sun.
- ☐ Ski cap.
- ☐ "Sou'wester" hat for rain.

Insulated Clothing
(The choice between down fill and synthetic fill is largely personal. Synthetic fill is preferred for wet climates.)
- ☐ Expedition parka, 16–20 oz. down or 20–30 oz. fiberfill, with hood. Must fit over bulky clothing.
- ☐ Medium-weight parka, 10–12 oz. or 16–20 oz. fiberfill.
- ☐ Down or fiberfill vest or sweater.
- ☐ Down or fiberfill overpants with zipper and/or snaps on the legs.
- ☐ Skiers' warmup pants or quilted underwear.
- ☐ Warm jacket or parka.

Foul Weather Gear
(With ANY rain garment, make sure the seams are sealed.)
- ☐ Light, collapsible umbrella
- ☐ Gore-tex parka for rain and wind; or anorak, mountain parka, or cagoule. Large enough to fit over bulky sweater or insulated clothing.
- ☐ Poncho—lightweight but sturdy.
- ☐ Backpack rain cover.
- ☐ Waterproof (not just water repellent) rain suit including parka, pants and hat (e.g., traditional nautical foul weather gear).
- ☐ Rain pants (not necessary if you bring windpants).

Handwear
- ☐ Silk or nylon glove liners.
- ☐ Polypropylene gloves.
- ☐ Cotton garden gloves for sun/wind protection.
- ☐ Expedition overmitts (must fit over polypropylene gloves).
- ☐ Overmitts—must be wind-and-water-proof and fit over polypropylene mitts.

Socks
- ☐ Heavy duty socks, at least 80% wool.
- ☐ Cotton athletic socks.

Boots and Shoes
(Boots should be waterproofed, well broken in and worn with one lightweight & one heavyweight pair of socks.)
- ☐ Tennis or running shoes.
- ☐ Comfortable walking shoes.
- ☐ Light hiking boots, with padded ankle and lug sole (size 9 weighs approx. 3 lbs. 8 oz.)
- ☐ Medium-weight hiking boots (size 9 weighs approx. 4 lbs. 10 oz.).
- ☐ Alpine, heavy mountaineering boots or model like Koflach "Viva" double boot. (size 9 weights approx. 5 lbs.)
- ☐ Double plastic boots (Koflach "Ultra" with alveolite liner).
- ☐ Korean vapor-barrier boots with lug soles (also called K-boots or bunny boots—U.S. Army made). Include a patching kit.
- ☐ Booties—down or fiberfill.
- ☐ Rubber boots. Sturdy, calf length, weigh about 3 lbs.

Gaiters and Overboots
- ☐ Overboots with rugged bottoms, insulated with foam or ensolite (for single alpine heavy mountaineering boots.)
- ☐ Full length gaiters up to the knee.

Sleeping Pads
(select from below)
- ☐ Open cell foam, 3/4 length or full length, 2″ thick with waterproof cloth cover (not recommended for cold weather or water trips.
- ☐ Closed-cell, like "Ensolite" 3/4 length, 3/8″ thick.
- ☐ Closed-cell, like "Ensolite" full length, 3/4″ thick (if on snow, Thermobar recommended.)
- ☐ Air mattress, top quality, 3/4 or full length (e.g., Therma-Rest, Air-Lift).
- ☐ Ground sheet.

Sleeping Bag

(with waterproof stuff sack)

☐ Expedition weight, temperature rating: −10F to −25F.
☐ Medium weight, temperature rating: 0F to +15F.
☐ Lightweight , temperature rating: +20F to +30F.
☐ Sleeping bag sheet liner (recommended for trips in hot climates as occasional substitute for sleeping bag).

Climbing Expeditions

(only for Grade D or Grade E)

☐ Ice axe (70–90 cm., as required by your height). Metal or fiberglass shaft recommended. Sling for wrist or body attachment of ice axe.
☐ Crampons (10 or 12-point HINGED, not rigid). With good straps (Neoprene) which have an extra 4″ so the ends can be easily grasped by a mittened hand. They must fit your boot perfectly (with overboots, if needed).
☐ Carabiners.
☐ Locking carabiner.
☐ Ascenders—Jumars, Gibbs, etc.
☐ Prusik loops—5 feet finished length, 12 feet in circumference of 5–6 mm Perlon joined with double fisherman's knot or grapevine knot.
☐ Slings—runners of 2.5 cm (1 inch) nylon tubular webbing, approx. 1.5 meters in circumference, ends to be joined with water knot.
☐ Swami belt (5 meters of 2.5 cm tubular webbing) or seat and chest harness (adjustable).
☐ Climbing helmet.
☐ Avalanche cord—20 meters with directional markers.
☐ Ice screw (one).

Winter Travel

☐ Snowshoes—aluminum (e.g., Sherpa, Black Forest, Early Winters); make sure lacings are well coated with plastic or resin to protect from abrasion.
☐ Ski poles.
☐ Cross country skis.
☐ Alpine skis.
☐ Appropriate waxes.

Packs and Bags

☐ Expedition framepack, with top quality aluminum frame, padded hip belt, roomy outside pockets (approximately 4500 cu in. capacity).
☐ Backpacking framepack, outside pockets (approx. 3800 cu. in. capacity)
☐ Large internal frame rucksack—approx. 4100 cu. in. capacity.
☐ Day pack with approximately 1500 cu. in. capacity to carry bulky jackets, camera gear, etc. One with waistbelt preferable.
☐ Small day pack, approx. 1000 cu. in. capacity.
☐ Duffle bag—made of strong material with full length zipper and wraparound straps. A padlock is also suggested. Size: medium (12'' x 30''), large (15'' x 33''), or extra-large (18'' x 36'').

Eating Utensils

☐ Cup, large, heavy duty plastic.
☐ Spoon, fork, bowl (plastic).
☐ Pocket knife with can opener and scissors.
☐ Leakproof plastic water bottle (1 or 1.5 qt. capacity).

Accessories

☐ First aid kit.
☐ Toilet kit—soap, toothbrush, toilet articles. Disposable towelettes (e.g., Wash n' Dries) are useful for hygiene.
☐ One roll of toilet paper per camping week.
☐ Insect repellent
☐ Repair kit—needle, thread, 1/8″ nylon cord, ripstop tape, etc.
☐ Regular sunglasses. Spare pair if you wear prescription lenses.
☐ Sunglasses or goggles for high altitude and snow travel with DARK (85% absorbency of visible light) lenses.
☐ Sun-blocking lotion—(e.g., Coppertone, Pre-Sun, Eclipse.)
☐ Glacier cream or zinc oxide to screen ultraviolet rays.
☐ Sun-blocking lip creme (e.g., A-Fil, Labiosan).
☐ Flashlight—with spare batteries and bulb.
☐ Head lamp—lightweight for night climbing or reading, plus spare batteries and bulb.
☐ Fire producer—2 butane lighters or waterproof matches.
☐ Whistle (plastic coaches' type).
☐ Compass (good quality, light and simple).
☐ Maps (if desired).
☐ Waterproofing boot sealer (e.g., Sno Seal).
☐ Small lockable suitcase for city clothes (can be stored in hotel while on the trail).
☐ Stuff bags of assorted sizes and colors; good for keeping gear dry and in order.
☐ Plastic bags—various sizes, heavy duty, ziplock for film, books, small items.
☐ Baggage tags—one per bag (supplied by Mountain Travel).
☐ Towel.
☐ Swimsuit.
☐ Camera and film. Bring an ample supply of film as purchase abroad is difficult and expensive.
☐ Binoculars.
☐ Watch.
☐ Reading material, writing material, playing cards.
☐ Money belt.

Packing Tips

We recommend that you hand-carry on the plane (in your daypack or hand luggage) your boots, camera, important documents, medicines and other irreplaceable items. Make sure you attach a Mountain Travel baggage tag to all luggage. It is also a good idea to have identification inside your checked bags.

Equipment courtesy of Wilderness Experience, Chatsworth, California.

Aer Lingus AeroPeru

AIR-INDIA Alaska Airlines

Reservations

A $250 deposit, along with a completed Trip Application, will reserve a place for you.

A second payment of $500 is due four months before departure.

Final payment of Land Cost and air fare is due two months before departure.

Prices are quoted in U.S. dollars. All payments must be made in U.S. dollars.

Reservations for most trips are accepted up to 21 days before departure. However, we encourage *early* bookings: they help to guarantee a trip's departure!

If you purchase a copy of our 1986 *Adventurous Travelers' Guide* and take a 1986 Mountain Travel trip, we will credit you for the cost of the book. Just attach your book receipt to the Trip Application.

See Your Travel Agent

Any travel agent can book a Mountain Travel trip for you. It costs no more to use a travel agent, and an expert agency can provide many special services for you free of charge.

Multiple Reservations

If you have sent in a deposit on a trip for which the departure is in doubt and wish to be covered on a second-choice trip, you may reserve space on the second-choice trip by sending in an additional $250 deposit. If your first-choice trip does not go, all funds will be transferred to the second-choice trip. The process works in reverse if your first choice trip does go—all funds will automatically be transferred to that trip. Should you cancel from your first-choice trip, handling fees will be charged as per cancellation policy.

Trip Waitlisting

If you cancel your reservation while still waitlisted, the full deposit will be refunded. Upon notification of confirmation, you must advise us within 15 days if you do not wish to remain on the trip roster. If you cancel your reservation after this 15-day period, the usual cancellation policy will apply.

Trip Information Supplements

The following material is sent out to participants.

Immediately After Sign-up:

Detailed itinerary, medical certificate, Health Matters bulletin.

Four Months Before Departure:

Equipment list, documentation, baggage and insurance information, air itinerary, medical immunization recommendations, invoice for 2nd deposit and final payment.

One Month Before Departure:

Last minute information on the trip, including air tickets, baggage tags, trip roster, rendezvous instructions, insurance policy (optional) visaed passports (if required), and maps if available.

Visas

Mountain Travel will process the necessary visas for your trip. If for some reason a visa is not granted to you, Mountain Travel is not responsible if you must therefore cancel your trip.

Land Cost

The American Express Card:

We accept The American Express Card for payment of Land Cost. You may charge on your usual basis or on an Extended Payment Plan of up to 24 months (see Trip Application Form).

Tier Pricing:

While we make every effort to fill each trip to the point of maximum economy for everyone (and do all possible to avoid cancelling trips with low signup), we tier-price some of our tours in order to operate them with smaller numbers of passengers.

Tier pricing is based on the number of full revenue tour members. Not included are guests or staff of Mountain Travel, the trip doctor (if applicable), or members of the press or media who are occasionally invited to join our tours.

If a member cancellation reduces the group size to a higher tier within 29 days of departure, remaining members will not be charged the resulting higher Land Cost.

Rates quoted are per person, based on sharing a double room or tent.

Share Basis for Single Travelers:

If you are traveling alone and wish to share accommodations, we will assign you a roommate, if one is available. If there is no one with whom you can share, you must pay a Single Supplement Fee which will be listed in the itinerary.

Land Cost Includes:

The following is a generalization of what Land Cost includes. Any variations from this will be listed in the Trip Itinerary.

In the Cities:

Hotels with private bath where available, airport transfers for members using the group flights, baggage porterage and hotel porterage, all sightseeing arrangements as indicated in the itinerary, entrance fees, leadership, local guides, visas, permits. All meals included on China, Mongolia, and USSR trips.

In the Field:

All camp meals, porters or pack animals (if applicable), guides, cooks, ground transport, community camping and commissary equipment.

Not Included:

Meals in the cities (except China, Mongolia, and USSR) to allow for individual choice of restaurants, tips to camp staff, cost of medical immunizations, insurance of any kind, excess baggage charges (if any), airport taxes (if any), alcoholic beverages, laundry charges and other items of a personal nature.

Any variations from the above list will be listed in the Trip Itinerary.

Medical costs (except for the ordinary services provided on trips), evacuation by helicopter or other conveyance or costs of hospitalization are not covered in the Land Cost.

If any trip has to be delayed because of bad weather, trail conditions, river levels, road conditions, flight delays, government intervention, sickness or other contingency for which Mountain Travel or its agents cannot make provision, the cost of delays is not included.

Validity of Land Costs:

Land Costs listed herein are subject to change. They are estimates only and are not valid. Most Land Costs will remain the same but since these trips are planned so far in advance, exact costs cannot be determined at this time and may be adjusted in the individual Trip Itineraries which are made for each trip. Contact Mountain Travel for current Land Costs.

Transfer & Cancellation Policy

At the time we receive written notice that you must cancel your trip, the following fees will apply:

More than 180 days before departure	$50
90 to 180	$100
60 to 89	$200
30 to 59	20% Land Cost
14 to 29	30% Land Cost
1 to 14	75% Land Cost
No show	100% Land Cost

If you transfer from one trip to another, between 180 and 60 days before departure (of the trip you are transfering from), the Transfer Fee is $100. If you transfer within 59 days of departure, you are subject to the usual Cancellation Fees outlined above (appropriate to the date you notify us that you want to transfer). We recommend that you purchase Trip Cancellation Insurance to protect yourself.

Trip Cancellation Insurance:

We encourage you to take out Trip Cancellation Insurance. This insurance protects all deposits and payments for both Air and Land Cost should you have to cancel your trip due to personal or family illness. Trip Cancellation Insurance costs $50 per $1000 of Air and Land Cost. We will mail you the necessary forms on request. We recommend that you purchase it soon after signing up.

Baggage and Accident/ Life Insurance:

(Sample rates): $69 for 30-day $1000 baggage insurance: $26 for 30-day $25,000 accident/life and illness insurance.

Cancelled Trips:

Mountain Travel reserves the right to cancel any trip due to inadequate signup which makes the trip economically unfeasible for us to operate. In such a case, a full refund of land cost is given, but Mountain Travel is not responsible for additional ex-

penses incurred by members in preparing for the trip (i.e., non-refundable "Advance Purchase" air tickets, visa fees if applicable, equipment, medical expenses).

Refunds:

No partial refunds will be given for unused hotel rooms, meals, sightseeing trips or trek arrangements for any reason whatsoever. Land Cost is quoted as a package and credits are not given for services not used.

Air Travel

Mountain Travel has a specialized agency staff and a fully automated computer system for handling ticketing and reservations worldwide. Our staff is experienced in scheduling air travel to the most remote and obscure destinations. In addition, we can book hotels and other services in most cities in the world.

Write or call for the latest fares.

You may purchase your air tickets with any major credit card. See the Trip Application Form. ALL AIR FARES QUOTED (in U.S. dollars) ARE SUBJECT TO CHANGE. They are valid as of May 1, 1985. Contact Mountain Travel for the most current information.

Sample Air Fares

Asia

Round trip to
Nepal, India and Pakistan

Pakistan via PIA:
N.Y./Rawalpindi
(14/120-day exc.) $1288
S.F./Rawalpindi
(14/120-day exc.) $1567

India via British Airways, TWA or Pan Am:
N.Y./Delhi
(14/120-day exc.) $1415
S.F./Delhi
(14/120-day exc.) $1704

Nepal via Thai International:
S.F./Bangkok/Kathmandu . $1667

Nepal via Air India, TWA or Pan Am:
N.Y./Delhi/Kathmandu
(14/120-day exc.) $1275
S.F./Delhi/Kathmandu
(14/120-day exc.) $1876

Round Trip to Japan and China
S.F./Tokyo (Apex) $930
S.F./Beijing (Apex) $1206

Africa

Round Trip to Africa
via British Airways and KLM:
N.Y./Nairobi
(Apex) $1368
N.Y./Johannesburg
(Apex) $1527
N.Y./Kilimanjaro (Tanzania)
(Apex) $1544
N.Y./Tamanrasset (Algeria)
(Apex) $850
N.Y./Cairo $899

Europe

Round Trip to England, Ireland, Switzerland, Paris, Athens, Oslo and Moscow via SAS, Aer Lingus, Air France, TWA and Aeroflot:
N.Y./London
(Apex, 7/60-days) $579
N.Y./Ireland
(Apex, 14/45-days) $559
N.Y./Athens
(Apex, 7/60-days $849
N.Y./London/Oslo
(Apex, 14/45-days) $697
N.Y./Geneva $876
S.F./Paris
(Super Apex) $1192
N.Y./Paris
(Apex) $769
N.Y./Moscow
(Apex) $969

South America

Round Trip to South America
via Eastern and Pan Am:
Miami/Cuzco
(YLE 150 exc.) $459
Miami/Cuzco/Puerto Maldonado
(YLE 150 exc.) $509
L.A./Cuzco
(YLE 150 exc.) $899
Miami/Quito/Guayaquil
(Apex) $512
L.A./Quito/Guayaquil
(Apex) $790
Miami/Punta Arenas
(Patagonia) $1428

Round Trip to Costa Rica and Mexico via Pan Am, Lacsa and Mexicana:
S.F./Mexico City $415
Miami/Costa Rica $355

North America

Round Trip to Alaska
via Alaska Airlines:
Seattle/Anchorage $489
Seattle/Juneau $328
Seattle/Fairbanks $594

Round Trip to Hawaii
via World Airways:
S.F./Honolulu $439

Equipment

Mountain Travel provides all group camping equipment such as tents and cooking gear. Trip members must supply their own sleeping bag.

A detailed list of recommended clothing and suggested personal equipment is made up specifically for each trip.

Baggage:

Most major carriers have "piece" baggage restrictions. Under these rules, Economy Class passengers are permitted free baggage allowance for two bags, total dimensions not exceeding 106 inches. Carry-on baggage (one or more underseat bags not exceeding 45 inches) is also permitted free. More detailed information will be sent to trip members.

Medical & Health

It is vital that persons with medical problems make them known to us well before departure. The trip leader has the right to disqualify anyone at any time during the trip if he feels the trip member is physically incapable and/or if a trip member's continued participation will jeopardize the safety of the group. Refunds are not given under such circumstances.

Mountain Travel will endeavor to secure the services of a doctor on every trip where the need is obvious (such as some South American and Himalayan treks). Medical attention and drugs will be administered free of charge to trip members by these trip doctors in the field.

Hospital facilities for serious problems are often unavailable and evacuation can be prolonged, difficult and expensive. Mountain Travel assumes no liability regarding provision of medical care. Trip members will receive our "Health Matters" bulletin, and a medical certificate which must be filled out by both the trip member and his/her doctor (not necessary for "A" trips) and returned to us.

Once you have been confirmed on a trip, there will be no refunds if your doctor does not approve your medical certificate.

Responsibility

Of Trip Members

Trip members have certain responsibilities to Mountain Travel and to other trip members: trip members are responsible for comprehending the conditions implied in the Mountain Travel trip grading system and selecting a trip (perhaps in consultation with Mountain Travel) which is appropriate to their interests and abilities; for preparing for the trip by studying the itinerary and supplemental trip information sent by Mountain Travel; for bringing appropriate clothing and equipment as advised by Mountain Travel; for following normal standards of personal hygiene in order to lessen risk of travelers' diseases, as advised by the trip leader and trip doctor (if a trip doctor accompanies the trip); for following normal social behavior patterns with fellow trip members; for acting in an appropriate and respectful manner in accordance with the customs of countries visited; for completing the trip itinerary as scheduled (or as adjusted in the field as necessary).

At the leader's discretion, a member may be asked to leave the trip if the leader feels the person's further participation may be detrimental to the trip or to the individual.

Of Mountain Travel Please Read Carefully

Mountain Travel, Inc., (its Owners, Outfitters, Agents, and Employees) give notice that they act only as the agent for the owners, contractors, and suppliers providing means of transportation and/or all other related travel services and assume no responsibility howsoever caused for injury, loss or damage to person or property in connection with any service resulting directly or indirectly from: acts of God, detention, annoyance, delays and expenses arising from quarantine, strikes, thefts, pilferage, force majeure, failure of any means of conveyance to arrive or depart as scheduled, civil disturbances, government restrictions or regulations, discrepancies or change in transit or hotel services over which it has no control. Reasonable changes in the itinerary may be made where deemed advisable for the comfort and well-being of the passengers. On advancement of deposit to Mountain Travel, Inc., the depositor therefore agrees to be bound by the above recited terms and conditions.

Airline Clause

The airlines are not to be held responsible for any act, omission or event during the time passengers are not on board their planes or conveyance. The passage contract in use by the airlines concerned, when issued, shall constitute the sole contract between the airlines and such purchasers of these tours and/or passenger. Such conveyance, etc. is subject to the laws of the countries involved.

Why Join A Mountain Travel Trip?

We offer a truly *different* travel experience. Our groups are small—averaging 8 to 12 members, which helps to ensure mobility and comfort. We are pleased to report a repeat clientele of more than 35% (warning: Mountain Travel trips can be habit forming!).

Expert Leadership

Our leaders are an important part of what makes Mountain Travel trips work so well. They come to us with a wide variety of backgrounds. Some are well-known authors or naturalists. Some are chosen for their knowledge of local language or culture, others for their outdoor skills. Above all, they are chosen for their ability to assure a safe, enjoyable and successful trip.

A Quality Experience

Even though the major focus of our trips is outdoor travel, we don't skimp on the amenities. We hire experienced cooks and camp assistants to make outdoor living a pleasurable experience. We outfit every camping trip with the finest quality tents, roomy enough to comfortably accommodate two people and all their gear. On the vast majority of our trips, we hire porters and/or pack animals to carry all your personal gear, so you are free to walk, photograph and enjoy the scenery unencumbered by a heavy pack.

We will endeavor to secure the services of a doctor on every trip where the need is obvious (such as some South American and Himalayan treks). Medical attention and drugs will be administered free of charge to trip members by these trip doctors in the field.

In the cities, we stay in First Class hotels and sightsee by private car or small mini-bus with the best available guides.

Mountain Travel reservations staff: L. to R.: Ann, Herb, Kate, Marsha, Dave (not shown: Gary).

Good Food

Yes, you can have "gourmet" dinners in a tent at 12,000 feet! Whether in Peru, Nepal, China, Africa or Alaska, our cooks are experienced professionals. We can't guarantee that the food will be exactly what you like, but our cooks often come up with delightful culinary treats. Some examples in the past have been home-made wonton soup at camp in China, a *pachamanca* (whole barbequed lamb) on the trail in Peru, cheese omelets served by a roaring stream in Nepal, just-caught salmon and crisp salads in the wilds of Glacier Bay, Alaska. Food on the trips is as varied as the trips themselves.

Who Goes On These Trips?

Basically, our trips are made up of active, healthy people who love the outdoors. Most enjoy physical activities as an integral part of their lives (hiking, jogging, tennis, skiing) and they like the idea of being able to remain physically active while on vacation. They come from all walks of life and from all over the country. About 50% of our trip members are between the ages of 30 and 50. Anyone in good health who has a spirit of adventure is welcome on our trips. There is no upper age limit for participation.

Books, Maps, Etc.

Write for our complete book and map list. We sell more than 80 books and 25 maps pertaining to the trips we offer.

T-shirt

Made of the best quality heavyweight cotton with the circular M.T. logo (taken from a Tibetan coin) silkscreened on the front. Short sleeved, color-fast, and washable, it makes a great gift. Color: Navy blue with orange & light blue design. Send check or money order for $7.95 postpaid (California residents add applicable sales tax). Specify quantity and size (Men: S,M,L,XL: Ladies: S,M,L,XL).

Private Trips

In addition to the trips listed here, Mountain Travel assists in setting up privately organized trips for small groups in East Africa, Nepal, Peru, Costa Rica, India, the Galapagos Islands, Alaska and other areas.

Write for details.

Mountain Travel has been at the same address for over 10 years. Albany is adjacent to Berkeley, ten minutes north of Oakland off of Interstate 80 and twenty minutes from San Francisco via the Bay Bridge.

Drop by if you're in the neighborhood.

Member

Mountain Travel Is A Full-Service Travel Agency

Our task, as experts in "adventure travel," is to smooth your way through the maze of details involved in travel to the most remote regions of the world. We will procure your visas and permits, advise you on questions of clothing and equipment, book your airline tickets and make any independent travel reservations you desire in conjunction with your Mountain Travel trip. Our staff handles the needs of every trip member on an individual basis.

We welcome
The American Express Card.

References

BANK OF AMERICA
Albany Branch,
1615 Solano Avenue
Albany, CA 94706

ALBANY CHAMBER OF COMMERCE
1108 Solano Ave.
Albany, CA 94706

How To Sign Up

See the Trip Application Form in this book (if you don't find one, call us—toll-free outside California at 800-227-2384—and we'll send you a copy). Fill out the Application Form and send it in with your deposit of $250 per person. We'll handle the rest.

If you have a favorite travel agency, take your Application Form to them and they'll be glad to book your Mountain Travel trip for you.

Write:

MOUNTAIN TRAVEL®
1398 SOLANO AVENUE
ALBANY, CALIFORNIA 94706
TELEX: 335-429
CABLE: MOUNTAIN ALBANY CALIFORNIA

Call:

800 227-2384 *(toll-free outside CA)*
415 527-8100 *(inside CA)*

1986/87 Trip Application

Please print all information and mail with your deposit of $250 per person payable to Mountain Travel or your Travel Agent.

Name of Trip: ______

Departure Date: ______

Applicant's Name(s): ______

Mailing Label Account No: ______
(if available)

Address: ______

City: ______

State/Zip: ______

Phone: *(day)* ______ *(evening)* ______

Age: ______ **Sex:** ______ **Ht:** ______ **Wt:** ______

Smoking Preference: ☐ *(Non smoker)* ☐ *(Smoker)*

Occupation: ______

Passport Number: ______

Issue Date: ______ **Expiration Date:** ______

Place of Issue: ______

Citizenship: ______

Date of Birth: ______ **Place:** ______

In Case of Emergency Please Notify: ______
(include address and phone number)

State of Health: ______
(a medical questionnaire will be sent to applicants)

Describe Your Outdoor Background:
(camping, hiking, skiing. Not necessary for "A" trips).

Please List Previous Mountain Travel Trips:
(indicate date and name of trip leader)

For office use only:

$ Dep. ______ *Trip #* ______

Acct. # ______ *Ad Code* ______

Res. ______ *T.A.* ______

For travel agent bookings:
IATA or ATC # ______

Air Transportation:
Unless we hear to the contrary, we will assume that you wish Mountain Travel to prepare your airline tickets, including domestic space. It is usually best to have domestic and international ticketing done together due to fare concessions.

From: ______

Returning to: ______

You may use a credit card to purchase your air tickets. Please fill in the information below.

Name of Card: ______

Account No. ______

Exp. Date ______

Signature ______

Hotel Accommodations:
☐ OK for sharing double room. Share with: ______
☐ I prefer a single room.

Note: People who occupy single rooms, either by choice or by circumstance, must pay a Single Supplement Fee (which will be quoted on request). Hotels only; single tents are not always available.

Land Cost:
I wish to charge the LAND COST on The American Express Card

☐ *Regular Payment Plan* ☐ **Extended Payment Plan (circle number of months)*

3 6 9 12 18 24

**Non-U.S. Cardmembers: Extended Payment terms (if any) will be determined by your American Express Cardmember Agreement.*

Account Number: ______

Exp. Date: ______

Signature ______

Release and Assumption of Risk:

I am aware that during the mountain trip, expedition, ski tour, cruise, or other trip or vacation that I am participating in under the arrangements of Mountain Travel and its agents or associates, certain risks and dangers may occur, including but not limited to, the hazards of traveling mountainous terrain, accident or illness in remote places without medical facilities, the forces of nature and travel by air, train, automobile or other conveyance.

In consideration of, and as part payment for, the right to participate in such mountain trips or other activities and the services and food arranged for me by Mountain Travel and its agents or associates, I have and do hereby assume all of the above risks and will hold them harmless from any and all liability, actions, causes of action, debts, claims and demands of every kind and nature whatsoever which I now have or which may arise of or in connection with my trip or participation in any other activities arranged for me by Mountain Travel and its agents or associates. The terms hereof shall serve as a release and assumption of risk for my heirs, executors and administrators and for all members of my family, including any minors accompanying me.

I have read and agree to the conditions, especially noting the policy on cancellations and refunds, as stated under "General Information" in the Mountain Travel Catalog.

Signature: **Date:**
(Parent or legal guardian must sign for person under 21)